THE SEA WOLF

The Sea Wolf

The Life of

ADMIRAL COCHRANE

by

IAN GRIMBLE

Birlinn

This revised edition published in 2000 by
Birlinn Limited
8 Canongate Venture
5 New Street
Edinburgh
EH8 8BH

© The Estate of Ian Grimble 1978
Postscript: 'The Secret War Plan of Lord Dundonald'
© Charles Stephenson 2000

First published in 1978 by
Blond and Briggs

ISBN 1 84158 035 X

British Library Cataloguing-in-Publication Data
A catalogue record for this book is available from the British Library

Printed and bound by
Creative Print and Design Wales, Ebbw Vale

Contents

List of Illustrations

Sir Francis Burdett by A. Buck
(National Portrait Gallery)
Broadsheet against Lord Cochrane's sentence
(Hamlyn Group Picture Library)
Lord Ellenborough by Drummond
(National Portrait Gallery)
Cartoon of de Berenger, 21 May 1814, by G. Cruikshank
(Hamlyn Group Picture Library)
Katherine Corbett Barnes, wife of Lord Cochrane, by J. Holmes
(*Collection*: The Earl of Dundonald)
Maria Graham by T. Lawrence (National Portrait Gallery)
Drawings by Maria Graham (Hamlyn Picture Library)
View of the Chile coast
Lord Cochrane's house at Quintero
View of Valparaiso
General Bernardo O'Higgins
(*Collection*: The Earl of Dundonald)
General José de San Martín
(*Collection*: The Earl of Dundonald)
Simón Bolívar (Hamlyn Group Picture Library)
Pedro I on his Coronation Day at Rio de Janeiro
(*Collection*: Rex Nan Kivell, National Library of Australia)
Cutting out the *Esmeralda* from under the forts of Callao
(National Maritime Museum)
View of Rio de Janeiro, from a drawing by Maria Graham
(Hamlyn Group Picture Library)
The *Rising Star* (National Maritime Museum)
Slave market in Rio de Janeiro by Maria Graham
(Hamlyn Group Picture Library)
View of Rio de Janeiro by Maria Graham
(Hamlyn Group Picture Library)
Hanover Lodge, Regent's Park, London
(Photograph in the possession of the Earl of Dundonald)
H.M. Steam sloops *Rattler* and *Alecto* towing stern to stern to demonstrate the relative powers of the screw propeller and the paddle wheel (National Maritime Museum)
Model of the screw propeller of the *Rattler*
(The Science Museum)
Thomas Cochrane, 10th Earl of Dundonald, photographed in his eighties (*Collection*: The Earl of Dundonald)
Memorial tablet in Westminster Abbey
(The Dean and Chapter of Westminster)

Acknowledgments

I am deeply grateful to the 14th Earl of Dundonald for allowing me access to family papers that have never been seen by previous biographers of his great ancestor. A section of them had been passed by the widow of the 10th Earl to her youngest son, Captain Ernest Cochrane, from whom they descended to Richard Cochrane, Esq., of Redcastle. I owe a comparable debt of gratitude to Mr Cochrane for placing his collection at my disposal.

Some of the Dundonald muniments had already been deposited at the Scottish Record Office in Edinburgh when I began work on them; others have been added since. To the staff of H.M. General Register House, and also of the National Library of Scotland where other Cochrane MSS. are preserved, I would like to express sincere thanks for much help over many years. In London I have been indebted particularly to the librarians of the British Museum and of the Luso Brazilian Council at Canning House.

CHAPTER ONE

Apprenticeship

On 27 June 1793 the Royal Naval dockyard at Sheerness hummed with the activity of ships being made ready for sea. Across the English Channel revolution had broken out: the King of France had been guillotined in January and in February Great Britain had gone to war against the regicides.

Sheerness yard stood on the Isle of Sheppey where the River Medway flows into the Thames estuary through a maze of channels and mud banks. Farther up the Medway lay the principal arsenal of Chatham, whose commissioner was also responsible for Sheerness, and from the low-lying land between could be seen an almost continuous forest of masts and the wooden hulls of Britain's fleet.

The *Hind* was not conspicuous among them, for she was only a very small frigate of 28 guns, dwarfed by the hulk to which she was attached in the yard at Sheerness. On her deck stood a man dressed as an ordinary seaman, with a marlinspike slung round his neck and a lump of grease in his hand as he checked the ship's equipment on that day in June 1793. He was not in fact an ordinary seaman but John Larmour, First Lieutenant of the *Hind* and soon to become the Captain of a ship of his own. But honest jack Larmour was one of the few officers in the Royal Navy at that time to have been promoted from the lower deck and here he stood amongst the rigging of the *Hind*, continuing the same meticulous attention to his duties that had earned him his place in the wardroom. For the *Hind* would soon be at sea, and then it would be too late to discover whether the lives of her crew had been placed at risk by shoddy work on the part of the dockyard workers of Sheerness.

Lieutenant Larmour was interrupted by the arrival on board of his Captain, the Honourable Alexander Cochrane, escorting his nephew who was to be the new midshipman. Although he was only 17 years old Cochrane was already over 6 feet tall, with sturdy limbs, a prominent nose, ginger hair and blue eyes. He was introduced to Lieutenant Larmour by the courtesy title of Lord Cochrane, which he had enjoyed since birth as the eldest son and heir of the ninth Earl of Dundonald. In the eyes of such a man as Larmour he was an unpromising addition to the ship's complement, a young lordling who had never trod a deck in his life, introduced by the most flagrant nepotism. His uncle had entered the name of young Thomas Cochrane as a first-class volunteer in the *Thetis* when he was no more than 7 years old, and since then he had done bogus sea-time in three other ships by the fraudulent practice known as a false muster. To one who had worked his way up from the lower deck and who took such a pride in his profession as Larmour did, the incident could scarcely have been more provocative. He stood there with the uncle and his nephew for just so long as civility required, the lump of grease still in his hand, then turned to young Thomas and said curtly: 'Get your traps below.'

The Captain moved away to his own quarters, Thomas made his cramped way down the companion while his chest was manhandled along the deck behind him, and the First Lieutenant turned back to his rigging. But presently his eye fell on that chest, and Thomas heard from below the angry exclamation: 'This Lord Cochrane's chest? Does Lord Cochrane think he is going to bring a cabin aboard? The service is going to the devil. Get it up on the main deck.' The pent-up exasperation had found an outlet on which to expend itself, not the actual cause, as Larmour's words reveal so clearly, but one that would have to do. Thomas cringed in the midshipmen's quarters wondering what would happen next, until someone came to him and demanded the key of his chest. He handed it over and continued to wait, until an ominous sound of sawing brought him back on deck.

His possessions were scattered all over it, and a sailor was sawing one end off the chest, just beyond the keyhole, while Larmour stood surveying the havoc, still muttering expletives. When the chest was in two segments, Larmour turned to Thomas and pointed out that the keyhole in a ship's chest ought to be at one end, where it could be got at, and not in the middle. The new midshipman replied by thanking him for his kindness in imparting so useful a lesson, and the gravity with which he spoke contained no hint of insolence as he stood there beside his ruined chest and disordered kit. So Larmour turned to take a closer look at this outsize boy whom he had perhaps judged too hastily. And Thomas Cochrane, who never forgot the incident, could still recall over half a century later how honest Jack Larmour stood there 'evidently puzzled as to whether I was a cool hand or a simple one'.

What Larmour could not have guessed was that although Thomas was an Earl's heir his father was so poor that he had actually been obliged to borrow the hundred pounds which purchased that mutilated chest and its scattered contents. It was sheer ignorance, not affluence that led the lordling to bring a cabin aboard. Nor was Thomas to be unnerved by the sort of treatment he had just received from the First Lieutenant. He had lost his mother when he was 9, and since then he had received worse treatment from his eccentric father. In particular, his burning desire to go to sea had been stamped on with the utmost severity until finally, through the help of his uncle Alexander and his own persistence, his dream had at last come true on this magical day of June 1793. Compared with the triumph of standing in his first ship, the fate of his belongings strewn about the deck can have mattered little to him.

To have encountered such a man as Larmour was the greatest good fortune, a chance in a thousand. Thomas had not been sent to Eton or Harrow to grow up among his titled contemporaries. His father had been far too poor to give his sons an expensive schooling: indeed he had given them very little formal education at all. Thomas had grown up in the dilapidated mansion of Culross Abbey; and in the relatively egalitarian social world of Scotland he had preserved the Lowland Scottish accent of Fife, and an eye to personal worth, not inherited status. Nothing could have exceeded his respect for a sailor who had earned his promotion from the lower deck, or the sincerity of his thanks for the first lesson imparted to him. Jack Larmour would soon learn this when he found Lord Cochrane working beside him, also dressed in the rig of an ordinary seaman. When the *Hind* was ready for sea she was ordered north to Norwegian waters, and Cochrane lived in hope of an action with a French privateer or even a chance to harass an enemy convoy from the West Indies, sailing by the northern route round Orkney to avoid the British fleet in the Channel. He was disappointed: the *Hind* sighted no enemy vessels during that cruise. But it was the first time he had gone to sea, and there is no enchantment to be compared with the first fulfilment of a dream. He was able to participate in the intricate discipline of a team of men harnessing wind and sail against the forces of the ocean, study the routine of gunnery practice with the twenty-eight little 9-pounder guns that his ship carried, observe how efficiency and good morale are maintained amongst a haphazard assortment of men all compelled to live in an extremely confined space. The 17-year-old boy who was to perform such miracles with this kit of tackle, guns and human beings, did not need a sea battle at this stage in his apprenticeship, however much he would have enjoyed one.

As Cochrane recalled later with deep gratitude, it was Jack Larmour who was the making of him. Few relations in life are more satisfactory than those based on mutual esteem and a shared passion, and in addition the two men were united in their intention that Lord Cochrane should enjoy no further privileges because he was the nephew of the captain. Which of them first challenged the other is not clear. Either Cochrane boasted to Larmour that he would carry out his duties faultlessly despite his lack of previous service, or the First Lieutenant told Cochrane to watch his step, because he had never heard of such a thing as a faultless midshipman. Suffice to say, Larmour watched for the slightest shortcoming in Cochrane's behaviour, and young Thomas scurried to his duties, determined not to be caught. The game went on until once he went below when he thought Jack Larmour's back was turned. The moment he returned, Larmour called out to him: 'Mast-head, youngster.'

It was a bitterly cold day, and as Cochrane climbed the rigging to his windy perch above the sails he had an uneasy feeling that Larmour would leave him there a long time before calling him down again. He did: and Cochrane took care that he was never sent to the mast-head again.

They did not encounter heavy seas because the *Hind* spent most of her time in Norway's home waters, and among the offshore islands of that long coastline a ship can travel almost from one end of the country to the other without so much as meeting the swell of the open sea. As they sailed from one little Norwegian port to another, showing the British flag in a round of courtesy visits, Cochrane shared the wonder of all who set eyes on the deep fjords and towering mountains of western Norway. He also had ample opportunity to meet the inhabitants, 'for my uncle, though a strict disciplinarian, omitted no opportunity of gratifying those under his command, so that we spent nearly as much time on shore as on board'.

One aspect of Norwegian society struck him particularly. Here was the nearest equivalent in Europe to the world of the Scottish Highlands, with their chiefs of clans living in castles, and a social hierarchy of dependants beneath them descending to the mere tenants at will, who held their patches of land precariously, and often by the performance of unlimited servile labour. In the Lowland world of Fife where Cochrane had grown up things were certainly rather different, but his father the Earl of Dundonald was the chief of the name of Cochrane and he still lived in the tattered remains of feudal splendour at Culross Abbey. Here in Norway, by contrast, he found an entirely peasant society 'without any symptoms of that feudal attachment which then prevailed in Britain'. For centuries Norway had been the property of the Danish crown, and there were already Norwegians who dreamed of restoring her lost independence. But at least those who worked her land and fished her seas were peasant proprietors, not the tenants at will of an alien aristocracy, and Cochrane was able to recall later: 'I have never seen a people more contented and happy; not because their wants are few, for even luxuries were abundant and in common use.' Already the 17-year-old youth had discovered another of his lifelong enthusiasms, and one that was to be constantly at war with his passion for the sea. The politician had been born.

But he was still a boy, who could enjoy hurtling through the snow in a sleigh to the jingle of bells, the horses' hooves quite soundless in that vast silent world. He went shooting and fishing too, but he found the fish and game so plentiful that there was no sport in it. Once his uncle unbent so far as to take Thomas with him to a formal dinner at the house of a local magnate. The feast continued for about 5 hours and he was astonished to see his hostess standing at the head of the table, becoming increasingly flushed as she did all the carving herself. In Scotland servants were two a penny: not in this egalitarian society. Cochrane suspected that his hostess had also done all the cooking herself, and he anticipated the habits of a later age by suggesting that her menfolk might have lent a hand.

Captain Alexander Cochrane returned all this hospitality as well as he could aboard his little ship, and on one occasion this led to a hilarious accident. The ship's mascot was a parrot, which Jack Larmour hated because it had learned to imitate the pipes of the bosun's whistle, that excellent system for issuing orders in shrill notes that could be heard throughout the vessel. The parrot, having nothing better to do, would often throw the crew into confusion by issuing orders of its own and Larmour was helpless because the Captain had a partiality for the parrot—and possibly for its tricks too. But one day when a party of ladies was visiting the *Hind*, her mascot went too far. It watched as they were hoisted aboard in a chair, one after another, by means of a whip on the mainyard. A particularly unlucky young lady was ascending the side of the ship in her chair when the parrot suddenly piped from its perch in the rigging 'Let go.' Seamen are taught not to think, but to obey orders instantly, and so the unfortunate visitor went straight into the sea. If Jack Larmour had been present, the parrot would probably have perished on the spot, but it had thought of everything. The First Lieutenant happened to be ashore.

As the short northern summer drew to a close the *Hind* sailed home, where Captain Alexander Cochrane was given the command of the *Thetis*. He took Larmour and his nephew Thomas with him into his new ship's company, so that the young midshipman was able to do real service in the ship in which his name had been entered as a volunteer at the age of 7. She was a larger vessel than the *Hind*, though one of the smallest class of frigate, and she had returned from a tour the other side of the Atlantic to refit at Sheerness. Here, during the late autumn of 1793, honest Jack Larmour was to be seen, attending to his duties as usual while other officers were ashore on leave. But this time he had with him a tall eager youth with 'no more pride in my head than money in my pocket', also dressed in the rig of an ordinary seaman as he learnt the very pulse-beat of a wooden sailing ship equipped as a weapon of war.

Then at last the young midshipman took carriage back to London to visit the great-uncle, Colonel James Stuart, at whose home in Grosvenor Street he had spent his last night ashore before joining the *Hind* at Sheerness. Colonel Stuart would soon be departing for India, where he was to become a Lieutenant-General and the superior officer of the future Duke of Wellington in his campaign there. His sister the Dowager Countess of Dundonald had brought her grandson Thomas from Scotland to stay with the Colonel on his journey to his ship. He had left home a boy, in the care of relatives. That winter he returned to Culross a man.

His father's seat at Culross Abbey stood on a ridge of high ground looking south over the waters of the Forth. By the shore below stood the buildings of what remains to this day the most beautifully preserved ancient burgh in Scotland. The ruins of the old abbey church have also been restored as well as the centuries of destructive Calvinism have allowed, and in one of its transepts stands the memorial to Sir George Bruce, who had developed the coal-mines of Culross two centuries before. The Dundonald properties had belonged formerly to the Bruces, and today Culross Abbey is once more in the hands of Sir George Bruce's descendant, and during the interval these two families, chiefs of the names of Cochrane and Bruce, were repeatedly allied in marriage.

But the old mansion of Culross Abbey has been considerably rebuilt since the ninth Earl of Dundonald's time. Then, it was a somewhat unkempt block of three storeys with a tower at each end. The doorway had six windows on either side of it and the thirteen windows of the middle floor above were decorated with hoods of stone carving of the kind which the renaissance brought to Scotland. Inside, the ninth Earl lived in circumstances that had not yet been improved by the dowry which came with a second marriage, and he continued to indulge in new and ruinous scientific experiments.

The Earl was indeed a brilliant inventor, and had he possessed the slightest capacity for practical business, he might have made an enormous fortune. As it was, his son and heir looked on while 'our remaining patrimony melted like the flux in his crucibles' and Thomas inherited nothing from him except a title and a gold watch. Living above the coal-mines of Culross, it was naturally from this source that the Earl drew two of his most remarkable discoveries. First, he introduced the process of distilling tar from coal, with which he proposed that the wooden bottoms of ships should be coated as a preservative. Then, as his son Thomas recorded, 'having noticed the inflammable nature of a vapour arising during the distillation of tar, the Earl, by way of experiment, filled a gun barrel to the eduction pipe leading from the condenser. On applying fire to the muzzle, a vivid light blazed forth across the waters of the Forth.' Dundonald had discovered coal-gas, which would soon light the streets of Europe.

Thomas was in his father's company when he called to see James Watt, the Scottish inventor of the steam-engine, and told him of this discovery he had made at the tar-kilns of Culross, and it was one of Watt's assistants who introduced gas lighting years later in London. Now Thomas returned home a midshipman in the winter of 1793 to find his father immersed in fresh enthusiasm. His leaping mind had alighted upon such far-sighted targets as the means of converting peat moors into productive crop-lands, the malting of grain for cattle-feed and the use of salt refuse for manure. Anyone with such creative gifts ought to have been able to make an outstanding success of the principal function of all heads of noble families for centuries past; which was to maintain their landed properties as a profitable source of emolument to their whole family. But not the ninth Earl of Dundonald. When Thomas returned home from sea his father was preparing *A Treatise showing the intimate connection between Agriculture and Chemistry*, which he published in 1795. It anticipated the great Sir Humphrey Davy's *Elements of Agricultural Chemistry* by 18 years, but did nothing to relieve the indigence of an Earl whose name was worthy to rank with those of James Watt and Humphrey Davy, Joseph Priestley and Henry Cavendish, the forerunners of modern practical science. On the contrary, it merely helped to cement his local reputation as the Daft Dundonald.

But although Thomas returned to a widowed father from whom he had received scant material benefit, little affection and no encouragement to follow his chosen profession, he came to the source of one of his most enduring interests. For whether by precept or by heredity, he was to be his father's equal in practical invention, and unlike his father he was to put his ideas to the most stunningly effective use. In addition Thomas had the pleasure of seeing his younger brothers again, the youngest of whom, Archibald, was only 10, so that he could hardly have remembered his mother. The Earl's agent once remarked: 'It is true they have not had very much education, but they are strong and fine to look at and very sensible and will get on anywhere.' Throughout his life the unemotional Thomas was to retain a strong bond of loyalty and affection for his brothers.

In the spring he returned to Sheerness to board the *Thetis*, which sailed in May to Plymouth. So Cochrane at the age of 18 first set eyes on the port to which he would return one day like those Elizabethan sea captains who sailed home laden with the loot of the Spanish Main. His present tour of duty was to be comparatively uneventful. Captain Cochrane of the *Thetis* received orders to proceed to the North American station and guard the fisheries in the fog-bound waters off Newfoundland.

The first natural wonder that met his gaze there was a procession of icebergs, which stretched across their path as far as eye could reach in either direction. They encountered it at dawn, after a sudden drop in the temperature had warned them of the danger. As the *Thetis* altered course to pass round those walls of ice her crew saw an even more remarkable sight, no less than three ships cradled amongst them, the highest at least a hundred feet above the surface of the sea. But Cochrane did not merely lose himself in amazement at those sculptured shapes, or 'the wonderful display of reflected light which they present'. He noticed also, with his father's scientific precision, the dangerous indraught of water on their weather side, the heat caused by the sun's rays when the ship came within the angle of incidence of their reflection from the ice, the intense cold of the wind that had passed over it.

The monotony of his fishery protection duties was relieved when, within a year of his embarkation for this new tour of duty, he was transferred to the *Africa* with the rank of acting Lieutenant. She was a very much larger vessel than either of the two in which he had served already, with an armament of 64 guns, and it was an exceptional honour to have been promoted within two years of his entrance into the service. Thomas also had the satisfaction of knowing that this time he owed his rank entirely to his own merits, since the captain of the *Africa* had heard enough about his qualities to apply for him. It did, however, lead to one colossal disappointment. On 17 May 1795, almost exactly a month after his transfer, his uncle Alexander was involved with another frigate captain in an action against a squadron of five French ships, and captured two large store-vessels. It was the only important action in which he might have taken part during the entire five years he spent in the North American service, and he just missed it.

But he was not to know this at the time, as he adjusted to his new rank amongst a strange ship's company commanded by a man who was not his uncle. The experience which made the deepest impression on him then was the behaviour of his earliest recorded invention, during a cruise south along the coast of Florida. 'I had contrived a ball of lead studded with barbed prongs, for the purpose of catching porpoises. One day the doctor laid me a wager against hurling the missile a certain distance, and in the attempt a hook nearly tore off the fore-finger of my right hand.'

In his spare time at sea Cochrane tried to remedy the defects in his education by reading, and for one of his essentially practical mind he showed a somewhat strange taste for works of philosophy. Having nobody to guide him, he sometimes chose rather odd books, and he had just then read one by a philosopher who maintained that all pain was a delusion. Worse still, the young Lieutenant who had never been in action had preached this doctrine among people who knew better, and none more so than the ship's doctor. As he was dressing Cochrane's hand, the philosopher gave a cry of pain. 'What?' said the doctor, 'I thought there was no such thing as pain.' Cochrane replied lamely: 'My exclamation was not one of pain, but mental only, arising from the sight of my own blood.' The doctor chuckled, and Cochrane learnt to be more wary of exotic theories.

When he had served for just over 2 years aboard the *Africa*, Lieutenant Cochrane received another extremely gratifying transfer. On 21 June 1793 he was appointed to the Admiral's flagship.

Admiral Vandeput had obtained his present rank at the time when Cochrane first became a midshipman, after nearly 30 years' service as a Captain, and he had just been appointed to the command of the North American station when he summoned Cochrane to his ship. It was an elderly man whom Cochrane encountered there, a man who would die in harness 2 years later, before he could be invested with the honours to which his services entitled him. Cochrane was now 21 years old and possessed the growing confidence of a young man who has worked hard in his profession and received recognition for his efforts. But his experiences had not taught him how to conduct himself when he sat down to dine near an elderly Admiral in his flagship.

He made the familiar mistake of trying too hard. Admiral Vandeput turned to ask him what the dish before him contained: Cochrane told him, and enquired whether he might help him with it. Vandeput snapped back that when he wished for anything it was his habit to ask for it. In his embarrassment Cochrane asked the Admiral whether he would do him the honour of taking wine with him, only to be snubbed again. 'I never take wine with any man, my Lord,' said Admiral Vandeput. It was a trivial incident, and Cochrane accounted for it later by saying that Vandeput made a practice of displaying this intimidating façade at the outset. 'A very short time developed his true character— that of a perfect gentleman, and one of the kindest commanders living. In place of the hornet's nest figured in my imagination, there was not a happier ship afloat, nor one in which officers lived in more perfect harmony.' But in writing this, Cochrane revealed that he had not learnt the lesson so well as when he tore his finger on that barbed hook and discovered that pain is real. What he ought to have noticed was that he had said too much, and succeeded in antagonising a superior officer who would otherwise have remained perfectly well disposed towards him. It was the small but fatal flaw in his judgment, and because he could not cure it—did not even recognise it for what it was—it was to lead him to destruction. The Achilles heel of Thomas Cochrane was that he did not know when to keep his mouth shut, and in this apparently harmless context it had appeared already, during his very first professional encounter with an Admiral.

During the final year of Cochrane's North American service Admiral Vandeput shifted his headquarters from Halifax in Nova Scotia south to Chesapeake Bay, which divides the state of Virginia from Maryland. Relations between Britain and the United States were peaceful despite Britain's provocative habit of seizing seamen who had emigrated from the mother country and were serving in American ships. During that winter of 1797 Vandeput even found it possible to live ashore, and he used to invite his officers to stay with him in rotation for a week at a time. Cochrane was able to make himself acquainted with a society that had recently cast off its colonial status by force of arms, and yet remained in many ways more English than the English. There was hunting to hounds, though this sometimes led the riders through thick forests amongst perilous overhanging branches. There was shooting. There were dinner parties at which people drank as excessively as in the great houses of England.

Cochrane was an abstemious drinker and he boasted at the end of his days that he had never been drunk in his life. At one of these dinners the bottle circulated so fast that Cochrane resorted to a trick so that the other guests would not notice how little he drank. He leaned his head on his left hand as he pretended to drink, and poured the wine down the sleeve of his coat. How long he could have continued doing this before the wine would have begun to seep through to the lap of his neighbour was not put to the test. He was detected and condemned to drink a whole bottle as a penalty. Leaping from his seat, Cochrane darted out of the room, pursued by some of his companions: but he outstripped them and spent the night in a neighbouring farm-house. This was a time when a gentleman was supposed to be able to take his liquor, even if he was not able to hold it, and it says much for Cochrane's independence of character as a junior Lieutenant of 21 years that he was prepared to flout such a convention in public.

His loss of face on another occasion was more inadvertent still. While he was the guest of his Admiral he decided that he would go out and shoot a wild hog for his table. Off he strode to the forest with his gun, where he encountered what he took to be a wild sow with her litter of young pigs. He shot one of the pigs and before he could reload the sow charged him. He managed to scramble up a tree, but he had to leave his gun at the bottom where the sow remained also, on guard. Time passed, until the sow finally moved off to attend to the remainder of her family: but by then Cochrane returned far too late to provide roast sucking pig at the Admiral's table. He also had to offer an explanation for his long absence, and it provided much hilarity at his expense over dinner.

'It would be wearisome,' Cochrane ended his account of those years, 'to enter into further details respecting the operations of a squadron so ingloriously employed, or to notice the subordinate part which a junior Lieutenant could take in its proceedings.' When he transferred back to the *Thetis* to return home in the autumn of 1798, he had advanced dramatically in his naval career. But he had been relatively inactive in a distant station at a time when stupendous events had been occurring on the other side of the Atlantic.

The most alarming of these were the succession of mutinies that broke out in the British fleet. They assumed a character that had never been seen before when the Channel fleet was ordered to sea from Spithead on 15 April 1797, and sixteen ships of the line refused with disciplined precision. Their crews ran up the shrouds and gave three cheers as the signal for mutiny, unpopular officers were put ashore and two delegates from each ship met in the Admiral's cabin of the flagship *Queen Charlotte* to present their terms to the Board of Admiralty. It was in this very year that the great reforming Admiral, the Earl of St Vincent, wrote: 'the civil branch of the Navy is rotten to the very core'; and Britain's seamen had had enough of it.

Their wages had not been raised for over a hundred years, although the value of money had fallen considerably in the interval, and they had seen Army pay increased. They were sent to sea with rotten food provided by dishonest contractors, the sick and wounded were not properly cared for, they were not allowed adequate shore leave while their ships were in harbour. With remarkably well-organised persistence they insisted that these grievances should be redressed while politicians, civil servants and admirals scurried to and fro between London and Portsmouth. Finally the rise in pay was agreed, the proper issue of provisions, improved treatment of the wounded. 'But we beg to remind your Lordships,' wrote the mutineers, 'that it is a firm resolution that, until the flour in port be removed, the vegetables and pensions augmented, the grievances of private ships redressed, an Act passed, and his Majesty's gracious pardon for the fleet now lying at Spithead granted, the fleet will not lift an anchor; and this is the total and final answer.' They put no faith in the bland assurances of politicians.

The fleet was ordered to sea, and once again it refused to budge. It was not until a month later that the government sent the hero of Britain's recent naval victory of the Glorious First of June, Admiral Howe, with the Act of Parliament which the seamen demanded for their protection and plenary powers to settle the dispute. Two days later the fleet put to sea.

But only a few days after that a second mutiny broke out on an even larger scale, and this time the results were to be tragic. It was named after a sandbank at the mouth of the River Thames called the Nore, which lay near an anchorage between Sheerness and the open sea and gave its name to one of Britain's chief naval commands. The new mutiny broke out in the ships at the Nore and in the North Sea, and this time the delegates appointed as their president and spokesman a former midshipman called Richard Parker who had been court-martialled for misbehaviour in 1793 and discharged from the service in the following year on grounds of insanity. When the Admiralty accepted some of their demands but refused others, some of the mutineers expressed their defiance by firing at the fort of Sheerness. From the beginning there was an ugly hardening of attitudes on both sides.

The Admiralty sent a second conditional pardon if the men would return to duty, but Richard Parker rejected it, and for a few days longer the rebellious seamen paraded about the streets of Sheerness, holding meetings and cheering themselves with flags and music. Troops soon put a stop to that, and to Sheerness came the same Admiralty delegation that had formerly been sent to Portsmouth. Their attempts to reason with the mutineers merely provoked greater insolence until the commissioners departed for London, announcing that no further concessions would be offered. So the collision course continued to its fatal conclusion.

In the circumstances it is surprising that the rebel seamen did not sail their ships to an enemy port, since their fate was sealed so long as they remained where they were. But a creeping awareness of this only led them into increasingly disorganised and erratic courses. Some tried to coerce London into supporting their demands by blockading the port. Others tried without success to open negotiations with a ship's captain. Ships tried to escape from their incriminating neighbours and were fired on by them: they hauled down their red flags in a gesture of submission. There were bloody struggles aboard some of the ships before those who wished to submit gained the upper hand. Finally the ship in which Parker operated was taken by her crew under the guns of Sheerness, where a boarding party captured Parker with thirty of his delegates. He was tried and hanged on board, while other mutineers were imprisoned either in the Marshalsea or aboard a prison ship in the Medway.

The worst fate was suffered by those who were condemned to be flogged from ship to ship as a ghastly deterrent to the other seamen of the fleet. It was one of the most horrible methods that could have been devised for torturing a man to death slowly, in full view of his fellow-men. With elaborate ritual he was placed in a boat to be rowed from ship to ship, drums beating to deafen his screams as the lash was applied at measured intervals. The punishment might be anything up to 500 lashes, and it would have been relatively humane to allow the man to die under the punishment. But there was a doctor present to ensure that this did not happen. As soon as he judged that the culprit's life was in danger he was taken to hospital and nursed back to health before his punishment was resumed. It was not uncommon, however, for him to die under his second flogging. By the time Cochrane returned from the North Atlantic station, isolated mutinies still occurred, but they became increasingly rare, and there were no more on the scale of those at Spithead and the Nore. The reforms introduced after the one, and the savage punishments inflicted after the other, both played their part in this result.

By chance Cochrane had been separated by the broad Atlantic from one of the most dramatic conflicts between the Admiralty and its seamen in the whole of British history—he who was to wreck his own career in the British Navy by embarking on a similar course.

He had also missed a succession of major sea battles, including Britain's greatest naval victory of the eighteenth century, all of which had taken place despite the troubles in her home ports. The earliest was Admiral Howe's defeat of the French fleet on the Glorious First of June in 1794. Next came the news of Admiral Jervis' victory over the grand fleet of Spain off Cape St Vincent in 1797, while it was on its way to join the Dutch and French fleets and take part in the invasion of England. Before the year was out, the third triumph followed when Admiral Duncan captured more than half the strength of the Dutch fleet in a bloodthirsty engagement of Camperdown. These hammer blows removed the immediate threat of invasion, but they were nothing to the one which Nelson administered to the French fleet in August 1798 at the battle of the Nile. Here Napoleon's naval armament was virtually annihilated, and his plans for eastern conquest with it. Cochrane had lost the opportunity to take part in all these engagements while he had been gazing at icebergs or shooting at hogs on the other side of the Atlantic.

On the other hand he had gained a proficiency and a seniority unusual for his years, and he was about to enjoy another short-cut to fresh opportunity. For at the time of his return the second in command of the Mediterranean station happened also to be at home, and he too happened to be the son of a Scottish peer although he had been ennobled for his naval service with the title of Viscount Keith. Admiral Keith offered Cochrane the post of supernumary Lieutenant aboard his flagship, and so the fortunate youth found himself on 14 December 1798—his twenty-third birthday—approaching the goal of his dreams, the great rock of Gibraltar, arsenal of the Mediterranean fleet.

Presently he was taken ashore to meet Old Jarvie, the Commander-in-Chief, Earl of St Vincent since his victory over the Spanish fleet in the previous year. St Vincent was in poor health and it was understood that Keith would soon be taking over the Mediterranean command from him. He could be as curt as Admiral Vandeput at the best of times and he disliked favouritism in the service as much as any other form of corruption. Although he received Cochrane kindly at this first meeting, he is likely to have scrutinised his record with more than his customary thoroughness before confirming the appointment of an officer who had enjoyed such obvious favours. But evidently he was satisfied, for Cochrane was posted to the *Barfleur* when Keith shifted his flag to her at Gibraltar, and so embarked on the final period of his apprenticeship, with its omens for the future both good and bad.

The first ill omen bore a sinister resemblance to the episode, at Admiral Vandeput's dining table. 'Our First Lieutenant, Beaver,' Cochrane explained later, 'was an officer who carried etiquette in the wardroom and on deck almost to despotism. He was laudably particular in all matters visible to the eye of the Admiral, but permitted an honest penny to be turned elsewhere by a practice as reprehensible as revolting. On our frequent visits to Tetuan we purchased and killed bullocks on board the *Barfleur*, for the use of the whole squadron. The reason was that the raw hides, being valuable, could be stowed away in her hold in empty beef casks, as especial perquisites to certain persons connected with the flag-ship; a natural result being that, as the fleshy parts of the hides decomposed, putrid liquor oozed out of the casks and rendered the hold of the vessel so intolerable that she acquired the name of "the stinking Scotch ship".'

Out came Cochrane's Achilles heel. 'As junior Lieutenant, much of the unpleasantness of this fell to my share, and as I always had a habit of speaking my mind without reserve, it followed that those interested in the raw hide speculation were not very friendly disposed towards me.' For the second time Cochrane's memoir reveals a totally uncritical attitude to his fatal inability to keep his mouth shut, and this time the consequences were to enshrine the passing annoyance of an Admiral in the records of a court-martial.

Criticised by a junior officer, the Flag-Lieutenant had only to wait for an opportunity to strike back, and it came after Cochrane had gone ashore at Tetuan to shoot wild fowl. During the course of his sport he became covered with mud, and consequently did not join the other officers who returned from their shore-leave in the ship's pinnace, but waited for the launch. It was delayed, so that Cochrane reached the ship shortly after his leave had expired, as the Flag-Lieutenant observed from the gangway. Rather than report on the quarterdeck in his filthy condition, Cochrane first went below to change into a clean uniform, and from there repaired to the wardroom. Here Lieutenant Beaver asked him why he had not reported on the quarterdeck when he returned to the ship; Cochrane retorted that Beaver had seen him come up the side and therefore knew he was not in a fit condition to appear on the quarterdeck. Beaver's reply easily provoked him into reminding the Flag-Lieutenant that he himself had made a rule that matters connected with the service should not be discussed in the wardroom. From the insolence of this piece of logic it was a short step to Cochrane's fatal remark: 'Lieutenant Beaver, we will, if you please, talk of this in another place.' Cochrane was given one last opportunity to escape the consequences when the Captain intervened by suggesting that Beaver should accept an apology and allow the matter to drop. Cochrane insisted that he had no apology to make, and the result was a court-martial.

It was Lord Keith's disagreeable responsibility to sit as president of the court, and listen to the details of the squabble as the other men in the wardroom related it. 'Here are all the Flag Officers and Captains called together,' he remarked irritably, 'when the wind is coming fair and the ships ought to be under weigh. I think I am made the most ridiculous person of the whole.' The charge he had to consider was whether Cochrane had issued a challenge to the Flag-Lieutenant, and he dismissed it in the following words: 'The court having heard the evidence on behalf of the prosecution, and what the prisoner had to allege in his defence, and having maturely weighed and considered the same, is of opinion that the charges are not proved, and do therefore acquit the said Lord Cochrane.'

But in his exasperation Admiral Keith added some advice to his tactless young protégé that was unfortunately written down in the court record. 'I am directed by the court to say that officers should not reply sharply to their superior officers, and a First Lieutenant's situation should be supported by everyone. A ship is but a small place where six or seven hundred persons are collected together, and officers should in every part of it avoid flippancy.' A somewhat bizarre word for the fatal flaw in Cochrane's character. Now it was chalked up on the slate of his service record in the files of the Admiralty.

For the present, relieved by his acquittal, he probably thought little of it, especially as there was the exciting prospect that he would soon be engaged in his first fleet action. In the spring of 1799 Admiral Keith received intelligence that the French fleet had escaped from the British blockade of Brest and was sailing to join the Spanish fleet at Cadiz. With his sixteen ships Keith hurried to prevent a junction of thirty-three French sails with twenty-two Spanish ones, and Cochrane witnessed the superb audacity with which he placed himself between the two overwhelmingly superior forces. But instead of attacking him, the French Admiral continued south through the Straits of Gibraltar, while Keith gave chase. In the Mediterranean the British fleet was dispersed in scattered detachments, which St Vincent attempted to concentrate as fast as he could. But the French Admiral outwitted the two British ones by doubling on his course and sailing back through the Straits to join the Spanish fleet.

There has been much discussion ever since as to whether the fault was Keith's or St Vincent's: if indeed any blame can be attached to either. Cochrane later laid the blame entirely on St Vincent, and it is true that he was by now an extremely sick man who ought perhaps to have laid down his command before his health compelled him to do so on 2 June. He was certainly much criticised for sailing home ostentatiously in the largest ship of the Mediterranean fleet, a vessel of 110 guns, when its interests would have been better served had he merely travelled in a frigate. But neither these circumstances nor the dexterity of the French Admiral add up to grounds for blaming either of the British ones.

On 14 June 1799 Keith shifted his flag as Commander-in-Chief in the Mediterranean, from the *Barfleur* to the *Queen Charlotte*, a vessel of 100 guns and consequently the largest in which Cochrane had yet served. In the Admiral's cabin of this ship the Spithead mutineers had held their conferences with the delegates from the Admiralty just over 2 years before, and there were still many seamen amongst the crew who had been among the rebels. In his new flagship Admiral Keith sailed to Torbay, where he entrusted to Cochrane his despatches for the Commander-in-Chief of the Channel fleet. He was received on board by the Flag Captain, who instantly reprimanded him for infringing the quarantine regulations by coming aboard. Once again Cochrane failed to hold his tongue. He was still spending much of his leisure time aboard in reading the philosophers, and this was sharpening his naturally logical mind to a degree most hazardous in one who could not resist plain speech to superior officers. This time he escaped unscathed, but his account of the episode reveals that once again it had taught him nothing.

When the *Queen Charlotte* returned to her station she sailed east to Sicily, and there at Palermo Cochrane at last met that darling of the Neapolitan court, Lord Nelson. Several conversations took place between the two greatest British seamen of their age, the one so near to his death, the other poised upon the threshold of his career. Cochrane recorded only Nelson's advice: 'Never mind manoeuvres, always go at them.' And in reflecting on what he owed to Nelson's advice and example, he commented: 'It has been remarked that Trafalgar was a rash action, and had Nelson lost it and lived he would have been brought to a court-martial for the way in which that action was conducted.'

On 21 September Cochrane was at last given his first chance to fight the enemy. Keith observed a cutter being chased by some gunboats and privateers in the Bay of Gibraltar, and he ordered his ship's boats to be launched for an attack. On Cochrane he bestowed the honour of commanding the Admiral's cutter, while Lieutenant Beaver put out in one of the other boats. With his crew of sixteen, Beaver boarded his vessel successfully, and Cochrane laid his cutter alongside one of the enemy privateers and leapt aboard with an encouraging cry to his sailors. To his mortification not a sailor stirred, so that he was forced to jump back into his cutter and abandon the attack. Evidently the spirit of Spithead was not yet dead in the *Queen Charlotte*.

For Cochrane it must have been a numbing experience. The most confident and extrovert characters have their dark corners of self-doubt and his had been invaded by the strictures of superiors and by the indifference of those he had tried to lead in action. He had now served for over 6 years in the Navy, and in all that time his only opportunity to prove himself had ended in fiasco. In December his twenty-fourth birthday came and went.

To his delight his youngest brother Archibald joined the ship as a midshipman at this moment of gloom. At 17 Archibald had determined to follow in the footsteps of the brother he admired so much, and this time the Earl of Dundonald seems to have raised no objections. He had just made a second marriage which retrieved his fortunes for a brief space, and he may have found it convenient to dismiss the youngest child of his first marriage at such a time. At any rate, Archibald reached the *Queen Charlotte* just in time to share with his brother Thomas the adventure which was to launch him at last on the road to fame, wealth, the highest rank in his service, and the deepest degradation that his countrymen could have inflicted on him.

It was made possible by the confidence which Admiral Keith continued to place in him: a confidence quite independent of the favour he had shewn to the Cochrane brothers by placing them in his ship.

One of the French vessels that had escaped from Nelson at the battle of the Nile was the *Généreux*, of 74 guns. She was captured, in very poor shape, on 18 February 1800, and it was necessary to sail her at once to Port Mahon in Minorca so that she could be repaired and refitted for use in the British fleet. For such a service Keith could only spare the sick, lightly wounded and least competent of his own seamen, and it was to Thomas Cochrane that he entrusted this damaged vessel with its unpromising crew, on its 500-mile voyage to Port Mahon. He allowed Cochrane to take his young brother Archibald with him.

They had hardly left Gibraltar before the *Généreux* encountered a gale of such severity that the men refused to go aloft, so dangerously did the masts sway in that lunging ship. As there was an immediate danger that the ship would founder unless the sails were furled Thomas called to his brother Archibald and the two youths led the way up the rigging on their own. This time the seamen followed, the ship was saved, and by June she was back in service as a British vessel of war.

Meanwhile the brothers and their crew had escaped a more dreadful fate through their appointment to the *Généreux*. For during their trip to Port Mahon the Admiral sailed in his flagship to Leghorn on the coast of Italy, and there landed with a part of his staff. He contemplated an attack on the neighbouring island of Capraia, and accordingly ordered his captain to reconnoitre its shores. At 6 a.m. on the morning of 17 March, as the *Queen Charlotte* lay off Capraia, she caught fire and by

11 o'clock she had completely burnt out. The accident was thought to have been caused by some hay left under the half-deck, which was set alight by a match kept in a tub nearby to fire the signal guns. Of the 829 men on board only 156 were saved, and among those who perished were the Captain, two Lieutenants, the Captain of Marines, Surgeon, Purser, Master and Boatswain. Beaver the martinet survived to serve for another 14 years in the Navy and reach the rank of Captain, but 18 midshipmen were killed. Had the Cochrane brothers been aboard, their chances of survival would have been slight. The *Queen Charlotte* was not a lucky ship.

As it was, Thomas was reunited with his Admiral to receive a commendation for his service in the *Généreux* and to be appointed to his first command. On 10 May 1800 he sailed out of Port Mahon in the vessel whose name he was about to make as famous as his own throughout Europe. His apprenticeship was over at last.

CHAPTER TWO

First Command

Cochrane's new ship was a comic contrast to the *Queen Charlotte* with her armament of a hundred guns. She was a converted brig of a mere 158 tons, a burlesque of a ship as Cochrane described her, scarcely fit to rate as a vessel of war at all. She carried fourteen guns, but they were only 4-pounders, with the fire-power of a blunderbuss. Cochrane once amused himself by walking the deck with their total shot for a broadside in his pockets.

His cabin was only 5 feet high; and at the age of 24 Cochrane was now over 6 feet 2 inches in height, and bulky of limb. The remainder of the ship was equally congested with her crew of eighty-four men and six officers. But instead of being a junior officer in a ship containing over 800 men he was now in command of this crew which lived at close quarters with him, and it developed a wholly different dimension of his character. There were no longer senior officers to grow touchy over the larky behaviour of a privileged young peer in their midst, none to spark off the aggressive streak which his impecunious background and difficult father had engendered in him. In this little brig he was not separated from his seamen by the etiquette of a wardroom in an Admiral's flagship. They could see him as he really was, and they soon showed how impressed they were by what they saw.

Cochrane had equal grounds for satisfaction over his crew. It was his good fortune that the previous commander of the brig had been Jahleel Brenton, a seaman, no less professional and devoted to the service than himself, so that he inherited the enormous asset of a happy ship. Since this was her only asset, Cochrane gave all his attention to the possibility of adding a few others. When he tried to mount larger guns in her he found that they could not be operated in such a confined space, and anyway her decks would not stand the strain.

But at least he could force her to live up to her name, which was *Speedy*. He applied for a new mainyard, and was supplied with the fore-topgallant yard of the captured *Généreux*. The dockyard authorities decreed that it was too long for the *Speedy* and would have to be cut down, but Cochrane outwitted them by having the yardarms planed so that they appeared to have been shortened, and so enabled his brig to carry an exceptional spread of sail for her size. On 10 May he sailed out of Port Mahon and captured his first enemy vessel the same day, 'my first piece of luck', as Cochrane called it in his log.

It was now almost 2 years since Nelson's victory at the mouth of the Nile had destroyed Napoleon's dream of eastern conquest and restored Britain's naval power in the Mediterranean. But it was still far from paramount, and in particular the vital strategic island of Malta was still in French hands. Napoleon had been acclaimed First Consul, with dictatorial powers to mobilise his country's resources of which he made effective use. The entire Mediterranean coast of Spain and France was a Goliath awaiting the puny little *Speedy*, with her armament like David's sling. Cochrane gained his first prize east of the island of Sardinia: during the next 13 months he would capture over fifty vessels and more than 500 prisoners, and perform the feat which earned from Napoleon the epithet *le Loup de Mer*, the Sea Wolf.

Again and again the comic little *Speedy* struck, and her outsize commander sent his prizes to Lord Keith at Leghorn. Then, in August, the Commander-in-Chief sent Cochrane to harry the shipping off the Spanish coast. The *Speedy* was now entirely on her own, and as she pursued her solitary task, Cochrane drew upon the only and priceless legacy he had received from his father—an inexhaustible gift for invention.

He adopted the practice of remaining far from the enemy coast by day, sailing inshore during the night, and striking just before the first light of dawn. It had never been done before, perhaps because it had not been thought of, perhaps because of the danger of approaching too near a treacherous coast in pitch darkness. It certainly required strong nerves and high standards of seamanship, and before long it began to be necessary to add something more. For Cochrane remained alone in inflicting the terror of night attacks along the Spanish coast, so that it was only a matter of time before his tiny brig was identified as the source of the mischief and singled out for destruction. Gradually he became aware of the excessive attention he was attracting from enemy ships of war.

He met it with a stratagem that anticipated a trick of twentieth-century warfare by over a hundred years. He had noticed an innocuous Danish coastal brig that was well known in Spanish waters and he painted the *Speedy* in imitation of her. He even added a Danish quarter-master to his crew, and provided him with the uniform of an officer of that nation, an early example of the meticulous attention to detail that was to pay such rich dividends. In December his ruse was put to the test. Cochrane approached too close to a vessel that appeared to be a heavily laden merchantman, but proved instead to be a large Spanish frigate. To flee would have been impossible, so Cochrane blandly hoisted Danish colours and hailed the frigate. The Spaniards responded by sending a boat-load of armed men to board the *Speedy*. But while her crew watched its approach with bated breath, Cochrane ordered the quarantine flag to be hoisted and instructed his Danish quartermaster to explain that they had just sailed from Algiers, where the plague was raging. The Spanish boarding party lay tossing on the sea below the decks of the *Speedy* while the quartermaster imparted the awful news to them: then they rowed hastily back to the frigate. The *Speedy* was saved, and what was more, her crew gradually gained such confidence in their commander as a result of strokes like these that they came to believe in their own invincibility too.

By December, when the incident occurred, Malta had been recovered from the French, and Cochrane sailed to the island in the New Year of 1801 to enjoy the festivities. In the port of Valletta tickets were on sale for a fancy-dress ball, and he bought one of them. The disguise he chose was the very rig he had worn to work with honest Jack Larmour in the dockyard of Sheerness, the dress of a British seaman.

There was still no uniform costume issued to the sailors of the British Navy, but it was customary for them to wear white trousers, a blue jacket and a tarpaulin hat, and they could draw these items from the purser's stores. The familiar straw hat was just coming into fashion and dandies of the lower deck would bedeck it with ribbons. Beneath this finery they still wore a pigtail: even in the wardroom it did not go out of fashion until some years after that fancy-dress dance in Valletta, where Cochrane planted a lump of grease in his straw hat for good measure and adorned himself with a marlin spike.

Some officers of a French royalist regiment were standing near the entrance to the ballroom as he came in, and mistook him for an ordinary seaman. He must have been aware how effectively he could have soothed their sensibilities by explaining that he was an officer and what was more, a nobleman, but to have done this would have been right out of character. Instead, he observed that the costume of a British seaman was just as honourable as any of the other fancy dresses in fashion, and strode on into the ballroom. One of the officers tried to seize him: he received a cool look from the blue-eyed giant, and then Cochrane struck him. Immediately there was an outburst of Latin excitement. A French picket was called which carried Cochrane by force to the regimental guardroom without first establishing his identity. When he revealed it he was immediately freed, but the French officer whom he had struck demanded an apology and challenged

Cochrane to a duel when he refused it. They met the following morning behind the ramparts of Valletta, where Cochrane shot his adversary in the thigh and himself escaped with a bruised rib or two. 'It was a lesson to me in future, never to do anything in frolic which might give even unintentional offence,' he reflected. But most human beings do not alter their behaviour pattern as often as they repent it, and the only difference in Cochrane's case was that he so seldom repented.

It was an exceptionally stormy winter in the Mediterranean, increasing the hazard of operations at night. But still the log-book of the *Speedy* continued to swell with the record of Cochrane's depredations. Early in February he sighted in the bay of Tunis a French brig carrying arms and ammunition to Napoleon's army in Egypt. The brig sailed into a neutral port and there anchored. Flouting the laws of neutrality, Cochrane boarded her during the night and brought her out before the astonished crew could communicate with the shore authorities. The following day the ammunition destined for Alexandria was transferred to the *Speedy*, and in the evening Cochrane solved the problem presented by the captured French crew. He ordered the ship's launch to be left unguarded and made other discreet arrangements that encouraged the French sailors to plan an escape. During the night they succeeded in getting away in the launch, and were presently making their outraged report to the Bey of Tunis while Cochrane escorted Napoleon's ship-load of field pieces to Minorca.

He had scarcely left Port Mahon after handing over his prize when a large enemy frigate sighted the hated *Speedy*, and immediately gave chase. Fortunately for Cochrane it occurred at dusk, and all through the night he strained his sails and spars in an attempt to elude his pursuer. But there she was the next day to continue the chase, and by the time daylight died again she had gained perilously on the *Speedy*. So when it was quite dark Cochrane played another of his tricks. He dropped a tub overboard containing a lantern, and left the frigate to pursue it through the night while he abruptly altered course. Dawn broke the next day on an empty horizon.

But the next time the *Speedy* encountered an enemy frigate there was no escape. By this time her crew had been reduced in number to fifty-four men and boys (although this was not caused by casualties but by the detachment of prize crews), and this ship's company had reached such a pitch of enthusiasm and self-confidence that they actually clamoured to take the offensive against a warship with a crew of over 300 men. Apparently it meant nothing to them that their dozen or so little 4-pounder guns were opposed by an armament that included twenty-two 12-pounders and eight 8-pounders. Their infinitely resourceful captain would find some means of making their guns effective and frustrating those of the enemy.

He did just that, in an action which has been described as unique in naval history. It occurred on the morning of the 6 May 1801, when Cochrane had just captured a prize off Barcelona and returned to the same waters to pounce again. Suddenly, from behind a number of smaller vessels, there billowed a large Spanish frigate, *El Gamo*, which proceeded to give chase. Instead of attempting flight, which would have been useless, the *Speedy* turned to approach her, hoisting American colours to delay the *Gamo*'s first broadside for just long enough to enable the *Speedy* to pass out of range on the other tack. Cochrane then ran up the British ensign, sailed in through two broadsides without wasting any shot in return, and attached himself alongside the *Gamo*.

He had conceived an elaborate plan of action in the twinkling of an eye, and the speed of it was only equalled by the perfection of its details. He had not been too busy mystifying the enemy with his flags or ordering the movements of his vessel to notice that the maindeck of the *Gamo* lay a full 10 feet higher than that of the *Speedy*. As he sailed in, he ordered his little guns to be trebly shotted, and as soon as he was alongside he fired at point-blank range up the *Gamo*'s maindeck, killing both her captain and her bosun, while the guns of the *Gamo* sent their broadside whizzing harmlessly over his head.

The Spanish seamen were immediately ordered to board the *Speedy*, but above the din Cochrane heard the order, and he sheered off and raked the hull of the *Gamo* again before returning alongside. So it continued for upwards of an hour, the enemy alternately attempting to board the *Speedy* and firing through her rigging as Cochrane came and went like a wasp. The slightest error of judgment would have exposed him to the overwhelming force of over 300 men or 20 powerful guns, but Cochrane and his men worked with such mutual confidence and precision that all the resources of that great frigate were powerless against the little brig.

However, Cochrane knew that if the enemy's fire were to dismast his ship the game would be lost, and it was only a matter of time before such an accident would occur. He therefore ordered his crew of fifty men to board the vessel whose maindeck lay 10 feet higher than his own, and fight her crew of over 300 men, and such was their belief in him that they obeyed. The ship's doctor was left alone at the helm of the *Speedy*.

In describing the preparations he made for this assault, Cochrane remarked: 'No device can be too minute, even if apparently absurd, provided it has the effect of diverting the enemy's attention whilst you are concentrating your own'. He ordered some of his men to blacken their faces and to clamber aboard by the prow, cutlasses in their mouths. It was sufficiently astonishing to the Spaniards that so few men would dare to board their ship: but when they also saw such fearful apparitions emerging through the smoke of the bow guns, they stood unnerved for exactly the space of time that permitted Cochrane to lead the other assault party aboard in the waist of the ship and surprise them yet again in an attack from behind.

He had one trick more in store for them, and it proved to be decisive. He ordered one of his men to haul down the Spanish colours. Assuming that their colours had been struck by their own officers, the Spaniards thereupon surrendered. Cochrane had captured the *Gamo* with the loss of three seamen killed and one officer and seventeen men wounded. The casualties among the enemy amounted to more than the entire crew of the *Speedy*.

The only remaining problem was how to secure such an enormous prize despite the disparity in numbers. Cochrane drove the Spaniards into the hold of their vessel, pointed one of their own guns down the hatch, and placed a permanent guard with lighted matches beside them.

He hit upon a further solution. He could recall that his present position owed much to the task Admiral Keith had entrusted to him when he ordered Cochrane to sail the captured *Généreux* with her skeleton crew to Port Mahon. His brother Archibald had been permitted to join the *Speedy*, and he now gave Archibald exactly the privilege he had enjoyed himself—to sail the *Gamo* to Minorca while Thomas Cochrane escorted it there in triumph. As the two vessels made their merry journey, Cochrane looked forward with exhilaration to being promoted to the rank of Captain and placed in command of the captured *Gamo*. It was not an extravagant hope: officers were promoted for a great deal less than he had achieved.

The trouble was that his temperament was ill-qualified to bear with disappointment, and the next orders he received came as a bitter anti-climax. No sooner had the *Speedy* been repaired in Port Mahon than he was instructed to proceed on a diplomatic mission to the Dey of Algiers. It was about as cretinous an order as even the Admiralty of that day could have issued to an officer on active service. Neither the size of the *Speedy* nor the age or rank of her commander were appropriate to the mission of lodging a protest with the Dey of Algiers against acts of piracy. It was particularly tactless to send Cochrane, whose own depredations were notorious, and who had recently infringed the neutrality of a North African port. Indeed, the Admiralty's order would only have possessed any logic if the intention had been to send the most promising young officer in the Royal Navy to his death. It was only a matter of decades since an earlier Dey of Algiers had received a protest from the British government because he 'was detaining a British seaman in captivity, and responded by producing the miserable sailor before the Consul of King George III, tortured and mangled, as evidence of his contempt for such representations. The present Dey was a ruler of much the same stamp, and he gave Cochrane a sufficiently frightening reception. 'I was ushered through a series of galleries lined with men, each bearing on his shoulder a formidable-looking axe, and eyeing me with an insolent scowl, evidently meant to convey the satisfaction with which they would apply its edge to my vertebrae, should the caprice of their chief so will.'

But this time the Dey merely expressed his contempt by showering Cochrane with insults and then ordering an Algerian vessel to chase the *Speedy* from his shores. It was the Dey himself who later perished beneath those axes.

Cochrane returned from this humiliation to discover that he would not obtain command of the *Gamo*, which had been sold for a trifle to the very people who had just treated the British flag with such disrespect, 'whilst I was condemned to continue in the pigmy and now battered craft by which she had been taken. To have obtained command of the *Gamo*, even as a means of deception on the enemy's coast, I would scarcely have changed place with an admiral.' Worse still, the despatches describing his capture of the *Gamo* took 3 months to reach the Admiralty, with consequences for his promotion that were to deepen his resentment even further.

But he returned with a will to his raiding activities, and soon captured a Spanish privateer of six guns which he placed under the command of his brother Archibald as a tender to the *Speedy*. Shortly afterwards he fell in with the British vessel of war *Kangaroo* with significant consequences. For the *Kangaroo* was a larger ship, carrying eighteen guns, and her skipper, George Pulling, was the senior of the two Commanders. Presently they observed a Spanish convoy lying under the protection of a battery at Oropeso and Cochrane proposed that they should sail in at midnight and cut them out. Pulling could not know that Cochrane would one day rank as the greatest genius in the art of cutting out enemy vessels in the history of naval warfare, and despite the phenomenal success of his subordinate's night attacks, he refused to adopt his tactics.

Instead he deferred the attack until noon on the following day. The *Kangaroo* then anchored within range of the fort and bombarded it while Cochrane in the *Speedy* and his brother in the tender moved in to fire at the craft sheltering under its protection. Other Spanish ships arrived to take part in the cannonade and after about 9 hours several of the enemy boats were sunk, while the British ones ran almost entirely out of ammunition. They therefore advanced without further delay on some merchantmen and compelled these to run ashore. But there they were protected by Spanish troops on the beaches, and without ammunition it was impossible to fight for the stranded vessels. In a night raid Cochrane would probably have succeeded in cutting them out and carrying them off as prizes, but there was worse to it than that. Pulling had to report the loss of three officers and eight seamen in the *Kangaroo*, a heavier list of casualties than it had cost Cochrane to capture the *Gamo*.

Later, Cochrane was to publish an explanation for the failure of British warships to carry out night raids on the enemy's coastal shipping (or indeed daylight raids either) that had nothing to do with timidity or conventional thinking. He attached the blame to the dishonesty of the Admiralty courts whose responsibility it was to apportion the prize money for captured ships. The large number of prizes which the *Speedy* brought home from her night raids provided him with early and cumulative evidence of these peculations, and of their effect on the morale of seamen who risked life and limb, only to discover that they were enriching dishonest shore officials. 'The amusement of destroying the enemy's trading vessels, even under the excitement occasioned by protecting batteries, ceased to operate as a permanent incentive; and as a result, as may be seen by the logs of frigates, etc. stationed on the enemy's coast, was that their commanders avoided the risk of keeping their ships in contiguity with the shore, and adopted the only means of securing a comfortable night's rest by running into the offing. By daylight the coasting convoys got into some port or place of protection. Consequently the British cruisers, having nothing in sight, their ropes were coiled up, the decks were washed, the hammocks stowed, and at eight o'clock the order was given to pipe to breakfast. In addition to this, the daily journal consisted of little more than the state of the weather, accompanied by the comprehensive remark, "employed as usual".'

The log of the *Speedy* makes rather different reading, and there could have been few such restful nights aboard her. But her crew were rewarded for their unrelenting toil and their prodigies of valour by the prize money for their captures—diminished by the pickings of the Admiralty court officials. Gradually it became Cochrane's settled conviction, rightly or wrongly, that many other officers and their crews would not follow his example because they were unwilling to risk their lives for the benefit of such men. 'If it should be objected that I am deprecating the character of officers, I answer first, that I state only the truth: and secondly that I do not consider such truth as at all derogatory to their character. It is no reflection on their honour, and is creditable to their common sense. They could not reasonably be expected to sacrifice their rest, and to run their ships into danger and themselves into debt, for the exclusive emolument of the Courts of Admiralty.'

These remarks were not published until over 40 years later, but they naturally raise the gravest misgivings over Cochrane's relations with the shore authorities in the ports to which he returned in the Mediterranean, and the question whether the despatch upon which his promotion depended was held up for almost 3 months entirely by accident in its journey to the Admiralty. If he could not hold his tongue in the presence of senior officers aboard ship, is he likely to have exercised greater tact towards officials of the Admiralty courts whom he believed to be cheating him and his seamen over their prize money? What would George Pulling of the *Kangaroo*—soon to be promoted Captain like Cochrane himself—have thought of such explanations for his conduct if they had come to his ears? Gradually Cochrane's hornet's nest was growing in size, and it would not be long before he would be stung.

The successes of the *Speedy* under his command had continued unbroken for over a year and his ingenuity and luck could not last for ever. Indeed, it is a wonder that they did not expire sooner, when the slightest miscalculation could have been fatal in almost every major action in which he had engaged. Cochrane now commttted the error of judgment which brought the cruise of the *Speedy* to an end.

He had returned to Port Mahon in company with the *Kangaroo*, where he received instructions to convoy the mail packet from Minorca to Gibraltar. It was an appropriate enough task for such an insignificant vessel as the *Speedy*, but not for a Commander with Cochrane's record. He felt it to be much below his dignity: it also bored him. As he sailed west down the Spanish coast in the company of the mail packet, he used his superior spread of sail to dart off and explore the creeks and bays for enemy shipping that might be lurking there. They were about half-way to Gibraltar when he sighted some promising-looking ships off Alicante and immediately pounced on them. They quickly weighed anchor and ran ashore. It would have been impossible for Cochrane to refloat them and sail them out without failing in his instructions to convoy the mails, so instead he set fire to them.

That was his first error. One of the vessels contained a cargo of oil, whose flames illumined the night sky for miles. The blaze was seen by three French line-of-battle ships which had escaped from the blockade of Toulon and were sailing west towards the Straits of Gibraltar like Cochrane. They altered course to investigate and at daybreak he sighted them on the horizon. Ignorant that there could be French warships in these waters, he sped towards them to discover whether they were Spanish galleons filled with riches from South America. That was his second error. He expiated both in a last, heroic, hopeless attempt to save his little brig from the three leviathans that billowed towards him.

Never were the masts and spars of the *Speedy* burdened with more canvas, but it was to no avail. The wind dropped. To lighten ship Cochrane flung those useless 4-pounders overboard, then all his stores. But still the French warships gained on him, and then they separated on different tacks to encircle him. As they came within range, each fired a broadside, so that it was only a matter of time before one of them would sink the *Speedy* with a single salvo. Nevertheless Cochrane ran the gauntlet for over 3 hours, employing every subterfuge of seamanship that his fertile brain could devise.

Finally one of the warships sailed within musket range, and let fly a complete broadside of round and grape shot which would have sent the *Speedy* to the bottom had the enemy ship not turned too abruptly, so that her missiles cascaded into the water just ahead of the *Speedy*'s bow. By this time her rigging was shot to pieces and to have waited for the next broadside would have amounted to wanton sacrifice of the seamen who had served Cochrane with such courage. At last he hauled down his colours. He was rowed to the *Dessaix*, the ship that had so nearly sunk him. As he stepped aboard, he unbuckled his sword to hand it to her commander, Captain Pallière, who instructed him to continue wearing it as a prisoner saying: 'I will not accept the sword of an officer who has for so many hours struggled against impossibility.' He added that he had received special intructions to terminate the career of the *Speedy*.

Such was the atmosphere of compliment and mutual respect in which Cochrane began the novel life of a captive in an enemy vessel. He was an inactive observer now after more than a year of exceptional activity, with plenty of time to spend in reading and indulging his insatiable curiosity. 'During this cruise I had ample opportunity of observing the superior manner in which the sails of the *Dessaix* were cut, and the consequent flat surface exposed to the wind; this contrasting strongly with the bag reefs and bellying sails of English ships of war at that period.'

Soon he was privileged to observe something more interesting still.

The *Dessaix* and her two attendant battleships were bound for the Atlantic and the safety of Brest. But while the main packet which Cochrane had been ordered to protect reached Gibraltar in safety, these leviathans were less fortunate when they ran the gauntlet of the Straits. They managed to pass the Rock without incident, but the French Admiral decided to enter the bay of Algeciras, opposite Gibraltar, and there take in provisions before passing through the narrows. Here the three ships lay—one of 74 guns and two of 84—when six British warships of 74 guns under the command of Admiral Saumarez sailed into the bay. He had received an urgent message from Gibraltar where he lay off Cadiz warning him of the arrival of the three French ships, and had raced to intercept them. Captain Pallière was talking with Cochrane in his cabin when the topgallant masts and pendants of the British squadron were reported to be rounding the point.

'Do you think an attack will be made,' Pallière asked his guest, 'or will the British anchor off Gibraltar?'

'An attack will certainly be made,' Cochrane answered, 'and before night both the French and British ships will be at Gibraltar, where it will give me great pleasure to make you and your officers a return for the kindness I have experienced on board the *Dessaix*.'

In this atmosphere of friendly banter Cochrane witnessed a major fleet action from the deck of an enemy ship. Its greatest interest to him lay in the fact that it offered an opportunity to the British Admiral to cut out the French ships and carry them to Gibraltar. To avoid such a fate the French Admiral moved his ships inshore, under the protection of some Spanish coastal batteries. But since this manoeuvre had to be executed with extreme haste, all three ran aground, where their sterns were exposed to the approaching British warships.

In the stern cabin of the *Dessaix* Captain Pallière had invited Cochrane to sit down at table with him, remarking in his jocular way that the impending action should not be allowed to spoil their breakfast. They had not finished eating when a round shot came crashing through the stern and hit a wine-bin under the sofa, sending a shower of broken glass before it. Pallière and Cochrane leapt to their feet and ran to the quarterdeck in time to see a file of marines swept from the poop by British fire. Cochrane, who was the first to expose himself to danger in his own ships, saw no point in endangering his life as a prisoner of war, and went to observe the battle from a safer vantage-point.

It was shortly after 10 o'clock in the morning that Admiral Saumarez ordered the *Hannibal*, of 74 guns, to go in and rake the French. By the evening she had gone aground amongst the enemy, and although she maintained a gallant fire against every possible target and tried by every means to heave off, she was eventually captured. But now a most curious incident occurred. The French boarding party had neglected to take with them their national ensign, and for want of the *Tricolore*, they rehoisted the British ensign upside down. It seems unlikely that they gave thought to the fact that this was generally recognised as a distress signal, or that it would be interpreted as such by the authorities at Gibraltar. But that is what occurred. Every available craft was filled with artificers and seamen and sent across the bay to give assistance to the *Hannibal*. Pallière summoned Cochrane to ask him whether he thought they seriously intended to attempt to recapture the *Hannibal*. Cochrane, who foresaw that the entire dockyard staff at Gibraltar might soon be the prisoners of the French, replied discreetly that this was most probably their intention, and suggested that Pallière should warn them off by firing at them. But Pallière was too shrewd to be taken in by his advice. He allowed them to come on until every boat-load had reached the *Hannibal* and been taken prisoner.

It had not been an auspicious day for the British. By the time the action was discontinued, the odds between the two fleets no longer stood at six ships to three but at five to four, and all the skilled dock workers of Gibraltar were under hatches. The Flag Captain of Admiral Saumarez was Jahleel Brenton, from whom Cochrane had taken over the command of the *Speedy*. He now crossed over from Gibraltar with a flag of truce to request an exchange of prisoners. The French Admiral was far too astute to accept the proposal, but he did agree that Cochrane and other captured officers should be released on parole; that is, on condition that they would agree to take no further part in hostilities until they had been formally exchanged. So Cochrane left the agreeable society of his host Captain Pallière and was rowed across the bay to witness the next action from the Rock.

It was delayed for several days while the French awaited the arrival of Spanish reinforcements from Cadiz. In the interval they rightly claimed a major victory, which they confidently expected to turn into a hammer-blow against Britain's navy when six Spanish warships sailed round the point.

Dusk was falling as they entered the bay of Algeciras. Admiral Saumarez launched his fleet against them at once, although he was now outnumbered by two to one, and this time luck was with him. Two colossal Spanish warships, each of 112 guns, mistook one another for enemy vessels in the darkness and with ferocious enthusiasm they blew each other up. Only a handful of their crews were rescued by a British ship. Cochrane stood watching the tremendous firework display through the night from the garden of the Commissioner's house, and most of the inhabitants of Gibraltar did the same. By dawn the outcome became clear. The British fleet returned with the recaptured *Hannibal*, filled with the men of the dockyard. They also escorted a captured Spanish warship, for whose second Captain Cochrane was formally exchanged.

It had proved an unexpectedly happy outcome, both for British arms and for Cochrane personally. One further formality remained for him before he left Gibraltar, released from his parole to fight again. On 18 July 1801 he was acquitted of blame for the loss of the *Speedy* at a court-martial held on board the battle-scarred *Pompée*. Then he returned home after an absence of nearly three years to receive the reward for his outstanding services: and on his native soil he landed straight on his Achilles heel.

Admiral St Vincent, who had confirmed his first appointment in the Mediterranean, had been appointed to the Admiralty as First Sea Lord the previous February. As soon as the news of this reached Captain Alexander Cochrane on board the ship in which he lay at Alexandria, he wrote to St Vincent, inviting the First Sea Lord to promote his nephew. As it happened, Alexander's petition reached St Vincent before the despatch concerning the *Gamo*, so that the punctilious Admiral had only a file of rather different information concerning Commander Thomas Cochrane to study when he found the time to review his case. He found that Alexander had entered his nephew's name in the books of no less than four ships in which he had never served, a practice considered scandalous even in those days and particularly by St Vincent, who also abhorred corruption in any form. He discovered furthermore that Thomas had been court-martialled on a charge of insubordination, and acquitted with a caution: and St Vincent had once expressed himself on the subject of insubordination in the fleet in such strong terms that he was reproved by the Admiralty. He noted that Thomas had subsequently lost his ship to the enemy and was now a prisoner of war, so that no court martial had yet been held to convict or acquit him of blame. Admiral St Vincent did not so much as acknowledge Captain Alexander Cochrane's petition.

Unable to take the hint, he wrote again, over a week before his nephew's acquittal aboard the *Pompée* at Gibraltar.

'My Lord, I some time ago wrote to your Lordship in favour of my nephew Lord Cochrane, recommending his being made post.

'I hope your Lordship received my letter, and that you viewed Lord Cochrane's conduct in the light I did. But if my persuasions were not then judged of sufficient weight, I may now with much confidence come forward and claim for my nephew the palm of victory in both ways, by an act hardly equalled in this war of naval miracles, considering the great inequality of force between the *Speedy* with fifty-four men, and a xebec frigate of thirty-two guns and 319 men . . .'

It was Cochrane's misfortune to have an unpredictable father and several more uncles, and there is no knowing how far they went in increasing Old Jarvie's exasperation. It is a fact that St Vincent once exploded in a letter: 'The Cochranes are not to be trusted out of sight. They are all mad, romantic, money-getting and not truth telling.' This harsh judgment was to prove correct so far as one of the Cochrane uncles was concerned, but it need not have spilled over to include the 25-year-old Thomas if his relatives had left him to manage his own career. As it was, he returned to find that the newly appointed First Sea Lord had been thoroughly antagonised. Jahleel Brenton's brother noted that St Vincent 'was so much pressed on the subject of Lord Cochrane's promotion for taking the *Gamo* that it became almost a point of etiquette with the Earl *not* to make him a captain'. And when someone had the temerity to tell the First Sea Lord that he must promote Cochrane, The tetchy old Admiral snapped back: 'The First Lord of the Admiralty knows *no must*'.

Thomas found himself advanced to the rank of Post Captain in August 1801, almost as soon as he had returned home, but his promotion was not back-dated to the day on which he had captured the *Gamo*. As a result, his name appeared on the bottom of the list, below those of officers who had previously been his juniors. Undoubtedly this can be interpreted as an act of vindictiveness on the part of St Vincent, even if it helped to redress some of the unfair seniority Cochrane had gained earlier. What ought to have been made clear to the Cochranes was that St Vincent was immune to their solicitations.

It was not. The Earl of Dundonald now wrote to the First Sea Lord at inordinate length, complaining of his son's loss of seniority. 'I beg leave to call your Lordship's attention to what Lord Cochrane's feelings must be, and what the situation he will be placed in on service from this supersession; and whether his being thus postponed in rank will not have a tendency to detract from the merit of one of the most gallant actions during this or any other war? And whether it may not induce the public at large, or the Navy in particular, to believe that your Lordships have had cause to disapprove of Lord Cochrane's Conduct?' And a great deal more to the same effect.

Whoever drafted the reply to this interminable, querulous letter, St Vincent must have signed it with deep satisfaction. 'My Lord, I can have no difficulty in acknowledging that the capture of the *Gamo* reflects the highest degree of credit on Lord Cochrane and the officers and crew of the *Speedy*. The first account of that brilliant action reached the Admiralty very early in the month of August, previously to which intelligence had been received of the capture of the *Speedy* . . . Lord Cochrane was promoted to the rank of Post Captain on the 8th August —the day on which the sentence of acquittal for the loss of the *Speedy* was received—which was all that could under existing circumstances be done.' Thus the heads of departments of state justify their actions by invoking the regulations: and if St Vincent did the same as a means of explaining an act of spite, his reply ought at least to have taught the Cochranes a lesson.

But now it was the turn of the Post Captain himself. The Admiralty had effectively silenced any further complaint concerning his own promotion. But he had been particularly well served in the capture of the *Gamo* by the gallantry of the First Lieutenant, who had been severely wounded in the action. He had written from the Mediterranean, requesting Lieutenant Parker's promotion, without receiving any reply. On his arrival in London he had written again, without acknowledgment. After receiving his own promotion, he addressed a third application to St Vincent.

Such petitions caused the First Sea Lord genuine embarrassment. The Treaty of Amiens had just brought a year's respite in the war against France, and on 4 September 1801 he wrote to Cochrane's former Commander-in-Chief, Lord Keith: 'The list of Post Captains and Commanders so far exceeds that of ships and sloops, I cannot, consistently with what is due to the public and to the incredible number of meritorious persons of those classes upon half-pay, promote except upon very extraordinary occasions, such as that of Lord Cochrane and Captain Dundas'. Old Jarvie might be irascible, but he was fair-minded unless his prejudices were aroused.

If only he had replied to Cochrane in the same vein all might have been well. But he was a busy man, and he was irritated by the very name of Cochrane, and he was served by Admiralty bureaucrats, and through a combination of these causes, Cochrane received this astonishing answer to his representations on behalf of Lieutenant Parker: 'It is unusual to promote two officers for such a service—besides which, the small number of killed on board the *Speedy* does not warrant the application.'

It might almost have been a deliberate trap to lure Cochrane to destruction, with its monstrous argument, its false logic. In the circumstances he ought to have got drunk or taken a girl out for the night and forgotten about it. But Cochrane was not given to either of these pursuits: he read philosophy. It did not make him any more philosophical, but it sharpened his naturally logical mind, and he now treated St Vincent to the most devastating piece of logic ever inflicted on a First Sea Lord by a junior officer.

He ought, of course, to have reflected that it was improper for the Admiralty to divulge the grounds for its decisions, and that some sort of compliment had been paid to him, even in the statement of such a monstrous principle that an officer's merits were assessed there by the size of the butcher's bill. Had Cochrane been faced with such a danger at sea as this reply presented to him, he would have extracted from it both victory and safety. But he was on land again, with even less to challenge his enormous energies than when he had been a junior officer in the wardroom of the *Queen Charlotte*. So it was that his courage, his intelligence and his inability to hold his tongue found expression in the retort to the First Sea Lord that 'his reasons for not promoting Lieutenant Parker, because there were only three men killed on board the *Speedy*, were in opposition to his Lordship's own promotion to an Earldom, as well as that of his Flag Captain to knighthood, and his other officers to increased rank and honours: for that in the battle from which his Lordship derived his title, there was only one man killed on board his own flagship, so that there were more casualties in my sloop than in his line-of-battle ship'. Even the capture of the *Gamo* does not beat this in British naval records.

If it was unlikely that the Admiralty would look twice at a second recommendation on behalf of Lieutenant Parker after ignoring the first, it was inconceivable that any further application would be considered after this insulting letter to the First Lord. Yet Cochrane persisted until May 1802, when he was silenced with the snub: 'My Lord, I have received and read to my Lords Commissioners of the Admiralty your letter of the 27th inst., and have nothing in command from their Lordships to communicate to you.' For Lieutenant Parker the efforts of Cochrane proved to be the kiss of death, though St Vincent himself cannot be blamed for the refinement of cruelty with which he was subsequently treated, since he had been driven from the Admiralty himself. The real culprits are hidden among the civil servants who held up Parker's promotion to the rank of Commander for another four years and then played a most vicious trick on him. He was ordered to join a sloop in the West Indies. He sold all his household possessions and sailed to look for his ship, first in Barbados, then in the Bermudas. He never found her because no such ship existed: and so he returned home, a ruined man and died without ever receiving another appointment.

What Cochrane was too obsessed with his own and Parker's wrongs to appreciate was that Admiral St Vincent was just as incensed by the shortcomings of the civilian branches of the Admiralty as he was. He had described them as rotten to the core before he became First Sea Lord, and as soon as he entered that office he set out to reform them. 'I am sorry to tell you,' he thundered on one occasion, 'that Chatham Dockyard appears by what we have seen today a viler sink of corruption than my imagination ever formed. Portsmouth was bad enough, but this beggars all description.' In that year of peace in which Parker's promotion was refused, St Vincent introduced a Bill in Parliament to set up a committee to investigate dockyard abuses. His secretary has left a graphic picture of Old Jarvie's wrath when the cabinet opposed him. ' "My commission is rejected! But"—bending his fist, while his countenance personified his invincible firmness—"we'll read them a lesson on the Articles of War tomorrow, Sir," and then related the opposition he had met with; nor would he again sit on the Ministerial bench in the House of Lords till he had carried his point.'

This was exactly when Cochrane himself determined that he would take up the same cudgels as the chief whom he had made his enemy. 'Hitherto no naval officer had ventured to expose, in Parliament or out of it, this or indeed any other gross abuse of the naval service; and having nothing better to do, want of employment appeared to offer a fitting opportunity for constituting myself the Quixote of the profession.' The particular abuse to which he referred was the peculation of the Admiralty prize courts, which he had encountered so frequently in the Mediterranean. But while he prepared to embark on his lifelong task of tilting at windmills, the First Sea Lord was taking more practical steps to achieve the same end. St Vincent was indeed driven from the Admiralty, but not before he had secured the commission of enquiry which brought down the First Lord who succeeded him on a charge of corruption.

For a short space of time the conflict ceased between the two sailors, so different in age, appearance and background, so alike in character and in their ideals; whom circumstances and their own defects of temperament had turned into enemies when mutual respect ought to have bound them in friendship. After Cochrane had used his leisure to explore the same abuses that St Vincent had already laid before the cabinet, he went to Edinburgh to remedy the defects in his education. At a time when most young men home from sea would have been in search of feminine society, if not a wife, a driving sense of destiny sent him to the finest centre of learning in the country, just as it had impelled him to spend his leave learning his trade from Jack Larmour.

One day he would fall in love, and then it would be for life: there were no half measures with Cochrane.

The university buildings of Edinburgh, a new register house, and many squares and terraces had recently been built to the designs of the Adam brothers, and their classical style had invested the Scottish capital with the title—The Athens of the North. The famous Professor Dugald Stewart held the chair of Moral Philosophy when Cochrane enrolled at the university, Walter Scott had just published his first major work, the *Border Minstrelsy*, Scotland's most distinguished portrait painter, Henry Raeburn, was depicting the celebrities of the new Athens during her golden age. Cochrane had come to the right place at the right time, and he made the most of it. 'It was perhaps an unusual spectacle for a Post Captain fresh from the quarter-deck to enter himself as a student among boys. For my self-imposed position I cared nothing, and was only anxious to employ myself to the best advantage. With what success may be judged from the fact of my being but once absent from lectures, and that to attend the funeral of a near relative.' Here is the humility that contrasts so strangely with the arrogance in Cochrane's character, the underlying conscientiousness that he occasionally flung to the winds in outbursts of totally irresponsible behaviour.

There was an election during 1802, which must have been of particular interest to Cochrane in view of his ominous intention to enter politics himself. And since he was now living in Scotland he was able to observe the gerrymandering of the electoral system at its most corrupt. His country was in fact one vast rotten borough in the hands of Henry Dundas, who boasted, 'the means by which I govern Scotland cannot be dissolved by the breath of any Minister'. For the success with which he manipulated votes, Dundas was created Viscount Melville in December.

The most iniquitous part of this system in Cochrane's eyes was that votes were bought with the plunder of the service departments. Contracts were issued to men who committed every kind of fraud for their private profit. It is thought that two warships of 74 guns and one of 64 were lost with their crews because a contractor had inserted only the tops of the bolts that should have secured their fabrics. The deficiencies in food, medical supplies and other stores which the mutineers at Spithead had protested against were directly due to the operations of people known as Boroughmongers. These were precisely the scandals that St Vincent's commission of enquiry was designed to uncover. But young Captain Cochrane, ever a lone wolf, was preparing to attack them with the weapons of Don Quixote.

It was nearly 20 years since the death of his mother, and when he crossed the waters of the Forth to visit Culross Abbey he found a new Countess of Dundonald presiding in his home. She had been married to the Earl for 3 years during Cochrane's absence, and was to live for another 6 without bearing him any children, and during this period her dowry gave Culross an Indian summer before the house and what remained of the estate were finally sold. The Earl was proud of his eldest son, as he had demonstrated so ineptly, and Cochrane probably celebrated his twenty-seventh birthday in a more placid and orderly home than he could well remember.

The interlude ended in May 1803 when war was renewed between Britain and France, and Cochrane returned post-haste to London in the hope of being given a ship. The Marquess of Douglas wrote to St Vincent on his behalf, who replied that there were many senior captains whose claims must be considered first. The Earl of Dundonald returned to the attack, and was assured that his son would be employed, though it was not yet possible to say how soon. Uncle Alexander made his approach to another member of the Admiralty, saying 'Do, my good friend, send Lord Cochrane afloat. I do not care what ship is given him so she is not a block, as I trust if ever he has an opportunity he will not be behind hand with his brother officers.' All of them were at it again while St Vincent pursued his relentless purpose to resist all patronage and appoint on grounds of seniority, in very rare cases allowing priority to exceptional merit. Were the 3 months' seniority Cochrane had lost at the hands of the First Lord to be offset by his outstanding capabilities, reinforced by all this patronage? The answer of the Admiralty was No.

Cochrane's solution was to make a tour of the dockyards, and draw up separate lists of ships that were ready for sea, and of the others that were still being refitted for active service. Armed with these, he applied for a personal interview with the First Sea Lord, and the incredible thing is that it was granted. So Cochrane once again faced the irascible old man whom he had insulted in such terms that he was fortunate not to have been dismissed from the service. St Vincent had for a long time been the most stern, unbending and unpopular Admiral in the British Navy, and now he was crippled with gout and vexed with all the problems of preparing the fleet for the new war. His consent to the interview in these circumstances ought to have told Cochrane something about his character that he never learned.

The resentful young Captain stood before the First Lord, with his shock of ginger hair, his cold blue eyes and his Scottish accent, and produced his first list. The hunched figure before him stared back out of that gnome-like face with its nose as prominent as Cochrane's own, and replied that each of the ships had been promised to others. Cochrane produced his second list, and St Vincent told him they were too large to entrust to a Post Captain in his first command. As usual, Cochrane displayed his fatal inability to spot the right moment to hold his tongue. He began to enumerate other ships, until St Vincent cut him short by saying they were not yet in a sufficiently advanced state of preparation for any appointment to be made to them. Did this young man from Scotland really think he had not been attending to his business?

Faced with the confirmation of what the Admiralty had informed his well-wishers already, that there was no ship at present available for him, Cochrane indulged in one final outburst. 'I frankly told his Lordship that as the Board was evidently of opinion that my services were not required, it would be better for me to go back to the college at Edinburgh and pursue my studies with a view to occupying myself in some other employment.' St Vincent looked at him keenly, 'to see whether I really meant what I said', as Cochrane interpreted that long pause half a century later. But it is just as likely that he was considering whether it would not be best to give this young fanatic any vessel, however unfit for its duties. Had his uncle Alexander not recommended that he should be sent to sea in any ship, provided 'she is not a block'?

'Well, you shall have a ship,' said the First Lord at last. 'Go down to Plymouth, and there await the orders of the Admiralty.' It would be absurd to suppose that St Vincent had been saving up the parody of a warship which Cochrane found there, out of a mean spirit of revenge. Nor does Cochrane's own account of the interview make it appear in the least likely. But it was what his own persistence finally earned him.

She was an old converted collier that ought never to have been bought by the Admiralty in the first place: a symbol of the kind of abuse that St Vincent had secured a commission to report upon. She was named the *Arab*, and Cochrane took her to sea in the very month of December 1803 in which Lord St Vincent was superseded at the Admiralty.

'With a fair wind,' Cochrane remarked later, 'it was not difficult to get off Boulogne, but to get back with the same wind was—in such a craft—all but impossible. Our only way of effecting this was by watching the tide, to drift off as well as we could. A gale of wind anywhere from N.E. to N.W. would infallibly have driven us on shore on the French coast.' Nobody could doubt Cochrane's skill in seamanship. 'I wrote to the Admiral commanding that the *Arab* was of no use for the service required, as she could not work to windward, and that her employment in such a service could only result in our loss by shipwreck on the French coast.'

The Admiralty was ready with its solution. Cochrane was ordered to proceed North-East of the Orkney islands, there to protect the fisheries: and although there were no fisheries in those waters to protect, the Sea Wolf remained there until October 1804, a whole year from his appointment to the *Arab* and one in which his services might have been of the greatest value to his nation elsewhere. In so far as this was due to the civil servants of Whitehall, there is nothing surprising about it. Probably many of them thought that the Shetland Islands lay in the Moray Firth, where they were to be found inset in most maps, and it would have taken more than such a national emergency as the Napoleonic war to distract them from their petty peculations and petty spites. The question is whether Admiral St Vincent is to blame for having allowed it to happen in the first place. The most that can be said on his behalf (and it is much) is that he had been gravely provoked by Cochrane: and if he did not appreciate that the youth who captured the *Gamo* was the greatest seaman ever produced by these islands after Nelson, there are a great many people who still do not realise it over 150 years later.

During Cochrane's sojourn in Orcadian waters, his uncle Alexander was promoted to the rank of Rear Admiral, although it was not until 2 years later that he received the high honour of a knighthood of the Bath. Meanwhile the nephew whom he had endeavoured to help too much was left with his reflections during the long hours of winter darkness, and during nights lit by the northern lights and the prolonged sunsets of the Orcadian summer. It was a pity that he did not spend his leisure in reading the plays of Shakespeare, for he would have discovered in *Hamlet* a man who could at least recognise his fault, even if he could not correct it.

> So, oft it chances in particular men,
> That for some vicious mole of nature in them,
> As, in their birth—wherein they are not guilty,
> Since nature cannot choose his origin—
> By the o'ergrowth of some complexion,
> Oft breaking down the pales and forts of reason,
> Or by some habit that too much o'erleavens
> The form of plausive manners; that these men,
> Carrying, I say, the stamp of one defect,
> Being nature's livery, or fortune's star,
> Their virtues else, be they as pure as grace,

As infinite as man may undergo,
Shall in the general censure take corruption
From that particular fault.

Cochrane lived longer than Hamlet, and at the end of his days he wrote: 'To argue with a First Lord is no doubt an imprudent thing for a Naval Officer to attempt.' It was not exactly an abject confession, and it came too late.

CHAPTER THREE

The Golden *Pallas*

The man who succeeded St Vincent as First Sea Lord was none other than Henry Dundas, Viscount Melville. This master of parliamentary corruption was one of the few personal friends of William Pitt the Prime Minister, and he had held the office of Treasurer at the Admiralty from 1782 until 1800, as St Vincent's commission of enquiry had noticed with considerable interest. While Cochrane lay in the *Arab* off Orkney the Duke of Hamilton, 'my excellent friend, was so indignant at my ignominious expulsion from active service, where alone it would be beneficial to the country, that unsolicited by anyone he strongly impressed upon Lord Melville, the successor of Lord St Vincent, the necessity of relieving me from that penal hulk the *Arab* and repairing the injustice which had been inflicted on me, by employing me on more important service. Lord Melville admitted the injustice, and promptly responded to the appeal by transferring me from the wretched craft in which I had been for fifteen months in exile, to the *Pallas*, a new fir-built frigate of thirty-two guns.' Which proves that corruption in the form of personal influence can operate in the national interest in particular cases.

But Cochrane had hardly joined his ship at Plymouth before he found himself the victim of another gross abuse of his service. As he inspected the amenities of the *Pallas* he looked forward to receiving his instructions for her cruise from the Admiralty. But the Port Admiral at Plymouth was Sir William Young, another of those shore officials from whom Cochrane had suffered much in the days when he had escorted home his prizes in the *Speedy*. St Vincent had already noted Admiral Young's propensity for cashing in on the sailing orders of ships for his personal profit. 'I have a notion,' wrote Admiral St Vincent when he commanded the Channel fleet, 'that he wishes to have the power of issuing orders for their sailing, in order to entitle him to share prize-money.' Sir William Young now pounced on Cochrane's orders as soon as they reached Plymouth from the Admiralty, and copied them out so that they were transformed into orders issued under his own authority.

The year 1804 was drawing to a close when Cochrane boarded the

Pallas. She was of 667 tons burden and she carried twenty-six 12-pounder guns on her main deck, and twelve 24-pounders on her quarter-deck and forecastle. She would require a crew of over 200, whom Cochrane tried to attract by sticking up public advertisements that he would fill his seamen's pockets with 'pewter' and 'cobs', sailors' jargon for ingots and coin. He expected the men in the port taverns to remember the rich prizes of the *Speedy*. But their memories were too short: they reflected instead on the unprofitable rigours of the *Arab*'s cruise in northern waters, and neither the fine appearance of the *Pallas* nor anything they knew of her Captain attracted them aboard.

Cochrane therefore resorted to the distressing method of recruitment so commonly employed at this time. Using the force of his personality, he gathered a party of men whom he not only persuaded to serve in the *Pallas*, but also induced to act as a press-gang to conscript the remainder of the crew. 'They turned to with great alacrity to impress others,' Cochrane recorded, 'so that in a short time we had an excellent crew. This was the only time I ever found it necessary to impress men.' The borough records of Plymouth cast further light on the tall young Post Captain, scouring Plymouth for promising seamen with the men whom he had already talked into joining his ship. On New Year's Day 1805 a warrant for his arrest was issued upon a summons to answer charges of assault on two constables. The proceedings were delayed by Cochrane's absence at sea, and on his return he brought a counter-action for assault against the Mayor of Plymouth. He lost it and had the costs awarded against him. Evidently the civil authorities did what they could to protect innocent victims from the menace of the press-gangs and Cochrane did not use half-measures in securing his crew.

Later, he excused what he had been forced to do by pointing to the outcome. His men had been well rewarded, and they were quickly transformed from a diverse collection of resentful men into a triumphant team under his incomparable leadership. In fact it is astonishing that they should have displayed such seamanship so soon after putting to sea. He had inherited the ninety men of the *Speedy* as the legacy of that excellent sailor Sir Jahleel Brenton: the crew of the *Pallas* was his own creation.

She sailed from Plymouth on 21 January with orders to spend a month in training on the dark and stormy seas off the Western Isles of Scotland. Thereafter he received exactly the kind of independent assignment which offered the fullest scope to his genius. He was to harass enemy convoys in the Atlantic.

As soon as the training period had been completed to his satisfaction,

Cochrane made for the routes along which ships approached Europe from the Americas. He crossed the Bay of Biscay, ran west of Cape Finistere, and then worked his way towards the Azores. By 6 February the bonanza had begun. 'We fell in with and captured a large ship, the *Caroline*, bound from the Havannah to Cadiz, and laden with a valuable cargo. After taking out the crew, we despatched her to Plymouth. Having learned from the prisoners that the captured ship was part of a convoy bound from the Havannah to Spain, we proceeded on our course and on the 13th captured a second vessel which was still more valuable, containing in addition to the usual cargo some diamonds and ingots of gold and silver. This vessel was sent to Plymouth as before. On the 15th we fell in with another, *La Fortuna*, which proved the richest of all.'

Her gold and silver was valued at £132,000 and her merchandise at a similar sum, which was the equivalent of over a million at the present purchasing power of money. In Plymouth the Port Admiral could rub his hands over the care he had taken to copy out Cochrane's orders, soon to be rewarded with a share of all this wealth. The Spanish Captain and Supercargo of the *Fortuna*, on the other hand, were extremely crestfallen as they were rowed to the *Pallas*, especially as their entire life-savings were aboard the captured vessel. They explained to Cochrane that this was the second time such a misfortune had befallen them: their entire fortunes had been captured by a British ship at sea in 1779. With the impulsive generosity of his nature, Cochrane ordered the bosun to pipe all hands on deck as soon as he had listened to this story. He asked his crew whether they would agree to give their captives five thousand dollars each, and they shouted back: 'Aye, aye, my Lord, with all our hearts' and gave the Spaniards three cheers. The incident provides a revealing glimpse of their Lord's many-sided character. His penurious upbringing had hardened his resolve to make his own fortune, and many people were to echo St Vincent's charge against all the Cochranes, that they were 'money-getting', against Lord Cochrane himself. But all his life there was to be the contrast between his attitude to men like Sir William Young—anyone whom he believed to be attempting to cheat him—and to those people or situations that called upon the underlying generosity of his character.

The very next day the *Pallas* captured another Spanish vessel with coin on board and despatched her after the rest to Plymouth. Then an emergency occurred, horribly reminiscent of the circumstances in which the *Speedy* had been lost. The *Pallas* was now sailing home, and in the sub-tropical heat between the Azores and Portugal she ran into a haze which lay so low on the sea that the look-out in his crow's nest stood in the sunshine above it. Suddenly he reported the masts of three large ships in the distance, approaching through the haze. Cochrane immediately leapt up the rigging to the crow's nest with his telescope, to scan as much as he could see of the fore and topgallant masts that protruded above the dazzling quilt of cloud. He decided that they were French line-of-battle ships although they were flying no colours.

The *Pallas* was a very different vessel from the *Speedy*, but even so, how could she escape from such giants of the ocean? He changed course, added more sail: and then the wind rose and the frigate began to heave and plunge in a heavy sea. The maindeck guns became submerged, and even those of the forecastle and quarterdeck occasionally went under. But as the wind cleared the haze, Cochrane could see the strange ships gaining on him, hand over hand. Some means must be found of carrying more sail, despite the fact that the sea was already breaking over the plunging hull of the *Pallas*. He ordered that every hawser in the ship should be run up to the mast-heads and hove taut. As soon as the masts were secured in this way, the men on the yard-arms were ordered to release the last stitch of sail. Onward lunged the *Pallas* as the helmsman clung to his wheel through the lashing spray, the very forecastle went under, and the enemy ships came ever closer. Soon they could be seen flashing the priming of their guns: next they divided, one sailing to leeward, another to windward, each within half a mile, while the third remained slightly farther off.

Cochrane would have been trapped but for the speed with which he found a solution, and the skill with which his crew executed his orders. Everything depended on whether the masts would stand the strain of the stratagem he had in mind. The men clinging for their lives to the rigging were ordered once more to make certain every rope that secured them was as taut as could be, then they waited tensely to carry out Cochrane's latest trick. This was to clew up or haul down every sail in the ship at once, the moment the order was given. At the same instant the helm of the *Pallas* was tugged round so that her head swung away from the wind, leaving first her side exposed to the heaving seas, then her stern exposed to them. As the frigate stopped in her tracks and crossed the trough of the waves, a great shudder shook her timbers from stem to stern, but her masts held. The enemy ships shot past at full speed and ran on for several miles before they could shorten sail or alter their tack, while Cochrane contemplated the excellence of the crew he had press-ganged from the streets of Plymouth, and the seamen looked at their Captain with fresh wonder. They had contributed to another of his phenomenal achievements.

The ruse gave him a respite until nightfall, and then he repeated a trick that had once saved the *Speedy*. When it was pitch-dark he lowered a ballasted cask into the sea holding a lantern. He then held on the same course all night while the battle-ships pursued the lantern as it drifted on its own way. By daybreak the horizon no longer contained them and the *Pallas* reached Plymouth without further mishap. At her mast-heads Cochrane tied three golden candlesticks about 5 feet tall, intended by the people of Mexico for a church in Spain—fit emblems for the ship that became known as the Golden *Pallas*. Her Captain had earned for himself £75,000 in prize money in the course of ten days.

Sir William Young pounced on this treasure, and received half of what was apportioned to Cochrane as his share. 'Being then young and ardent,' Cochrane commented later, 'my portion appeared inexhaustible. What could I want more? The sum claimed and received by Admiral Young was not worth notice.' But elsewhere he claimed that Young's claim was improper, because his command had been limited to the port. In fact Young was probably within his rights; and whether he was or not, it was undoubtedly as well for Cochrane that he did not take issue with another Admiral at this stage of his career.

A more momentous contest had meanwhile engaged his enthusiasm. Another parliamentary election was at hand, and in the rotten borough of Honiton near Plymouth there was an opening for an independent candidate. The windmill of Don Quixote's dreams stood just over the hill from where he stepped ashore with money in his pocket, and at Honiton there were electors who would be able to help him spend it in return for their votes. His well-satisfied Admiral gave him ready permission to stand.

But things soon began to go wrong. One of the electors explained to Cochrane during his canvas: 'You need not ask me, my Lord, who I votes for. I always votes for Mr Most.' Standing as a radical and reforming candidate, Cochrane decided that he could not undertake to bribe the electors, and once he had made this clear he was defeated. But he took his first step towards future victory when he sent the bellman round Honiton to announce that he would pay 10 guineas to everyone who had voted for him 'as a reward for having withstood the influence of bribery'. His successful opponent had only paid 5 pounds for a vote. Leaving the electors to their sums, he then returned to his ship and sailed away on 28 May 1805 to continue his naval service.

This time it consisted of the less lucrative and exciting task of escorting a convoy to Canada. The most serious hazard was caused by the dockyard authorities, who had saved expense by surrounding the binnacle of the *Pallas* with iron bolts instead of copper ones while she was being refitted, so that her compass was made inaccurate. Providentially, Cochrane had invited a former astronomer from Greenwich to accompany him, and the weather proved clear enough to enable him to calculate their course by the stars. One may imagine how busy the astronomer was kept at other times, satisfying the eager young Captain's thirst for knowledge as the two of them leaned over the ship's rail night after night, scanning the heavens. For Cochrane sought a total knowledge of everything that concerned the sea, and more again for its own sake.

Despite the services of the astronomer he decided it would be advisable to steer for Halifax in Nova Scotia, and there have the iron bolts removed before the convoy encountered the fogs of the Canadian coasts. At Halifax the dockyard officials insisted that permission must be obtained from London before the work could be carried out. Cochrane retaliated by threatening to remain at Halifax with his convoy for the 6 months that it would take to obtain the required authority of the Admiralty. The copper bolts were then produced and the *Pallas* sailed on to Quebec with her convoy and a compass that was once more reliable.

While he was escorting another convoy back across the Atlantic, Cochrane devised the first of his inventions to be rejected by the Admiralty. It was a new kind of guiding light and prompted by his present duties. 'The carelessness of merchant captains when following a convoy can only be estimated by those who have to deal with them. Not only was this manifested by day, but at night their stern cabins glittered with lights, equally intense with the convoy light, which therefore was not distinguishable. The separation of the convoy on the following day was thus rather a matter of course than surprise. To remedy this I constructed a lamp powerful enough to serve as a guide in following the protecting frigate by night. The Admiralty, however, neglected its application or even to inspect my plan.'

What finally drove the Admiralty to take some action was the chorus of complaint arising from the loss of merchant vessels dispersed in convoys. A reward of £50 was offered to the inventor of the most suitable guiding light, and Cochrane took the precaution of submitting his model under another name. It was subjected to exhaustive tests at Spithead, Sheerness and St Helens, and then chosen as the winner. But when it became known that this was Cochrane's invention, it was at once abandoned. As a result, Cochrane remarked later, 'I am persuaded that millions of money were lost to the public during the war, by the scattering of convoys and consequent capture made of the dispersed vessels.' Such was the vendetta that Cochrane endured from faceless officials, from the day when he first menaced their pride and their pockets, until he finally became an Admiral and the Grand Old Man of the British Navy.

During the journey home from Canada Cochrane found the leisure to experiment with another invention, designed this time to promote speed. The device was a gigantic kite. 'A studding sailboom was lashed across a spare flying jib-boom to form the framework, and over this a large spread of canvas was sewn in the usual boy's fashion.' He admitted failure. 'My spars were of unequal dimensions throughout, and this and our launching the kite caused it to roll greatly. Possibly I might not have been sufficiently experienced in the mysteries of "wings and tail", for though the kite pulled with a will, it made such occasional lurches as gave reason to fear for the too sudden expenditure of his Majesty's stores.' But at least he was giving his seamen some fun during their present comparatively monotonous occupation.

Soon Cochrane would be one of the pioneers in the promotion of steam power in ships, nor would it be long before he found a better use for the kite, one that anticipated a technique of modern warfare by over a century.

The ships in Cochrane's convoy reached port safely, not because he managed to prevent them from separating, but simply because there was no enemy to catch them when they did. 'It blew so hard, with hail and rain, that no light could be kept in a common lanthorn, and my only expedient was to place candles in my cabin windows: and at last I could only bring one vessel home in convoy (called the *Ariadne*), which being the worst sailor, I kept in tow.'

During his absence, on 21 October 1805, Nelson was killed in the battle of Trafalgar, leaving Cochrane (as a fellow officer would one day declare) the greatest British seaman afloat. And on his return he was given orders which enabled him to demonstrate this with increasing resonance. In January 1806, exactly a year since he had first sailed in the *Pallas*, he was sent to join the squadron of Admiral Thornborough in the Channel, with instructions to operate off the French and Spanish coasts. Thus he returned to the pursuit of that central objective of British naval policy, of which he was now the supreme exponent, the dislocation of the enemy's sea communications and the destruction of her merchant shipping.

His perennial preoccupation with the weapon of speed prompted him to design a new craft to add to his striking power. It was a galley that he commissioned the boat-builders of Deal to construct for him at his own expense, carrying eighteen oars double-banked. This manned torpedo could be launched from the *Pallas* with a swiftness independent of wind-force, and Cochrane went so far as to describe her as 'perhaps the fastest boat afloat'. She soon became such an object of terror to the enemy that at the very sight of her ships were run ashore and their crews fled in their boats. Such was the precursor to his next invention of this kind, the explosive torpedo.

In April Cochrane embarked on the first of a series of feats that were to eclipse his capture of the *Gamo* in public estimation. He sailed from the Bay of Biscay into the broad estuary of the Gironde. At the inside end of this estuary, about 40 miles from the open sea, the Dordogne and Garonne rivers unite in their journey to the ocean. The river-mouth of the Garonne was considered one of the most difficult to navigate on that entire coast and it was protected by shore batteries. But when Cochrane learned that some French corvettes were lurking there, protected by a guard-ship as well as the forts, he determined to go in and capture or destroy them. Furthermore, he planned a night attack despite the notorious perils of that stretch of water. He kept the *Pallas* well out of sight as long as daylight lasted, and then brought her in under cover of darkness and anchored her as the base for his attack, manned by a skeleton crew of about forty men. The remainder rowed out in the ship's boats under the command of his First Lieutenant in the 18-oared galley, to capture the guard-ship from beneath the guns of two shore batteries.

This was one of the few occasions when Cochrane did not lead such an assault himself, and as the weather was thick and dark, he could detect nothing of the brief, gallant resistance when his men clambered aboard the guardship and caught her crew unawares. She proved to be the *Tapageuse*, of fourteen guns, and soon Cochrane could see and hear them firing in the darkness, though he could only guess what was going on in that hornet's nest. Other hornets had appeared in the form of two more guardships, and the First Lieutenant was holding them at bay with the guns of the captured *Tapageuse*.

As dawn broke, Cochrane found his predicament more perilous still as three more enemy ships came into view, sailing towards the mouth of the Garonne. With only forty men left aboard the *Pallas*, it would have been impossible for him to engage in a successful action against such odds, so instead Cochrane fooled the enemy out of attacking him by one of those instant feats of inspiration that so rarely failed him in such emergencies. He sent his skeleton crew scurrying aloft with great lengths of yarn, with which they secured the furled sails in such a way that they would all fall at once when the yarn was cut. As the enemy vessels advanced towards him, he weighed anchor but still lay there, sails furled.

Suddenly the French seamen saw an impressive—indeed, an intimidating—sight. A cloud of canvas fell from the masts and yardarms of the *Pallas* with a speed and precision that bespoke a most highly disciplined crew. Lest their gunnery should be of a similar order the enemy warships rapidly altered course and made off along the shore with the *Pallas* in pursuit. All three ran aground, a reminder to Cochrane of the risks he was running by sailing the *Pallas* in these waters as he steered in to carry away the *Tapageuse* and the seamen who had captured her. She was not a phenomenal prize, but the operation itself was a work of art.

As soon as he was safely clear of the Gironde estuary, Cochrane sat down to compose a despatch for Admiral Thornborough, giving special praise to his First Lieutenant. Thornborough forwarded the despatch to the Commander-in-Chief of the Channel fleet, adding his own commendations. This was none other than Admiral St Vincent, back on a quarterdeck after his stormy spell at the Admiralty. He read the details with his usual care, and sent the despatch on to London with the observation: 'The gallant and successful exertions of the *Pallas* therein detailed reflect very high honour on her Captain, officers and crew, and call for my warmest approbation.'

It was during the very month in which St Vincent sent this commendation to the Admiralty that the First Sea Lord who had succeeded him there was charged with corruption and impeached by the High Court of Parliament in Westminster Hall. Lord Melville had only been detected by St Vincent's commission of enquiry in a comparatively minor financial irregularity during the period when he had been Treasurer to the Admiralty, and his acquittal was easily managed. But he was the last man in Britain to suffer impeachment, and when the casting vote was given in favour of it in the House of Commons, his friend William Pitt drew his hat down over his eyes, knowing that the disgrace of it was enough. Besides, everyone knew the meaning of his prosecutor's words: 'By the foot of Hercules, you may judge of his size. By the finger of a giant you may form an estimate of his strength.' This was the man who had used his office at the Admiralty to buy seats at the Scottish elections, so that people quoted—or rather, misquoted— from the seventy-fifth psalm: 'Promotion cometh neither from the east nor from the west, nor yet from the south.' Paradoxically it was St Vincent, the enemy of corruption, who now commended Cochrane, although he had condemned him to the penal hulk off Orkney. Melville who had rescued him and appointed him to the *Pallas* was charged with the very corruptions that Cochrane so deeply abhorred. For human beings are more complicated creatures than Cochrane, in his incurable simplicity, could ever comprehend.

Meanwhile, as First Lords came and went, the bureaucrats at the Admiralty sat secure at their desks, filing the record of Cochrane's services with pursed lips, so that not a word of congratulation reached him. And it was natural that he should suppose St Vincent, Commander-in-Chief of the Channel fleet, was to blame. He was developing a persecution complex, which requires a culprit for its sustenance.

As Cochrane sailed north out of the Gironde basin in the Bay of Biscay, looking forward with confidence to the recognition that never came, he passed the fortified islands of Oléron and Ré and Aix. Land-ward of them run the waters known as the Aix and Basque Roads, whose shoals and tides reinforced the shore batteries that guarded the entrance to the great naval arsenal of Rochefort. It was an infinitely more dangerous trap than the entrance to the Garonne but into it Cochrane sailed, to examine those recesses in which so much enemy shipping found apparent safety: and he discovered that its security was increased further by a network of signal posts along the coast which could pass information about the movements of British warships to the local merchant marine and the French naval authorities. In a series of commando raids Cochrane demolished five of these signal houses, and so destroyed the chain of signals. For good measure he also launched his men in the ship's boats to destroy a shore battery. It was his first essay in amphibious operations, and its success was a portent.

So was the letter he wrote to Admiral Thornborough on 24 April as he lay off the isle of Aix. He had moved within gunshot of the French squadron that floated in the safety of Aix Roads, protected by their shore batteries, and he was pondering upon a means of destroying those ships, or even cutting them out. 'The ships of the line,' he wrote, 'have all their topmasts struck and topgallant yards across. They are all very deep, more so than vessels are in general for common voyages. They may be easily burned, or they may be taken by sending here eight or ten thousand men, as if intended for the Mediterranean. If people at home would hold their tongues about it, possession might thus be gained of the Isle of d'Oléron, upon which all the enemy's vessels may be driven by sending fire vessels to the eastward of the Isle of d'Aix . . .' Cochrane had worked out the formula that ought, in Napoleon's opinion, to have given Britain the most overwhelming victory in the whole of her naval history.

Cochrane's thoughts also returned to kites. Propaganda leaflets were issued to British ships in case any opportunity should occur to use them to sow dissension among the French. But before the invention of the aeroplane there was no means of distributing them inland amongst the civilian population. They could only be dumped on the crews of French fishing boats off-shore, who could scarcely be expected to run the risk of handing them around after they had landed, even if they possessed any inclination to do so. Cochrane constructed a number of small kites, to which he attached bundles of the leaflets. 'To the string which held the kite a match was appended in such a way that when the kite was flown over the land the retaining string was burned through, and dispersed the proclamations; which, to the great annoyance of the French government, thus became widely distributed over the country.' Recalling this ingenious prank in his old age, Cochrane perhaps over-estimated the annoyance of the French government. But he had used the propaganda weapon of the word with such telling force in the interval that his overstatement (if such it was) is excusable.

In May he was back off the isle of Aix, still examining those treacherous channels amongst which the French squadron lay, watching every detail of its activities, seeking some chink in the armour of their defences through which he could strike. There was a large French frigate named the *Minerve* of 40 guns and twice the tonnage of the *Pallas*, which he found an opportunity to bring to action on 14 May. This involved sailing within range of the battery on the isle of Aix, navigating a dangerous channel that his enemy knew better than he did, and then engaging a vessel with superior fire-power. Soon he had to reckon with three brigs also, which sailed to the support of the *Minerve*.

Cochrane dismantled one of the brigs with a single broadside, and then veered to attack the frigate and another of the brigs under the very fire of the shore battery. The water was filled with shoals which added to the danger as he tacked to and fro, firing at his targets whenever he had the opportunity. After about an hour, instead of having grounded or been bombarded into surrender, he had shot away the after-sails of the *Minerve* and incapacitated the boldest of the brigs. And it was now that he carried out one of those acts of calculated audacity that characterise his career as a seaman. First he sailed between the *Minerve* and the shore battery, raking her protected flank with a succession of punitive broadsides as he passed: next, he brought his ship alongside the enemy.

Unfortunately the order was carried out too impetuously, and unknown to Cochrane the *Minerve* had grounded on a shoal and become relatively immovable. The two ships collided with such force that the spars and rigging of both were seriously damaged, while the guns of the *Pallas* were driven back into their ports by the impact. But this did not prevent them from being instantly fired into the *Minerve* with such devastating effect that the French crew fled below for safety. Only three pistol shots answered the broadside, and nobody except the Captain, Joseph Collet, remained on deck. Gallantly, helplessly, with astonished admiration, Captain Collet raised his hat to Cochrane: and the Sea Wolf, who never forgot courage in others, retained the memory of that lonely figure until the day when he was able to pay his own compliment to the man he had humbled.

Now there appeared on the scene another sailor whose path was to cross Cochrane's more than once. Captain Seymour of the *Kingfisher*, later to become Admiral Sir George Seymour, was regarded by Admiral Thornborough as a man over-liable to take risks. Consequently Seymour had received strict instructions not to pass a certain lighthouse on that coast: how Cochrane came to be exempted from the same instructions is something of a mystery. But there lay Seymour in the *Kingfisher* like a greyhound on a leash, watching Cochrane's every move.

He studied the brilliant manoeuvres as Cochrane pirouetted among the enemy guns in that dangerous channel and finally closed on the *Minerve*. He saw the two enemy ships, each larger than the *Pallas*, bearing down to help the *Minerve* just as Cochrane was on the point of giving the order to board her. He watched the feat of seamanship as Cochrane limped away, his sails in shreds, his foresail lost altogether, the two undamaged frigates in pursuit. Then Seymour could bear it no longer: he passed the lighthouse and signalled to Cochrane that he was coming to his assistance. As soon as he was within range ropes were flung out and he took the *Pallas* in tow. Although each of the French frigates possessed a greater fire-power than the *Pallas* and *Kingfisher* put together, they instantly called off their pursuit and went to the assistance of the *Minerve*.

The great seven-volume history of the Royal Navy observes in its heavy fifth book: 'Cochrane's whole career is so wonderful—his judgment was so excellent, his resourcefulness so capable of surmounting any emergency—that one hesitates to accuse him of rashness in thus assailing an enemy of enormously superior force in full sight of a strong French squadron. But a lesser genius would probably have sacrificed his ship by such an act.' In contrast to this unusual panegyric, Cochrane ended his own despatch on the operation: 'The officers and ship's company behaved as usual; to the names of Lieutenants Haswell and Mapleton, whom I have mentioned on other occasions, I have to add that of Lieutenant Robins, who had just joined.' In his eyes the attempt had not succeeded, although it had taught him what must be done another time.

For once his recommendation was not the kiss of death. As the same naval history records: 'It is satisfactory to be able to note that Lieutenant Haswell was promoted on August 15th following; but Cochrane, being unpopular with the Admiralty, never received the thanks which he deserved.' What the Admiralty desk-men could appreciate least of all was the effect on enemy morale of such depredations in their safest anchorages.

When Cochrane reached Plymouth a week later he was ready to take his revenge—the revenge that would cost him his career in the British Navy, and his country their greatest living sailor in her hour of crisis. He returned with an even higher reputation than he had brought home with him in the *Speedy* after his capture of the *Gamo*, to find another general election pending. On 24 May 1806 there appeared an advertisement in Cobbett's *Weekly Register*, calling for a public-spirited candidate to stand for the rotten borough of Honiton, the constituency whose electors remembered the 10 guineas he had distributed to all who had voted for him at the previous election. It was too good an opportunity to resist, and any second thoughts that Cochrane might have had were stifled by the arrival of his uncle Andrew with William Cobbett himself from London.

It is easy to understand the fascination of Cobbett in Cochrane's eyes, with his country background and his sturdy independence of mind. He was the grandson of a farm labourer, though his father had risen to the position of a competent small farmer—a Jack Larmour of the land. Cobbett was as firm a supporter of the war against Napoleon as Cochrane was, and he had held Tory views until he criticised the enormities of English rule in Ireland and was fined £500 for his trouble. This in turn incensed him against the restrictions on freedom of speech, and soon he was equally angry about corruption in high places and the gerrymandering of elections. So he drifted into the radical camp, armed with his eloquent and lucid pen. But what this band of courageous, patriotic and compassionate men did not possess was a national hero who possessed inside knowledge of what went on inside the service departments. Cochrane was the answer to their prayer.

Uncle Andrew, the bane of Cochrane's career, was a very different kind of person. As was inevitable among the children of the crumbling estate of Dundonald, he had set out to make his own fortune, especially as he was the youngest brother of the eccentric ninth Earl. From

1797 until 1803 he had been governor of the island of Dominica in the West Indies—such perquisites were still available to the scions of noble houses—and during his tenure of that office he had stamped out a mutiny of negro troops. In the course of his career he dabbled in the slave trade, took part in extortionate sales of arms, and was cashiered from the Army for dishonesty. When he married the daughter of the Earl of Hopetoun he added the name of Johnstone to his own, and when he accompanied William Cobbet to Plymouth he was planning to enter Parliament himself by the purchase of the rotten borough of Grampound. He was only 8 years older than his nephew Thomas, Lord Cochrane.

William Cobbett and Andrew Cochrane Johnstone reached Plymouth on 7 June 1806, and the following day Cochrane made his triumphant entry into Honiton. A description of the carnival which heralded the tragedy of his life was published 3 years later. 'He set out from the port of Plymouth on this occasion in a true seaman-like style. He himself, accompanied by a couple of lieutenants and one midshipman all in full dress, as if engaged in actual service, proceeded in one carriage and were followed in another by his boat's crew, new-rigged and prepared for action. On the box sat the helmsman, who wished to regulate the steerage, which he doubtless lamented to see confided to two lubberly landsmen of postilions, with favours in their hats and boots on their legs; while the boatswain, perched on the roof of the carriage with his whistle in his mouth, kept the whole in order, and enabled all to cheer in due time, every blast being accompanied by a long huzza.' Not an outstanding sample of the journalism of the day, but it evokes the boyish sense of fun in Cochrane's character, which must have been one of the secrets of his extraordinary hold over his seamen.

There are two conflicting accounts of his election as Member for Honiton, but according to both it was an expensive luxury. In his old age he wrote that the electors did not bargain with him for their votes, remembering his munificence after his previous defeat. But after he was returned they asked him what they might expect.

'Not one farthing,' he replied.

'But my Lord, you gave ten guineas a head to the minority at the last election, and the majority have been calculating on something handsome on the present occasion.'

'No doubt. The former gift was for their disinterested conduct in not taking the bribe of five pounds from the agents of my opponent. For me now to pay them would be a violation of my own previously expressed principles.' But Cochrane was no match for the electors of a rotten borough. They asked him to give a public supper to his constituents, and he fell into the trap.

'By all means; and it will give me great satisfaction to know that so rational a display of patriotism has superseded a system of bribery which reflects even less credit on the donor than the recipients.' Fine words, as Cochrane discovered when he was taken to court for the cost of a dinner given to the entire town, and made to pay up.

Such were the memories of a man of over 80 years of age, and they were accurate so far as that dinner was concerned. But just over 10 years after the election, when he was an ardent parliamentary reformer, he gave a rather different account of that scandalous election, and it must be the true one. He admitted that he had bribed the electors in addition to incurring the colossal cost of that dinner, and he added: 'Though I am conscious that I did wrong, I assure the House that that was the way I was returned. If any Member disputes it, I can only say that I am willing to shew the bills and vouchers which I had for the money. I have no doubt but that there are very many in this House who have been returned by similar means. My motive, I am now fully convinced, was wrong, decidedly wrong, but as I came home pretty well flushed with Spanish dollars, I found this borough open, and I bargained for it, and I am sure I would have been returned had I been Lord Camelford's black servant or his great dog.'

Universal suffrage has been introduced since his time, leaving the parliamentary system exactly where it stood when Honiton was a rotten borough. That is, the deciding vote is still cast by those who vote for Mr Most. And another fundamental feature of parliamentary democracy remains unchanged. Those who succeed in politics are professional politicians, rarely those who enter Parliament to contribute some professional skill from other walks of life. As Cochrane was about to discover to his cost, few of these succeed in scrambling to the top without learning on the way how to deal with anyone who endangers their position, or the interests of those on whom they depend for their support.

Cochrane had no sooner set up house in Old Palace Yard, opposite the Houses of Parliament, than he was given some revealing glimpses of these men at close quarters. One of those who cultivated him most assiduously after he had arrived in London in the summer of 1806 as a Member of Parliament was an Anglo-Irishman called John Croker, Secretary to the Admiralty for over 20 years. Chronicler of the social world into which he insinuated himself with such dexterity, he fancied himself as a man of letters, though his literary reputation rests exclusively on the gossip he wrote about top people. As a literary critic he is chiefly remembered for his venomous attack on Keats, a poet who was neither fashionable during his lifetime nor well-born. It was said to have hastened Keats' death, so that Byron remarked:

'Tis odd the soul, that very fiery particle,
Should let itself be snuffed out by an article.

Croker was promoted to the Admiralty in 1809, and he obtained the post, characteristically, as a reward for his defence of the royal Duke of York when he was attacked in Parliament for allowing his mistress to sell commissions in the Army. In 1806 he was still on the look-out for political employment, and the young naval hero who was also a nobleman was an obvious target for his attentions.

Croker provides yet another illustration of Cochrane's inability to judge people soundly. 'This gentleman had an invitation to my table as often as he might think proper, and of this—from a similarity of taste and habit, as I was willing to believe—he so far availed himself as to become my daily guest; receiving a cordial reception, from friendship towards a person of ardent mind who had to struggle as I had done to gain a position.' No doubt Croker flattered Cochrane: it is stock-in-trade of such people. He also congratulated Cochrane on his excellent claret.

This claret was a perquisite of the solitary prize that the *Pallas* had taken on her second cruise. Croker asked whether Cochrane would be so kind as to give him some of it, and his host replied that as he had taken it from the French for nothing, Croker should have his claret for nothing too, paying only the duty and the cost of bottling as he had to do himself. But the incident occurred shortly before Croker found other friends and obtained his naval appointment, and he disappeared abruptly from Cochrane's dining table before he could collect his wine. 'Nor did I by any chance meet him till, some time afterwards, we encountered each other by accident near Whitehall. Recognising me in a way meant to convey the idea that he was now my master, our relations were slightly altered. I asked him why he had not sent for his wine. His reply was: "Why really, I have no use for it, my friends having supplied me more liberally than I have occasion for".' John Croker, one of the greatest masters of vituperation of his age, had joined the civil servants of the Admiralty who were watching Cochrane as a cat watches a mouse, and Cochrane had gained nothing by showing kindness to the social climber.

The chamber of the House of Commons in which he took his seat was burned down during his lifetime. The place where it stood is now called St Stephen's Hall, and it runs from one end of the ancient Westminster Hall to the central lobby. A Lancashire weaver paid a visit to the chamber when Cochrane sat in it, and left a graphic description of what he witnessed. 'On each side of this pit-looking place, leaving an open space in the centre of the floor, were some three or four hundred of the most ordinary-looking men I had ever beheld at one view. Some were striking exceptions; several young fellows in military dress gave relief to the sombre drapery of others.'

But it was the lack of decorum that shocked the young weaver from the north most. 'Some talked aloud; some whinnied in mock laughter. Some called "Order, order", some "Question, question"; some beat time with the heel of their boots; and one old gentleman in the side gallery actually coughed himself from a mock cough into a real one, and could not stop until he was almost black in the face. And are these, thought I, the beings whose laws we must obey? This the most illustrious assembly of free-men in the world?' The House of Commons was in fact very much the same then as now: except that it then contained such orators as are not to be heard in it today. Their statues line the new St Stephen's Hall—Sheridan, the dramatist, whose orations rivalled those of ancient Greece; Edmund Burke, whose speeches have become monuments of English literature though they sent Members to sleep when he uttered them; those two great rivals, William Pitt and Charles James Fox.

Cochrane had just missed the spectacle of their long conflict. Pitt had died earlier in the year, weighed down by the hammer blows of Ulm and Austerlitz, and by the death of Nelson at Trafalgar. Charles James Fox had succeeded him as Prime Minister but by the summer he was dying too, of dropsy. During his brief term of office Fox tried to discover whether the war could be brought to an end by a negotiated peace, and Napoleon was to remark in exile: 'Fox's death was one of the fatalities of my career.'

It occurred in September 1806, and in August Cochrane had been appointed to a ship twice the size of the *Pallas*, a captured Spanish frigate called the *Impérieuse* of over a thousand tons. Back he went to Plymouth, and it would have been well for him if the *Impérieuse* had been ordered to some distant station where he might have pursued his true vocation far from the political world of Westminster. But as luck would have it the *Impérieuse* returned to port on 11 February 1807, and Parliament was dissolved in April.

During the interval the seat made vacant by the death of Charles James Fox had been offered to one of his most devoted supporters, Samuel Whitbread, who had turned it down. Whitbread was one of the most selfless philanthropists of the day, and was to become one of Cochrane's most loyal friends in his time of greatest need. He was a pioneer of educational and prison reform, one who turned his gaze on the plight of destitute children, the families of soldiers, the prisoners of war. He had played the leading part in the impeachment of Lord Melville during that very year, and he could hardly have been offered a more flattering token of appreciation for his services to the nation than to be offered the seat of Charles James Fox in the House of Commons. But he was already one of the Members for Bedford, in the county that used to be called Whitbreadshire in recognition of his devotion to its interests: and with the constancy that was the hallmark of his character, he refused to abandon his friends for his own convenience and prestige.

The seat of Fox would have been ideal for a man whose brewery lay in London, and its prestige was without equal in the British Isles. For it was one of the two seats for the city of Westminster, a constituency whose 10,000 rate-paying electors could not be bought like those of the rotten boroughs. Consequently it had a long record of independence and radicalism which the government proved powerless to undermine. When Whitbread declined the invitation to stand there as a candidate, the electors turned to Cochrane instead.

It is some measure of the reputation he now enjoyed, not merely as a naval hero, but also as a fearless opponent of corruption, if not yet a radical in his political opinions. Unfortunately Whitbread's reason for refusing operated in reverse in Cochrane's case. So far from being bound by a sense of loyalty to the electors of Honiton, he was already aware of the mistake he had made in ever becoming involved in their affairs. The error had been a costly one for him, but at least the invitation from Westminster gave him the opportunity to cut his losses without delay. Besides, it was an even higher compliment to him than to a man of Whitbread's standing, for Cochrane had been far less than a year a Member of the House of Commons. It proved irresistible: Cochrane accepted.

Unlike the campaign for a rotten borough in distant Devon, the Westminster election was headline news. There were five candidates. The first was Sir Francis Burdett, the immensely rich baronet with principles that periodically involved him in swingeing fines, and even imprisonment. From this moment he was to become one of Cochrane's lifelong supporters and friends. The next most formidable contestant was Richard Brinsley Sheridan, the dramatist, bosom friend of Fox and Treasurer at the Admiralty during his brief administration. So Cochrane the young, inexperienced naval officer, was in effect competing for the second Westminster seat against an old hand, an outstanding parliamentary orator.

The actual polling went on for 15 days, during which Cochrane's character and actions were torn to shreds in the manner of those times. Sheridan's supporters declared that naval officers were unfit to be representatives of the people in Parliament, and Cochrane asked who else was more competent to attack naval corruption in the legislature. When Burdett and Cochrane came top of the poll, Gillray drew a cartoon showing 'the Republican Goose at the Top' of a greasy pole, 'the Devil helping behind' with the words Deceit and Sedition written on his wings. Such was his delineation of that feather-brained philanthropist, Sir Francis Burdett. From now on Cochrane would be smeared with the same epithets, as he began his parliamentary partnership with the well-meaning but eccentric baronet. In Gillray's cartoon he appeared below the goose on the greasy pole, dressed in naval uniform, his red hair showing beneath his gold-rimmed captain's hat, brandishing a cudgel on which is written the word Reform 'lent to him by Cobbett'.

Gillray has treated Cochrane more kindly than any of the other candidates; and especially more than Sheridan, who is savagely depicted as 'an old Drury Lane Harlequin, trying in vain to make a spring to the Top of the Pole, his Broad Bottom always bringing him down again'. Sheridan was approaching his middle fifties by this time and it was decades since he had written the witty comedies on which his fame rests. Although his conversation was as delightful as ever, his appearance showed the effects of habitual drunkenness while his friendship with the Prince of Wales undermined his popularity in Westminster. However, the Prince put up most of the money to console Sheridan with a rotten borough, and the harlequin of Drury Lane forgot the animosities of the contest more quickly than Cochrane did, although he had so much greater cause for resentment. With the characteristic generosity of his nature he supported the motion which Cochrane introduced in the House of Commons within a fortnight of taking his seat, calling for a Committee to enquire into all sinecures, perquisites and offices paid out of public money.

In doing this he aroused antagonism amongst both the Whigs and the Tories, from the party in power that enjoyed these blessings and from the one in opposition that wished to see them still intact when their turn should come. At sea, Cochrane had taken the offensive against overwhelming odds: and he had been victorious time and time again because his calculations had been exact to the last detail, his judgment sound and swift in every emergency. In politics he was equally impetuous, but in this sphere he possessed neither the training nor the flair, and instead of being faced with seamen whom he could inspire to hero-worship by his courage and ability, he was amongst politicians, a subtle species whose behaviour patterns he never throughout his life began to comprehend.

But among them was the huge, amiable bulk of Samuel Whitbread, and 50 years later Cochrane still remembered with gratitude how Whitbread stepped in to save his motion from defeat. The principal cause of Whitbread's own unpopularity was that he hated war, and openly proposed a negotiated peace with Napoleon. But none could feel a deep antipathy to a man of such decency, courtesy and compassion, and he prevailed on this occasion, as Cochrane recalled. 'Mr Whitbread, a most excellent man, and a great peacemaker when practicable, came to the rescue by stating that though he concurred in principle with my motion, yet it might be sufficient to refer it to a Committee of Finance, with instructions to enquire into and report upon the matters therein contained. Such a course would be useful without being invidious, and a report based upon such alteration would probably be attended with beneficial results.' The most beneficial would be that no dirty linen would be exposed to the public gaze.

The alternative was seized upon by the Prime Minister. His name was Spencer Perceval, and his chief claim to fame is that he was assassinated in the lobby of the House of Commons 5 years later. Cochrane continued to press for his original motion, asserting that corruption ought to be made public. But he expressed himself moderately, without any of the long-winded ranting that would later distress his friends more than it annoyed his enemies. 'A general feeling exists in the country regarding the corruption of the House of Commons. It is notorious that commissions in the Army and Navy have been given for votes in this House, and to such an extent is the system carried that the best way to preferment is considered to be the purchase of a house or two in usually contested boroughs.' Sheridan and Whitbread were among those who supported his motion, which is impressive in both cases. But it was lost, and the Prime Minister's adopted in its place. This resolved merely that a list should be drawn up of everyone holding places and pensions of over £250 a year, except for those serving in either the Army or the Navy.

Undeterred by the amount of hostility he had aroused for such a trifling gain, Cochrane immediately proceeded to introduce a second motion which struck directly at those Admiralty officials who already regarded him with such vindictive hatred. 'Rotten to the core', 'a viler sink of corruption than my imagination ever formed', Lord St Vincent had said of the civilian branches of his service. But when he had tried to use his position as First Sea Lord to introduce reform, he had been driven from office. Now the 31-year-old Captain Lord Cochrane proposed to take up the same task in his capacity as Member for Westminster. He gave graphic instances of the naval abuses which required examination, and particularly appalling details of the suffering caused by inadequate medical facilities. 'All such grievances may seem slight and matter of indifference to those who are here at their ease. But I view them in a different light, and if no one better qualified will represent subjects of great complaint I will do so, independent of every personal consideration.'

It is difficult to decide whether his reference to persons better qualified was aimed at the naval officers who sat listening to him in the House. There was Eliab Harvey who had been Captain of the Fighting *Téméraire* at Trafalgar, immortalised by Turner's painting. He had been promoted Rear Admiral immediately after the battle, and he would soon meet Cochrane at sea in circumstances that prove they were at least united in mutual esteem. There was John Markham, who had been promoted Rear Admiral a few months earlier, and there was Captain Sir Samuel Hood, who would be promoted Rear Admiral later in 1807. None of these were pavement admirals of the corrupt stamp of Admiral Young, but gallant seamen who respected courage and ability in others. Perhaps they sympathised with much that Cochrane said, but it is obvious from their interjections that he forfeited sympathy by some of his allegations, and above all by his critical references to Admiral St Vincent. Cochrane was as incapable of assessing the character of Old Jarvie as of John Croker, and his judgment was darkened further by resentment. But worse than this, he was permitting a personal animosity to undermine the merits of a good case.

All he achieved was an immediate posting to the Mediterranean in the *Impérieuse*. Napoleon was to state that the death of Fox was the fatality of his career. Hindsight reveals that it caused the destruction of Cochrane's as well, when the electors of Westminster honoured him with unlimited leave of absence instead of choosing another Member to occupy the seat in which he had followed Charles James Fox in the House of Commons.

CHAPTER FOUR

The *Impérieuse*

At Wimbledon House near London there lived a rich West Indies merchant named Joseph Marryat, who was a Member of Parliament and also colonial agent for the island of Grenada. These activities brought him into contact with Admiral Sir Alexander Cochrane, who had been appointed to the West Indies station after his promotion; Andrew Cochrane Johnstone, the former governor of Dominica and now Member of Parliament for Grampound; and their nephew the Member for Westminster.

Marryat was blessed with a family of fifteen sons and daughters of whom one, named Frederick, showed Cochrane's youthful desire to go to sea. Like Cochrane, Frederick Marryat met strong opposition from his father until his persistence finally won him his heart's desire. At the age of 14 he made the same journey by coach to his ship that Cochrane had made when he was 3 years older: such a journey as he described graphically in one of his novels, and a far longer one than Cochrane's for it took him all the way to Plymouth. In his novel the Captain is aboard the coach also, as Cochrane may well have been, since he was appointed to the *Impérieuse* on 23 August 1806 and the 14-year-old midshipman joined her to begin his first voyage under his hero's command on 23 September. At the moment when Cochrane was reaching the zenith of his skill as a seaman, his character and career were to be studied and chronicled by the most outstanding and popular naval writer the English language had ever known.

Midshipman Marryat joined a happy and enthusiastic crew. The men whom Cochrane had been driven to impress by force to serve in the *Pallas* all clamoured to be taken aboard the *Impérieuse*. But since she was a much larger ship, Cochrane also had to post an advertisement on the dockyard walls to attract the extra hands required:

Wanted. Stout, able-bodied men who can run a mile without stopping with a sackful of Spanish cobs on their backs.

From the applicants he was able to pick and choose until he had made up his complement of 284 men, including thirty-five marines. Guthrie the surgeon, who had held the helm of the *Speedy* when the *Gamo* was captured, was still serving with Cochrane but now he had an assistant. Another midshipman who joined with Marryat was Houston Stewart, who would become an Admiral one day; while the Master's Mate, the Honourable William Napier, was destined to be Britain's first ambassador to China. 'A giant amongst us pigmies,' Marryat recalled him, 'one of the best navigators in the service, he devoted his time and talents to those who wished to learn. At the same time as he laughed and played with us as children, he ensured respect; and although much feared, he was loved much more. . . . Well do I recollect the powerful frame of Napier with his claymore, bounding in advance of his men and cheering them to victory.' There was, in fact, a strong Scottish element aboard: but Marryat also found Henry Cobbett there, nephew of Cochrane's English radical friend.

Frederick Marryat's story of his naval service opens with the latest stroke Cochrane was to suffer at the hands of that old rogue Sir William Young, the Port Admiral at Plymouth. Whether or not he was carrying out instructions from officials of his own stamp at the Admiralty, he forced the *Impérieuse* to sail before she had been properly serviced in the dockyards. 'How nearly,' wrote Marryat, 'were the lives of a fine ship's company, and of Lord Cochrane and his officers, sacrificed to the despotism of an Admiral who *would* be obeyed.'

For the 14-year-old boy making his first trip to sea it was a frightening experience. 'The signal for sailing was enforced by gun after gun; the anchor was hove up and with all her stores on deck, her guns not even mounted, in a state of confusion unparalleled from her being obliged to hoist faster than it was possible she could stow away, she was driven out of harbour to encounter a heavy gale. A few hours more would have enabled her to proceed to sea with security, but they were denied. The consequences were appalling; they might have been fatal. In the general confusion some iron too near the binnacles had attracted the needle of the compasses; the ship was steered out of her course. At midnight, in a heavy gale at the close of November, so dark that you could not distinguish any object however close, the *Impérieuse* dashed upon the rocks between Ushant and the Main. The cry of terror which ran through the lower decks; the grating of the keel as she was forced in; the violence of the shocks which convulsed the frame of the vessel; the hurrying up of the ship's company without their clothes; and then the enormous wave which bore her up and carried her clean over the reef will never be effaced from my memory.'

Admiral Young became Sir Hurricane Humbug in Marryat's novels, while Cochrane himself is drawn to the life as Captain Savage in *Peter Simple*. 'A sailor every inch of him. He knew a ship from stem to stern, understood the character of seamen and gained their confidence. He was besides a good mechanic, a carpenter, a rope-maker, sail-maker, cooper. He could hand reef and steer, knot and splice: but he was no orator. He was good tempered, honest and unsophisticated, with a large proportion of common sense and free with his officers.' Many others who knew him were to confirm that this man who could be so rancorous in his public life was by nature affable, courteous in his manners and considerate. His reported speeches provide the best evidence that he often ruined a good argument by his way of presenting it.

Marryat also drew attention to another quality that Cochrane demonstrated on so many occasions. 'I never knew anyone so careful of the lives of his ship's company as Lord Cochrane, or any who calculated so closely the risks attending any expedition. Many of the most brilliant achievements were performed without the loss of a single life, so well did he calculate the chances; and half the merit he deserves for what he did accomplish has never been awarded him, merely because, in the official despatches, there has not been a long list of killed and wounded to please the appetite of the English public.'

It would be hard to find any other commander, either on land or on sea, who possessed this particular gift in such an eminent degree as Cochrane did: and naturally it was the men who shared with him the dangers of active service who were so deeply impressed by it, not the civilian parasites of the war game. For instance, Jahleel Brenton, who had commanded the *Speedy* before him and whose own services were to make him a Knight of the Bath, a Baronet and a Vice Admiral. 'Bold and adventurous as Lord Cochrane was,' Brenton noted particularly, 'no unnecessary exposure of life was ever permitted under his command. Every circumstance was anticipated, every caution against surprise was taken, every provision of success was made; and in this way he was enabled to accomplish the most daring enterprises with comparatively little danger and still less actual loss.'

The chorus of praise from those best able to assess his qualities heaps coals of fire on the men who spent their time denigrating his character— an occupation that has still not ceased. Sir Jahleel's brother Captain Edward Brenton's comments have a particular interest because he published the first biography of Admiral St Vincent, and might have yielded to prejudice against the critic of Old Jarvie. But on the contrary, he added his own illustrations of Cochrane's wonderful gift.

'No officer ever attempted or succeeded in more arduous enterprises with so little loss. Before he fired a shot he reconnoitred in person, took soundings and bearings, passed whole nights in the boats, his head line and spy glass incessantly at work. Another fixed principle of this officer was never to allow his boats to be unprotected by his ship, if it were possible to lay her within range of the object of attack. With the wind on shore he would veer one of his boats in by a bass hawser (an Indian rope made of grass, which is so light as to float on the surface of the water). By this means he established a communication with the ship, and in case of reverse the boats were hove off by the capstan, while the people in them had only to attend to the use of their weapons.' Such were the feats of ingenuity and seamanship that inspired the future Captain Marryat to write his tales of naval adventure.

He recalled the thrill of his first experience of the sea, so different from Cochrane's placid initiation among the Norwegian fjords. 'The cruises of the *Impérieuse* were periods of continual excitement from the hour in which she hove up her anchor till she dropped it again in port. The day that passed without a shot being fired in anger was with us a blank day. The boats were hardly secured on the booms than they were cast loose and out again. The yard and stay tackles were for ever hoisting up and lowering down. The expedition with which parties were formed for service; the rapidity of the frigate's movements day and night; the hasty sleep, snatched at all hours; the waking up at the report of the guns, which seemed the only key note to the hearts of those on board; the beautiful precision of our fire, obtained by constant practice; the coolness and courage of our Captain, inoculating the whole of the ship's company . . . when memory sweeps along those years of excitement, even now my pulse beats more quickly with the reminiscence.' Such was life aboard the *Impérieuse* when she sailed to join the fleet of Admiral Collingwood in the Mediterranean in September 1807, after Cochrane's interlude at the hustings of Westminster. She travelled in state, having a convoy of thirty-eight merchantmen to escort, some to Gibraltar, the remaining fifteen as far as Malta. Warned by past experience both offensive and defensive, he ran no risks with the ships under his protection, but fired repeatedly at stragglers to bring them back into position.

Of all the Admirals with whom he ever came in contact, there was none for whom he expressed such unqualified admiration as Collingwood; and the respect between these two men, so utterly unlike in character, was mutual. Vice Admiral Lord Collingwood had taken over the command at Trafalgar after the death of Nelson, and had since been appointed to the extraordinarily difficult task of blockading the French fleet in Toulon and stamping out both enemy trade and piracy. He had not revisited his home since 1803, and as his health declined he made repeated requests for leave to do so. But the government found him so irreplaceable that he was kept in harness until he died aboard his ship off Port Mahon in 1810. He opposed the use of flogging and the press-gang, and he treated his crews with such kindness that they called him 'father'.

At a time when communications were slow it was a perpetual problem for Collingwood to determine which ships should be respected as friendly, and which attacked as enemy ones. Officially all ships not flying the British ensign could be regarded as hostile, but a government directive of January 1807 laid down that British commerce was to be safeguarded as far as possible. To promote this, licences were issued to vessels that smuggled British manufactures into foreign markets; which increased the confusion and gave rise to widespread abuses. Cochrane soon had disquieting evidence of them. Soon after he had deposited the remainder of his convoy at Malta he encountered a Maltese privateer off Corsica named the *King George*. She was heavily armed, and in fact a £500 reward had been offered for her capture. Cochrane sent three unarmed boats to enquire her business. Furiously, he informed Collingwood of what followed:

'I am sorry to inform your Lordship of a circumstance which has already been fatal to two of our best men, and I fear of thirteen wounded, two will not survive. These wounds they received in an engagement with a set of desperate savages collected in a privateer, said to be the *King George* of Malta, wherein the only subjects of his Britannic Majesty were three Maltese boys, one Gibraltar man, and a naturalised Captain; the others being renegadoes from all countries, and great part of them belonging to nations at war with Britain.' They had allowed Cochrane's crew to come alongside, under the command of Napier, who was among the wounded, before receiving them with 'a volley of grape and musketry discharged in the most barbarous and savage manner, their muskets and blunderbusses being pointed from beneath the netting close to the people's breasts. The rest of the men and officers then boarded and carried the vessel in the most gallant manner. The bravery shown and exertion used on this occasion were worthy of a better cause.'

Worse was to follow. Somebody with a financial interest in the *King George* brought his influence to bear on that sink of iniquity, the Maltese Court of Admiralty, and a licence was produced under which Cochrane was fined for having interfered with what was described as a British vessel. Marryat described the fight for the *King George* in his most famous novel, *Mr Midshipman Easy*, and he recalled elsewhere: 'I never at any time saw Lord Cochrane so much dejected as he was for many days after this affair.'

The system of granting licences to ships that traded in the Mediterranean not only gave raise to genuine confusion, it also offered a
huge temptation to dishonesty. For so long as some merchant vessels
received the privilege of passes, the authorities who granted them were
bound to be exposed to attempts to bribe or influence them. There was
also the question of whether a pass was genuine. This was the next
difficulty that Cochrane encountered, when Collingwood appointed
him to the command of the Corfu squadron whose responsibility was
to enforce the blockade off the Ionian islands. He was to succeed
Captain Patrick Campbell, an officer who was only a year older than
Cochrane, and who would also reach the rank of Admiral.

It was the first time Cochrane had ever been appointed to the
command of a squadron, and the commission reflects Collingwood's
confidence in him. Cochrane sailed from Valletta early in December and
arrived off Corfu to discover that preparations for the transfer of the
command had not been completed in the squadron there. Disliking
inactivity, Cochrane obtained leave from Campbell to reconnoitre
north of Corfu and there, to his surprise, he encountered thirteen
merchantmen sailing along the blockaded coast as confidently as if
they had been British vessels. Cochrane singled out the three nearest
for inspection, and discovered to his further astonishment that each
carried a pass from Captain Campbell. Cochrane sent them to Malta for
examination by the Court of Admiralty.

Whether or not it had been proper for Captain Campbell to issue
those passes, the action he took when he heard what Cochrane had
done was not merely an ill-mannered breach of professional etiquette
but a grotesque over-reaction for anyone with a clear conscience.
Without waiting to discuss the matter with the officer who had come
to succeed him, he immediately sent a ship to Admiral Collingwood
with a letter complaining that Cochrane's want of discretion rendered
him unfit to be entrusted with a single ship, much less with the command of a squadron. As a comment on another officer of about the
same age and seniority, this would appear impertinent even if that other
officer had not been Cochrane: but such backstairs libel was by no
means uncharacteristic of those times. Nor can it be taken as evidence
of guilt any more than Campbell's subsequent promotion to the rank
of Admiral is evidence that he acted with invariable good sense or
integrity.

Collingwood recalled Cochrane without any preliminary enquiry.
Homesick, his health ebbing away, his days harassed by a hundred
problems, he acted in a typically constructive and conciliatory manner.
He was bound to have heard already of Cochrane's reputation for

insubordinate and quarrelsome behaviour. It was as a loner that he had become a legend in this war, and Collingwood perhaps blamed himself for not having given him the right appointment in the first place. He wasted no time now over an angry confrontation between his two Scottish subordinates—particularly since news had just arrived that Russia had declared war on Britain as Napoleon's ally. He did not even discuss with Cochrane the grounds for his recall, but expressed his confidence in him by sending him back to Malta to revictual his ship and thence to harass enemy shipping off the coasts of France and Spain in total independence. With such an exciting prospect, Cochrane easily forgot his disappointment that he would not command a squadron after all, especially an inactive squadron whose only responsibility was to blockade a few frigates.

There followed the marvellous climax to Cochrane's services in the British Navy, remembered so vividly by Marryat that 'even now my pulse beats more quickly with the reminiscence'. The dawn strike after a night of preparation; the daylight chase under billowing sails; the boarding party's scuffle on deck; the exploration of holds stacked with merchandise and munitions; the prizes carried off for adjudication; such was the ceaseless round of activity, upon which Cochrane was later to reflect: 'One ship well officered and manned is more effective than two of the opposite description and will cost less to the nation. The true strength of the navy is not in a multitude of ships, but in the energies and alacrity of officers and crews.' His exploits in the *Impérieuse* have been studied ever since as the supreme example of the truth of this axiom.

One of the tasks he undertook was to destroy the coastal fortifications on the islands of Majorca and Minorca. The ship's boats that he had sent in on one occasion returned after failing to assault the enemy position. At the gangway Cochrane turned to the coxswain and asked:

'Well, Jack, do you think it impossible to blow up the battery?'

'No, my Lord, it's not impossible,' he replied. 'We can do it if you will go.'

Cochrane immediately leapt into the cutter and ordered the assault party to return to the shore, where he and his men made good the coxswain's words.

On 31 May the *Impérieuse* sailed into Gibraltar for a much-needed overhaul, and she had hardly arrived when Cochrane heard news of vast import. Napoleon had attempted to place his brother Joseph Bonaparte on the throne of Spain, and the country had risen in revolt. It was the signal for Wellington to land at Oporto and begin the Peninsular war which ended with his triumphant entry into Paris. From

Admiral Collingwood Cochrane received instructions that he was to
give the Spaniards all the assistance in his power in their resistance to
French rule. As Cochrane returned east along the coast he must have
wondered what sort of reception he would receive from people to
whom he had been such a menace hitherto. He need not have worried.
As soon as his frigate reappeared amongst his erstwhile enemies with
British and Spanish colours flying, delighted officials rowed out to
make him welcome, and received him ashore as though El Cid had
arisen from his centuries of sleep to fight for them again. They knew
the value of their new ally from harsh experience. The man who had
captured the *Gamo* was now on their side.

Cochrane concentrated his attention on the province of Catalonia,
all the principal strongholds of which remained in French hands, and
thus began an association with a foreign people that was to be the
most satisfactory of his entire career. The Catalans were scarcely less
distinct from the Spaniards than the Basques who bestrode the other
end of the Pyreneean frontier with France. At frequent periods in their
history they had lived under French rule, and they possessed the spirit
of independence innate in all frontier peoples. To this day their somewhat ugly and abrupt speech is markedly different from Castilian
Spanish; their abundant folklore is all their own; their churches are
filled with their rich and original arts. History and geography have
combined to give them a character that a Lowland Scot such as
Cochrane could salute as much resembling his own.

'The Catalans made capital guerilla troops,' Cochrane recalled,
'possessing considerable skill in the use of their weapons, though
previously untrained. A character for turbulence was often attributed
to them; but in a country groaning under priestcraft and bad government the sturdy spirit of independence, which prompted them to set
the example of heroic defence of their country, might be, either
mistakenly or purposely—the latter the more probable—set down for
discontent and sedition. At any rate the descendants of men who, in a
former age, formed the outposts of the Christian world against
Mahomedism in no way disgraced their ancestors, and became in the
end the terror of their enemies. One quality they predominantly
possessed, patience and endurance under privation; and this, added to
their hardy habits and adventurous disposition, contributed to form an
enemy not to be despised—the less so that they were in every way
disposed to repay the barbarities of the French with interest.' These
were the kind of people Cochrane understood and liked and knew how
to lead. The partnership began in mutual esteem and was quickly
cemented by success.

The principal stronghold of Catalonia was the great seaport of Barcelona, less than a hundred miles from the French border. As it was garrisoned by French troops, Cochrane could do no more than hearten the inhabitants by sailing to a point just out of range of the shore batteries, hoisting British and Spanish colours, and firing a salute of 21 guns. As he did so, he could see the inhabitants crowding excitedly on the housetops and gathering in the public squares, while French cavalry and foot-soldiers were hastily dispersed to intimidate the menacing crowds. From the coastal batteries began a cannonade which merely sent jets of water flying in the air between the *Impérieuse* and the shore. Not knowing how effective the French military presence in Barcelona was, Cochrane made one further gesture to stimulate its citizens. He hoisted British colours over French, and then Spanish colours over French, to the sound of an additional salvo. Then, seeing that a civilian uprising in the capital was out of the question, he departed to explore the situation in the neighbouring towns, and particularly along the road which linked them all to France.

Since the interior was rendered unsafe by guerillas, this road was the indispensable supply route for the French garrisons. So now Cochrane flung himself into the novel trades of engineer and instructor of guerillas, while he maintained the *Impérieuse* as a floating battery, ever ready to bombard any who should attempt to use the road. First he landed with a party of his crew to blow up bridges and dislodge overhanging rocks with gunpowder until the road was blocked. Then he trained local Catalans to continue the same task, which they did with glee. So long as the *Impérieuse* remained at hand to fire on those who attempted to repair the damage, the supply route to Barcelona remained completely blocked.

But Cochrane was called away by intelligence that a French General was approaching with a strong force to augment the garrison at Barcelona. He determined to take possession of the fort of Mongat before the enemy could reach it and hastened there, only to discover that the French advance party had occupied the fort already. There followed the first combined operation in which British seamen and Catalan guerillas together executed one of Cochrane's impromptu master-strokes. There was a band of 800 of these patriots lurking in the neighbourhood, who eagerly agreed to storm the fort of Mongat with British support. But first Cochrane took the precaution of blowing up the road between Barcelona and Mongat so that the separated French forces would be unable to lend one another assistance; then, as the French general still advanced from the other direction, he went ashore to reconnoitre the ground from a hill above the fort. Finally he returned to bring the *Impérieuse* close inshore for the bombardment.

As always, he combined speed with precision and attention to detail, and these precautions proved too great a strain for the impatient Catalans. He had not yet returned with his party of marines when they dashed up a hill to assault a French outpost. The enemy troops hung out flags of truce, but the guerillas would have none of it: they continued their impetuous charge to storm the position, whose defenders maintained a ragged, desultory fire behind their flags to keep the Catalans at bay. Cochrane on the other hand signalled his acceptance of the truce as soon as he had leapt ashore, and was immediately conducted to the castle. He found the troops in it drawn up on either side of the gate, and the French commandant hurried towards him, begging him not to allow his Catalan allies to enter with him, and saying that he would surrender to Cochrane alone. He and his soldiers had reason to be thankful that Cochrane exercised such a magnetic influence over the guerillas, for they outnumbered his marines by over twenty to one and yelled for vengeance upon the hated occupiers of their land. And the recorded horrors of the Peninsular war tell what that vengeance might have been like. As it was, the French suffered no more than the abuse of the Catalans as Cochrane escorted them to the boats which would carry them to the safety of the *Impérieuse*. He also carried off four brass field pieces and threw the iron guns over their parapets before blowing up the fort of Mongat.

It was the first of the outstanding services of a wholly novel kind that Collingwood reported to the Admiralty with mounting encomiums. There the despatches were filed away in stony silence to await the day when generations of seamen would be trained from the example of his methods, while further generations would be inspired by the same story as it was related by Captain Marryat. And in his old age Cochrane himself could reflect: 'It is wonderful what an amount of terrorism a small frigate is able to inspire on an enemy's coast. Actions between line-of-battle ships are no doubt very imposing, but for real effect I would prefer a score or two of small vessels well handled to any fleet of line-of-battle ships.' Prophetic words.

As a result of the severance of the coastal route from France to Barcelona, achieved by a single frigate, the French troops were compelled to march to the Catalan capital by a circuitous inland route on which they were exposed to the ferocity of the guerillas. The feelings of the Catalans had been further enraged by the steps which the French had taken to repair the coast road. They had not only rounded up the local country people to shift the great blocks of stone, but they had forced them to fill up the holes with everything movable that they possessed, even their agricultural implements, furniture and clothes. Then, in an attempt to frighten them out of blocking the road again, they had sacked and burned every home in the neighbourhood. The only consequence, of course, was to inspire the Catalans to more furious resistance, and provoke them into more horrible atrocities whenever French soldiers fell into their hands.

By blocking the road and capturing the fort of Mongat, Cochrane had fulfilled the threat he had made off Barcelona a month before when he had hoisted the flags of Britain and Spain over that of France. By mid-August in 1808 the *Impérieuse* had passed beyond the cliffs of the Spanish frontier with France, and lay in the bay of Marseilles. It was Cochrane's intention to destroy another vital means of enemy communication, the signal stations that relayed information about British naval activities up and down the coast, as well as their own military secrets. It was a game that some of his men had learned to play on France's Atlantic seaboard, and they returned to it with enthusiasm.

They demolished their first station without opposition on the 16th, and the following day Cochrane despatched ninety men in boats to attack another on an island in the delta of the river Rhône. Its defenders fled, and the station was demolished with such ease that Cochrane sent the same party to blow up a third the same afternoon. This time they were not only met with a running fire of musketry but bogged down in mud up to the knees as they waded through the swamps of that gigantic estuary at the end of a tiring day. And it is a measure of the fitness and enthusiasm they had attained under their indefatigable Captain's leadership that when they returned 4 hours later, caked with mud and not a man missing, they had accomplished their task.

Without delaying for even a night's rest, Cochrane sailed down the coast through the darkness to surprise his next victims before any warning could reach them. Only when he found their stations guarded by troops did he stay his hand in order not to endanger the lives of his men. But during one night raid he only pretended to retire when his boats were showered with grape shot as they rowed towards the beach. He waited until he judged that the enemy would be off-guard, confident that they had frightened the intruder away, then he personally led his men back, blew up the signal station, and took them along the shore to surprise the battery that had fired on them earlier. Napier was there with his claymore, and Gilbert, the assistant surgeon, who far preferred ploys of this kind to hanging about in the *Impérieuse* waiting for the rare occasion when he and Guthrie had an operation to perform on the table of the midshipmen's mess.

As soon as the men in the battery became aware that the pest had returned—which the explosion from the signal station told them—they opened fire again. But they naturally assumed the assault party was hurrying back to the sea, and so they fired into the darkness in the wrong direction until those leaping figures pounced on them and silenced their guns.

Among these were two brass 24-pounders, which Cochrane was preparing to carry back to his ship in the first light of dawn when the silence was once more broken, this time by a solitary warning shot from the *Impérieuse*. The look-out in the frigate, peering landward through the ebbing darkness, had detected movement which appeared to be that of cavalry advancing over a nearby hill. Although Cochrane could not know the exact nature of the emergency, he could guess that the earlier firing would have alerted French troops in the neighbourhood. But he did not abandon his brass guns: he and his men redoubled their efforts to roll them down to the shore on captured barrels of powder, and they were already being manhandled into the boats by the time the enemy horsemen reached the beach. As usual Cochrane had provided in advance for just such an emergency, by mounting 9-pounder guns in his boats to cover a retreat under attack. The cavalry were kept at bay by these guns while the remainder of the men leapt aboard and the weary oarsmen pulled them out of range. There was only one casualty and it was not achieved by a Frenchman. Seaman Hogan had a box of powder secured to his waist which caught fire as the fuses were lit, blowing him to bits. The rest of the party reached the safety of their ship at 7 o'clock in the morning 'somewhat fatigued by the night's adventure', as Cochrane conceded.

The British gained a long-term advantage from these operations, through the care Cochrane took to deceive the enemy over the fate of their code books. On each occasion when he destroyed a signal station he found the time to scatter all the papers in them in a half burnt condition, in such a way as to convince the French that these books had also been destroyed in the fire. He forwarded them to Admiral Collingwood who was able to read all the information in the enemy semaphores about the movements of French and British ships from the promontory of Italy northwards, simply because nobody thought necessary to alter the code.

While Cochrane returned to report to Collingwood where he lay blockading the French fleet in Toulon harbour, the tale of his achievements leaked far beyond the implacable files of the Admiralty, and his fellow-countryman Walter Scott was the first to give it to the world. 'Lord Cochrane during the month of September 1808, with his single ship, kept the whole coast of Languedoc in alarm—destroyed the

numerous semaphoric telegraphs, which were of the utmost consequence to the numerous coasting convoys of the French, and not only
prevented any troops from being sent from that province into Spain,
but even excited such dismay that 2000 men were withdrawn from
Figueras to oppose him, when they would otherwise have been
marching farther into the peninsula. The coasting trade was entirely
suspended during this alarm; yet with such consummate prudence were
all Cochrane's enterprises planned and executed that not one of his
men were either killed or hurt, except one, who was singed in blowing
up a battery.' Poor Seaman Hogan was more than singed: but Cochrane's autobiography, which records his fate, was not published until
long after Walter Scott's death.

In the stern cabin of his flagship off Toulon Admiral Collingwood
received Cochrane for the last time, to enjoy his personal account of
these phenomenal successes; then despatched him to continue his
operations in complete independence. But shortly after the *Impérieuse*
had returned to the waters of Marseilles she fell in with the *Spartan*
commanded by Jahleel Brenton, and the two captains decided to try
some team work. The results were of the kind that heartened the ailing
Collingwood to write: 'The activity and zeal of those gallant young
men keep up my spirits, and make me equal to bear the disagreeables
that happen from the contentions of some other ships. Those who do
all the service give me no trouble; those who give the trouble are good
for nothing.'

In view of the recurrent failure of personal relations between
Cochrane and men of the same profession and social order—Lieutenant
Beaver who had brought him to a court-martial, the French officer who
challenged him to a duel, Captain Campbell who libelled him behind
his back—this new, voluntary partnership with an officer 5 years older
than himself and slightly senior in rank is of particular interest. Jahleel
Brenton proved in the end to be a more distinguished sailor than either
Beaver or Campbell, and he was not jealous of his junior's well-earned
fame. He fell in with Cochrane's methods in the most co-operative
manner, so that their first combined attack in a signal station defended
by troops was an entire success.

The practice it gave them in using two ships and separate contingents
of marines enabled them to carry out a more complicated operation at
Vendres with even greater precision. The coast where this port lay was
defended by shore batteries, cavalry, infantry and even armed peasants.
The exploit began as usual with the destruction of a defended signal
station followed by a night assault on one of the batteries. Seamen
reinforced the marines as they carried the fortification by assault,

spiked the guns, destroyed their carriages and blew up the barracks, with such speed that they had embarked again by the time an over-whelming body of troops arrived on the scene with cavalry and artillery.

As they sailed along the coast, only just out of range of the enemy guns, they saw the troops massing everywhere, determined not to be caught napping again. So this time Cochrane and Brenton decided they would alter their tactics by luring the cavalry away before they got on with their main job. The stratagem was just such a lark as Cochrane loved, and no doubt his men did too. The ships' boys of both the *Spartan* and the *Impérieuse* were dressed up in the scarlet jackets of the marines and despatched in the small boats and the rocket boats to a point well to the right of the real target, as though they intended to make a landing there. Sure enough, as this miniature armada rowed down the coast a body of cavalry set off to receive them. The two frigates meanwhile moved in towards the town they had selected for attack, and although they were hit by the guns from the shore batteries they held their fire until their own broadsides could take full effect. The bombardment continued for an hour, but it did not bring the cavalry back since it was clearly not here that the assault was planned: this was merely a diversion while the marines made their assault farther up the coast.

Then suddenly the real marines were landed in the larger boats that had been kept in reserve for the purpose. As soon as they touched the shore the enemy fled from their guns. While they were being destroyed the enemy cavalry could be seen galloping back to their defence. What these horsemen could observe was that the landing-party was still ashore; the guns were silent; the two frigates now lay close inshore. But they were in far too great a hurry to repair their mistake to evaluate this situation—until they came within musket range of the ships and were mown down by grape shot. Those who retained their saddles fled out of range, leaving the marines to return to the *Spartan* and the *Impérieuse* as though from a spell of shore leave. The ships' boys too rowed back to their ships after their delightful outing in scarlet uni-forms.

Jahleel Brenton's co-operation had enabled Cochrane to demonstrate how much more he would have been able to achieve with a squadron than with a single frigate, and Collingwood was not slow to read the same lesson to the Admiralty. 'Nothing can exceed the zeal and activity with which his Lordship pursued the enemy. The success which attends his enterprises clearly indicates with what skill and ability they are conducted, besides keeping the coast in constant alarm—causing a general suspension of trade, and harassing a body of troops employed in opposing him.' Collingwood might have saved his ink.

Cochrane returned to destroy coastal shipping, signal stations and shore batteries on the Spanish side of the frontier on 15 November 1808. The army of occupation there had enjoyed a respite of over 3 months which it was time to terminate. When he sailed back into the bay of Barcelona he discovered that the French were still maintaining themselves uneasily in one quarter of the city, molested by the Catalan peasantry, and he gave them what cheer he could by firing into this sector. He was interrupted 4 days later by news that the enemy were endeavouring to capture the frontier fortress of Rosas, the key to the coast road to Barcelona, and at once sailed there to enact the spectacular finale of his service in the Mediterranean. In it he passed beyond the functions of a naval leader of marine commandos to play the part of a besieged garrison commander.

He arrived at a moment of extreme emergency. The Catalan freedom fighters awaited the approach of an army of 6000 Italian troops in the French service. In an attempt to stiffen their resistance the gallant Captain West of the *Excellent*, a frigate with almost twice the armament of the *Impérieuse*, had flung every man he could spare from his ship into the two principal strongholds of Rosas—the citadel in the town and Fort Trinidad beyond it. This formidable and picturesque fortification climbed up the cliffs from the sea and Cochrane's own description of it can scarcely be improved upon. It was constructed, he found, 'with walls some 50 feet high. Behind this and joined to it rose another fort to the height of 30 or 40 feet more, the whole presenting the appearance of a large church with a tower 110 feet high, a nave 90 feet high, and chancel 50 feet. The tower having its back to the cliff as a matter of course sheltered the middle and lower portions of the fortress from a fire of the battery above it.' This battery had already been established by the French on cliffs behind the fort that were even higher than the tower, but although they subjected the tower to a sustained bombardment they found it to be bomb-proof and therefore could not assail the lower portions of the fort beyond.

The citadel of Rosas was in more immediate danger. Captain West had set his marines to work to make it as defensible as possible and they had defended it with great gallantry against French assault despite its wretched state of repair. The French troops were busy digging entrenchments and bringing up guns with which to batter the citadel into submission when Captain West was superseded by Captain Bennett of the *Fame*, another frigate as well armed as the *Excellent*. But neither of these officers could contribute more than a few dozen men to the defence of Rosas, and the most they hoped to achieve was to retain possession of the two key-points in the hope that a Spanish relieving army would appear before those 6000 Italian troops. When no such help came Bennett withdrew his marines as West had done, and it was immediately after this policy of disengagement had been carried out that Cochrane sailed into the wide semicircle of Rosas bay.

For him to adopt a course that had been abandoned by the future Admiral of the Fleet Sir John West and Captain Richard Bennett, both senior officers and each possessing far superior resources to those of the *Impérieuse*, was virtually to convict them of an error of judgment. At the very least Bennett might have restrained Cochrane on the grounds that he would be entering a death-trap. The wind also exercised a restraining hand, for the *Impérieuse* found herself becalmed almost as soon as she entered the bay: but Cochrane immediately had himself rowed ashore in a gig to make his own appraisal and then returned to lay his plan before Captain Bennett, and found him as co-operative as Jahleel Brenton had been. Bennett did not return himself to take part in the defence of Rosas, but he allowed his junior to embark on the courageous and hazardous attempt.

The wind freshened as Cochrane rowed back to his ship, enabling him to use his favourite weapon—speed. His principal concern was to bring what relief he could to the beleaguered citadel until Spanish troops should arrive to relieve it and to this end he had made a careful study of the positions of the French batteries that were bombarding it and of the trenches that surrounded it. In the rising wind he brought the *Impérieuse* to a range of 600 yards, from which he fired with such effect that the firing of the battery guns was interrupted and the enemy troops were impeded in their digging operations.

At the same time he prepared to re-occupy Fort Trinidad, and the entire operation was executed with such despatch that he had obtained possession of the fort with fifty of his seamen and all his marines the very day after Captain Bennett had evacuated it, before the French could make a move to anticipate him. It was still possible to enter the nether-most of the chain of forts from the beach in perfect safety, but by this time the enemy battery on the hill above their topmost tower had already made a dangerous breach in it. However, the elevation of the guns in this battery was such that the hole was well up the tower wall—as though it were the great west window in Westminster Abbey, as Cochrane explained so graphically. He had brought ashore no guns with which to fire back at the battery on the hill. He concentrated instead on making Fort Trinidad impregnable against attack.

The hole in the tower happened to breach its wall just above a strong stone arch which vaulted the interior 50 feet above its base. Cochrane set his men to smash this arch so that if the enemy should reach the breach they would face a yawning chasm, and as he surveyed his man-trap other devices crowded into his inventive mind. 'I got together all the timber at hand and constructed a huge wooden case, exactly resembling the hopper of a mill—the upper part being kept well greased with cooks' slush from the *Impérieuse*, so that to retain a hold on it was impossible. Down this, with the slightest pressure from behind, the storming party must have fallen to a depth of fifty feet and all they could have done if not killed would have been to remain prisoners at the bottom.' The skeleton crew aboard his ship must have wondered what on earth their Captain would be up to next as they consigned their greasy refuse to Fort Trinidad, and it would not be long before they received their next surprise.

Catalan patriots, seamen and marines entered with gusto into these hectic preparations for an attack, and presently they were joined by a contingent of fifty Irishmen serving with the Spanish forces. In relative safety they repaired the breach as fast as it was widened by French bombardment, but Cochrane himself was hit in the face by a splinter of stone which forced his great nose right back into the cavity of his mouth and caused him intolerable pain. Guthrie the surgeon was summoned to restore it to its original prominence, but to the garrison of Fort Trinidad their commander must have presented a fearsome appearance, with his two black eyes and smashed nose.

After providing for the immediate danger of an assault through the hole in the tower, Cochrane prepared for the contingency of an emergency evacuation. He placed powder in the tower with a train lasting ten minutes, and explosives to demolish the bottom end of the chain of fortifications as soon as the last boat-load of men should have left the shore. Then surveying his handiwork, almost as an afterthought, he invented barbed wire. He ordered ship's chains and a pile of fish-hooks to be brought from the *Impérieuse*, and festooned the chains across the man-trap in the tower so barbed with the fish-hooks that no man caught in them could hope to free himself before he was shot.

During the 2 days that were spent in making these preparations the French had not been idle on their hill above the tower. First they installed a second battery there which enabled them to enlarge their breach faster than the defenders could repair it. They they seem to have had second thoughts because they suddenly launched a night attack, not against Fort Trinidad, but on the town of Rosas.

Captain West, who had begun the defence of these two positions, still kept his 74-gun frigate the *Fame* in company with the *Impérieuse* in the wide bay. Although he was little more than a year older than Cochrane he had obtained his captaincy nearly 5 years earlier. He nevertheless exhibited the same generous and unselfish patriotism as Jahleel Brenton and Richard Bennett had done in giving his support to the operations of his brilliant junior. The *Fame* now accompanied the *Impérieuse* as she sailed into close range once more, and the two frigates reopened fire on the besiegers. From his fort Cochrane was able to study the enemy's gunnery. 'The practice of the French when breaching the walls of Rosas was beautiful. So skilfully was their gunnery conducted that, to use a schoolboy similitude, every discharge "ruled a straight line" along the lower part of the walls. This being repeated till the upper portion was without support, as a matter of course the whole fell in the ditch, forming a breach of easy ascent.' By dawn the French were in possession of Rosas, just before an army of 2000 Spaniards arrived for its relief. As Cochrane recalled bitterly, 'six hours earlier would have saved the town, the preservation of which was the only object in retaining the fortress'.

But it was not in Cochrane's character to relinquish his foothold without a struggle, even when the Spanish army tamely disappeared back into the hills. The French were now able to bring four more batteries from Rosas to the hill overlooking Fort Trinidad and through the growing din of their bombardment the little garrison waited for the inevitable assault. Twice there was silence as the French ceased firing to offer terms of honourable surrender under flags of truce: twice they were refused.

Cochrane had evidently decided that Frederick Marryat was now old and mature enough to include among his garrison troops, though he could scarcely have dreamed that by doing this he had brought his chronicler with him. Three days after the fall of Rosas the 16-year-old midshipman stood on watch, peering through the dawn mists. As usual the wakeful Cochrane was on the prowl. 'The Captain came out and asked me what I was looking at. I told him I hardly knew; but there did appear something unusual in the valley, immediately below the breach. He listened for a moment, looked attentively with his night-glass, and exclaimed in his firm voice but in an undertoned manner, "To arms! They are coming." In three minutes every man was at his post; and though all were quick there was no time to spare, for by this time the black column of the enemy was distinctly visible, curling along the valley like a great centipede; and, with the daring enterprise so common among the troops of Napoleon, had begun in silence to mount the breach.'

Cochrane gave them particular credit for their silence as they placed their scaling ladders against the walls and 1200 men gathered beneath them. The defenders also made no sound and in this breathless hush of expectancy the first enemy soldiers reached the rim of the breach and saw by the first light of dawn that horrifying chasm with its greased hopper and the barbed chains. At first they could not retreat because their comrades were pressing up the ladders behind them, and so about forty men were swept off their perch by the defenders' fire. Cochrane was looking through the sights of his musket at the officer who stood on the parapet, sword aloft, leading his men. It was a sight reminiscent of the courageous Captain of the *Minerve*, alone on his quarterdeck, who had raised his hat to Cochrane in tribute. 'I never saw a braver or a prouder man,' thought Cochrane to himself, and lowering his musket he shouted to the Frenchman that he was not meant to be shot down like a dog, and was at liberty to return down the ladder. At this the officer 'bowed as politely as though on parade and retired just as leisurely'.

Lest any more should be tempted to scale those ladders, Cochrane now ignited the devices he had prepared with his customary foresight for their discouragement. These were shells suspended from ropes on the outer walls, and to the horror of their explosion was added a hail of hand grenades and musket fire. The dense mass of troops at the base of the tower wavered for a few minutes longer, then they retreated amidst the raucous cheers of the defenders. There were far too many dead bodies to carry away, but Cochrane watched with admiration as they risked their lives to take their wounded comrades with them.

He left the fort himself to bury the French dead, taking with the burial party Midshipman Marryat who commemorated this startling experience in *Frank Mildmay*. Although this was a novel, Marryat's account has always been accepted as an exact description of what occurred that morning below the walls of Fort Trinidad. While the British seamen were digging graves for the corpses the French began to fire at them and Cochrane at once ordered his men to run back to the fort. But 'he himself walked leisurely along through a shower of musket balls'. Marryatt described Cochrane as the bravest man he ever met in his life, but such people can be disquieting company. 'As his aide-de-camp I felt bound in honour, as well as duty, to walk by the side of my Captain, fully expecting every moment that a ball would hit me where I should have been ashamed to show the scar. I thought this funeral pace after the funeral was over confounded nonsense, but my fire-eating Captain never had run away from a Frenchman, and did not intend to begin here.'

The resistance of Fort Trinidad not only held down vastly superior forces of French troops; it also prevented these men from concentrating on the reduction of the citadel of Rosas, which still held out despite the capture of the town. But Cochrane was dealing with no novices in the art of war. After their failure to assault his fort they turned all their batteries on the citadel until all at once the boom of their guns was succeeded by an ominous hush, which told Cochrane that the defenders of the citadel were negotiating terms of surrender. As this would release the entire French strength to concentrate on Fort Trinidad and perhaps prevent its garrison from escaping, Cochrane thereupon ordered immediate evacuation.

In the bay of Rosas the *Fame* and *Impérieuse* had been joined by the frigate *Magnificent* of 74 guns. At a signal from the fort all three moved towards the landing-place and the first boats were rowed to the shore under the protection of their guns. The French had read Cochrane's signals and they kept a close watch on the movements that followed. Presently they ceased their fire from the batteries above the tower and despatched a contingent of troops to capture the fort at the moment when Cochrane was despatching his men by rope ladder from the nethermost tower to the boats that awaited them on the beach. Here they were safe from the enemy, protected by the higher ramparts of the fort. It was only as they rowed out into the bay that they ran the gauntlet of the enemy batteries. Cochrane sent the Catalan troops down the ladders first because they had served longest in the fort. Next followed the men from the Irish brigade, while the marines and seamen of the *Impérieuse* were the last to leave. Then the fort was empty except for Cochrane and a gunner, who went to light the trains that would blow up the fort from end to end.

The French troops could by now have reached the breach in the tower, but they had such experience of Cochrane's lethal devices that they hung back warily. It was as well for them that they did, for the first explosion blew up the tower they had been breaching while the garrison was clambering aboard the British ships. Unfortunately the shock affected the portfire which ought to have set off the second explosion, so that Cochrane's plan to demolish the fort entirely was frustrated. When the French had waited long enough to satisfy themselves that the lull did not presage another of his infernal tricks they made their entry at last. As Cochrane sailed out of the bay of Rosas he had the mortification of seeing the *tricolore* flying from Fort Trinidad.

But he had held it from 24 November until 5 December after it had been judged untenable, had repelled the assault of an immensely superior force with the loss of three men killed and three seriously injured, and had evacuated his garrison of three nationalities without a

single casualty. Trained exclusively as a sailor, he had achieved one of
the most exemplary combined operations in British naval record.

Collingwood rammed this down Admiralty throats in despatch after
despatch. He told them on 14 December, before he had yet received
Cochrane's detailed report: 'Captain Lord Cochrane has maintained
himself in possession of Trinity castle with great ability and heroism.
Although the fort is laid open by the breach in its works, he has sustained and repelled several assaults, having formed a sort of rampart
within the breach with his ship's hammock, cloths, awnings etc. filled
with sand and rubbish. The zeal and energy with which he has maintained that fortress excites the highest admiration. His resources for
every exigency have no end.' Evidently he had not yet learnt of the
chance invention of barbed wire, as a new and terrible weapon of war.

Cochrane's report of 5 December reached him at the speed of sail
after he had written those words. 'The citadel of Rosas capitulated at
twelve o'clock this day. Seeing, my Lord, farther resistance in the
castle of Trinity useless and impracticable against the whole army, the
attention of which had naturally turned to its reduction; after firing the
trains for exploding the magazines, we embarked in the boats of the
Magnificent, Impérieuse and *Fame*.' Those terse words reveal the speed
with which he had made and executed his decision to evacuate.

Admiral Collingwood forwarded them with the footnote: 'The
heroic spirit and ability which have been evinced by Lord Cochrane in
defending this castle, although so shattered in its works, against the
repeated attacks of the enemy is an admirable instance of his Lordship's
zeal.' With unintentional irony he added, it 'will doubtless be very
gratifying to my Lords Commissioners of the Admiralty'.

While the Commissioners of the Admiralty concealed their gratification behind a wall of silence, the Spanish government in Gerona
gave Cochrane the first of the encomiums he was to receive from so
many foreign countries throughout the world. In so doing it made the
common mistake concerning Cochrane's identity as heir to a Scottish
chiefship. 'This gallant Englishman has been entitled to the admiration
and gratitude of this country from the first moment of its political
resurrection.' The Spanish gave a special reason for their gratitude.
'The extraordinary services which we owe to his indefatigable activity,
particularly this city and the adjacent coast, in protecting us from the
attempts of the enemy, are too well known to be repeated here. It is
sufficient eulogium upon his character to mention that in the defence
of the castle of Trinidad, when the Spanish flag hoisted on the wall
fell into the ditch under a most dreadful fire from the enemy, his
Lordship was the only person who, regardless of the shower of balls

flying about him, descended into the ditch, returned with the flag and happily succeeded in placing it where it had been.'

Why was the lesson of Rosas and of Cochrane's other operations on the enemy coast so completely lost on the British High Command? Perhaps if Admiral Collingwood had lived to return home he might have succeeded in enlightening those who controlled the direction of the war better than written despatches could do. As it was, these were addressed to William Wellesley-Pole, brother of General Wellington and First Secretary of the Admiralty. He was in regular correspondence with his brother in Spain, and it was only natural that he should have shared the general pre-occupation with the military commitment of Britain in the Peninsula. It took Walter Scott, that Tory patriot, to point out as vigorously as any radical could have done the monumental harm caused to the war effort because the Tory war cabinet would not learn the lesson of Cochrane's career.

'The event might have been different had there been a floating army off the coast—the whole of the besieging force might then have been cut off. Of the errors which the British government committed in the conduct of the Spanish war, the neglect of this obvious and most important means of annoying the enemy and advantaging our allies is the most extraordinary. Five thousand men, at the disposal of Lord Cochrane or Sir Sydney Smith, or any of those numerous officers in the British Navy who have given undoubted proofs of their genius as well as courage, would have rendered more service to the common cause than five times that number on shore, because they could at all times choose their points of attack, and the enemy, never knowing where to expect them, would everwhere be in fear and everywhere in reach of the shore in danger.'

Ever since the letter Cochrane had written to Admiral Thornborough from the golden *Pallas*, he had been exploring the immense possibilities of such a strategy on paper, as well as experimenting with it in action as often as he could find an opportunity. He continued to do so when he returned to his routine duties off the Spanish coast after sailing away from Rosas. On one occasion he pounced on an army of no less than 5000 men who were marching along the coast road in the course of a foraging expedition, and scattered them into the interior with extraordinary loss. On another he went ashore to learn what he could from watching a battle between 40,000 Spanish troops and a French army of 10,000, and what he learnt was plenty. The Spaniards were routed and he barely escaped capture as he hurried back to his ship. Admiral Collingwood continued to brief William Wellesley-Pole at the Admiralty without the slightest effect.

Finally Cochrane decided to return home as his own advocate, and applied for leave to do so. 'My reasons for the application were various, the ostensible grounds being the state of my health, which had in reality suffered severely from the incessant wear and tear of body and mind to which for nearly two years I had been exposed.' But he also admitted that 'my chief motive for wishing to return to England was that during our operations against the French on the Spanish coast I had seen so much of them as to convince me that if with a single frigate I could paralyse the movements of their armies in the Mediterranean—with three or four ships it would not be difficult so to spread terror on their Atlantic shores as to render it impossible for them to send an army into Western Spain'. Half a century later he made a more stupendous claim for this strategy than had never been used. 'Had this permission been granted, I do not hesitate to stake my professional reputation that neither the Peninsula war nor its enormous cost to the nation from 1809 onwards would ever have been heard of.'

By the time he wrote that in his old age he had employed his strategy with a success unparalleled in naval history, so that nobody could say it was an extravagant claim although it was far too late to prove whether or not he was right.

It was not merely as a naval hero that Cochrane sailed home to Plymouth, but as a Member of Parliament for Westminster eager to resume his seat 'in order to expose the robberies of the Admiralty Courts in the Mediterranean, the officials of which were reaping colossal fortunes at the expense of naval officers and seamen, who were wasting their lives and blood for official gain'. Their colleagues in Whitehall struck first: 'In place of approbation I was reproached for the expenditure of more sails, stores, gunpowder and shot than had been used by any other captain in the service'.

CHAPTER FIVE

Aix Roads

During February 1809, the month before Cochrane sailed the *Impérieuse* back into Plymouth harbour, the Lords of the Admiralty found themselves with a crisis on their hands. Eight French battleships escaped from the blockade of Brest during a storm that struck the rocky coast of Brittany and scattered the ships of the Commander-in-Chief of the Channel fleet, Admiral Lord Gambier. The eight runaways released other French ships from the blockaded port of Lorient farther down the Breton coast, and this armada continued south to add the Rochefort squadron in Aix Roads to its strength.

For a while the British remained entirely ignorant of the whereabouts of this fleet, and a fear began to possess them that the French planned a massive attack on the West Indies where Admiral Sir Alexander Cochrane was in command. Lord Gambier returned in a panic to Plymouth and sent another admiral to search for the missing fleet, first at Cadiz then as far afield as Madeira. He drew a blank but the mystery was resolved by Admiral Stopford, who encountered the runaways with a fleet of only half their number. It proved sufficient however to persuade the enemy to retire into Aix Roads, where Stopford blockaded them with his seven ships until Gambier arrived with another twelve.

The British government was understandably nervous. It was only a year since Villeneuve had succeeded in breaking out and sailing to the West Indies, while the British Navy had gained no great victory at sea since the death of Nelson. As Cochrane gazed from his quarterdeck at the approaching landmarks of Plymouth Hoe, the Lords of the Admiralty were pondering the dangers and opportunities which that concentration of the French fleet at the great arsenal of Rochefort presented. They suggested to Admiral Gambier that the British fleet should enter Aix Roads to bombard the French vessels at their anchorages, using fireships—just as Cochrane had proposed to Admiral Thornborough 3 years earlier in the letter he wrote to him from Aix Roads.

Admiral Gambier's reply to the Admiralty was a masterpiece of querulous indecision. 'A trial was made six years ago, when a Spanish squadron lay at the same anchorage, but without effect. The report of it you will find in the Admiralty . . . The enemy's ships lie much exposed to the operation of fireships, it is a horrible mode of warfare, and the attempt hazardous, if not desperate; but we should have plenty of volunteers in the service. If you mean to do anything of the kind, it should be done with secrecy and quickly, and the ships used should be not less than those built for the purpose—at least a dozen, and some smaller ones.'

The author of that abysmal letter was in his early fifties and had been an admiral for nearly 14 years. He had held the office of a Lord of the Admiralty during the years in which its administration was more flagrantly corrupt than at any other period in its history, the years of St Vincent's vehement denunciations and of the great mutinies at Spithead and the Nore. But in 1807 Gambier was appointed to the Baltic command when the British fleet bombarded the city of Copenhagen and destroyed some of its finest buildings before the Danes were driven to surrender. This is now considered to have been one of the grossest acts of vandalism in British naval history, and it required neither nautical skill nor a gift for strategy. But the surrender of the Danish Navy, which prevented the total destruction of the Venice of the north, also confused the British government into believing that Gambier was a competent fleet Commander. He was raised to the peerage, and in January 1809 he was appointed Commander-in-Chief of the Channel fleet; by March, when he wrote that despatch it had been reduced to as dismal a condition of disarray as could well be conceived.

Admiral Lord Gambier was a man of exceptional piety, and as he gradually lost his grip he took refuge in increasingly morbid and eccentric religious exercises. Faced with the escape of the French ships and then their concentration in the waters of Rochefort, his solution was to assemble his crews for religious devotions and distribute fundamentalist tracts amongst them. When the Admiralty suggested a line of positive action to him, he merely dithered. When the ebbing morale of the fleet found expression amongst his most senior officers, he parried it with disarming politeness, for he was a man of truly Christian charity. None found this more exasperating than Admiral Eliab Harvey, who had been equally vexed by the criticisms which he had heard Cochrane declaiming in the House of Commons. Lying in the supine fleet of Lord Gambier off Rochefort, Harvey had ample leisure to compare his superior with Lord Nelson and the demoralised fleet with the one in which Harvey had commanded the *Téméraire* at Trafalgar.

It was in these circumstances that Cochrane received a most surprising letter from London as soon as he stepped ashore at Plymouth. Although it came from the Admiralty its message was very different from the reprimand of the civil servants over the quantity of stores he had expended during his tour of duty. It was sent to him by the retiring Second Lord, William Hope, the son of another Scottish Earl, who would rise like Cochrane to the rank of Admiral and to the honour of knighthood of the Bath. As a naval officer rather than a politician or a civil servant, Hope had been able to appreciate the accounts of Cochrane's services which had been reaching his department at intervals without worrying about the waste of fish-hooks and chains, or dreading the increased popularity of the Member for Westminster.

'My Dear Lord,' wrote William Hope. 'I congratulate you on your safe arrival after the fatigues you underwent at Trinity. Be assured your exertions there were highly applauded by the Board, and were done most ample justice by Lord Collingwood in all his despatches.

'There is an undertaking of great moment in agitation against Rochefort, and the Board thinks that your local knowledge and services on the occasion might be of the utmost consequence, and I believe it is intended to send you there with all expedition; I have ventured to say that if you are in health you will readily give your aid on this business.

'Before you can answer this I shall be out of office, and on my way to Scotland, as I found I could not continue here and keep my health.'

This letter proves that the Board of Admiralty had already decided to employ Cochrane himself, as well as the plan he had outlined to Thornborough 3 years earlier, when they proposed it to Admiral Gambier. The Lords of the Admiralty were reading his reply on the very day—19 March—on which Cochrane was digesting William Hope's letter in Plymouth.

Gambier's equivocations were brushed aside in instructions forwarded to him on the same day. Twelve transports were being adapted as fireships, he was informed, and William Congreve, the inventor of the new war rocket, would accompany them in person with some of his missiles. 'These preparations,' wrote the Admiralty's Secretary, 'are making with a view to enable your Lordship to make an attack on the French fleet off Isle d'Aix if practicable; and I am further commanded to signify their Lordships' directions to you to take into your consideration the possibility of making an attack upon the enemy, either with your line-of-battle ships, frigates and small craft, fireships, bombs and rockets, or separately, by any of the above-named means.' But there was one fatal omission in these instructions. They ordered Gambier to drop his Bible and get on with it without warning him of the intention to send a comparatively junior Captain to execute the task: and it would not be Gambier himself who would be most deeply angered by this information when it came, but all those officers in his fleet whom such an appointment labelled as incompetent, cowardly, or slothful. Cochrane spotted the danger as soon as he read William Hope's letter.

Why then did the Lords of the Admiralty not foresee it? For one thing, there had been no less than five successive First Sea Lords there during the period of less than 6 years since Cochrane had last travelled to Whitehall to meet St Vincent in the Admiralty, and such a turnover does not make for a well-conducted department. In addition the present First Lord was a civilian politician, Lord Mulgrave, who had inherited a barony and enjoyed the office of Secretary of State for Foreign Affairs before passing on to this office at the Admiralty and to the subsequent reward of an Earldom. On the one hand, he had the insight to promote Cochrane's project for the destruction of the French fleet at Rochefort at exactly the moment when its concentration there offered the finest opportunity since it had been conceived; on the other, he showed that he had not the slightest conception of the state of affairs in the Channel fleet, and having no experience of service life he could not take Cochrane's warnings seriously.

The meeting between the two men was extremely affable, and doubly gratifying to a junior Post Captain whose previous meeting with a First Lord at the Admiralty had been so humiliating. As soon as Cochrane had hurried from Plymouth summoned by telegraph signals, to keep his appointment with Lord Mulgrave, he found himself flattered with the most confidential information. The Board feared, Mulgrave told him, that the French fleet might slip out of Aix Roads, just as it had escaped previously from Brest and Lorient Various officers had been consulted about the feasibility of destroying it with fireships, said the First Lord with tactful vagueness, and their response had been discouraging.

'Now,' said Mulgrave, coming to the point, 'you were some years ago employed on the Rochefort station and must to a great extent be acquainted with the difficulties to be surmounted. Besides which, I am told that you then pointed out to Admiral Thornborough some plan of attack, which would in your estimation be successful. Will you be good enough to detail that or any other plan which your further experience may suggest?' It was a stupendous compliment, the opportunity of a lifetime, but it left wide open the question of who would execute the plan when the Channel fleet was commanded by a Bible-thumping buffoon, presiding over an increasingly disaffected body of officers and seamen. Mulgrave showed that he was not unaware of this when he made his most confidential gesture of all. He picked up Gambier's ridiculous letter of 11 March and read it out to Cochrane.

So Cochrane learned that he was being invited to prepare a plan that the Admiral responsible for its execution considered 'hazardous, if not desperate', and 'a horrible mode of warfare' in addition. He reassured Lord Mulgrave that an attack by fireships in Aix Roads would be successful, and at the First Lord's invitation he outlined it in more detail. And this raises the question, when did Cochrane first think of the new invention which gave him such confidence in the outcome? Barbed wire had been a sudden inspiration—and so were many other and infinitely more intricate devices that snatched success from a grave emergency. On the other hand, 2 days had elapsed between the moment when Cochrane read the Honourable William Hope's letter and this interview, and he must have spent the interval in deep thought. Out of that fertile mind, at some time during this interval, there was born the invention of the explosive torpedo. Mulgrave praised the 'novelty and completeness' of Cochrane's plan and invited him to reduce it to writing so that he could carry it straight to the Board of Admiralty, which was actually in session in another room. Nothing could have been more bizarre than that gathering of impotent Commissioners, waiting to learn what the *enfant terrible* of the service might have devised to extricate them from their difficulties after years of neglect and insult.

Then Mulgrave made one last proposal, and one which must have appeared to him the most flattering of all, though it merely reveals his total ignorance of the realities within the fighting service over which he presided. He invited Cochrane to undertake the execution of his plan. Cochrane reminded the First Lord that the appointment of a Post Captain to such a task would arouse a furore amongst senior officers in the fleet, only to have his objection brushed aside.

'The present is no time for professional etiquette,' Mulgrave retorted blandly. 'All the officers who have been consulted deem an attack with fireships impracticable, and after such an expression of opinion, it is not likely they would be offended by the conduct of fireships being given to another officer who approved of their use.' If every naval officer had resembled Brenton, West and Bennett this might have been true, but Cochrane already knew that they did not, even if he did not know that Admiral Harvey was not among the officers who had been consulted. He contented himself with pointing out another false premise in the First Lord's argument: it overlooked the fact that these officers had not been able to assess the impact of his new secret weapon.

'The plan submitted to your Lordship was not an attack with fireships alone, and when the details become known to the service, it will be seen that there is no risk of failure whatever, if made with a fair wind and flowing tide. On the contrary, its success on inspection must be evident to any experienced officer, who would see that as the enemy's squadron could not escape up the Charente, their destruction would not only be certain but in fact easy.' For a while even Lord Mulgrave seems to have had second thoughts, while the Lords of the Admiralty sat in another room, waiting for the outcome of this extraordinary interview.

'Although I do not believe Lord Gambier would feel hurt,' Mulgrave conceded at last, 'at your undertaking to put your own plan in execution other officers might not be well pleased that its superintendence should be committed to a junior officer.' He promised to reconsider the matter, and presumably the Lords of the Admiralty did the same when he finally went to report to them. The very next day Mulgrave summoned Cochrane again, to communicate their fatal decision to him.

'My Lord, you must go. The Board cannot listen to further refusal or delay. Rejoin your frigate at once. I will make you all right with Lord Gambier. Your confidence in the result has, I must confess, taken me by surprise, but it has increased my belief that all you anticipate will be accomplished. Make yourself easy about the jealous feeling of senior officers. I will so manage it with Lord Gambier that the *amour propre* of the fleet shall be satisfied.' Empty words. The intimation which reached Lord Gambier, signed by Wellington's brother William Wellesley-Pole, paid no more regard to the *amour propre* of senior officers than this: 'My Lord—My Lords Commissioners of the Admiralty having thought fit to select Captain Lord Cochrane for the purpose of conducting, under your Lordship's direction, the fireships to be employed in the projected attack on the enemy's squadron off Isle d'Aix, I have their Lordships' commands to signify their direction to you to employ Lord Cochrane in the above-mentioned service accordingly, whenever the attack shall take place.'

So instead of taking the rest he had promised himself or returning to his seat in the House of Commons, Cochrane rode back to Plymouth only a matter of days after he had left there for London, to board the *Impérieuse* once more. By this time the twelve fireships were ready on the south coast waiting for a favourable wind, and William Congreve, a man after Cochrane's own heart, was there too with his rockets. The directive announcing their imminent arrival reached Lord Gambier off Rochefort, and it had no sooner done so than the pent-up feelings of his officers erupted. Admiral Harvey went straight aboard the

Commander-in-Chief's flagship and offered to take charge of the operation himself. With his unfailing courtesy Gambier explained that the Lords of the Admiralty had entrusted the command to an officer junior to every single Captain in his fleet.

'If I am passed by,' Harvey replied, 'and Lord Cochrane or any other junior officer appointed in preference, I shall immediately desire to strike my flag and resign my commission.' When Gambier tried to soothe him with further explanations, Harvey shouted back that he would impeach the Commander-in-Chief for his disgraceful manage-ment of the fleet and take his own flagship into Aix Roads alone to attack the enemy there. When Cochrane arrived in the *Impérieuse* and reported aboard Lord Gambier's flagship the storm was at its height. Harvey's 'abuse of Lord Gambier to his face was such as I had never before witnessed from a subordinate', he recalled. 'I should even now hesitate to record it as incredible, were it not officially known by the minutes of the court-martial in which it sometime afterwards resulted.' Cochrane noted the unshakeable patience, amounting to inertia, with which Gambier merely replied: 'The Lords of the Admiralty having fixed on Lord Cochrane to conduct the service, I cannot deviate from their Lordships' orders.' He heard accusations from Harvey's lips that augured ill for his project—that Gambier had made no attempt to sound the channels in which an attack would be made, examine the enemy defences or train his crews in gunnery. Instead they had been mustered for religious exercises. 'Had Nelson been here,' stormed the gallant Trafalgar officer, 'he would not have anchored here at all, but would have dashed at the enemy at once.' The tragedy of these two officers who were so soon to be dismissed the service for the remaining 6 years of the war against Napoleon is that if Harvey had now been commanding the Channel fleet, he and Cochrane would undoubtedly have won the most overwhelming victory in Britain's naval history.

His passion spent, Admiral Harvey strode from the quarterdeck to the cabin of Gambier's Flag Captain Sir Harry Neale. Cochrane followed in embarrassed silence, until Harvey reassured him by saying that he intended no reflection on him personally, but he had already volun-teered for the same service and been refused. The last occasion on which the two men had bandied words had been in the House of Commons; here in the cabin of a flagship their relations remained amicable despite the tempest that raged about them. Cochrane made what apology he could for his unwelcome presence.

'The service on which the Admiralty has sent me,' he said, 'was none of my seeking. I went to Whitehall in obedience to a summons from Lord Mulgrave, and at his Lordship's request gave the Board a plan of attack, the execution of which has been thrust upon me contrary to my inclination, as well knowing the invidious position in which I should be placed.'

'Well,' replied Harvey, 'this is not the first time I have been lightly treated, and that my services have not been attended to in the way they deserved; because I am no canting Methodist, no hypocrite, nor a psalm singer. I do not cheat old women out of their estates by hypocrisy and canting.'

'Permit me to remark,' Cochrane interjected, 'that you are using very strong expressions relative to the Commander-in-Chief.' If Admiral St Vincent had been present he might at least have raised an eyebrow, but it was the Flag Captain who was placed in the embarrassing position of witness to this conversation.

'I can assure you, Lord Cochrane,' Harvey went on, 'that I have spoken to Lord Gambier with the same degree of prudence as I have now done to you in the presence of Captain Sir Harry Neale'—He maintained a discreet silence and eventually attained the ranks of Admiral and Knight Grand Cross of the Order of the Bath. Cochrane was left to speak the advice that he so often found difficulty in heeding himself.

'Well, Admiral, considering that I have been an unwilling listener to what you really did say to his Lordship, I can only remark that you have a strange notion of prudence.' But the most imprudent man of all had been Lord Mulgrave in the Admiralty. He had assured Cochrane that he would take steps to avoid this fracas, and done nothing whatever to implement his promise. Most unforgiveable of all, he had not informed Lord Gambier that Cochrane would be employing a new and secret weapon; which provided the sole and sufficient means of reconciling senior officers in the fleet to his appointment. For the explosive torpedoes had not been made in a British dockyard to be sent across the Channel with the fireships. Cochrane would construct them himself on the spot, so that not a whisper of them would reach the enemy in advance.

As soon as the stormy interview was over Cochrane stepped down into his launch to return to the *Impérieuse*, watched by resentful eyes from the ships that lay at anchor, their sails furled, all around him. Had he been a prey to the manic depression so common in the human species, his reaction to the extraordinary scenes he had just witnessed aboard the Commander-in-Chief's flagship might have been other than they were. But in extreme adversity he always acted with flinty resolution, and his mind was now filled with the grandest design it had ever conceived, which lay there like an intricate jigsaw puzzle, every piece in place. He lost not a second in preparing to execute his plan.

On the very evening of his arrival and of his interview aboard the flagship he sailed the *Impérieuse* as close as he dared to the island of Aix. It was 3 years since he had explored those waters in the *Pallas*, and as he peered among the masts and spars of the enemy ships in the distance, the ideas that occurred to him grew ever more ambitious. Despite the stresses of that exhausting day he hurried down to his cabin to write the First Sea Lord a long, brilliant, astonishing letter.

'My Lord—Having been very close to the Isle d'Aix, I find that the western wall has been pulled down to build a better. At present the fort is quite open, and may be taken as soon as the French fleet is driven on shore or burned, which will be as soon as the fireships arrive. The wind continues favourable for the attack. If your Lordship can prevail on the ministry to send a military force here, you will do great and lasting good to our country.

'Could Ministers see things with their own eyes, how differently would they act; but they cannot be everywhere present, and on their opinion of the judgment of others must depend the success of war— possibly the fate of England and all Europe.

'No diversion which the whole force of Great Britain is capable of making in Portugal or Spain would so much shake the French government as the capture of the islands on this coast. A few men would take Oléron; but to render the capture effective, send twenty-thousand men who, without risk, would find occupation for the French army of a hundred thousand.' The advice poured on from a junior Captain to the First Sea Lord, from a radical Member for Westminster to the Tory administration. The strategy which Walter Scott first publicly and in print blamed the war cabinet for not having adopted, and which Cochrane himself eventually described in his autobiography, was set out in detail in the Captain's cabin of the *Impérieuse* and sent to Lord Mulgrave at the precise moment when it ought to have been implemented.

Cochrane must have been extremely weary by the time he ended his letter. 'I hope your Lordship will excuse the way in which I have jumbled these thoughts together,' he wrote in conclusion. 'My intentions are good and if they can be of any use, I shall feel happy.'

If the French identified the *Impérieuse* on the evening of 3 April 1809 as she sailed close to the island of Aix, it was their first intimation that the Sea Wolf had appeared on the scene. A week later they observed the arrival of the twelve fireships, and the French Admiral Allemand issued thorough directions for the protection of his fleet. His ships were moored in three lines between the two little islands of Aix and

Madame that lie on either side of the entrance to the river Charente, and they all faced north in the direction of the open sea beyond the island of Aix. Unknown to the British, these ships were protected by a gigantic anchored boom of floating cables half a mile in length, and this surprise obstacle was covered by a formidable array of at least 30 guns, including a preponderance of long 36-pounders and some heavy mortars. Most of these were mounted on the isle of Aix, which was also garrisoned by about 2000 troops; and when Admiral Allemand learnt of the arrival of the fireships he immediately increased this garrison. If Admiral Gambier had bothered to survey these defences before writing his jeremiads to the Admiralty he would have found satisfying grounds for his pessimism.

The French had corresponding cause for confidence. 'You may quiet your apprehensions that the enemy will attempt something against the isle of Aix,' Napoleon had written 4 years earlier. 'Nothing can be more insane than the idea of attacking a French squadron at the isle of Aix.' Napoleon and Gambier seem, in fact, to have been of one mind on the subject. The element which both men left out of their reckoning was the arrival on the scene of a young and junior Captain.

By the time the fireships reached Gambier's fleet on 10 April, Cochrane had converted three transports into his secret weapon. Here is his own description of it. 'The floor was rendered as firm as possible by means of logs placed in close contact, into every crevice of which other substances were firmly wedged so as to afford the greatest amount of resistance to the explosion. On this foundation were placed a large number of spirit and water casks, into which 1500 barrels of powder were emptied. These casks were set on end and the whole bound round with hempen cables, so as to resemble a gigantic mortar, thus causing the explosion to take an upward course. In addition to the powder casks were placed several hundred shells, and over these again nearly three thousand hand grenades; the whole, by means of wedges and sand, being compressed as nearly as possible into a solid mass.' Such was the instrument which would, at one stroke, burst the protecting boom and petrify the crews in the ships beyond with panic.

Soon after midday on 11 April the *Impérieuse* sailed to a point less than 2 miles from the nearest French ship, at the entrance to Aix Roads between the islands of Aix and Oléron. At her stern she towed one of the explosion vessels and she was accompanied by three other frigates. Most auspiciously, one of these was the golden *Pallas* in which Cochrane had entered Aix Roads 3 years earlier to attack the *Minerve*, and her present Captain was none other than George Seymour who had come to his rescue then in the *Kingfisher*. While other captains in Gambier's fleet nursed their injured pride, Seymour had leapt forward to share the last, greatest and most tragic triumph of his friend's service in the British Navy.

Six miles away on the horizon lay Gambier's ships, still at anchor: the fireships had been placed no more than a mile closer to their target. Although the French Admiral was confident that fireships would be unable to breach his boom, he had ordered his fleet to take all the usual precautions against fire. The four frigates in the van were on the alert for instant action and about seventy smaller vessels were stationed where they would be able to board and tow away the fireships at a moment's notice. The ten line-of-battle ships behind them had struck their topmasts, brought their topgallant yards to the deck, and bestowed their sails so as to protect them from risk of fire. Launches rowed through the night, patrolling the boom. Admiral Allemand had provided for every eventuality except the element of terror, astonishment and consequent disarray on which Cochrane always depended for his victories.

His own greatest menace lay in the powerful batteries mounted on the isle of Aix, but he possessed a knowledge that Admiral Gambier had never made the slightest attempt to acquire. 'From previous employment on the spot on several occasions I well knew there was room in the channel to keep out of the way of red-hot shot from the Aix batteries even if, by means of blue lights or other devices, they had discovered us.' This discovery reveals the far-sighted care with which he had explored those waters years before in the *Pallas*, when there was no immediate prospect that he would ever have an opportunity to use his knowledge.

The night on which Cochrane launched his attack turned out black and stormy with a heavy sea, so that the risk of discovery was greatly diminished. He reserved the most dangerous part for himself, setting out in the first and largest of the floating mines with four seamen who had volunteered, and a Lieutenant who was promoted to the rank of Commander from that very night for the part he played. The twelve fireships had been signalled to sail in so that they would become an integral part of the armada and thus contribute to the central deception on which Cochrane based his plan. For he anticipated with complete accuracy 'that the officers and crews of the line-of-battle ships would be impressed with the idea that every fireship was an explosion vessel, and that in place of offering opposition they would, in all probability, be driven ashore in their attempt to escape from such diabolical engines of warfare, and thus become an easy prey'.

A mounting wind and tide carried Cochrane and his infernal flotilla towards the hidden boom, while he strained his eyes for a glimpse of the nearest enemy ships. He was followed by one other explosion vessel commanded by a Lieutenant with Midshipman Marryat as his assistant. The third remained attached to the stern of the *Impérieuse*, waiting for Cochrane to return and sail it to its target once the fireships had provided illumination. As he lunged forward through the wind and spray in his unwieldy vessel he looked back and observed that several of these were being grossly mismanaged by their crews. But while they scattered without ever reaching within 2 miles of the French fleet, five or six of them were admirably handled, and they proved sufficient to achieve his purpose.

He was still unable to make out exactly where the French ships lay in the darkness ahead when his instinct told him that it was time to light the fuse and abandon his torpedo. He ordered his crew into the gig and remained alone on board to kindle the port-fires. Then he leapt into the gig and all six seamen strained at the oars with all their might to row clear of the coming explosion. According to an account that appeared in the press, Cochrane saw a dog aboard his explosion vessel as they began to pull away, and returned to rescue it. He himself recorded that the fuses were timed to burn for fifteen minutes but the strong wind caused them to burn through in half that time. In addition, they were hampered by the strength of the wind and tide against which they contended. As a result they were still quite close to their mine when it exploded, and as it transpired, this was what saved their lives. It also transpired that Cochrane's mysterious instinct had led him to fire his torpedo right on the boom itself, although he had no knowledge of its existence.

'For a moment,' Cochrane recorded, 'the sky was red with the lurid glare arising from the simultaneous ignition of 1500 barrels of powder. On this gigantic flash subsiding, the air seemed alive with shells, grenades, rockets, and masses of timber, the wreck of the shattered vessel; whilst the water was strewn with spars shaken out of the enormous boom, on which, on the subsequent testimony of Captain Proteau, whose frigate lay just within the boom, the vessel had brought up before she exploded. The sea was convulsed as by an earthquake, rising in a huge wave on whose crest our boat was lifted like a cork and as suddenly dropped into a vast trough, out of which, as it closed on us with a rush of a whirlpool, none expected to emerge. The skill of the boat's crew however overcame the threatened danger, which passed away as suddenly as it had arisen, and in a few minutes nothing but a heavy rolling sea had to be encountered, all having become silence and darkness.' Miraculously, all those fragments of shells, rockets and grenades had passed over their heads because they were still so close to the explosion vessel, and had landed in the sea beyond them.

Ten minutes later, as they rowed back to the *Impérieuse*, there came a second explosion to cheer them and add to the terror of the French. Marryat's torpedo had run into the boom before her crew knew where they were and her Lieutenant had thereupon lit the fuse and rowed away safely with his men. Next Cochrane had the satisfaction of seeing two fireships pass him, already blazing, and pass through the gap he had made in the boom. By their light he could also see a third fireship pass through the broken defences, though he could not tell that it was not the third explosion vessel since it had not yet been ignited. He rowed on exultantly, knowing that his plan had succeeded to perfection.

Just how devastating its impact on the French fleet had been he could not apprehend. Like him, the enemy did not know that the third vessel which bore down upon them was merely a fireship and not one of those infernal engines of destruction. Panic seized them as that awful shadow on the dark stormy sea came closer, imperfectly lit by the fireships. Some ships actually began to fire on one another: many went aground, exposing their hulls as sitting targets; they collided with one another; crews threw water on their powder to prevent an explosion and thus rendered their vessels defenceless. As Captain Proteau in the nearest frigate testified later, this self-inflicted ruin was brought about entirely by psychological means, for Cochrane's fireworks had themselves done no damage whatever except to breach the boom. Proteau had been keeping such attentive watch that he observed Cochrane's explosion vessel reach the boom at 9.30 p.m. though he naturally could not tell what it was. He deposed that 'the explosion occurred all of a sudden and projected a quantity of rockets, grenades and shells which exploded in the air without doing us the least harm, although we were no more than a cable's length away.'

By 10 o'clock Admiral Allemand's own flagship was among the great men-of-war which had grounded to the rear of Captain Proteau's frigate. Almost immediately one of the two fireships that had penetrated this far grappled the flagship's exposed stern while her fire was at its height; the second fireship attached herself to another of those stranded hulls. At once there was a pandemonium of activity aboard the two menaced vessels. Fire engines were manned, pumps played on the poop to prevent it from going up in flames, spars were brought to shove off the fireship, men hacked feverishly with axes at the grapplings lashed to her yards. But a fence of spikes still kept the flaming vessel glued to her stern while the flames enveloped the menaced poop and turned the water from the pumps into clouds of vapour. While her crew expected every minute that they would be burned to death in their ships, two other great battleships collided with her, breaking her bowsprit and destroying her main chains. But what appeared to be an additional calamity proved the flagship's salvation.

The fireship's crew drew their flaming vessel round from the stern to the starboard side where she lay in the angle between two of the enemy warships and might have reduced both to ashes. But the Admiral made no attempt to detach her when she had reached as far as the damaged bowsprit, concentrating instead on giving the two other line-of-battle ships time to sail clear of the danger. He did take the precaution of ordering the taps to be opened in order to wet the powder and prevent an explosion, and it is a measure of the disorder on board his ship that no less than fifty seamen fell into the sea and were drowned in the course of carrying out this order, while others had to be rescued by boat. But it is possible that the diversion saved the French flagship.

The heroism of the seamen who brought their fireships into the middle of the French fleet cost them heavy casualties. Some were killed, others severely burned: one seaman was blown clear of his vessel with burns from which he never recovered, an officer and a seaman actually died of fatigue. Most of those who survived only regained the safety of the *Impérieuse* and her attendant frigates with great difficulty. Here Cochrane found himself menaced soon after his return by a fireship which had been set alight prematurely and then allowed to sail out of control. By this time Marryat had returned safely also with the crew of the second explosion vessel and was evidently in a high state of excitement over the adventures of the night, for Cochrane ordered him back into his gig with four fresh hands, saying that since he seemed to be enjoying the fun so much he could go and rescue the *Impérieuse* from the danger of the fireship which was bearing down on her. She was flaming from end to end by the time Marryat boarded her, but he succeeded in placing her back on course. When he returned to the *Impérieuse*, speechless from the smoke in his lungs and covered with soot, Cochrane congratulated him curtly and asked him whether he had found it warm, and Marryat treasured the incident for his sea stories and the portrait of his hero which they contain.

As the first glimmer of dawn appeared Cochrane strained his weary eyes down Aix Roads. He could not yet make out the full extent of the havoc he had created: he was not to know that since midnight every ship in the Roads except two had been aground, while several of them were severely damaged. But he could see enough to know that he had made good his promise to Lord Mulgrave, that he had given Lord Gambier the easiest opportunity in Britain's naval history to destroy an enemy fleet in its entirety, if not to capture it in its own stronghold. At 5.48 a.m. he signalled to the British Commander-in-Chief the message which such a pious man might well have interpreted as an answer to prayer. 'Half the fleet can destroy the enemy. Seven on shore.' The number was in reality much greater.

Admiral Gambier had not bothered to move nearer to the action in which all those brave seamen in the fireships and the explosion vessels had risked their lives for him through the night. He still lay at anchor 12 miles to the north. In one of his latest, longest and most lugubrious letters to the Lords of the Admiralty he had affirmed his willingness to fight if they ordered him to do so against his better judgment. 'I am ready to obey any orders they may be pleased to honour me with,' he pronounced patriotically, 'however great the risk may be of the loss of men and ships.' Now the moment had come to make good his promise, and all he did was to acknowledge Cochrane's signal. For a whole hour the men who had achieved such a miracle by their skill and valour stood straining their eyes for any sign of movement in the distant British fleet, and at the end of this time it was light enough to see how much greater the damage was to the enemy fleet than they could have supposed possible.

At 6.40 a.m. Cochrane signalled again to Gambier: 'Eleven on shore', and once again Gambier acknowledged the information and did nothing. An hour later still, Cochrane was able to tell him of a state of affairs that had actually existed since the previous midnight. 'Only two afloat.' For the third time there was no response. The doomed French fleet possessed, after all, a secret weapon as effective as the explosive torpedo, and its name was Gambier.

To Cochrane, exhausted by his night's work, the ebbing away of those vital hours must have been amongst the most terrible experiences of his career. Two more of them now passed before the opportunity to destroy or capture the entire French fleet at Rochefort had been lost forever. The despair of a sailor deprived of a victory as overwhelming as any Nelson had won is compressed into the laconic message he sent Gambier at 9.30 a.m.: 'Enemy preparing to heave off.'

It was now that Gambier began to stir. The fireworks that he may or may not have troubled to observe through the night from such a safe distance had not brought him an inch nearer to the scene of action, neither had a series of messages over a period of 4 hours that read like an invitation from the Lord of Hosts. But at a signal that the French fleet was recovering from its helpless plight Gambier ordered his own to prepare to weigh anchor, though not to make ready for action. Next he summoned all his captains aboard his flagship, as effective a way of wasting more precious time as he could have devised. At 11 o'clock Cochrane saw Gambier's ships weigh anchor at last, only to drop them again when they were still 6 miles away from the nearest enemy ships. To everyone in the four British frigates that lay off the isle of Aix the act could only have given the appearance of mutiny or treason.

By now Cochrane had been given many hours to consider the possibility that he might be left to continue the battle against the enemy without any help whatever from Admiral Gambier, and despite the attrition of prolonged sleeplessness and of his labours during the night, his mind remained equal to the emergency. His most dangerous enemy was not the French Admiral any longer but the British one, who might countermand his actions, and nothing he ever did demonstrates his clarity of mind under great stress more than the plan he now adopted. It is also generally regarded as the bravest action of a career in which it is extremely difficult to make such a choice.

He had determined that if necessary he would sail in to attack the entire French fleet in his frigate single-handed, and it was necessary to do this in such a way that if Gambier were to drop his Bible and look, he would not notice what Cochrane was doing. He therefore weighed anchor and allowed his ship to drift with the tide stern foremost towards his enemy, although this required a singular feat of helmsmanship in those channels. Only when it became absolutely essential to recover full control of his vessel did he give the tell-tale order to unfurl the sails. As it happened, the skilful subterfuge proved unnecessary because Gambier was paying not the slightest attention to what he was doing until he was prodded into action by a series of three signals, hoisted in rapid succession.

1.30 p.m. The enemy's ships are getting under sail.

1.40 p.m. The enemy is superior to the chasing ship.

1.45 p.m. The ship is in distress, and requires to be assisted immediately.

While Gambier was still making up his mind what action to take, if any, the *Impérieuse* anchored in such a position that she was able to discharge her broadside into the French magazine ship *Calcutta*, while her forecastle and bow guns fired into two other French ships. Captain Lafon of the *Calcutta* thereupon climbed to safety from the stern cabin of his vessel, for which he was afterwards convicted of cowardice and shot. Admiral Gambier was roused from his torpor by the strange spectacle of a single British frigate anchored in the middle of the French fleet, and firing with apparent impunity in all directions. He determined to send assistance, as he had been requested to do at 1.45 p.m., and so it was that the 44 gun *Indefatigable* sailed in with attendant frigates and small craft, and passed the *Impérieuse* at 3.20 in the afternoon —over 8 hours later than they ought to have come in for the kill. As they did so, the exhausted crew of the *Impérieuse* rent the air with a mighty cheer.

Marryat recalled the immaculate appearance of the *Indefatigable* as she appeared from the begrimed and shot-torn decks of his frigate. 'One of our ships of the line came into action in such gallant trim, that it was glorious to behold. She was a beautiful ship, in what we call "high kelter"; she seemed a living body, conscious of her own superior power over her opponents, whose shot she despised as they fell thick and fast about her, while she deliberately took up an admirable position for battle. And having furled her sails and squared her yards as if she had been at Spithead, her men came down from aloft, went to their guns, and opened such a fire on the enemy's ships as would have delighted the great Nelson himself.' The *Indefatigable* was commanded by Captain John Rodd, who would rise to the rank of Vice Admiral and a knighthood of the Bath.

At this moment a boat was on its way from the *Impérieuse* to board and take possession of the French magazine ship *Calcutta* as fast as she was being abandoned by her own crew. This they were able to do without the slightest difficulty, but they were driven to leave the ship again when the fire from the newly arrived British vessels exposed them to the danger of an explosion that would have blown them all to bits. It was the sort of muddle that might not have occurred if the Commander-in-Chief had been directing operations on the spot.

At 5 o'clock Rear Admiral Stopford was also allowed to join the assault in the *Caesar*, one of whose gunners secured immortality by leaving one of the rare, vivid accounts that survive from the lower decks. Other British warships sailed in, and at 5.30 two more French ships were struck. Half an hour later a third was abandoned by her crew and shortly afterwards blew up. An enemy frigate did so at almost the same instant, and an hour later Gunner Richardson in the *Caesar* observed the 'dreadful explosion' as the magazine ship *Calcutta* went up in flames. 'Fortunately,' wrote Richardson in the account that would be published a century later as the story of a *Mariner of England*, 'none of her fiery timbers fell on board our ship; everything went upwards, with such a flash of red colour as illuminated the whole elements.' Admiral Gambier had as much to entertain him from his vantage point 6 miles away as when he had sat in the Baltic, watching Copenhagen burn.

It was a complete vindication of the first signal that Cochrane had sent him at 5.48 that morning—'Half the fleet can destroy the enemy.' But now six great French warships, including Admiral Allemand's flagship which had been crippled at midnight, were safely afloat again and lying in the mouth of the river Charente. In the *Impérieuse* three men had been killed in the afternoon's engagement, while Dr Guthrie and his assistant were attending to the wounds of eleven others. The remainder of the crew must by now have been far too weary even to carry out repairs on their damaged vessel.

It was Admiral Stopford in the *Caesar* who took the initiative. Fireships were what were needed to get at those great ships in the mouth of the Charente, but they had all be expended the night before and there only remained Congreve's bomb-vessel the *Aetna*. Stopford hurriedly converted three transports into fireships, but he was discouraged when the *Caesar* became grounded at dusk and remained stuck until 10.30 p.m. By the time Stopford was able to manoeuvre his vessel once more, it was the fireships that caused further delay, and by the early hours of the morning the wind had veered to a direction which made it impossible to employ them against the line-of-battle ships which cringed in the mouth of the Charente. So they were used instead to set fire to two other French ships, which suffered the further misfortune of being fired on by their own countrymen who mistook them for other British fireships as they blazed in the darkness. A third French ship became so panic-stricken that her crew abandoned her after setting her on fire.

Amidst all this din and conflagration the Captain and crew of the *Impérieuse* had evidently snatched some rest during the night, and Cochrane was back on deck in fighting mood when the *Indefatigable* sailed past him at 5 a.m. He signalled to Captain Rodd, proposing that they should go in and attack Admiral Allemand's flagship, but Rodd replied that his ship had a shot through her main topmast, that she lay too deep in the water to approach the mouth of the Charente, and that he could not act without superior orders in the presence of two senior captains. The only one of these three objections that might really have disabled him from joining Cochrane in the attack was the one that concerned his damaged topmast, and ships went into action despite more serious injuries than that. What Captain Rodd's reply reveals yet again is the impossible situation in which Cochrane had been placed by the First Sea Lord, and the extent to which Gambier had made matters worse by sulking in his tent throughout the battle that nobody but he had the authority to command.

As the *Indefatigable* sailed away in company with all those other ships commanded by senior captains, Cochrane acted on his own initiative for the third time. From the golden *Pallas* Captain George Seymour signalled to ask him whether he should remain, and Cochrane begged him to do so unless he had contrary orders. So these two gallant comrades set off on their last ploy together, accompanied by Congreve's rocket-ship *Aetna*, the little *Beagle* of 18 guns, the gunbrigs and other small craft. From 11 o'clock until they were driven away by the ebbing tide, that brave little band engaged the great French flagship and the two battleships that lay nearest to her. The *Beagle* suffered more heavily than any as she clung close to the flagship's stern through a battering that continued for 5 hours: so that it seems almost miraculous that not a single casualty occurred aboard her.

While this was going on, Admiral Gambier sent a succession of five ships to Cochrane, not to lend him any assistance, but to bring him a series of extraordinary messages. The first despatch bordered on lunacy. It consisted of a public and a private message, the first of which ordered him to attack the French flagship in exactly the manner in which he had been doing for some time, though 'I do not think you will succeed; and I am anxious that you should come to me, as I wish to send you to England as soon as possible. You must, therefore, come as soon as the tide turns.'

The private letter urged Cochrane to do the opposite to what he had ordered in his public despatch—to give up at once and return. 'My Dear Lord—You have done your part so admirably that I will not suffer you to tarnish it by attempting impossibilities.' The opinion that Gambier had expressed to the Admiralty before Cochrane ever arrived on the scene remained virtually unaltered by anything that had occurred in Aix Roads during the past 2 days. 'You must, therefore, join as soon as you can, with the bombs etc., as I wish for some information, which you allude to, before I close my despatches.'

Cochrane replied tersely: 'My Lord—I have had the honour to receive your Lordship's letter. We *can* destroy the ships that are on shore, which I hope your Lordship will approve of.' Gambier had allowed them to slip through his fingers when they were last aground, and he did not intend to allow the same to happen again, now that they were stranded in the mouth of the Charente. By this time the water was so low that his little fleet could only watch from a distance while the French flung their guns overboard to lighten ship, so that they would be able to refloat at the first opportunity; when British vessels of lighter draught would have been able to approach them. Many of them had destroyed their powder, some were now without guns also, and the sea around them swarmed with fishing boats scrambling to rescue stores from derelict vessels. Cochrane lay in wait until the following morning, when salvation reached the French from the usual quarter.

Gambier sent another Captain to relieve Cochrane of his command in an order couched in terms of characteristic courtesy. 'My Dear Lord—It is necessary I should have some communication with you before I close my despatches to the Admiralty. I have therefore ordered Captain Wolfe, to relieve you in the services you are engaged in. I wish you to join me as soon as possible that you may convey Sir Harry Neale to England, who will be charged with my despatches.' To his credit, Captain Wolfe tried to implement Cochrane's plan to destroy those warships; though he did not succeed, nor did he live to reach any higher rank in the service.

Eleven days had passed since Cochrane had tried to restrain the imprudence of Admiral Harvey in the flagship of the Commander-in-Chief. Now it was his own turn to throw prudence to the winds. He had been dragged from the forefront of a battle in which for 3 days and nights of unremitting toil and danger he had tapped every reserve of energy and invention to maintain the initiative against the enemy, and to overcome the reluctance of his own seniors to support him. His impertinence to Admiral Gambier when he reached the quarterdeck of the flagship was at least constructive in its intention. Cochrane reminded the Admiral of the basic trouble from the start: that he was a junior Captain whose appointment had probably aroused jealousy in the fleet. He begged Gambier to send Admiral Stopford to complete the task from which he had been recalled.

Gambier, who had never sailed within 6 miles of the battle, and who would not have attacked at all in the wake of the fireships if Cochrane had not forced his hand by drifting alone into the middle of the enemy fleet, was fixed in his opinion that the action had been successfully completed on the previous day. Cochrane had merely delayed his smug despatch to the Admiralty by ignoring his orders to return earlier, and now he had the impertinence to offer the Commander in-Chief criticism and advice. With the cunning of such pettifogging minds Gambier warned Cochrane: 'If you throw blame upon what has been done, it will appear like arrogantly claiming all the merit to yourself.'

Cochrane answered that he had no such intention: his sole considera-tion was the destruction of the enemy's ships. But this argument brought even Gambier's patience to an end: he terminated the inter-view abruptly and sent Cochrane written instructions to convey Sir

T..S.W.—H

Harry Neale to Plymouth on the morrow in the *Impérieuse*. And because
seamen will talk of their adventures when they return home, and the
public there will pass their tales from mouth to mouth faster than
semaphore, Lord Gambier was a hissing and a scorn to his countrymen
by the time he arrived 5 days later, while Cochrane was the hero of the
hour.

It was only just over 50 years since Admiral Byng had been shot at
Portsmouth for precisely the offence which Gambier had committed,
and such an event could not have been forgotten in Britain's ports nor
in the country at large. Byng was acquitted of both cowardice and
disaffection at his court-martial, but condemned to death on the charge
of failing to do his utmost in battle and in pursuit. Gambier's self-
righteous despatch contained not the slightest hint that he had a
guilty conscience over these or any other failings, but too many
sailors had witnessed them for days with mounting fury to keep them
secret.

What saved Admiral Gambier from the fate of Byng was that the
present government did not require a scapegoat for its own failures as
the government had done when it sacrificed Admiral Byng. On the
contrary, it needed a naval victory to announce to an increasingly
restive public; the last thing it could afford was any talk of bungling or
failure, and as the dreadful whispers began to circulate in the corridors
of Whitehall Gambier's reputation became increasingly identified with
that of the Admiralty and of the government. A whole batch of
promotions was announced in celebration of the victory of Lord
Gambier at Aix Roads, dated from the night on which Cochrane had
brought his secret weapon to breach the boom. He himself was created
a Knight of the Bath—not even Nelson, only St Vincent, had ever been
invested with this high honour at the mere rank of Captain. For
Gambier was reserved the fanfare which a government could so easily
stage-manage for propaganda purposes: he was to receive the formal
thanks of the two Houses of Parliament.

On both sides of the Channel the suggestion aroused equal contempt.
A leading article in *The Times* exploded:

'Lord Cochrane's signal, as we learn from the *Gazette*, to the Admiral
of the fleet, was that "seven of the enemy's ships were on shore, and
might be destroyed". The question which hereupon naturally suggests
itself to the mind is, "Why, then, if seven might be destroyed, were
there only four?"

'The despatch proceeds: "I immediately made the signal for the
fleet to unmoor and weigh." Indeed! Had Admiral Lord Gambier to
unmoor at the time he received this intelligence? Did he not expect

this might be the case? Or with what view was Lord Cochrane sent up the Roads?'

The leader writer could not know that Gambier had lied in his despatch when he stated that he gave the order to weigh anchor immediately. The only question is whether the whole series of lies he told concerning his part in the battle were the natural mistake of a man of sufficient stupidity, or whether one who made such a parade of moral probity could have stooped to utter them deliberately.

The verdicts of every French naval historian, which have been as annihilating as those pronounced by his own countrymen, were anticipated by Napoleon himself. 'If Cochrane had been properly supported,' he asserted during his years of exile, 'he could not only have destroyed all the French ships, but he could have taken them out.'

It would have been the greatest naval feat in Britain's history, and Cochrane's disappointment was not assuaged by the Order of the Bath nor by the public adulation in which he basked. Neither could he be reconciled to Gambier by the despatch which declared that his services in Aix Roads 'could not be exceeded by any feat of valour hitherto achieved by the British Navy'. It was not enough that five French ships had been destroyed and a sixth wrecked when the entire fleet might have been taken out but for the *mollesse*—the inertia—of Admiral Gambier, as the French themselves testified. Cochrane went to see Lord Mulgrave at the Admiralty and told him that as a naval officer he could not comment on the conduct of a senior officer, but that he must oppose a vote of thanks to Gambier in Parliament as a Member of the House of Commons.

The First Lord treated the national hero with extreme tact. He already had the scandal of Admiral Harvey's court-martial on his hands to remind him that the troubles in the Channel fleet had been largely due to his own ignorance of the conventions within the fighting arm of a service department, and his consequent mishandling of the situation. Waiving his dignity he tried by every means in his power to woo the irate young Captain to a more amenable frame of mind. He reminded Cochrane that the public would not recognise the distinction between a Member of Parliament and a naval officer if he were to attack his Commander-in-Chief, and that he himself was to be included in the vote of thanks. Finding Cochrane at his most obstinate, Mulgrave gave him time to cool before extending his next olive branch.

In this, the most tragic error of judgment of Cochrane's long and varied life, all the elements in his character, the simple and the complex, the vicious mole of nature in him and his most admirable qualities, combined inexorably to drag him down as in a Greek tragedy. He was self-willed and arrogant; he loved courage and hated cowardice; he possessed not a particle of tolerance for inefficiency in the service that was still his only passion, but what was most fatal was that he possessed the rare gift of unshakeable loyalty; and the same loyalty that he displayed all his life for his relatives, however unworthy, and for his friends, was given now to the men with whom he had cast his lot when he became a radical Member of Parliament. They were all men of whom their country can still be proud even if some of their opinions do not command equal respect, and this is a great deal more than can be said of most of the politicians who then enjoyed positions of profit and power. These men endured public abuse, colossal fines, even imprisonment on frivolous charges, and Cochrane considered that it would be an act of cowardice and of self-interest to desert them now, when he was the natural spokesman of a major public scandal. The difference between him and Samuel Whitbread or Sir Francis Burdett was that he was not a private civilian but a servant of the administration that he proposed to attack, by virtue of his commission.

It is one of the anomalies of Cochrane's character that he could assess a situation with such lightning clarity when his feet were on a quarterdeck, yet could not now perceive how false his stance was on land: that he thought he could accept service in a department of the government and then attack its administration in a different capacity. Lord Mulgrave certainly did his best to enlighten him when he summoned Cochrane again and proposed a solution to his dilemma that would be honourable to himself and most advantageous to his country. He suggested that Cochrane should return at once to the task he had left with such reluctance at Lord Gambier's bidding.

'If you are on service,' he told Cochrane, 'you cannot be in your place in Parliament. Now, my Lord, I will make you a proposal. I will put under your orders three frigates with *carte blanche* to do whatever you please on the enemy's coasts in the Mediterranean. I will further get you permission to go to Sicily, and embark on board your squadron my own regiment, which is stationed there. You know how to make use of them.'

How the course of history on both sides of the world would have been altered if Cochrane had accepted that offer there is no saying; the only certainty is that it must have been very different. But Cochrane thanked Lord Mulgrave for his offer and declined it, saying that to accept would be interpreted as evidence that he could be bribed to hold his tongue.

So oft it chances in particular men; and Cochrane was the most particular man whom the British Navy possessed. Never would the Sea Wolf trouble Napoleon again.

CHAPTER SIX

Crusader

A few months before Cochrane's return home the country had seethed with the news that the mistress of the royal Duke of York, Commander-in-Chief of the British Army, had been selling military commissions and also places of preferment in the Established Church of England. When Mary Ann Clarke made her capricious disclosures Samuel Whitbread introduced a motion in the House of Commons for a Select Committee of enquiry, supported by Colonel Wardle. 'The plague is amongst us,' called Whitbread. 'Bring incense quickly. The House of Commons can alone stand between the living and the dead. Bonaparte is a flea bite compared to internal corruption, and if we do not prevent its spreading, we are a lost nation.'

The scandal was more embarrassing to the government than any which had yet leaked out of the Admiralty, involving as it did a royal family that had already dragged the British monarchy to a lower level of disrepute than it had ever reached before. King George III was on the brink of the final spell of madness in which he passed the last 10 years of his reign. His heir, the Prince of Wales, had entered into a secret canonical marriage with a Roman Catholic, which could have barred him by statute from the succession if the marriage certificate had ever been disclosed. He had subsequently made a bigamous marriage with a first cousin who shared with him the family insanity, and the undignified public quarrels in which the pair indulged aroused almost as much animosity as the gigantic debts that Parliament was periodically called upon to pay on the Prince's behalf. By contrast, the King's sailor son William, Duke of Clarence, lived in relative respectability with his mistress Mrs Jordan and their large brood of children. Since Clarence remained a bachelor and had consequently not received a marriage allowance, poverty frequently drove Mrs Jordan back to her profession on the stage in order to augment the family income. The Duke went to the House of Lords to speak with more vehemence than skill in favour of slavery whenever William Wilberforce's tireless efforts for abolition succeeded in getting a Bill as far as the Upper House. It is impossible to believe that even a member of such an eccentric family would have troubled to do this unless he was being bribed by the slavery interest, especially one who was in such constant and desperate need of bribes.

As though all this were not enough, the peccadilloes of his brother of York were now the talk of the land, and it was not merely that they compromised a service department of a nation at war, and the Church upon which the Protestant succession of the house of Hanover rested. The Duke of York was married to a Princess of the house of King Frederick the Great, a respectable little squirrel of a woman who was the first to introduce the practice of exchanging Christmas presents in Britain.

While the Ministers of the government listened in embarrassment to the indictment of Samuel Whitbread and Colonel Wardle, a new Member who had reached the benches behind them a mere matter of months earlier surveyed the same scene with the expectancy of one whose opportunity has arrived. Whitbread had called for incense and John Croker possessed exactly the recipe for the incense the government required, a rancorous tongue and pen, tireless industry, and an entire lack of scruple. He leapt to the defence of the Duke of York, and thereby earned in addition the patronising acquaintance of the royal family. It was impossible to refuse the Select Committee which Wardle and Whitbread demanded, but it was possible to manage the votes when its report was presented, so that the Duke was acquitted by 278 to 196. In the circumstances this amounted to a conviction just as the acquittal of Melville had done, and like Melville the Duke resigned, in March 1809.

A month later the Admiralty and its Commander-in-Chief replaced the War Office and its Commander-in-Chief as a general subject of gossip, in the columns of William Cobbett's *Weekly Political Register* and of *The Times*, in the corridors of the Houses of Parliament, in the coffee houses and drawing rooms, and in the streets where the ballads were hawked in Cochrane's praise. As soon as Admiral Gambier heard of Cochrane's intention to oppose the vote of thanks in Parliament he demanded a court-martial, but the administration had already decided upon a more ambitious demonstration to take the public's mind off the scandals of the two service departments and to restore their credit. They could see that the plan which Cochrane had sent Admiral Thornborough 3 years before had proved staggeringly apt in conception. Since then he had sent a more recent proposal to Lord Mulgrave from Aix Roads. With 20,000 men, he had prophesied, the British could capture the islands that guarded the French arsenal of Rochefort and not merely destroy the enemy fleet, but hold down an army of 100,000.

While the authorities were rigging the court-martial which would whitewash Lord Gambier, they also prepared a re-enactment of the drama at Aix Roads on the extended scale which Cochrane had suggested. To ensure success they planned the repeat performance on such a gigantic scale that it must surely bring overwhelming victory and appear to the public as the operation for which Aix Roads had, after all, been a mere rehearsal. So the planners assumed in their folly as they prepared to play Hamlet with a cast of thousands, but without the prince.

The target chosen was the French fleet lying on the Scheldt between the island of Walcheren and distant Antwerp, farther up the river. 40,000 men, double the number suggested by Cochrane, including 3,000 on horseback, were brought to the Downs to await transport across the Channel to the Netherlands. Warships were adapted to carry the horses. Thirty-seven sail of the line, twenty-three frigates, nearly 400 transports and numerous other vessels were put in order to accompany the expeditionary force. It was the largest armada that had ever left England.

Total secrecy would have been impossible when all this was going on, and as Cochrane demonstrated after some time—and also told Lord Mulgrave in his letter from Aix Roads—secrecy and surprise were the most important weapons of all. But the men who were planning the operation were no more aware of this than they understood the importance of their own weapon—Cochrane himself. Lord Mulgrave had proposed sending him to the Mediterranean; nobody suggested that he should go to the Scheldt, or even consulted him about the plan he had outlined in the stern cabin of the *Impérieuse* when he was almost too weary to put his thoughts together.

Of course he knew very well what was in the wind. The newspapers were discussing the enterprise from May onwards, two months before the armada sailed. Cochrane could not resist sending Lord Mulgrave suggestions for the most effective use of the assembled forces, but it would have taken another genius to have seized such a priceless opportunity after all that had occurred during the past weeks, and Lord Mulgrave was no genius. He ignored Cochrane's advice and appointed another officer to take the *Impérieuse* to the Scheldt. She sailed with the enormous fleet on 28 July, 2 days after the court-martial of Lord Gambier opened.

Behind the ceremony of the proceedings that began in Portsmouth on the 26th, the gold braid of the dress uniforms, the doors guarded by marines in their scarlet jackets, a proceeding as vile as any which has disgraced the senior service began its course. The President of the court is perhaps more to be pitied than blamed: he was a personal friend of Gambier's so that personal loyalty was added to his sense of duty. But no such excuse can be made for the senior Admiral on the board, the man whose money-making tricks Admiral St Vincent had once pointed out, whose failings as a Port Admiral Cochrane had exposed in Parliament, the egregious Sir William Young. His character is preserved with horrifying clarity in the records of the trial.

Cochrane himself had made a tactical error of the kind he so rarely committed on sea, so frequently on land. When the court-martial of Gambier had been determined, the Admiralty wrote to Cochrane, asking him for details of his charges. But he did not want to be placed in the invidious position of prosecutor of his commanding officer so he replied that the log books of the fleet provided all the evidence the Admiralty could need—which they certainly do. But Cochrane had forfeited the right to introduce the evidence which he ought to have realised the prosecution would suppress.

With Cochrane muzzled before the trial had opened, it was only necessary to select the witnesses with care. One of those who were known to hold the most severe opinion of Gambier's conduct was Captain Maitland of the 36-gun *Emerald*, later to become Rear Admiral Sir Frederick Maitland; by 26 July he had been posted to a distant station. Captain Austen was not called as a witness although he was present; and after he had been promoted Admiral of the Fleet Sir Francis Austen he placed on record the evidence which the court-martial did not wish to hear. Gambier, he asserted, ought to have advanced to a position just clear of the batteries on the isle of Aix where he could have seen the position of the enemy ships, rather than remain at such a distance that he depended on the reports of others. And he told Cochrane something that was fundamental to the purpose of the court-martial. 'I must in conscience declare,' wrote Austen, 'that I do not think you were properly supported, and that had you been the result would have been very different. Much of what occurred I attribute to Lord Gambier's being influenced by persons about him who would have been ready to sacrifice the honour of their country to the gratification of personal dislike to yourself, and the annoyance they felt at a junior officer being employed in the service.' This was the cat that must not be allowed to escape from the bag. Incompetence was one thing, deliberate dereliction of duty another, and the gossip of the seamen after they came ashore had filled the country with the suspicion that there had been quislings in the flagship.

'I was fifth or junior Lieutenant of the *Valiant*,' wrote one of the officers who was present throughout the action in Aix Roads, but not called as a witness, 'and can bear testimony to the indignation which pervaded the whole fleet in witnessing the total want of enterprise and even common sense of duty, which then permitted so many of the enemy's ships to escape when they were entirely at our mercy.' He confirmed that Gambier would not have moved at all if Cochrane had not forced his hand with the manoeuvre that has been called the bravest action of his life. 'There was universal conviction that but for the ingenious ruse adopted by your Lordship of running in singly with the *Impérieuse*, and then making a signal of distress, or rather of want of assistance, nothing whatever would have been effected against the French fleet.' The issue which faced the court-martial was as simple as it was grave, the evidence available was overwhelming, and most of it was public knowledge before the proceedings began.

The real interest of the trial record lies in tracing the subterfuges by which this evidence was suppressed, and the deliberate mendacities that were introduced whenever it was necessary and feasible to resort to them. For it was inevitable that, however carefully the questions were framed, naval officers who were accustomed to telling the truth would let slip uncomfortable facts. On the subject of those dawn signals from the *Impérieuse*, Captain William Broughton of the *Illustrious* observed: 'It would have been more advantageous if the line-of-battleships, frigates and small vessels had gone in at half flood, about 11 o'clock. There were nine sail ashore, and if the British ships had been ordered in, it would have been more advantageous.' Worse still, Captain Broughton invoked Gambier's Flag Captain to confirm what he had just said. 'I told Sir Henry Neale on board the *Caledonia*, when the signal was made for all the captains in the morning, that "they were attackable from the confused way in which the French ships were at the time".' Captain Neale was instructed not to give evidence to corroborate Broughton, and when Cochrane attempted to do so instead he was rudely silenced by Sir William Young.

One of the most embarrassing witnesses was Captain George Seymour of the *Pallas*, whom the President of the court instructed to speak only of what had occurred after he had sailed to join Cochrane in the middle of the French fleet on 12 April, and not of the events he had witnessed from the moment of the night attack on the 11th.

Seymour: From what period am I to give my answer?

President: From the time of your being sent in to attack the enemy, and your having remained there.

Seymour: Without going back to the 11th?

President: No. I take it from your going in on the 12th.

Nevertheless Seymour stuck to the facts that really mattered, and to his credit the President did not stop him.

Seymour: I think the ships might have floated in sooner; that they might have come in on the last half of the flood-tide.

President: How much sooner would that have been than the time they actually did go in?

Seymour: At eleven o'clock.

President: What time did the line-of-battle ships go in?

Seymour: Within a short time after two o'clock.

A third officer insisted on speaking out, and so helped to preserve the credit of his service even if he could not influence the outcome of the proceedings. Captain Malcolm of the 74-gun *Donegal* later became Admiral Sir Pultney Malcolm and he was a worthy brother to that outstanding Indian servant General Sir John Malcolm, whose monument dominates a hill-top above Langholm in their native Dumfriesshire. 'I saw the enemy's three-decker on shore,' Malcolm deposed. 'Till about noon she was heeling over considerably, and appeared to me to be heaving her guns overboard. She got off about two o'clock. All the ships got off except those that were destroyed. Had it appeared to me that there was no other chance of destroying those ships but by such an attack, I certainly think it ought to have been made.'

The real facts were more dramatic than Malcolm himself knew. At one time during the night of the torpedo attack there was nobody left aboard the stranded enemy flagship except the quartermaster. A midshipman came to take a look at her in his jolly-boat and the quartermaster called out to him: 'Qui vive?' Had the midshipman realised that the quartermaster was alone in his ship, he might have captured the three-decker with his crew of four men. But the court had heard enough from Broughton, Seymour and Malcolm alone to satisfy any honest judge.

The defence against such apparently unassailable evidence was provided by three officers who had never been present during the action, who had never entered Aix Roads in their lives, and evidently possessed no knowledge of them. These were supported by the perjured evidence of two chart masters called Stikes and Fairfax, whose fabricated charts were introduced to lend weight to Admiral Gambier's muddled references to the dangers of shoals and currents.

Gambier's statements are the most interesting of all in the trial record. He asserted that it was a fireship that had burst the boom on the night of the 11th, not Cochrane's explosion vessel. However great his desire to discredit Cochrane it is almost incredible that he should have stooped to such a falsehood, not merely because there were so many witnesses to the truth amongst his own profession, but also because he ought to have known that a fireship would not have been capable of injuring the boom. Certainly he had displayed sufficient ignorance to make this extraordinary blunder in his first despatch to the Admiralty after the action. But by the time of the court-martial he had enjoyed ample time to correct his error. Similarly his defence that the batteries on the isle of Aix would have exposed his ships to unnecessary danger was discredited in advance. In his reports to the Admiralty before Cochrane ever reached his fleet he had stated first that these batteries offered no danger, then that they did, without making any attempt to discover whether they did or not during the interval. At the court-martial evidence was given that the menace of the fortifications on the isle of Aix had proved illusory; then Gambier came forward to assert the opposite. It is possible that an impartial court might have convicted the Admiral on his own evidence alone, without requiring other witnesses.

In the event it ruled that 'his general conduct and proceedings as Commander-in-Chief of the Channel Fleet in Basque road, between the 17th day of March and the 29th day of April 1809, was marked by zeal, judgment, ability, and an anxious attention to the welfare of his Majesty's service, and did adjudge him to be most honourably acquitted'.

The reassurance, for what it was worth, came none too soon. Already the first tidings of appalling disaster were beginning to trickle home from the Scheldt, and not even the news that Wellington had won another victory in the Peninsula at Talavera could soften the impact.

The expeditionary fleet was commanded by Admiral Sir Richard Strachan, the army by Lieutenant General the Earl of Chatham, elder brother of the late Prime Minister William Pitt. After the fiasco a popular lampoon blamed both men equally.

> Lord Chatham, with his sword half-drawn,
> Stood waiting for Sir Richard Strachan.
> Sir Richard, longing to be at 'em,
> Stood waiting for the Earl of Chatham.

Rumour treading hard on the heels of the event cannot always apportion the blame accurately. Admiral Strachan was in fact a splendid seaman; it was Chatham who displayed the fatal inertia and lack of initiative of a Gambier, and as at Aix Roads, it was the government that was principally to blame for mishandling the entire operation. But at least Gambier had preserved the lives of his men, and at least there had been a Cochrane at Aix Roads to inflict heavy damage on the enemy fleet.

In the Walcheren expedition 14,000 British soldiers fell sick with malaria as they waited inactive in the Dutch islands, and over 3000 died of it. The damage to the French fleet was negligible. Cochrane thundered: 'Had one half of the troops been placed, as suggested in my letter to Lord Mulgrave, on the islands of the French coast, and had one half of the frigates alone been employed as had been the *Impérieuse* and other vessels in the Mediterranean, not a man could have been detached from Western France in the Spanish peninsula, from which the remaining portion of the British army might have driven the French troops already there.' Such a ruse would have restored the essential element of surprise when the French were long prepared for an attack at the Scheldt, and it might have relieved Wellington in the Peninsula when he was in serious need. He had won at Talavera the day after the fleet had sailed to the Scheldt but 'never was there such a murderous battle', he told his brother.

Even if it was beyond the capacity of the British High Command to entertain Cochrane's plan to strike back at Aix, it might yet have found salvation in the alternative suggestions he offered for the conduct of the Scheldt operation. 'Had my recommendation been adopted,' Cochrane asserted in later years when he had proved his right to speak with such confidence, 'even though not carried out under my supervision, nothing could have saved the French fleet in the Scheldt from a similar fate to that which had befallen their armament in Aix Roads. Even—as with the disaster in Aix Roads fresh in remembrance is probable—had the French fleet in the Scheldt taken refuge above Antwerp, it would only have placed itself in a *cul-de-sac*; whilst there was ample military and naval force to operate against the dockyards and fortifications during the period that my appliances for the destruction of the enemy's fleet were in progress; for I in no way wished to interfere with the operations of the General or Admiral commanding, but rather to conduct my own independently of extraordinary aid from either.'

Economy of means, both in lives and materials, was one of the most distinctive merits of any plan that Cochrane conceived. 'The cost of this plan to the nation would have been ten rotten old hulks, some fifty thousand barrels of powder, and a proportionate quantity of shells. The cost of the expedition which failed—in addition to the thousands of lives sacrificed—was millions; and the millions which followed by the prolongation of the war.'

As the haggard faces of the survivors from the death-camps of Walcheren appeared in the south coast ports, and the great armada returned without the slightest success to its credit, the government's reputation sank to new depths. The public anger was not allayed when the victor of Talavera was created Viscount Wellington, Baron Douro, a Portuguese Marshal and a Spanish Captain-General; and when he was also voted a pension of £2000 a year by Parliament the gift was publicly opposed by the Common Council of the City of London. It was pointed out that the victory had achieved nothing except prestige and little enough of that since Wellington had been compelled to retire into Portugal.

The Prime Minister rode out the storm until October when he resigned and died. He was a total nonentity called the Duke of Portland who owed his position exclusively to his rank and wealth, and who had first been placed in Downing Street on the grounds that he was a 'convenient cipher'. He was replaced by Spencer Perceval and when the new session of Parliament opened a new Prime Minister who sat in the House of Commons was joined on the front bench by the assiduous John Croker, replacing William Wellesley Pole as First Secretary to the Admiralty. To these men would fall the principal responsibility of piloting the vote of thanks to Lord Gambier through the lower House, now that his name had been officially cleared and the importance of his 'victory' at Aix Roads had been enhanced by the fiasco in the Scheldt and the doubts about Talavera.

The vote was introduced in the upper House by Lord Granville on 25 January 1810, and it received a hostile reception from the Whig peers. Prominent among these was Samuel Whitbread's brother-in-law Charles Grey, who had recently inherited his father's earldom. A tall stately man, who would one day pilot the Great Reform Bill through Parliament, Grey rose to declaim in his fine voice and cool, aristocratic manner: 'I am glad to find from the humble and chastened tone of Ministers that they appear to feel some remorse for the numerous miseries which, by their imbecility and misconduct, they have inflicted on their country.' The First Lord, Lord Mulgrave, proceeded to compound their misconduct by describing the action of Aix Roads in terms which, even by the standards of his time, are breath-taking in their mendacity. Ominously the Whig magnate Lord Holland pointed to the evidence that must in the end confound the prevarications of the First Lord and the fabrications of the court-martial:

'What said Lord Cochrane in his reply to the Admiralty? "Look at and sift the log-books, and not ask me for accusations".'

Lord Melville, son of the impeached First Lord and a future First Lord himself, repeated another truth that Cochrane had been the first to state: 'I conceive the Admiralty to have acted extremely wrong in giving to Lord Cochrane a command so contrary to the usual rules of the service, and which must have been so galling and so disgusting to the feelings of other officers in Lord Gambier's fleet.' Admiral Harvey had been dismissed the service for repeating the same criticism aboard Gambier's flagship, and Admiral Austen was subsequently to give it as the reason why Cochrane had not been properly supported at Aix Roads. Lord Darnley rose to utter a third uncomfortable truth. The government, he remarked, was only pushing this vote of thanks in a miserable attempt to enhance its own credit. The motion was then passed without a division, probably to save the House of Lords the embarrassment of acting as a jury on one of its own peers.

As a compliment to Lord Gambier or a fanfare for the government these proceedings fell short of what either could have desired, and they must have anticipated worse in the Commons. Here Captain Lord Cochrane sat in his place among the radicals, and he was ably supported by Samuel Whitbread when he demanded that the minutes of the court-martial should be laid before the House. Of course he could have torn them to shreds: it was out of the question that they should be exposed to public view.

William Wilberforce came to the Commons' rescue, protesting that to ask for the minutes would be to throw 'a stigma on all the members of the court-martial' and Whitbread argued in vain that Members must be allowed to assess the merits of Lord Gambier's conduct for themselves if they were to be asked to give him a vote of thanks.

This odd intervention from Wilberforce was characteristic of him. The man who devoted his life to the abolition of slavery, who inherited substantial wealth and yet died too poor to maintain a home of his own, was a devout opponent of the radicals. He attacked inhumanity, and vested interests in the dreadful form in which they flourished in his time, yet showed scant concern over the lesser manifestations of both on his own doorstep. This was due partly to his fear for the traditional order of church and state, menaced by revolutionary forces abroad and by social unrest at home; partly to his single-mindedness, which may have dismissed local injustices as trivial compared to the stupendous horrors of the slave trade. In the present instance it was natural that he should fly to the rescue of a devout Christian Admiral, attacked by men who were constantly threatening the Establishment.

The attitude of the saintly Wilberforce was almost identical in this context to that of the evangelical Hannah More, one of those pests who are reincarnated at regular intervals as a plague to society, who wrote to a cousin of Gambier's: 'Terrible as Buonaparte is, I do not fear him so much as these domestic mischiefs—Burdett, Cochrane, Wardle and Cobbett. I hope, however, that the mortification Cochrane etc.

have lately experienced in their base and impotent endeavours to pull down reputations which they found unassailable, will keep them down a little.' Even the present government probably preferred to manage without that kind of support, but Wilberforce in the House of Commons was a frequent source of moral strength and the alliance at least achieved this good objective—that it secured support for the negro slaves which would otherwise have been denied them.

Opposite the new Prime Minister, Perceval, the new Admiralty Secretary John Croker and Wilberforce amongst their supporters sat that trio of trouble-makers, the massive, benevolent bulk of Samuel Whitbread, the tall, stringy, handsome Burdett, and the young, ginger-haired Scottish peer. As impotently as Hannah More could have wished, Burdett rose to ask:

'Has there been anything said to make out a reason for the vote demanded? Where is the evidence of the Commander-in-Chief's intrepidity or skill? Of that boldness which bursts its way through all obstacles? Of that genius before which obstacles vanish? In place of this the House has been insulted with a dry catalogue of negatives, and an account as to how the noble Admiral inspected the action at a distance of seven miles.'

But in effect it was Lord Gambier who was insulted. Thirty-nine Members opposed the vote of thanks in the Commons and the remarks that had been made about his services at Aix Roads in both Houses were such that he might well have wished they had not been debated in Parliament at all. He received no other form of recognition, and after his command of the Channel fleet had run its 3-year course he was not employed in the navy again. The government's credit was not enhanced either: it was Wellington who reaped the benefit of its ill-concealed disgrace. His letters from the Peninsula expressed constant anxiety lest the administration should alter its war strategy and recall him from his relentless struggle to drive the French out of Portugal and Spain. But now that Cochrane had been discredited by the rehabilitation of Gambier, and his alternative strategy through the fiasco in the Scheldt, Wellington remained as the sole, irreplaceable hope of salvation in the war against Napoleon. So far from withdrawing its support from him, the administration greeted each new victory in the Peninsula with almost hysterical relief and loaded the victor with such honours and emoluments that he rapidly became the most richly rewarded public servant in the whole of Britain's history.

With comparable hysteria the Ministry also rounded on the men whom Hannah More feared more than Napoleon himself—though she probably regarded him as the devil incarnate. The world of the Hannah

Mores is filled with devils, often extremely bizarre in their variety. One of these was an obscure and harmless man called John Gale Jones whose delight was the discussion of current affairs. He had been a member of a Corresponding Society until it was suppressed as subversive by William Pitt, and he had since organised a debating society in Covent Garden where he was known as Citizen Jones. He was the sort of man who possesses an insatiable appetite for the dreariest debates in Parliament, and he hungered to listen to those in which the failure of the Walcheren expedition was discussed. When the government tried to conceal its shame by closing the public galleries Jones displayed a handbill protesting against what he considered an infringement of democratic rights. The House of Commons ruled that this was an affront to its dignity and ordered Jones to be flung into Newgate prison without any form of trial. The incarceration of Citizen Jones took place in February 1810, just after Gambier had received his vote of thanks.

But John Jones was merely the sprat which served to catch the mackerel. Sir Francis Burdett rose in the House of Commons to declare that its action had been an infringement of Magna Carta and of the fundamental rights of citizens under the law. William Cobbett published his speech in the *Weekly Political Register*, together with an address from Burdett on the same subject to the electors of Westminster. The Ministry responded by passing a motion in the Commons for Burdett's committal to the Tower of London. Sir Francis denounced the Speaker's warrant as illegal and barricaded himself in his mansion in Piccadilly.

Popular fury brought out the largest crowds ever seen in London to protect Burdett from arrest. They pelted passers-by who refused to cheer him, and filled the government with such fear that the Horse Guards were called out to patrol the streets, then the Foot Guards and Light Dragoons. By day and night they went about their invidious task, doing their best to disperse groups of people wherever they assembled by striking them with the flats of their swords. Mutual animosities between these different bodies of troops added to the confusion, while tension was increased by the mounting of batteries of artillery in Berkeley Square, St James's Park and Soho Square. The Tower of London was fortified, all cavalry and infantry within a hundred miles of London ordered to the capital. Would it become necessary to recall Wellington from the Peninsula to stamp out revolution at home? Ever since the fall of the Bastille in France this had always been an imponderable danger, haunting the Establishment.

One of the gifts which contributed most to Cochrane's successes in war was an instinctive flair for demoralising his opponents and exploiting their panic to the full. The delighted crowds of London now saw their hero practising this art. He arrived at Burdett's house in a hackney carriage, and presently the spectators who hung around in spite of the troops, waiting for something exciting to happen, saw the 34-year-old giant who was a radical politician, a naval genius and a peer, manhandling a barrel of gunpowder from the carriage to the cobblestones, and thence through a side door into the besieged house. They raised a mighty cheer, then waited expectantly to see what would happen next.

Within, Sir Francis Burdett was keeping strange company. Francis Place, the London tailor, was 4 years older than Cochrane and his energetic life filled the same long span before he died in his eighties. A self-taught economist, a utilitarian and a radical, he espoused such diverse and dangerous causes as contraception and universal suffrage, and in his patient promotion of education for the working man and of the organisation of skilled artisans he presented a far more real menace than Citizen Jones. Place was conferring with Burdett about the next move when Cochrane entered breezily with his barrel of gunpowder, and began knocking a hole in the front wall of the house to make a trap for anyone who should try to force an entry.

Neither of these two civilians had seen what Cochrane had seen of life; the consequences of standing one's ground, of calling an opponent's bluff. They watched him in growing alarm, and debated whether they ought to run the risk of bloodshed if their hands were forced. It did not occur to them, apparently, that panic-stricken Ministers might be discussing the same with a great deal more trepidation, or that Burdett's initial resistance to the Speaker's warrant had been pointless if he did not mean to maintain his stand. Cochrane tried to explain all these things to them, but in vain. They prevailed on him to cease turning Burdett's residence into another Rosas, and presently the spectators outside the house saw him leave, taking his barrel of gunpowder with him.

On 9 April, after a 3-day siege, a constable managed to climb in through a window. Troops poured in after him, the warrant was served, and amid ugly scenes the Member of Parliament for Westminster was carried away to the Tower of London. He remained in captivity there for two and a half months, during which Cochrane went continuously to the House of Commons to protest, often heartened by a wildly cheering crowd.

By this time he had become a deadly nuisance to the Commons. 'The civil branch of the navy is rotten to the very core,' Admiral St Vincent had said in 1797, and despite the report which led to the impeachment of Melville it was still true 13 years later. John Croker himself had exposed a fellow official at the Admiralty who had embezzled £200,000 of public money—several millions at its modern value—soon after taking office as First Secretary. Cochrane knew from first-hand experience that the prize courts were among the worst centres of corruption, and on 19 February he moved for papers concerning them in the House of Commons.

His threat caused disarray on the benches opposite. Sir William Scott, who was an Admiralty Court judge, assured the House that Cochrane's accusations were totally unfounded. George Rose, by contrast, who had been Treasurer of the Navy since 1807, rose from the front bench to confess that the scandal had vexed him ever since he had taken office, and that he had already collected much evidence, some concerning the Court of Sir William Scott himself. He accepted Cochrane's motion in a modified form. 'Sir William Scott, however, never forgave me,' Cochrane recalled. Not surprisingly.

On 11 May, while his fellow Member for Westminster was a prisoner in the Tower of London, Cochrane delivered what is possibly the most impressive speech of his parliamentary career. John Croker had proposed the vote for the Ordinances of the Navy, and whereas Cochrane sometimes spoke under the dangerous spell of resentment and without the careful preparation that he never neglected before going into action at sea, on this occasion he was cool, well-briefed and consequently devastating.

'An Admiral worn out in the service,' he informed the House, 'is superannuated at £410 a year, a Captain at £210, a Clerk of the Ticket Office retires on £700 a year. The Widow of Admiral Sir Andrew Mitchell has one third of the allowance given to the widow of a Commissioner of the Navy.' Such was the discrepancy in pay between those who did the fighting and the civilians who were responsible for so many of their other hardships; and their pickings were nothing compared with the sinecures enjoyed by well-connected magnates.

'Thirty-two flag officers, twenty-two captains, fifty lieutenants, one hundred and eighty masters, thirty-six surgeons, twenty-three pursers, ninety-one boatswains, ninety-seven gunners, two-hundred and two carpenters, and forty-one cooks, in all seven hundred and seventy-four persons, cost the country £4028: less than the net proceeds of the sinecures of Lords Arden—£20,358—Camden—£20,536—and Buckingham—£20,693. All the superannuated Admirals, Captains and Lieutenants put together have but £1012 more than Earl Camden's sinecure alone. All that is paid to the wounded officers of the whole British Navy, and to the wives and children of those dead or killed in action, do not amount by £214 to as much as Lord Arden's sinecure alone: that is, £20,358. What is paid to the mutilated officers themselves is but half as much.'

Cochrane now referred to the family of the most richly rewarded man in British history, the future Duke of Wellington. His present rewards were only a part of the final total, and few now protest that they were excessive in view of the magnitude of his services to the nation. But he was only one of the five Wellesley brothers, sons of the impoverished Anglo-Irish Earl of Mornington, and at the time when Cochrane included them in his indictment the opposition press had already singled them out as greedy plunderers of the public purse. Long before the genius of Wellington had begun to tower above the varied talents of the others, the whole consortium of brothers had operated as a team, sharing what pickings it could in Ireland, Westminster, India, and now Spain. When the future Duke was in India there were three Wellesley brothers there, assisted by another in the government at home. When Wellington took command in Spain he was joined by two of his brothers, one in the capacity of Ambassador to Spain, the other as Minister to Portugal; a fourth sat in the Cabinet. Byron scoffed:

> How many Wellesleys did embark for Spain,
> As if therein they meant to colonise?

There was nothing exceptional in this except the relative success of the Wellesley brothers. The Cochrane family operated as a family unit too, under the comparable pressure of an impoverished earldom. But it was relevant to enquire where some of the Wellesley's money was now coming from, and Cochrane provided the answer.

'I find upon examination that the Wellesleys receive from the public £34,729, a sum equal to four hundred and twenty-six pairs of Lieutenants' legs, calculated at the rate of allowance of Lieutenant Chambers' legs. Calculating for the pension of Captain Johnstone's arm—that is £45—Lord Arden's sinecure is equal to the value of one thousand and twenty-two arms. The Marquess of Buckingham's sinecure alone will maintain the whole ordinary establishment of the victualling department at Chatham, Dover, Gibraltar, Sheerness, Downs, Heligoland, Cork, Malta, Mediterranean, Cape of Good Hope, Rio de Janeiro, and leave £5460 in the Treasury.'

The tornado swept on, engulfing fresh victims as it went. 'Mr Ponsonby, who lately made so pathetic an appeal to the good sense of the people of England against those whom he pleased to call demagogues, actually receives, for having been thirteen months in office, a sum equal to nine Admirals who have spent their lives in the service of their country; three times as much as all the pensions given to all the daughters and children of all the Admirals, Captains, Lieutenants and other officers who have died in indigent circumstances, or who have been killed in the service.'

When Cochrane finally resumed his seat, William Wellesley Pole, the late Secretary to the Admiralty, rose to defend his family. He stated that the sinecure to which Cochrane referred was held by the eldest brother who had been created Marquess Wellesley in addition to being heir to the earldom of Mornington. The chicaneries of the Marquess in India had disgusted the future Duke of Wellington, and his private life was such that Wellington told his brother Wellesley Pole that he ought to be castrated. 'Lord Cochrane has thought proper to make an attack on the Wellesley family of which I am a member,' William Wellesley Pole told the House. 'In answer to this I must observe that no member of the Wellesley family except the noble Lord at the head of it possesses a sinecure. That noble Lord certainly did, many years go, receive the reversion of sinecure which has since fallen in, when he was about to go to a distant part of the world, in a most arduous and important public situation. He was at that time in a delicate state of health and had a large family.' Thus Wellesley Pole, a member of the administration as well as of the Wellesley team, assessed a sum of £34,729, equal to perhaps half a million pounds of money today, as a combination of sick benefit and family allowance.

The former First Secretary to the Admiralty went on to hint at the way in which Cochrane might serve his own best interests. 'Let me advise him that adherence to the pursuits of his profession, of which he is so great an ornament, will tend more to his honour and to the advantage of his country than a perseverance in the conduct which he has of late adopted, conduct which can only lead him into error, and make him the dupe of those who use the authority of his name to advance their own mischievous purposes.' Outside Parliament like-minded people burdened Cochrane's conscience with the same reproof. 'The worst injury the radical reformers have done this country,' said the Edinburgh *Annual Register*, 'has been depriving it of Lord Cochrane's services, and withdrawing him from that career which he had so gloriously begun.'

Behind such compliments lay a very real threat. Sir Francis Burdett was already a prisoner for all his wealth, his rank, and his status as a Member for Westminster in the following month it was the turn of William Cobbett. During 1809 he had got away with all he had written in the *Weekly Political Register* about the sale of army commissions and positions in the Church of England, and even when he published

Burdett's speech of protest against the treatment of Citizen Jones and the address on the subject to the electors of Westminster he continued to enjoy a charmed life. Then, in June 1810, he was brought to trial for what he had published about the flogging of five militia-men at Ely because they had complained of a stoppage in their pay. He appeared before Lord Ellenborough, who sentenced him to 2 years' imprisonment and a fine of £1000.

It is a curious paradox that while Britain was locked in one of the most monumental struggles in her history, her government was one of the most inadequate on record. In the Peninsula Wellington lived in constant fear that it would fail to support the objectives that he saw so clearly and implemented with such tireless skill, while Cochrane and his associates attacked its manifold corruptions in Parliament. Of all the servants of that administration Ellenborough was the most despicable. He was no needy adventurer from some Irish rotten borough like John Croker but the son of an English bishop, and he earned outstanding distinction at the English bar before he was appointed Attorney General and then raised to the peerage as Lord Chief Justice in 1802.

The foundation of all civilised societies is the integrity of their legal institutions. There may be bad laws—there generally are—but one of the most pernicious forms of corruption is the manipulation of the law by a man responsible for administering it. Francis Bacon was disgraced for accepting bribes when he was Lord Chancellor, but this has never been considered so heinous a crime as that of George Jeffreys who held the same office and bent the law savagely for political reasons. Lord Ellenborough was a Judge Jeffreys. On the bench his behaviour became notorious for its harshness, for his brow-beating of counsel in the cases heard before him, and above all, for his bias in political cases. When he received a seat in the cabinet in 1806 while continuing in his office of Lord Chief Justice, there was an outcry of indignation not merely because such a combination of functions was improper, but because the man who held them both was Ellenborough. The administration lost office in the following year and such a scandal has never occurred again in British public life. But Ellenborough remained Lord Chief Justice, and William Cobbett was only one of his victims.

He was able to live comfortably enough in Newgate at his own expense, and even continued to write for the *Weekly Political Register* there; but the very fact of his confinement on such a charge greatly embittered him. In his final article written in gaol on 8 July 1812 he said: 'I have just paid a thousand pounds fine to the King: and much good may it do his Majesty.' One day, in identical circumstances, Cochrane would put it more forcibly than that.

For the present he was still subjected to more flattering forms of persuasion, and they came from a new First Lord who sat in the House of Commons. For Lord Mulgrave left the Admiralty in May after a term of office made memorable by his part in the Scheldt fiasco and by his mendacious account in the House of Lords of the action in Aix Roads which he and Gambier had bungled, and passed on to other offices and an earldom. So it was Charles Yorke, who tried to induce Cochrane to quit his seat in Parliament at once and return to sea. He wrote on 8 June: 'I request that your Lordship will have the goodness to inform me as early as you can what day next week it is your intention to join your ship, as His Majesty's service will not admit of her sailing being much longer postponed.'

At this time there were twenty-four officers in the British Navy sitting in Parliament, of whom only four were on active service, while none of them had the responsibility of representing a constituency whose other Member was in prison without trial. The only possible pretext that the First Lord could use for singling out Cochrane was his outstanding value to the service; its weakness was that he had not been given the command of his own ship during the Scheldt operation when his employment might have been crucial to its success. Nevertheless Charles Yorke only allowed Cochrane 4 days of silence before writing again: 'I shall be much pleased to receive an answer in the affirmative, because I should then entertain hopes that your activity and gallantry might be made available for the public service. I shall be much concerned to receive an answer in the negative, because in that case I shall feel it to be my duty to consider it as your Lordship's wish to be superseded in the command of the *Impérieuse*.' It was not Cochrane's wish, but he was not going to allow himself to be bundled off to the blockading fleet at Toulon before the prorogation of Parliament. The *Impérieuse* sailed away and with her the last opportunity (as it was to prove) for him to fight in the Napoleonic war from a quarterdeck. He had remained true to his ideals: he had fought gallantly for his country, for the efficiency of his service, for the welfare of seamen; he had remained loyal to his friends and colleagues under the greatest stress. He had lost his first passion, the command of a ship of war.

After Parliament had risen an order was given for Sir Francis Burdett's release from prison, and Cochrane witnessed once again how the Baronet's courage could suddenly fail at critical moments. Francis Place, the tailor, organised a triumphal procession for his journey home through the city from the Tower of London to Piccadilly. But for the time being he was weary of martyrdom and slipped away across the river unnoticed in a rowing-boat. It was Citizen Jones, recently discharged from Newgate, who set a brave example in his place by sitting on the roof of a coach, the centrepiece of a merry demonstration.

So that storm blew itself out, and now Cochrane embarked on a period of latency, the first he was to enjoy in a home of his own after the years he had spent in almost ceaseless activity since he had stepped aboard the *Hind* at Sheerness. The strongest constitution must have rest, and the most restless may hanker for a hearth fire and a home-acre. Cochrane had recently acquired these at Hamble on Southampton water, near to the farm at Botley where he had visited William Cobbett before his imprisonment. While he was a guest there the young writer Mary Russell Mitford had chanced to call, and she left a delightful picture of him in this year in which he was 'in the very height of his warlike fame, and as unlike the common notion of a warrior as could be. A gentle, quiet, mild young man was this burner of French fleets and cutter-out of Spanish vessels as one should see in a summer day. He lay under the trees reading Seldon on the Dominion of the Seas, and letting the children (and children always know with whom they may take liberties) play all sorts of tricks with him at their pleasure.' Since Mary Mitford was over 10 years younger than Cochrane, and could yet describe him in his thirty-fifth year as a young man, his arduous life at sea and the injury to his nose can have left few marks on his face and done little to undermine his vitality.

But he had reached a turning-point in his career, the time to take stock of the strange, ambivalent position to which his past actions had led him. Mary Mitford had noticed that he possessed the attributes of a devoted family man, and during these 6 months which he spent by Southampton water during the latter half of 1810 he may well have put down the book he was reading from time to time and wandered through the empty rooms, wondering how one looked for a wife. For there is no evidence that he ever adopted the course that is second nature to most young men, of pursuing young women at every opportunity for pleasure or for matrimony. He simply waited for the miracle to happen when he would suddenly set eyes on one girl amongst many in a public place, and know that she was the one he had been waiting for. But she did not happen to be anywhere in the neighbourhood of Southampton water, did not even happen to be yet of marriageable age. So Cochrane was left to his thoughts about other things, and by the New Year they had led him to a decision on his next course of action.

This time the Sea Wolf would strike alone, and his target would be the most evil centre of corruption in the entire navy, the Admiralty prize court at Malta.

This was one of the few periods during Cochrane's life when he appears to have been totally free of financial worries. In addition to his home at Hamble he had purchased a captured French vessel called the *Julie* which he used as his yacht, and in her he sailed to Gibraltar. There he left her while he continued his journey to Valletta in the greater safety of a British warship. The enthusiasm with which British naval officers and seamen abetted him in the enterprise he was undertaking expressed the general disgust throughout the service over the peculations of the Maltese prize court, and provides a striking contrast to the obstructiveness of senior officers in Gambier's fleet at Aix Roads.

In defending the rights of British sailors to their prize money Cochrane was, of course, also looking after his own interests and it was precisely his own legal rights that he was in a position to enforce as a test case. As soon as he landed at Valletta he applied to the Admiralty court for an adjudication of all prizes of the *Speedy* and the *Impérieuse* according to the authorised table of fees. According to statute, a copy of these scales of fees ought to have been hung up in court for public scrutiny, but there was no such table to be seen, nor would the court officials adjust their accounts to conform to the missing code.

Cochrane therefore entered the court one day when it was not sitting and confronted Dr Moncrieff, the Judge-Advocate, in person. When Moncrieff denied all knowledge of the statutory table of fees, Cochrane prowled about the premises of the court-house in an attempt to discover where it was hung. Finally he penetrated to the inner sanctum of the Judge's robing-room, where there was still no sign of it. He was on the point of leaving when he noticed a door which opened upon the Judge's private lavatory and there, glued to the back of it, was the missing table of fees. Here the Admiralty court Judge could sit and elevate his thoughts far above the bodily functions that detained him there, as he worked out the means by which he and his colleagues could embezzle the money that sailors risked their lives to win. Cochrane detached the table carefully, folded it up, put it in his pocket and departed.

Dr Moncrieff had been watching his movements about the building with relief that alternated with consternation as Cochrane moved nearer or farther from the hidden document whose very existence he had denied. When he saw that Cochrane must have found it he summoned up the courage to try to prevent him from leaving. Cochrane, who could probably have lifted him in the air with one hand, soothed him with the assurance that he had no quarrel with the Judge-Advocate who himself was burdened with no responsibility to act as custodian of the Judge's lavatory. Dr Moncrieff discreetly agreed, but added that he must go instantly to inform the Judge of what had occurred. While he was doing this Cochrane hurried to the harbour and handed the table of fees to an officer who was on the point of sailing in his ship to Sicily, where no more interesting reading matter could have been seen in the wardrooms for a long time.

The Admiralty Judge was named Dr Sewell and when news of the disaster reached him he acted with more haste than discretion. He ordered Cochrane's arrest on a charge of insulting his court. Cochrane retorted that since the court was not sitting when he removed the document, he could not have insulted it. A more serious irregularity appeared when Marshal Jackson received his instruction to arrest Cochrane, for it transpired that this official was also the Proctor. The Deputy Marshal was likewise Deputy Proctor, and he held the post of Deputy Auctioneer as well. Gradually the whole machinery of fraud came to light, the interlocking functions through which the same official could place money in his own pocket under such headings as 'fees paid by the Proctor to the Marshal'.

When Jackson arrived to arrest him, Cochrane warned him that his exercise of the office of Marshal was rendered illegal by his tenure of that of Proctor, and that if he dared to lay a finger on him, Jackson would be treated as a private individual without authority, committing an assault. It transpired that Jackson's double appointment was not even known in England, still less endorsed there; he prudently refrained from pushing his luck any farther with Cochrane.

If Dr Sewell had possessed any flair for analogy, he might by now have read the writing on the wall that had replaced what was missing from his lavatory door. But he evidently knew nothing of Cochrane's capacity for following through any undertaking on which he embarked to its ultimate goal—the capacity which his fellow Member for Westminster lacked in common with the majority of mankind. Judge Sewell listened to Marshal Jackson's excuses for not having executed the arrest warrant, and then impatiently summoned Deputy Marshal Chapman to carry it out instead. This time Cochrane was able to improve on his retort to Jackson. Chapman, he informed him, was not merely deprived of any authority because he held two offices illegally; he was also guilty of combining these with the post of Deputy Auctioneer, which he exercised on behalf of a sinecurist in London who lived opulently on two-thirds of the prize court fees won by seamen on active service in war. Gradually Cochrane was plumbing the depths of the cesspool.

He kept his friends in the fleet constantly informed of every development and there was not a seaman in Valletta harbour who did not watch with delight and expectancy for the next move in this exciting game. For 2 days, then 3, those who had shore leave could observe Cochrane going about Malta with impunity while Deputy Marshal Chapman, bolder than Jackson, followed him like a shadow. Judge Sewell found himself an object of increasing ridicule but could not think of any means of extricating himself. Finally he ordered Chapman to arrest Cochrane on pain of being committed to prison himself for neglecting to carry out the orders of the court. Chapman responded by resigning from the post of Deputy Marshal, and thus inspired the solution which Dr Sewell had previously sought in vain. A man of the name of Stevens, unconnected with any other official position, was appointed in his place with the most careful formality, and then sent to serve the order of arrest on Lord Cochrane.

Cochrane happened to be visiting the naval Commissioner when Stevens arrived with his warrant, and he accepted it at once. He was particularly satisfied to discover that it was signed by Jackson, for this oversight provided the evidence he needed of Jackson's illegal exercise of plural functions. At Stevens' request he was taken to an inn, where he was informed that he would be allowed to remain on parole. Cochrane replied that he had no intention of offering his parole, and that if the authorities wished to detain him, they could only do so by placing him in the town gaol. The embarrassed Stevens suggested that in this case they had better proceed there.

'No,' Cochrane replied. 'I will be no party to an illegal imprisonment of myself. If you want me to go to gaol, you must carry me by force, for assuredly I will not walk.' The inn was filled with naval officers all watching with the greatest hilarity the difficulties of the wretched Stevens. First he sent for a carriage, then he found he would require a picket of Maltese soldiers as well, to lift Cochrane bodily in the chair in which he was sitting and deposit it in the carriage with his prisoner.

While ridicule continued to mount in the fleet at the expense of the men who had been robbing them for so long with impunity, Judge Sewell began to discover what a costly mistake he had made by committing Cochrane to prison. He was given comfortable quarters on the top floor where the jailor, 'a simple worthy man, civilly enquired what I would please to order for dinner'. But he was not facing a Burdett, one who would lose his nerve at the last moment. 'Nothing,' replied his prisoner. 'As you are no doubt aware, I have been placed here on an illegal warrant, and I will not pay for so much as a crust; so that if I am starved to death, the Admiralty court will have to answer for it.' At this the worthy turnkey stood aghast for a few moments, then rushed to report Cochrane's words to Marshal Jackson who had shewn earlier how easily he could crumble when he was intimidated. This time his panic led him into an expensive error of judgment. He gave the gaoler an order to a neighbouring hotel-keeper to supply Cochrane with whatever he chose and within the hour his prisoner had in his hands the necessary authority to banquet every officer in Malta at the expense of the Admiralty prize court. There followed days and nights of feasting, 'at what cost to the Admiralty court I never learned nor enquired; but from the character of our entertainment the bill when presented must have been almost as extensive as their own fees. All my friends in the squadron present at Malta were invited by turns, and assuredly had no wardroom fare. They appeared to enjoy themselves the more heartily as avenging their own wrongs at the expense of their plunderers.'

The officials who were being made such a laughing stock at the same time as they were being relentlessly exposed appealed to the Governor of Malta to persuade Cochrane to surrender the table of fees, so that he could be released. To His Excellency the Governor Cochrane replied that since he had been imprisoned illegally he must insist on being brought to trial, and this was accordingly arranged as a last desperate expedient on 2 March. Nearly every commanding officer in the Navy present at Valletta accompanied Cochrane to the court to hear two clerks, one a German and the other Maltese, depose that they had seen a man whom they believed to have been Lord Cochrane in possession of a folded paper. Their evidence was enlarged into the fabrication that Cochrane had entered the court registry and stolen it from there.

Cochrane pleaded waggishly that since the table of charges was required by statute to be displayed in open court, it was impossible that he could have taken it from the registry or anywhere else. He also demanded the right to cross-question his accusers, who were nowhere to be seen. Judge Sewell retaliated by ruling that Cochrane should instead answer his own questions, at which his prisoner protested that the entire proceedings were illegal. The astuteness of all his previous moves was in fact matched by the skill with which he pleaded his case in court, so that in the end the Judge tried to withdraw from a losing battle by inviting the accused to go free on bail. Cochrane refused, until his case should be properly tried.

There is no saying how the deadlock would have been broken, had not Cochrane's naval friends intervened. Their concern was the growing restiveness of the seamen in the port as they watched the treatment of their hero at the hands of men they detested. The officer in command at Malta was Captain Rowley, one of three officers of that name who attained the rank of Admiral during this period. One day he visited Cochrane in his prison and said:

'Lord Cochrane, you must not remain here. The seamen are getting savage, and if you are not out soon they will pull the gaol down, which will get the naval force into a scrape. Have you any objection to making your escape?'

'Not the least,' replied Cochrane, 'and it may be done. But I will neither be bailed nor will I be set at liberty without a proper trial.' So it was arranged that the bars on the windows should be filed away, which took 3 or 4 days—and nights. Then, after a farewell night of feasting, 'I passed a double rope round an iron bar, let myself down from the three-storey window, pulled the rope after me so that nothing might remain to excite suspicion, and bade adieu to the merriest prison in which a seaman was ever incarcerated.' A gathering of naval officers was waiting beside the *Eagle*'s gig at the quay to say good-bye. Cochrane remembered that it was an exceptionally dark night, the sea smooth as glass. The gig rowed him to a packet bound for England, where he arrived a full month before the officials of the Maltese Admiralty court could lodge their own version of events. He even found time on his way to delight the Gibraltar garrison with the tale of his adventures.

Many people, from that day to this, have shaken their heads over the escapade, scolding Cochrane for behaviour that was undignified, harmful to his personal career, or barren in its result. But it can also be seen as the only work of art he executed on land and in a civil capacity comparable to all of those he performed at sea and as acts of war, which give him his place among the incomparable human beings of the world.

As for the report he brought to the House of Commons, it did force the Admiralty to give an undertaking that the matter would be investigated although its spokesmen added in Parliament to the lies forwarded to them from Malta. In the course of his submission Cochrane was at last able to give appropriate publicity to the episode which proved that there was absolutely nothing to which the Maltese officials would not stoop—the case of the ship *King George* which he had captured in the *Impérieuse* after members of the boarding party had been treacherously shot at, killed and wounded. This vessel had actually operated for the profit of British government servants, who secured an adjudication in the Maltese Admiralty court which left Cochrane 600 crowns in debt. Indulging his taste for pranks, he unrolled the account along the floor of the House of Commons until it extended from one end of the chamber to the other. This was a sample of the Proctor-Marshal's self-remunerating work, he explained.

'This Proctor acts in the double capacity of Proctor and Marshal, and in the former capacity fees himself for consulting and instructing himself as counsel, jury and judge, which he himself represents in the character of Marshal; so that all those fees are for himself in the one character, and paid to the same himself in the other.'

Cochrane picked out items from the document that lay at the feet of his audience. Here, he indicated, was an article in which the court had deducted 50 crowns and charged 35 crowns for doing it. Then he turned to other evidence in support of his indictment: 'A vessel was valued at 8608 crowns: the Marshal received 1% for delivering her, and in the end the net proceeds amounted to no more than 1900 crowns out of 8608. All the rest had been embezzled and swallowed up by the prize court.' This time the Member of Parliament who was also an Admiralty Judge, Sir William Scott, did not clash with the Treasurer of the Navy in an attempt to discredit the evidence Cochrane had laid before them. He left that to his brother, who sat on the Woolsack in the House of Lords.

John Scott, Lord Eldon, had first become Lord Chancellor in 1801, and it was thought that his violent opposition to Catholic emancipation had much to do with the appointment. Two other motives governed his life, the preservation of his own power and opposition to change of any kind. Almost the only laws he helped to place on the statute book were those that empowered the government to coerce the public, and it was Lord Eldon who denied to Byron the protection of the law of copyright on the grounds that his poetry was too blasphemous. By the time of Cochrane's return in 1811 Lord Eldon swayed the Cabinet of nonentities almost as though he had been Prime Minister himself, and he continued to do so until Canning became Premier 16 years later and Eldon at last resigned from the post of Lord Chancellor that he had held for so long. From the Woolsack Lord Eldon described Cochrane's disclosures magisterially, in the tuneful voice that a Northumbrian burr made more attractive still, as 'a species of mummery never before witnessed within these walls, and altogether unbecoming the gravity of that branch of the legislature'. The more popular Cochrane became with officers and men in the British Navy and with the people of Westminster, the more enemies he made in high places; the more effectively he crusaded, the greater the menace he represented in their eyes.

Cochrane now turned his attention to the seamen serving in the lower decks, whose conditions had hardly improved since they provoked the mutinies of Spithead and the Nore. Not only was their pay still inadequate, which had been one of their original grievances, but they did not receive it until they returned from foreign service. This hardship was increased by the inordinately long periods that some ships spent at sea.

'I have in my hands,' Cochrane rose to announce one day in the House, 'a list of ships of war in the East Indies. The *Centurion* has been there eleven years, the *Rattlesnake* fourteen years, came home the other day with only one man of the first crew. Not one farthing of pay has been given all that period to all those men. I have made a calculation on the *Fox* frigate, and supposing only one hundred of the men returned, there would be due to the crew £25,000, not including the officers. What has become of these sums all the while? The interest ought to be accounted for to Government or to the seamen themselves. The *Wilhelmina* has been ten years, the *Russell* seven years, the *Drake* six years—of which the men will be exiles from England for ever— and another vessel four years.' This is another speech comparable in quality to his masterpiece on the subject of naval pensions. 'The seamen,' Cochrane pointed out, 'from want of their pay have no means of getting many necessaries of the utmost consequence to their health and comfort.'

Charles Yorke, who had replaced Lord Mulgrave as First Lord, held that office for less than 2 years with almost as little distinction as his predecessor, but it was long enough to enable him to dismiss Cochrane's evidence with the excuse that it was too late in the session to consider such details. 'As to ships being detained so long upon foreign and distant stations,' he observed, 'it is much to be regretted, but it is often unavoidable.' How often, the First Sea Lord showed not the faintest inclination to find out.

Cochrane espoused another cause that was a particular concern of his friend Samuel Whitbread, pioneer of prison reform. It was one that Captain Edward Brenton, Sir Jahleel's brother, also brought to public notice a little later in his *Life of Lord St Vincent*. 'The charge of sick and wounded prisoners of war,' he wrote, 'fell into the hands of a set of villains whose seared consciences were proof against the silent but eloquent pleading of their fellow-creatures—sick and imprisoned for no crime, in a foreign land, far away from their friends and relations.' Cochrane made a visit to Dartmoor where one of the prisoner-of-war camps lay, and when he was refused admittance he climbed a neighbouring hill in an attempt to make a plan of the prison and to observe what went on inside it. With what evidence he could gather, despite the deliberate obstruction offered to a Member of Parliament pursuing a humanitarian objective without any political motive, he returned to address the House of Commons.

'The health of the prisoners has suffered by exposure to heavy rains whilst standing in an open space for several hours receiving provisions issued at a single door; the cooking-room being several hundred yards from the prison, which now contains six thousand prisoners divided into messes of six.' Cochrane must have stood in the same heavy rain making those calculations. 'Consequently one thousand are soaked through in the morning, attending to their breakfast, and one thousand more at dinner. Thus a third are consequently wet, many without change of clothes.' His analysis gives some insight into the care he must have taken to look after his own men at sea, in the cramped quarters from which they erupted to perform such prodigies of vitality and valour on his orders.

When his excursions did not take him farther afield, Cochrane divided his time between his new home on Southampton water and that of his uncle Basil in London. Basil Cochrane was the sixth son of the eighth Earl of Dundonald, so that even if the family estate had been more prosperous he could have been expected to earn his own living. At the age of 16 he had been placed on the Madras civil establishment of the East India Company, in which he had succeeded so well that he had been able to live there in sumptuous style. He had returned to Britain in 1807, where he immediately paid all the outstanding debts of his brother the ninth Earl, purchased an estate in Scotland for himself, and made his home at number 12 Portman Square. In it he installed a Turkish bath, which he recommended to others in 1809 in a pamphlet entitled: 'An Improvement in the mode of Administering the Vapour-bath, and in the apparatus connected with it.'

Basil had remained unmarried in India, but he was evidently a gay dog, as the number of illegitimate children he left at his death bears witness. So did his vapour bath, which featured in criminal proceedings during the year 1813. Basil Cochrane had received a series of letters in the previous year, demanding blackmail on the grounds that he had urged a girl to use it as means of procuring an abortion. She was described in the press as 'a very elegant figure and prepossessing countenance, about 26 years of age' and it was disclosed in court that she had been Basil's mistress for about 7 years, and had borne him two children who were then living. It appears that she had since taken a younger lover, who had incited her to fleece the nabob in this manner. Had they not been too greedy, but 'had listened to the overtures made on the part of Mr Cochrane's family, who did not wish the business to come before the public' (as the court was informed), everyone might have been satisfied. As it was, Basil testified 'that he did not believe the steam bath would procure abortion but, on the contrary, would strengthen the mother; that he had shewn it to several medical men who had approved of it', and the culprits were convicted. The establishment at 12 Portman Square sounds a somewhat bizarre home for the chaste young Member of Parliament and naval Captain, but it is clear that his relations with the uncle whom he did not meet until he was over 30 years old were of the friendliest.

From Portman Square Cochrane could ride conveniently to Parliament when it was in session, through a neighbourhood that did not yet contain its Regency architecture although the Regency had by now begun. The building of Regent Street commenced in 1813, Belgrave Square was completed in 1825. Between Hyde Park Corner and Chelsea there still lay open ground while many of London's million inhabitants had not yet moved away from the crowded city. In Portman Square Cochrane's uncle lived in the fashionable outskirts of that world of wealth and fashion which Beau Brummell still dominated and Byron was about to take by storm with his poetry and his personality. It was not the west end of Nash that Cochrane saw when he visited Sir Francis Burdett or Samuel Whitbread or the Houses of Parliament, but one still dominated by the magnificent buildings of Henry Holland. The residence he had designed for the Prince of Wales facing St James's Park was considered by Horace Walpole to be the most perfect palace in Europe, and opposite to Carlton House, between Whitehall and the Park, stood his enlarged Melbourne House, now transformed into the Scottish Office. Between St James's Palace and Piccadilly ran that main artery of the world of fashion, St James's Street, in which Lord Byron took up his residence when he came to London. Several of the buildings that Cochrane saw there still remain, including the premises of those exclusive clubs, Brooks' and White's.

The people who stepped out of these elegant buildings into their carriages or strolled about in their fashionable clothes were assailed by the dust and filth of unpaved streets. At night they faced the dangers of dim street lighting or no lighting at all, aggravated by the fogs that so many chimneys generated. What London needed were the two inventions that Cochrane's father had made at Culross, tar to cover the streets and gas to light them. But Cochrane's own ideas about this matter were pushed to the back of his mind by another of such appalling consequence that for a time he did not dare mention it to anybody.

During his active service he had invented a succession of devices to meet immediate emergencies: barbed wire, explosive torpedoes, convoy

T.S.W.—K

lights, kites to drop propaganda leaflets over enemy territory. It was in relative tranquillity that he thought of an equivalent of the modern nuclear deterrent and was faced with the moral dilemma which it presented. On 2 March his Memorial of that date was sent to the Prince Regent, imparting the secret to him. The Regent swiftly appointed a select committee to investigate Cochrane's invention in utter secrecy. Its members were the Regent's brother the Duke of York, who had been bedevilled by such an indiscreet mistress; Cochrane's former chief in the Mediterranean, Admiral Lord Keith; Admiral Lord Exmouth, who had recently been appointed to the Mediterranean command with its responsibility for watching Toulon; and William Congreve, Cochrane's colleague of Aix Roads when he had brought his rockets there in the *Aetna*. Of all of these men Congreve most nearly resembled Cochrane himself as an inventor. The son of a Lieutenant General and heir to a baronetcy, he was a favourite of the Regent's, to whom he had been appointed Equerry in the previous year when he was also elected a Fellow of the Royal Society. Cochrane's invention had brought the dangerous radical, the shunned outsider, back into the bosom of the Establishment overnight.

Upon its effectiveness the committee were agreed: what they had to decide was whether it was too inhuman to use, a dilemma which haunted Cochrane all his life. The case for its use he put like this: 'No conduct that brought to a speedy termination a war which might otherwise last for years, and be attended by terrible bloodshed in numerous battles, could be called inhuman . . . The most powerful means of averting all future war would be the introduction of a method of fighting which, rendering all vigorous defence impossible, would frighten every nation from running the risk of warfare at all.'

For the device which had entered the mind of Cochrane, inspired by his observations of the collateral effects of the Sicilian sulphur industry the previous year, a phenomenon immediately impressing on his fertile mind its adaptation to warlike purposes, was poison gas.

His most incisive description of it was this: 'All fortifications, especially marine fortifications, can under cover of dense smoke be irresistibly subdued by fumes of sulphur kindled in masses to windward of their ramparts.' This would not have been as lethal as the mustard gas of the Germans, and it also comprehended the new device of the smoke screen which his countrymen did use in the following century with gratifying effect.

The committee reported Cochrane's ideas to be 'so perfectly new to us that we cannot venture an opinion'. Congreve considered them technically sound, and Keith invited Cochrane to prepare a plan for their experimental use against the French naval base at Toulon. But Cochrane was opposed to disclosing his terrible secret to the enemy except with overwhelming effect and he submitted a plan which relied on the use of explosive torpedoes. Admiral Exmouth rejected it, and there the matter ended, except that the responsible manner in which Cochrane had acted and the fresh powers of invention he had displayed restored some of the respect he had lost in official eyes. In June 1812 new elections were held and the voters of Westminster renewed their compliment by returning him again as one of their Members.

And it was at about this time that he happened to set eyes on a 16-year-old girl who was walking through Hyde Park in a school crocodile and fell in love with her. The real identity of Katherine Corbett Barnes remains something of a mystery, but it is conjectured that she was the daughter of a business-man, of the surname she used, by a Spanish dancer. Cochrane called her 'the orphan daughter of an honourable Midland family' and it was certainly as an orphan that she was brought up by her guardian in Portland Place. Years later she was to write to Cochrane: 'How much more happy should I have been had I been brought up under the affectionate eyes of a fond Mother, rather than by relations who only felt for me in the moment of childhood and left me to support in ignorance and poverty my growing years.' The young girl and the man 20 years her senior possessed, in fact, remarkably similar backgrounds. Both had been deprived of maternal love when they were young, and had grown up in financial insecurity without an education to meet the demands of their natural intelligence. The fact that one was heir to an earldom, the other perhaps a foreign dancer's bastard, was not of the least consequence compared with so much deeper grounds for mutual understanding; nor was Cochrane ever concerned by such considerations, the mainsprings of so many people's lives.

Unfortunately for Cochrane his uncle Basil was deeply moved by them, and at least he possessed an altruistic motive in this case. For Cochrane was heir to the impoverished estate which was the fount of his family's position in society, the source of marriage settlements for the girls, of endowments for the young men of his name. Basil Cochrane shared the preoccupation of most people of his class at this time, the honour and prosperity of the dynasty of which he was a cadet, and he had already decided how the earldom of Dundonald could be restored to its ancient splendour. The heir would marry an heiress and he would endow the couple with the fortune he had won for himself in the East Indies. He had already selected Cochrane's wife for him when his nephew fell in love with Kitty Barnes. She was, of all choices, the daughter of an Admiralty court official.

So it was that Thomas Cochrane's courtship of Katherine from his uncle's house in Portman Square was almost as clandestine as that of Romeo and Juliet. How he obtained his first introduction to her can only be guessed but soon he was able to unfold his uncle's plans for his marriage to an heiress. Cochrane's powerful constitution rarely succumbed to physical illness and he seems to have been immune to the ordinary stresses of danger and fatigue. But nervous strain was another matter. One day a servant hurried round to Katherine's home to inform her that Cochrane was gravely ill, and to beg her to walk past 12 Portman Square so that he could look at her through his bedroom window. She did so and saw him there, propped up and looking like a corpse. Such were the pangs of a man who had fallen in love for the first and the last time in his thirty-sixth year.

As soon as he had recovered Katherine agreed to his proposal that they should travel secretly to Scotland where he could contract a legal marriage with her. It was a bold step for such a young girl to take but, as she explained later in life, 'I had no right and I had no reason to doubt the word of the most honourable man I have every known. I loved him.' So on the evening of 6 August Katherine entered a carriage with her servant Ann Moxham and travelled north in it with her bridegroom, while his own servant Richard Carter rode on an outside seat. They travelled night and day, sleeping in their carriage when they felt tired, until Cochrane was able to inform them that they had crossed the border into a land with different marriage laws.

'Well, thank God, we are all right,' he said. He already had a pet name for the exquisite young creature who, compared with him, was so tiny. 'It is all right, Mouse, we are all right now. Moxham, mind you get a comfortable room for Lady Cochrane at the Queensberry Arms. We shall soon be there.' For a while he was silent, then he said, 'You are mine now, and you are mine for ever.'

They arrived at Annan on the evening of the 8th and alighted at the Queensberry Arms, where Cochrane and his bride went to separate rooms. While Katherine washed and tidied herself, Cochrane wrote out the marriage documents, then sent Carter to call the two women. So they solemnized their marriage with their servants as witnesses and as soon as these had been dismissed Cochrane broke into a hornpipe and said again:

'Now you are mine, Mouse, mine for ever.'

'I do not know,' Lady Cochrane answered. 'I have had no parson or church. Is this the way you marry in Scotland?'

'Oh yes,' Cochrane assured her, 'you are mine sure enough. You cannot get away.' Then he became as business-like as though he were back on a quarterdeck. 'I have no time to spare, I have no time to lose, for I must be back on the 10th to my uncle's marriage. He is going to be married and he will be married on the 11th or 12th. I have not a moment's time to lose, and therefore I must leave as fast as I can. I have given all my instructions to Dick, and he will bring you back as soon as he can.'

Then he kissed her and left without conducting her to her room, leaving her in the care of their servants Richard Carter and Ann Moxham. There was no bath to be had at the Queensberry Arms, and so Katherine went directly to her bed, to spend her wedding night alone.

Back in London, Cochrane tried to reconcile his uncle Basil to the choice that he had just made irrevocable. 'Please yourself,' Basil Cochrane warned him. 'Nevertheless, my fortune and the money of the wife I have chosen for you would go far towards reinstating future Earls of Dundonald in their ancient position as regards wealth.' Basil cut his nephew out of his will, but such were the characters of the two men that their close relationship remained in other respects unimpaired. Nor did Cochrane ever regret his sacrifice. 'I did not inherit a shilling of my uncle's wealth, for which loss however I had a rich equivalent in the acquisition of a wife whom no amount of wealth could have purchased.'

Evidently Lady Cochrane's guardian, the man whom Cochrane described as 'her first cousin Mr John Simpson of Portland Place and also of Fairborn House in the county of Kent', was also reconciled to the runaway marriage. As for Kitty, whatever misgivings she may have entertained when she was left alone on her wedding night, after being taken so far for such a strange ceremony, a letter she wrote to the man she called her Ever during a separation 16 years later tells how completely they were laid to rest.

'I am content with the blessings God has been pleased to grant me without wishing for more. Yet I cannot help *informing you* that I am *not stone* and the sooner I find my little head on your bosom the sooner I shall be content. Do not however let this little wish alarm you, or believe that if I were a widow as many years as I have been days that I should seek consolation elsewhere. You know, my Ever, nature will be nature and I am human and you know that little secret.' There was not really much of the mouse in Katherine, but rather the intelligence, beauty and spirit of a Siamese kitten—and she was all woman.

Returning to London in August, Lady Cochrane and her husband were spared any immediate embarrassment from the curiosity of the fashionable world, because it had scattered to its country retreats throughout the length and breadth of Britain. This was the first summer of Byron's London fame, who left a graphic description of that mighty exodus.

> The turnpikes glow with dust: and Rotten Row
> Sleeps from the chivalry of this bright age:
> And tradesmen with long bills and longer faces
> Sigh, as the postboys fasten on the traces.

Society had much to preoccupy it that season, apart from the handsome young peer whom it was preparing to acclaim as the greatest poet since Shakespeare. In March 1812 the Regent's fiftieth birthday had been celebrated in the *Morning Post* by a panegyric poem which described him as an Adonis of Loveliness amongst other extravagances. Leigh Hunt had responded by calling the Prince 'a violator of his word, a libertine over head and heels in debt and disgrace, a despiser of domestic ties, the companion of gamblers and demireps, a man who has just closed half a century without one single claim on the gratitude of his country or the respect of posterity'. These strong words were published in the radical *Examiner*, which was edited by his brother John; and however reprehensible they may now appear, they were by no means exceptional in the time in which they were written. Public figures were often lampooned in such savage language as well as in cartoons of extreme viciousness, and the royal family were not exempt from such attacks.

The Regent was indeed angry, but his domestic life was not just then a suitable theme on which to focus further public attention. His quarrels with his estranged second wife had centred upon their daughter the Princess Charlotte, heir to the throne, and at the very time of the election in June a deplorable episode occurred when the Princess rushed alone out of her father's palace, summoned a hackney carriage, and fled in it to her mother's home. It was not until society had forsaken London (and Cochrane had installed Katherine in his home by Southampton water) that it was considered opportune to make an example of Leigh Hunt and his brother. For words published in March they were charged on 9 December before Lord Ellenborough, who sentenced them to a fine of £500 each and to two years' imprisonment, one in Surrey, the other in Middlesex. By the time the Cochranes returned to London in 1813 the Hunts had replaced Citizen Jones, Burdett and William Cobbett as the martyrs of the day. In the world of literature and the arts the indignation was such that their most distinguished practitioners turned the prisons in which the Hunts were confined into places of pilgrimage.

Leigh Hunt was released on 2 February 1815, so that he was still a prisoner when Cochrane was committed to gaol under sentence of the same judge. But he could have had no inkling of the fate in store for him as he busied himself during 1813 in taking out the first of a succession of patents for gas lamps, based on his father's patent of 1781. It was his intention that the streets of Westminster should be lit twice as brightly by half the number of lamps. He also continued his experiments for the improvement of convoy lamps at sea, for although Wellington was fighting his victorious way across Spain throughout this year and entered France in October, Britain had meanwhile gone to war with the United States of America.

In the new year of 1814 Admiral Sir Alexander Cochrane was appointed to the command of the North American station, and he invited his nephew to accompany him as his Flag Captain. Happily married, his affairs prosperous, Cochrane would even be able to resume his naval career. The cup of his happiness was brimful at the moment when it was dashed from his lips.

CHAPTER SEVEN

Downfall

The war with the United States was another of the British government's monumental blunders, into which the Ministry fell by degrees through a combination of arrogance and stupidity.

For some time previously the French and the British had both offered provocations to the new nation of North America, as each sought to injure the commerce of the other by forbidding trade with neutral countries. But British high-handedness took an especially vicious form for she enforced a right of search in American vessels, not merely to inspect the goods they carried, but also to seize their seamen. The conditions of service which Cochrane described in the House of Commons naturally led to wholesale desertion despite the appalling penalties for those who were caught, and the successful deserter's loss of all his back pay. Many of the deserters took service in American vessels.

But a large proportion of their crews consisted of British emigrants who had become American subjects, and it would have been difficult for the press gangs which boarded American vessels to determine which were which, even if they had tried. It has been estimated that about 2500 British seamen succeeded in making their way into the American marine every year, and during the same space British war-ships managed to hi-jack about 1000 seamen from American vessels, sometimes on the high seas, sometimes within brazen gunshot distance of the American coast. The British Minister in the United States gave his government timely warning of the barbarities that were being perpetrated by his countrymen 'in the very harbours and waters of the United States'. Not only was his advice ignored, but timid American protests and ineffectual attempts to protect American ships and sailors merely provoked the reactions of the bully. The ineffable *Morning Post* had suggested as early as 1807 that Britain's former colony ought to be made to see 'her folly by a necessary chastisement of her insolence and audacity'.

A particularly nasty episode occurred when an American ship put to sea and encountered a British vessel commanded by someone who shared the opinions of the *Morning Post*. American seamen were warned to be on their guard and as they became angrier, so it was inevitable that they should also have become trigger-happy. During the spring of 1811 in which Cochrane was disclosing the iniquities of the Maltese prize court, in the very waters in which that British ship had set upon an American one without cause, the American frigate *President* stumbled upon the British sloop *Little Belt* in the dark. The action began almost accidentally but the Americans were taking no chances. The *Little Belt* was knocked to pieces.

It was a portent to which the British government paid no more attention than to their Minister's advice from Washington. They stopped short of a course so ruinous to Britain's commerce and war effort as a declaration of war, but they allowed the tension to mount, hand over hand, until the United States declared war instead on 18 June 1812, when Cochrane was courting Kitty Barnes. There followed 9 months of disaster for British naval power in the Atlantic.

The rejected Mother Country possessed a régime utterly unaware of the quality of seamanship which the United States had acquired through desertion and emigration. The infant nation had not indeed developed yet a strong sense of national unity or patriotism; but a large number of her sailors had stripes on their backs and empty pockets to remind them what they were fighting against, and in 7 months they inflicted greater damage on the morale of the British Navy than it had suffered in 20 years of war against the great powers of Europe. They achieved it in five single-ship actions, the form of warfare of which Cochrane was by now the supreme living exponent.

The fratricidal war continued through 1813, until Wellington's invasion of France brightened the prospect: Britain might soon have her hands free to repay the humiliation she had suffered from her former colonists. The first step towards this objective was the replacement of Admiral Sir John Warren commanding in the Atlantic, a man whom some considered to have been too elderly for the emergency that had been thrust upon him. At the age of 56 Sir Alexander Cochrane was several years younger and he also possessed valuable past experience of the American hemisphere. Hence his appointment early in 1814.

After Lord Cochrane had accepted his uncle's invitation to become his Flag Captain he stayed at the home of his other uncle, Basil in Portman Square, where the sudden change in his future plans involved him in a multiplicity of tasks. In the first place, the flag ship *Tonnant* of 80 guns was being refitted at Chatham, and Admiral Cochrane arranged to leave her for his nephew to sail across the Atlantic when she was ready for sea, while he went on ahead to take up his appointment.

Secondly, Sir Alexander had been ordered to undertake convoy duties whenever opportunity permitted, and this required that his nephew should hurry on the manufacture of the convoy lamps he had designed so that they would be ready by the time he sailed.

He became involved in a third complication by chance, although it did not really concern him. Because it had been reported that the Americans placed sharp-shooters in their masts to fire down upon the seamen of the ships with which they engaged in close combat, Admiral Cochrane accepted a proposal that his own crews should be trained in the same tactics. The instructor recommended to implement it was a former acting adjutant in Lord Yarmouth's regiment of sharp-shooters, a foreigner called Captain de Berenger. After the downfall of the French aristocracy in the revolution, the country was filled with exiles possessing titles of nobility, not all of which were genuine, and de Berenger was among those who somewhat diffidently permitted himself to be addressed as a Baron. Lord Cochrane and his wife happened to be dining at their uncle Basil's table one evening, in company with the Admiral and his wife, when de Berenger was a guest, and the presence of the Admiral is sufficient evidence of the reason why he had been invited.

In ordinary circumstances Cochrane would probably have welcomed such an acquaintance. His relations with foreign officers were almost invariably cordial, and de Berenger was an inventive man like himself. Years later, in 1835, he published a book on the use of firearms in self-defence, and the reason for his presence at that dinner table was one which was bound to arouse Cochrane's professional interest. Yet in spite of the fact that de Berenger found an opportunity to meet him on a second occasion in Basil Cochrane's house (this time the Admiral was not present), and although de Berenger tried to enter into a correspondence with Lord Cochrane concerning his inventions, he was politely rebuffed: 'If you will go to America with me, we will talk on the subject over on the passage,' Cochrane told him. Either Cochrane was too preoccupied already to add to his social commitments, or there was something about de Berenger that he did not like, when he dismissed him in this manner.

There was certainly one concern to overshadow all others. His wife was expecting her first child in April, and he must consequently provide a home in which she could live in London with their baby during his absence. In the middle of February they moved out of Portman Square into the house at 13 Green Street, and here Cochrane spent his hectic days, travelling down to Chatham to inspect the progress of work on the *Tonnant*, visting the factory in Cock Lane in which Mr King was constructing his lamp, and ordering his financial affairs for the support of Lady Cochrane during their absence.

His broker's name was Richard Butt, a man whom he had first met in 1812 when Butt had been a pay clerk at Portsmouth dockyard and had doubtless made Cochrane's acquaintance during his residence at Hamble. It was on Butt's advice that Cochrane began investing in government securities in October 1813, and he then instructed Butt to sell in the event of a one per cent rise in the value of the shares. There was a reasonable prospect of such a rise as Wellington's invasion of France steadily increased the likelihood of Napoleon's downfall.

There was a statutory prohibition on selling stock for which the holder had not yet paid, designed to prevent speculators from earning profits from transactions which they did not possess the means to underwrite, though in practice this rule was largely ignored by brokers. On 12 February, just as Cochrane was preparing to move from Portman Square to Green Street, he contracted Butt to purchase £100,000 of Omnium, and by the 21st he had increased these holdings to £139,000. As soon as they rose in value by over one per cent, Richard Butt sold them in accordance with the instructions he had been given the previous autumn. The total profit to Cochrane was £2,470—nothing compared to what it might have been if he had been able to foretell an event which suddenly sent share prices leaping.

But there were others who were well able to foresee such a rise and they included Cochrane's uncle Andrew Cochrane Johnstone, Richard Butt with whom he also had dealings on the stock exchange, and Captain de Berenger. Having succeeded in recommending himself to Admiral Cochrane as a sharp-shooter and failed to ingratiate himself with Lord Cochrane as an inventor, de Berenger had succeeded in passing himself off on Andrew Cochrane Johnstone as a financial wizard. The motive which drove de Berenger to these shifts was insolvency: for the previous 9 months he had been lodging with a family of the name of Davidson 'within the Rules of the King's Bench' as it was called when such a man was allowed to live freely within a restricted area, his host standing surety for his debts should he abscond. He was now pinning his hopes on a family which enjoyed genuine nobility, two seats in the House of Commons, considerable wealth and an ability to offer him immediate professional employment. Happily for what de Berenger had in mind, it also contained one rogue who was willing to conspire with him in his plan to solve his financial problems.

This was the uncle who had accompanied William Cobbett to Plymouth to help persuade Cochrane to stand as candidate for Honiton nearly six years earlier, Andrew Cochrane Johnstone. Like de Berenger he was in financial difficulties, but unlike him he was immune from arrest as Member of Parliament for the rotten borough of Grampound. He possessed a home in Great Cumberland Street and property on the site now occupied by Madame Tussaud's wax-work museum which de Berenger offered him suggestions for developing profitably. Whatever else he proposed, Cochrane Johnstone now purchased government stock on an immensely larger scale than his nephew had done, and so did Richard Butt their broker, as a comparison of the figures demonstrates:

	Omnium	Consols
Lord Cochrane	£139,000	
A. Cochrane Johnstone	£410,000	£100,000
Richard Butt	£224,000	£168,000

Under instructions that Cochrane had given to Butt the previous autumn and never altered he stood to gain, on a one per cent rise, about double the amount he had spent on his wine bill for the *Tonnant*. Should there be a fall, he could easily meet his liabilities. For the other two men it was the jack-pot or ruin, and 23 February was settlement day.

At 1 a.m. on the morning of the 21st the landlord of the Packet Boat inn at Dover heard a knocking on the door of the Ship inn across the street and peered with friendly rivalry to see what was going on there. He observed that it was opened by a man wearing a red coat ornamented with a star order, a man who did not whisper his business in the depths of the night. On the contrary, he called resonantly for a post-chaise with four horses, and also for an express horse and rider to be sent instantly to Admiral Foley at Deal. The stranger thereupon entered the Ship inn, announcing that he was Lieutenant Colonel du Bourg, and sat down to write a letter to Admiral Foley informing him that he had just crossed the Channel with the news that the French had been defeated and Napoleon killed. After leaving the room with his letter lying open on the table for all to read, du Bourg returned to despatch it to the Admiral before setting off immediately by coach to London. Admiral Foley operated a semaphore system which passed messages from station to station until they reached the roof of the Admiralty, so that he would be able to send the news much faster than du Bourg would be able to bring it by coach. Since it was confidently expected that Paris would soon fall to the allies the news would cause delight, but not astonishment.

There was fog in the southern counties on the morning of 21 February, as a result of which the news had not reached London by signal before Colonel du Bourg entered Lambeth at nine o'clock. But rumours accompanied him and although they began to give way to doubts towards midday when the Lord Mayor had still received no official confirmation, these were dissipated by the appearance of a coach drawn across London Bridge by four horses decorated with laurels, and carrying three French officers with white cockades in their hats. The price of Omnium rose to 32 and did not fall to its original level of 26½ until 2 days later. Yet Butt sold Lord Cochrane's entire holdings, as he had been instructed, when they had risen a mere 1¼ per cent, thus forfeiting a fortune and proving beyond question that Cochrane could not have been a party to the hoax that had been perpetrated.

That morning Cochrane had breakfasted with his uncle Andrew and Richard Butt, a pleasant social custom among early risers that has since fallen regrettably into disuse. He then travelled with them to the stock exchange by carriage, and after dropping them there continued to his lamp factory in the city. He could not possibly have received the slightest intimation of du Bourg's news by the time he arrived to consult with Mr King about his convoy lights, and a man who based every stratagem on secrecy and surprise would not have chosen that morning for a public demonstration of his relationship with two men who were his partners in a criminal conspiracy.

Suddenly Cochrane was interrupted at the tin factory in Cock Lane by the arrival of a servant bringing an unsealed message. It informed him that a visitor had come to his house who wished urgently to see him. If Cochrane had asked the servant for a description of the man, he would have learned that he was a foreigner wearing some form of regimentals. It entered his mind with misgivings that the stranger might be bringing him news of his brother Major William Cochrane, who had been ill in Spain since January. The previous news was that there was little hope of recovery. Cochrane hurried home to discover that the man waiting for him in his parlour was Captain de Berenger.

All his life Cochrane preserved a reputation for courtesy to everybody who visited him, whether in a ship or on shore, and seldom could his politeness have been tested more severely than when he discovered who was now wasting his time. De Berenger was in a high state of agitation as he explained to Cochrane that he was in danger of arrest for a debt of £8000, and begged to go aboard the *Tonnant* at once. Cochrane replied that this was impossible without the consent of the Admiralty. De Berenger then confessed that the uniform he was wearing might lead to his identification and arrest, and asked Cochrane to lend him civilian clothes to conceal it. Since Green Street lay outside the area in which de Berenger was permitted to wander under the restriction of the King's Bench rules, the request possessed a plausible explanation. Had Cochrane been previously aware that de Berenger was du Bourg, perpetrator of the stock exchange hoax, had he possessed any means of divining it at that moment, this interview and its outcome would have been inconceivable. Never in his life did Cochrane take part in a plan that was not properly constructed in every detail, or fail to find an instant solution for every emergency. Only complete innocence could have led him to fetch a hat and a black coat for de Berenger to wear as he left the house and stepped into the very carriage in which Cochrane had driven from the city.

On the 22nd, when it was clear that the value of shares had been affected by the spreading of a false rumour on the previous day, the Committee of the Stock Exchange appointed a body to investigate the matter, while *The Times* reflected the public indignation over the trick played by the mysterious Colonel du Bourg. 'If this person should be recognised he will probably be willing to save himself from the whipping post by consigning his employers to the pillory, an exaltation which they richly merit and which, if indicted for conspiracy, they would doubtless attain.'

Investigation disclosed the large sales of shares by Butt and Cochrane Johnstone, and the lesser but still considerable sales of Lord Cochrane's shares. It was discovered that smaller sales had been made by Holloway and Sandom, wine merchants, and also by Alexander M'Rae, and this led to their identification as the men who had driven through London dressed as French officers. On 4 March the Committee of the Stock Exchange offered a reward for information leading to the identification and capture of Colonel du Bourg, and but for de Berenger's incompetence in visiting Cochrane's house, it might never have been claimed. On 8 March Cochrane obtained leave of absence from Chatham, where he had spent much of his time since the fatal 21st, in order to make an affidavit concerning the events of that day.

Cochrane believed all his life that he was responsible for identifying de Berenger with du Bourg in his affidavit, and indeed there is no obvious means by which he could ever have learned otherwise. But a few days earlier someone else did come forward with the information, and received the reward for it. The most likely candidate is Isaac Davis, a negro servant, who had recently left Cochrane's service but who happened to be at Green Street when de Berenger called there, and could remember him from his visits to Portman Square. He returned almost immediately afterwards to the West Indies, which strengthens the surmise that it was he who collected the reward.

A warrant was issued for de Berenger's arrest on 17 March and he was taken at the port of Leith in Scotland on 8 April. His stratagem had been brilliant in its boldness and simplicity, and yet it had been marred by careless mistakes throughout its execution which would have been unthinkable in such an operation if Cochrane had had any hand in its direction. It also possessed two particular features that would have involved Cochrane's acting completely out of character if he had taken any part in it knowingly. In the first place he had sacrificed his naval career, the first love of his life, in order to stand as the apostle of probity and the enemy of peculation and corruption. Before he could have abetted such a scheme he would have had to abandon the principles for which he had made such a heavy reckoning, merely for something like double the price of a wine bill. And he would have had to be capable of succumbing to such a temptation just after he had turned down an heiress and suppressed his invention of poison gas in the public interest. Secondly, the conspiracy involved hoaxing an Admiral into telegraphing false news for monetary gain, and it would have been equally out of character for a naval officer with Cochrane's respect for the service to be a party to such a despicable trick.

All the real culprits had been caught, the three bogus French officers with their white cockades, the counterfeit colonel with his news from France, Richard Butt and Andrew Cochrane Johnstone who needed urgently to sell their stock at a profit before settlement day on 23 February. Lord Cochrane's accidental association with these men did not provide the necessary criminal evidence upon which an impartial court would have been able to convict him, neither has the most painstaking research ever brought such evidence to light from that day to this. But the government had been presented with an opportunity, as though by the hand of providence, to discredit the man who had been discrediting the government, to drag down the national hero who had previously been beyond their power to attack. John Croker wrote to Cochrane in March, informing him that the Lords of the Admiralty were not satisfied with the explanations in his affidavit. He offered to amplify them and was snubbed for his pains while the Attorney General prepared what amounted to a government prosecution of the Sea Wolf, just when he was about to return to his true profession at last.

In the *Weekly Register*, on 21 March, William Cobbett sprang to the defence of the three men who were now being judged guilty of the stock exchange hoax in advance of any trial—Richard Butt, Andrew Cochrane Johnstone and Lord Cochrane. 'Under no wild democracy,' he fulminated, 'under no military despotism, under no hypocritical or cunning oligarchy, under no hellish tyranny upheld by superstition, was there ever committed an act more unjust or more foul than that which has during the last three weeks been committed in the City of London, through the means of the Press against these three gentlemen.' His *Rural Rides* makes better reading than this, but Cobbett's words raise a further question of the utmost importance concerning Cochrane's character.

William Cobbett preserved all his life a consistent record as a fearless opponent of dishonesty, and he suffered more than once for his courage. He was among Cochrane's closest friends, a man whose respect Cochrane would not have forfeited lightly. During the 3 weeks to which Cobbett referred he must have consulted Cochrane before he wrote those words, and if Cochrane had been guilty of criminal conspiracy he must either have set out deliberately to deceive Cobbett, or Cobbett must have entered with him into the same conspiracy. Since neither alternative is conceivable, it follows that up to the moment of their publication, which was over a fortnight before the arrest of de Berenger at Leith, Cochrane shared Cobbett's belief that his uncle and his broker were as innocent as he was.

The most significant mystery that remains unsolved in this whole affair is exactly when and how Cochrane first discovered that his uncle was guilty, and to what shifts he was consequently driven by his intense feeling of family loyalty. Over 40 years later, after Cochrane's rehabilitation, Andrew Cochrane Johnstone's daughter Elizabeth, Dowager Lady Napier, wrote to him: 'O my dear Cousin, let me say once more while you are still here, how ever since that miserable time I have felt that you suffered for my poor Father's fault—how agonising that conviction was—how thankful I am that *tardy justice* was done you —may God restore you fourfold for your generous tho' misplaced confidence in him and for all your subsequent forbearance.' Her words make it plain that she had always known Cochrane to be the innocent victim of her father's guilt, and that when he discovered this guilt his sense of family loyalty remained paramount.

On 18 April, amidst all the anxiety and turmoil, Lady Cochrane gave birth to her first child and it was a son. In St George's Church, Hanover Square, he was baptised Thomas Barnes, heir to an ancient title over which hung the shadow of dishonour. His mother confessed after five children had been born to her that childbirth was no trifling matter for her, but none of her confinements can have imposed a greater strain on her spirits than this one in 1814, when she was an 18-year-old girl reaching the end of her first pregnancy in an atmosphere of impending catastrophe. Just over a week later, on the 27th, her husband was indicted with the conspirators in the stock exchange hoax. Their case would be heard before Lord Chief Justice Ellenborough, and the man briefed as prosecuting solicitor was Germain Lavie, who had played an obedient and disgraceful part in the Gambier court-martial.

The trial opened at 9 o'clock in the morning of 8 June at the Guildhall. The Admiralty had suspended Cochrane from his naval duties and appointed an acting Captain in his place, but in those days the accused was not allowed to give evidence and he did not attend the court. Neither did his uncle, who had fled the country. Among counsel who represented them were James Scarlett, a future Lord Chief Baron of the Exchequer; Henry Brougham, a future Lord Chancellor; and William Best, a future Chief Justice of the Common Pleas. These were formidable witnesses to the manner in which the trial was conducted and to the nature of the evidence on which the verdict was given. Like all those Captains at Gambier's court-martial who would one day become Admirals, these barristers would become the judges of a reformed age and then they would speak their minds.

The case against Cochrane centred on the part he had played in providing de Berenger with a disguise when he was masquerading as Colonel du Bourg. He had been seen at Dover wearing a scarlet uniform with a star, and this very costume had been dredged up from the Thames, cut into fragments, before the trial started. Cochrane deposed that when de Berenger visited Green Street he was wearing a green one, which might simply have indicated that he had found time to change into the costume of Lord Yarmouth's regiment, either in the coach in which he travelled to London, or at one of the post-houses at which he stopped on the way. Alternatively the explanation might have been that all Cochrane saw of the regimental dress was a green collar emerging from his great-coat, for these collars were then absurdly high and frequently of a different colour from the remainder of the jacket. If Cochrane were innocent, he would hardly have been likely to give his attention to such details in the circumstances in which he met his visitor. But if he were guilty, it could appear that he had committed perjury in his affidavit in an attempt to prove that de Berenger in the green uniform could not have been du Bourg in the scarlet one. This was the explanation that the prosecution laid before the jury despite the fact that Cochrane's affidavit would have provided the only evidence that de Berenger was du Bourg if no one else had come forward as a witness of his visit to Green Street, and Cochrane would hardly have countenanced his visit there at all if he had been a party to his charade.

The most important witness to the dress in which de Berenger arrived at Green Street was the driver of the hackney carriage, a youth called William Crane who had recently been suspended from driving for 3 months on conviction of cruelty to his horses. The evidence was so shocking that the judges observed they had never heard of a more atrocious case, so it is a wonder he was treated so leniently. Since he was heard to boast before the trial that 'he would swear black was white if well paid for it', it is worth following Crane's subsequent relations with the law. In 1826, when he was still only 33 years old, he was sentenced to 7 years' transportation for theft, so that it is odd to find him discharged in 1830, upon a petition to the Secretary of State, and enabled to drive his father's hackney carriage again. Such was the career of the youth whose evidence helped to destroy Cochrane's.

The prosecution spent all day presenting its case against every defendant lumped together as a single group of conspirators—the three counterfeit French officers, the bogus colonel, the three shareholders. If the rest were guilty, Cochrane would fall with them. The Guildhall was packed with spectators, and large crowds had gathered outside despite the junketings that were in progress in the west end of London, for the public could recognise evidence of system as easily as the law did and remembered the fate of Citizen Jones and Sir Francis Burdett, William Cobbett and Leigh Hunt. They were eager to discover how the administration had succeeded in framing a man more obnoxious to them than any of these.

The rival spectacle would have emptied the public galleries in the Guildhall had Ellenborough and his jury been deciding anything less exciting than the fate of Lord Cochrane. For by this time Paris had fallen to the allies and on the day of the trial the sovereigns of Russia and Prussia arrived in London to celebrate their victory with that lover of pageantry, the Prince Regent. As usual the revelry was somewhat marred by the Regent's troubles with his womenfolk. His estranged wife Princess Caroline presented the greatest hazard, since she was as popular with the public as her husband was detested, and there was no metropolitan police to control public demonstrations in those days. The Prince's reigning mistress, the Marchioness of Hertford, proved to be another source of embarrassment. He had installed her with a refinement of cruelty to his canonical wife Mrs Maria Fitzherbert, compelling Mrs Fitzherbert to act as her companion for the sake of propriety until that long-suffering woman could stand no more of it.

Lady Hertford was a woman of ostentatious piety, and careful of her personal reputation, so that it was necessary for the Regent to give careful thought to the means of securing for her a respectful reception from the royal visitors. As soon as the Emperor of all the Russias reached London, the Regent appointed Lady Hertford's son Lord Yarmouth to him as his personal aide. The device failed: Tsar Alexander snubbed his aide's mother at the very first encounter. To make matters worse, it would have been impossible for Lord Yarmouth to avoid attending the Guildhall as a witness, to explain his association with de Berenger.

Here the prosecution were elaborating their second scrap of circumstantial evidence against Cochrane with great emphasis. When de Berenger was apprehended at Leith many bank notes of one pound each were found in his possession, and it was shown in court that these had previously been drawn by Cochrane. Long before Cochrane could explain that he had paid these notes to Richard Butt in settlement of an account, the inference had been planted in the minds of the jury that he had not only provided de Berenger with a disguise in which to make his escape, but also with ready cash for his expenses.

The prosecution case lasted until nearly 10 o'clock at night, when Counsel for the defence asked for an adjournment until the next day before presenting its submissions. Lord Ellenborough refused, and so the defence counsel were compelled to unfold their case before the exhausted jurymen between 10 at night and 3 in the morning.

Ellenborough's ablest apologist could find no better explanation for this monstrous ruling than that he was trying to protect the interests of the man in his court who stood closest to the Prince Regent. Naturally Lord Yarmouth was present: he had an older and a closer association with de Berenger than any of the Cochranes, and it was solely through this association that de Berenger had been able to infiltrate his way past Admiral Cochrane to his brother and nephew. Doubtless Yarmouth's connection with de Berenger was a perfectly proper and professional one, just as Lord Cochrane's might well have been. At the very least it would be necessary for Lord Yarmouth to give evidence about the green uniform of his regiment and about de Berenger's connection with it. He was also asked to give evidence of handwriting. Ellenborough's apologist explained that the Chief Justice could not have permitted the court to rise before the son of the Regent's mistress was able to leave it without a stain on his character, and return to his attendance upon the Russian Tsar.

The national interest, not to mention the cause of justice, might have been better served if Lord Cochrane had been released with similar despatch to sail in the *Tonnant* to the North American station. There is something excessively bizarre about the excuse given for a Judge who kept his court in session half the night, not because it contained his country's greatest sailor at a time when there was a war in progress which had urgent need of his services, but in order to protect a young man who shared the popular odium of the Regent as a member of his set. The following day Lord Ellenborough did what he could in his directions to the jury, to transfer the odium to one of the most popular men in London by securing his conviction on charges of peculiarly dishonourable conduct.

At this time John Campbell, who subsequently rose to the office of Lord Chancellor, was keeping the records of jury trials which he published later in four volumes of *Reports*. Lord Campbell described Ellenborough's performance on that day in these words, in the third volume of his *Lives of the Chief Justices*: 'The following day, in summing up, prompted no doubt by the conclusions of his own mind, he laid special emphasis on every circumstance which might raise a suspicion against Lord Cochrane, and elaborately explained away whatever at first sight might seem favourable to the gallant officer. In consequence the jury found a verdict of guilty against all the defendants.'

Another future Lord Chancellor who left an equally severe verdict on this perversion of justice was Henry Brougham, who had been present throughout the trial as Cochrane's defence counsel. Like Campbell, Brougham gave Ellenborough the benefit of the doubt he may have entertained concerning Ellenborough's genuine conviction of Cochrane's guilt, but he added: 'I must however be here distinctly understood to deny the accuracy of the opinion which Lord Ellenborough appears to have formed in this case, and deeply to lament the verdict of guilty which the jury returned after three hours' consultation and hesitation.' Brougham confirmed from his inside knowledge that family loyalty played a major part in Cochrane's downfall, though he did not descend to particulars. 'I take upon me to assert that Lord Cochrane's conviction was mainly owing to the extreme repugnance which he felt to giving up his uncle, or taking those precautions for his own safety which would have operated against that near relation. Even when he, the real criminal, had confessed his guilt by taking to flight, and the other defendants were brought up for judgment, we the Counsel could not persuade Lord Cochrane to shake himself loose from the contamination by giving him up.'

Ellenborough's apologist accused Campbell of inaccuracy and Brougham of political bias, since he was a Whig who would naturally find fault with a Tory administration. But Cochrane's other counsel James Scarlett became a member of the Tory Ministry which opposed the passage of the Great Reform Bill of 1832 before his promotion as Chief Baron of the Exchequer with the title of Lord Abinger. He told Earl Fortescue: 'As one of Lord Cochrane's counsel and fully acquainted with all the facts of the case, I was satisfied of his innocence, and I believe it might have been established to the satisfaction of the jury if the judge had not arbitrarily hurried on the defence at a late hour.' In this case the apologist hinted that Lord Abinger may have been drunk when he uttered his opinion. He had been anticipated by another of his profession, Thomas, Lord Erskine, who had held the office of Lord Chancellor several years before the trial took place, and who wrote to Cochrane after he had triumphed in new fields: 'No man has more sincerely rejoiced than myself at the prosperous results, both to yourself and to the world, which have followed the disgraceful oppression and injustice over which your spirit and talents have enabled you so completely to triumph. I was so sorry at the time that my station at the bar had gone by when you suffered so much in the Courts.' The apologist, never at a loss, suggests that Lord Erskine was jealous of one who had been his rival at the bar.

But however improper the various motives of three contemporary Lord Chancellors and a senior judge who criticised the conduct of the trial and its verdict, they expressed a consensus of opinion all the more devastating for the restraint with which it was worded. When such an opinion was held by these men, it may easily be imagined what sort of reputation Lord Ellenborough enjoyed in the country at large, and it was not until almost a century later that his family attempted to rescue it as an act of piety. One of his grandsons engaged a lawyer who was also a scholar called J. B. Atlay to prove Cochrane's guilt, and the Chief Justice's great-grandson, the fifth Lord Ellenborough, celebrated the centenary of the trial by publishing a book in 1914 suggestively entitled *The Guilt of Lord Cochrane in* 1814. The entire enterprise was misconceived, since the reputation of Lord Chief Justice Ellenborough would not be other than it is if Cochrane had never existed. But the harm would not have extended beyond its perpetrators if their work had not been used by a Judge writing under the pseudonym of Henry Cecil for his book *A Matter of Speculation* which revived the controversy in 1965. Cecil's book is inaccurate in its facts: those of Atlay and Ellenborough are not. But all three make the same fatal admission.

The man whose character was so well documented for posterity, could not have been guilty of the offence of which he was convicted, and so all three authors depict a wholly different kind of character, a man who could and would have committed the offence, and consequently totally unrecognisable as Thomas, Lord Cochrane. Before the third book was published another Lord Chancellor, F. E. Smith, Earl of Birkenhead, had answered all three of them: 'Was he guilty? I cannot—I do not believe that he was. His whole life negatives that suspicion.' It was Cochrane's deepest consolation as he surveyed the ruin of his life that most of his fellow-countrymen thought the same at the time.

His counsel helped him to prepare an appeal for a retrial in which his case would be heard individually. He presented it in person on 14 June before the Judges of the King's Bench, over which Ellenborough presided as Chief Justice. For the first time Cochrane stood before him, arguing his own case before a man whom the procedure of justice required to listen to an appeal against himself and decide it in consultation with his brother judges. They rejected Cochrane's appeal on the grounds that all the defendants in the previous trial were not present. Lord Campbell remarked, 'such a rule had before been laid down, but it is palpably contrary to the first principles of justice and ought immediately to have been reversed'. It was unfortunate for Lord Ellenborough that he had not established a reputation for impartiality on the bench in other cases by the time it fell to his lot to join with his colleagues in quashing an appeal against himself.

Another distinguished judge gave his opinion on the probable outcome of such an appeal. Fitzroy Kelly began studying law 5 years after Cochrane's conviction, and when he had become Lord Chief Baron he reflected: 'I have thought of it much and long during more than forty years, and I am profoundly convinced that, had he been defended singly and separately from the other accused, or had he at the last moment, before judgment was pronounced, applied with competent legal advice and assistance for a new trial, he would have been un-hesitatingly and honourably acquitted. We cannot blot out this dark page from our legal and judicial history.'

On 20 June Cochrane appeared in court again, this time to receive judgment. His conviction made him more blameworthy than any of the other accused. As the prosecuting counsel so rightly emphasised, the most disgraceful element in the charge was that he, a naval officer, should have tried to palm off the false intelligence 'upon that very Board of Government under the orders of which he was then fitting out on an important service, and still more as if to dishonour the profession of which he was a member, he attempted to make a brother officer the organ of that falsehood'. Even if the Admiral at Deal had been the nefarious Sir William Young, rather than Sir Thomas Foley, it would not have excused Cochrane for attempting to trick him in this way.

Before he was sentenced, Cochrane made his only speech to the court. It was a moderate and moving one in which he tore to shreds the thin tissue of circumstantial evidence on which he had been convicted.

'The pretended du Bourg,' he remarked, 'if I had chosen him for my instrument, instead of making me his convenience, should have terminated his expedition and found a change of dress elsewhere. He should not have come immediately and in open day to my house. I should not rashly have invited detection and its concomitant ruin.' But he seems to have realised that he was wasting his time, as he addressed his words to a more distant tribunal.

'I look forward to justice being rendered my character sooner or later; it will come most speedily, as well as gratefully, if I shall receive it at your Lordships' hands. I am not unused to injury; of late I have known persecution; the indignity of compassion I am not yet able to bear. To escape what is vulgarly called punishment would have been an easy thing; but I must have belied my feelings by acting as if I were conscious of dishonour. I cannot feel disgraced while I know that I am guiltless.'

As Captain Marryat observed, Cochrane was no orator but he spoke with dignity even though his words laboured under the stress of his terrible predicament. When he had finished, one of Ellenborough's brother judges sentenced him and those convicted with him to a fine of £1000, to a year's imprisonment, and to stand in the pillory for an hour opposite the Royal Exchange in the City of London. With disgusting alacrity the officials at the Admiralty struck the name of their most gallant officer off the Navy List.

Cochrane's personal misery quickened his sympathy for his uncle Andrew's daughter Elizabeth. He wrote to her from prison on 25 June: 'My dear Eliza—The feelings which you must have experienced, unused as you have been to the lamentable changes of this uncertain life, must have even exceeded that which I have suffered in mind from the unexpected and unmerited ruin in which I am unhappily involved. Shocked as I am, and distressed as I am, yet I feel confidence. God is my judge that the crime imputed to me I did not commit. Had I been accessory to the deception practised on the exchange I should not have protested my innocence in the manner I have done.'

He could assure her of his own innocence: he could give her no such assurance of her father's. 'My dear Eliza, try by all means which your truly religious sentiments and your strength of mind afford to bear up against this dreadful calamity. I am distressed on your account more than on my own; for knowing my innocence, and unable to speak of the private acts of any other, I cannot bring myself to believe that I shall be disgraced and punished without a cause.'

With vociferous loyalty William Cobbett risked a second prison sentence from Lord Ellenborough by filling his *Weekly Political Register* with material in Cochrane's defence. In the House of Commons his friends introduced a motion calling for the records of the trial and Cochrane's statements and affidavits, but the Attorney General replied that this would turn the House into a Court of Appeal. On 5 July something very like it occurred when the Commons debated the expulsion of their two convicted Members.

Cochrane had been released from his prison in the King's Bench in order to attend, and the Speaker directed him to take his usual seat. Andrew Cochrane Johnstone had been summoned also, but information was given that he had been seen last at Calais. The Speaker invited Cochrane to address the House in his own defence and he rose to read his statement from a written paper in his hands. Then, suddenly, the self-command which he had exercised in so many actions and sustained through the increasing strain of the past four months forsook him utterly. He reached his breaking point there, in that pit-like crowded chamber in which he had so often inveighed against the peculations of others, and in which he now stood convicted of far more disgraceful conduct himself. His friends listened appalled as he tossed his prepared statement aside and launched into a tirade which the Speaker himself was unable to restrain. Exactly what he said will never be known because when his storm had blown itself out Lord Castlereagh rose to warn the reporters that if they published his words outside the House they would expose themselves to prosecution for libel. The official report is consequently spattered with asterisks, and it is only possible to guess the language which he heaped upon Lord Ellenborough and his jury.

He did recover his self-command sufficiently to end his speech: 'I solemnly declare before Almighty God that I am ignorant of the whole transaction and uniformly I have heard Mr Cochrane Johnstone deny it also.' In public he remained loyal to his unworthy uncle to the last. What else he had done in an attempt to protect him after discovering his guilt can only be guessed, with the aid of some of the discoveries unearthed by the latter-day sleuths of the Ellenborough family.

After he had sat down, the Leader of the Opposition, George Ponsonby, rose to oppose Cochrane's expulsion from the House and began by observing that his bitterest enemy could not have done more to injure his cause than Cochrane had just done himself. Sir Francis Burdett and Samuel Whitbread remained loyal in their support and the surprising number of forty-four Members voted against his expulsion. Cochrane gratefully preserved their names, while those of the 140 who voted in favour have been lost. Nobody in the House voted against the expulsion of Andrew Cochrane Johnstone.

One of Cochrane's forty-four defenders now gave notice that he would move for the remission of the pillory sentence, on the grounds of Cochrane's outstanding services to his country. The Member's name was Lord Ebrington and he was supported by Lord Nugent, no radicals either of them, but men who were concerned for the reputation of Parliament and the honour of their nation. But in Cochrane's eyes this savoured of pity and 'as for pardon', Creevey the diarist noted, 'he will die sooner than ask for it'. The permanent scars in Cochrane's wounded character had already been exhibited to the assembled House of Commons, and his well-wisher was given another distressing glimpse of them as soon as Cochrane heard of his proposal.

'I had flattered myself,' he wrote to Lord Ebrington on 13 July, 'from a recent note of your Lordship, that in your mind I stood wholly acquitted; and I did not expect to be treated by your Lordship as an object of mercy on the grounds of past services, or severity of sentence.' At least he had recovered his natural dignity. 'If I am guilty, I richly merit the whole of the sentence which has been passed upon me. If innocent, one penalty cannot be inflicted with more justice than another. If your Lordship shall judge proper to persist in the Motion of which you have given notice, I hope you will do me the justice to read this letter to the House.'

Lord Ebrington did both, but the debate on his Motion was delayed during the exciting days in which the electors of Westminster exercised their right to express their own opinion about the expulsion of their Member of Parliament. Byron, enjoying his final year of fame in London, noted that 'Sherry means to stand for Westminster, as Cochrane (the stock-jobbing hoaxer) must vacate. Brougham is a candidate. I fear for poor dear Sherry. Both have talents of the highest order, but the youngster has *yet* a character. We shall see, if he lives to Sherry's age, how he will pass over the redhot ploughshares of public life.' But when Cochrane in his prison accepted an invitation to stand again himself, both Sheridan and Brougham stood down to enable him to be returned unopposed.

Sir Francis Burdett spoke eloquently in his favour at a mass meeting attended by 5000 electors. Burdett had already told his bank manager that it was fortunate none of his stock had been sold on 21 February, otherwise he would probably have shared Cochrane's fate. Now he informed the delighted crowds that if Cochrane should be taken to stand in the pillory, he would accompany him. His promise brought a burst of applause that lasted for many minutes.

At the same public meeting Alderman Wood made a most interesting disclosure. 'I have heard from one of the jury that had evidence since produced been brought forward at the trial, or had Lord Cochrane been in court and made his own defence, it would have been impossible to have found him guilty.' The Alderman and his unnamed juryman were child's play to the Ellenborough scholar who could knock down Lord Chancellors like skittles, but they illustrate the mood of the election. If the Alderman's gossip was merely an election device, it was nothing compared to one of those employed by Cochrane's enemies.

By this time the Chief of the name of Cochrane, that brilliant but impractical inventor the ninth Earl of Dundonald had degenerated into a drunken haunter of taverns. His second wife had died without issue 6 years earlier; her dowry was spent. Culross Abbey and the remainder of his property was sold. On the eve of the election the *Sun* newspaper published a series of accusations that Daft Dundonald was alleged to have uttered in his cups: that he had been left in penury by his affluent son, that he had been kicked downstairs when he tried to warn his son against Uncle Andrew, that the stratagem of Aix Roads had been his own idea although his son had denied him any recognition of it. Even by the standards of political infighting during the Regency such an attack was prodigious, and William Cobbett employed his pen to flay those responsible. Cochrane himself, ever loyal to his father, confined himself to a bare denial of the charges, stating that he had in fact contributed £8000 to his father's support during the previous 10 years.

Cochrane was returned to Parliament once more by the electors of Westminster, while public fury turned upon his persecutors. Once Lord Chancellor Eldon was menaced in his coach by a hostile crowd which mistook him for Ellenborough. It was the pillory sentence which excited the strongest resentment, as Lord Campbell recalled after he had reached the Woolsack. 'The award of this degrading and infamous punishment upon a young nobleman, a Member of the House of Commons, and a distinguished naval officer, raised universal sympathy in his favour. The judge was proportionately blamed, not only by the vulgar, but by men of education on both sides in politics, and he found on entering society and appearing in the House of Lords that he was looked upon coldly. Having now some misgivings himself as to the propriety of his conduct in this affair, he became very wretched.' It has been generally doubted whether Lord Ellenborough would have suffered such qualms of conscience as Campbell so charitably attributed to him.

Certainly they would not have been shared by the administration of which he was such a staunch supporter, which suspended the pillory sentence simply out of fear of the possible consequences of attempting to carry it out. It was Castlereagh who made the announcement on 19 July, 3 days after Cochrane's re-election, at the close of the debate on Lord Ebrington's Motion. He rose to announce that the Royal Pardon had been extended not only to Cochrane, but to all who had been sentenced to the pillory, and that sentence has never been imposed in Britain since. Six months later Ebrington happened to be speaking with the fallen Emperor Napoleon in his exile on the isle of Elba, who congratulated him on his part in defending Cochrane. 'You were right: such a man should not be made to suffer such a degrading punishment.'

It would have been much to the credit of the Prince Regent if he had shared Napoleon's sentiments and exercised the royal mercy as a genuine act of grace towards one who had so recently given fresh proof of his patriotism when he invented poison gas. But the Prince went out of his way to inform the world that his attitude was quite different— by including in his speech at a public function, before all those foreign potentates, insulting remarks about Cochrane that had no place on such an occasion. The government devised a no less contemptible alternative to the ignominy of the pillory sentence. On 11 August, by order of a Secretary of State, Cochrane's banner of a Knight of the Bath was removed from his stall in the Henry VII chapel of Westminster Abbey, his coat-of-arms, helmet and sword were likewise torn from their places and all these emblems of his family's honour and his own were kicked down the steps of the abbey.

In the misery of such afflictions it was small consolation to Cochrane that he was accommodated in two comfortable rooms on the upper floor of the King's Bench prison. In the *Speedy* he had lived happily in a cabin 5 feet high, standing with his head and shoulders protruding through the sky-light to shave with tackle spread out on the deck before him. William Cobbett and Sir Francis Burdett were among his constant visitors, and although Cochrane sought to deprive himself of the solace of his wife's company in order to spare her the pain of visiting a prison, she would come there, heavily disguised to avoid recognition.

On 14 October 1814 he wrote to her: 'My lovely Kate. You know the inconveniences of this place, and how impossible it is for me to make a single room in a prison comfortable to you. I would not willingly put you to inconvenience, and induce you to sacrifice anything to my satisfaction. No, not for the whole world. This is not a place favourable to morality. I wish you to remain, as you are, uncorrupted by the wickedness of this world; I wish to see you good, sensible in point of education, and in every respect blessed, Kate. Oh! my dear soul, you do not know how much I love you and my dear Tom. My conduct may not have shewn it, distressed as my mind has been, but I have felt towards you as I ought to feel, my lovely Kate.'

Cochrane had always turned the intervals of leisure in his breathless career to full account, and now when he lacked society he continued to remedy the deficiencies in his education, to enjoy the pleasures of reflection, and to work on his inventions, especially his various lamps. During the third month of his confinement he had the satisfaction of learning that gas lamps of his design had been installed in the parish of St Ann's, Westminster, and to his wife he expressed the hope that these would serve to rescue them from the financial ruin that threatened them. 'I have nothing new to tell you, but I believe and anxiously hope that our lamps will answer. I have been writing an advertisement today for the papers. It will be a happy thing for us both if God blesses us with independence from such a source, after the punishment he has been pleased to inflict upon me.'

But however systematically Cochrane employed his time, incarceration was bound to undermine the patience of so active a spirit, and the news that reached him in prison could only make him more fretful still. During this final year of the American war the coast was raided, plundered and blockaded from Maine in the north to the Mississippi in the south. Sir Alexander Cochrane incurred enduring odium because it was under his orders that Washington was captured and the Capitol and the White House destroyed by fire. The Americans proved powerless to repel such attacks, except at the mouth of the Mississippi where the genius of Andrew Jackson saved them. This was the war in which Cochrane should have been taking part, and although it went well the other side of the Atlantic, the time came when enemy privateers repaid the British in their own waters. By 11 February 1815 *The Times* was reporting: 'They daily enter in among our convoys, seize prizes in sight of those that should afford protection, and if pursued "put on their sea wings" and laugh at the clumsy English pursuers. To what is this owing?' asked *The Times*, to which a partial answer was that Lord Cochrane was in prison. 'It must indeed be encouraging to Mr Madison to read the logs of his cruisers. If they fight, they are sure to conquer; if they fly, they are sure to escape.'

Cobbett fed Cochrane's impatience by urging him to break out of prison as he had done in Malta. It was an absurd suggestion: but Cochrane possessed a temperament extremely ill-suited to prolonged inactivity, he loved a lark, and he understood the value of a demonstration as a weapon better than he could now assess what its limits ought to be. On 6 March 1815 he vanished from his rooms in the King's Bench prison.

A rope was smuggled in easily by one of his visitors and he possessed ample training among the masts and spars of sailing ships to enable him to use it. Unlike so many 39-year-old aristocrats of the Regency he was still energetic and fit. Below his windows ran a narrow street with a high wall on its farther side surmounted by spikes. Cochrane waited until he had heard the night watchman making his rounds, then he threw his rope, looped with a slip-knot, over one of those spikes. Unfortunately, whoever had obtained that rope for him knew less about such gear than he did. It proved to be defective, and after holding Cochrane as he swung himself across the street to the wall opposite it snapped as he was letting himself down on the farther side. He fell on his back from a height of 25 feet. But with the same fortitude that he displayed on other occasions when he was gravely injured, he crawled to the house in which his old nurse lived and lay here for several days until he was sufficiently recovered.

It was at this precise moment that news arrived of Napoleon's escape from the island of Elba. The American war was brought to an end as Britain and her allies prepared to face the new menace.

But not even such events could overshadow the escape of Cochrane in the minds of Londoners. He was the idol of the people, the war hero, the fearless denouncer of injustice, the friend of reform. His conviction on a disgraceful charge had done nothing to sully this image in the eyes of the public: on the contrary he was looked upon as the latest martyr of an utterly disreputable government. Although bills were posted everywhere offering a reward of 300 guineas for information leading to his capture, nobody came forward to earn this colossal sum. Yet Cochrane made no attempt to conceal himself: as soon as he was well enough he travelled openly to his home in Hampshire and lived there for a fortnight with his wife and child without being reported by anyone. The newspapers purveyed rumours that he had fled abroad, that he was staying with William Cobbett, that he was anywhere except where he was most likely to be—until he brought speculation to an end on 20 March by walking into the Houses of Parliament to take his seat. He entered in the plain civilian clothes in which he was usually seen there—a frogged coat and grey pantaloons—for he had never been one of the dandies of Beau Brummell's set.

To this day the legislature meets in a royal palace, set aside by the sovereign for the deliberations of her peers and faithful commons, and administered by the Lord Great Chamberlain. Her officials there are still designated Clerks, as in Tudor times, and the senior Clerk to the Commons sits below the Speaker, a belted knight, to advise him on matters of Parliamentary procedure. The Clerks are assisted by burly officials holding the office of badge messengers, their badge a silver-gilt plaque bearing the royal coat-of-arms which hangs round their necks by a chain and lies on the stout chests of men who are in many instances retired Regimental Sergeants Major. The oldest of these plaques date from the reign of George III and may have faced Cochrane when he puzzled the officials of the palace of Westminster by making his unexpected entry.

They played for time by pointing out to him that he had not taken the oath since his re-election. He went to the office of the Clerk to the Commons to repair this omission where he was told that the writ of his re-election would have to be fetched from Chancery Lane. Cochrane was kept waiting for 2 hours by this subterfuge while officialdom conferred, sent messages in all directions, made up its mind and executed its plan. Bow Street runners entered the building, reinforced by a posse of tipstaves and informed Cochrane that they had come to arrest him where he sat in the House of Commons.

He protested that his arrest was illegal and refused to move from his seat. The tipstaves were ordered to carry him away bodily and they took the precaution of first searching him for arms. All they found was a packet of snuff in his pocket. As they examined it, Cochrane exclaimed: 'If I had only thought of that before, you should have had it in your eyes.' The incident has been variously interpreted. The government press asserted that Cochrane had brought it with him deliberately with the intention of blinding the tipstaves, in spite of the fact that it was they who took it out of his pocket. A more sympathetic comment is that he made his remark in a burst of temper when it was taken from him in such unceremonious circumstances. More probably his words are just another example of his impish sense of humour.

His Westminster constituents saw him being driven away peaceably enough in a hackney carriage, accompanied by four constables, but he was not taken back to his comfortable appartments in the King's Bench prison. A Member of Parliament of the name of Bennet, who was then serving on a Committee for the investigations of conditions in prisons, inspected the prison in which he was now placed and reported: 'I found Lord Cochrane confined in a strong room fourteen feet square, without windows, fireplace, table or bed. I do not think it can be necessary for the purpose of security to confine him in this manner. According to my own feelings it is a place unfit for the noble Lord, or for any other person whatsoever.'

If Cochrane's new prison had not been described by such a competent witness it would scarcely be possible to believe he was being treated in this way, and the question arises whether his enemies were moved by fear or merely by the same mean spirit of revenge which provoked them to kick his honours of the Bath down the steps of the Abbey. Soon the fate of the people's idol became public knowledge, and anger was inflamed by the address which Cochrane issued to his constituents on 12 April, describing his condition. The very next day two eminent doctors were sent to examine him, and their reports caused even greater disquiet.

'This is to certify,' wrote Doctor Buchan, 'that I have this day visited Lord Cochrane, who is affected with severe pain of the breast. His pulse is low, his hands cold, and he has many symptoms of a person about to have typhus or putrid fever. These symptoms are, in my opinion, produced by the stagnant air of the strong room in which he is now confined.' As soon as this diagnosis was published the authorities bowed to the mounting storm and transferred Cochrane to more salubrious premises. On 20 June, the anniversary of his sentence, they told him he could leave as soon as his fine was paid. The battle of Waterloo had been fought and won 2 days earlier, but even this news could not altogether stifle the public interest in Cochrane's war against authority. He had been compelled to serve out his prison sentence; he could still resist the payment of his fine.

It was the entreaties of his supporters that broke him this time— of his wife and his uncle Basil, of Cobbett, Burdett and the many others who had remained so loyal to him in his adversity. On 3 July he yielded to their advice and despatched a note for 1000 pounds with a final challenge scribbled on the back of it. 'My health having suffered by long and close confinement, and my oppressors being resolved to deprive me of property or life, I submit to robbery to protect myself from Murder, in the hope that I shall live to bring the delinquents to justice.' The note is still preserved in the Bank of England, an example of the creeping corrosion of rancour that had invaded Cochrane's personality and would embitter him progressively until it found its fullest expression in the autobiography he composed in his old age.

Three days after he had written it, Cochrane witnessed the fate of another radical who had endured years of official disapproval. Samuel Whitbread had been amongst his most staunch supporters. He confessed to having spent more sleepless nights on Cochrane's case than on any of the other causes which his infinite spirit of compassion embraced, before becoming convinced of his innocence. Having reached his conclusion he flung himself into Cochrane's cause with his usual energy and courage.

But Samuel Whitbread, ever such a tower of strength to others, was gradually succumbing to persecution mania within himself. It was not the obstruction of his humanitarian reforms that undermined him; his attempts to improve the lot of the industrial poor, the mentally defective, the orphans and the prisoners of war. His Achilles heel was his pacifism, and the hostility to which this exposed him in time of war. Whitbread had proclaimed that his country could not defeat Napoleon and ought to make peace with him. When the news of Waterloo reached London, Whitbread began to speak strangely. One day he turned to his wife on their doorstep and said: 'They are hissing me. I am become an object of universal abhorrence.' He was the prophet whose prophecies had been disproved. A few days later he suddenly remarked to his companion in Piccadilly: 'The world will point and scoff at me. The populace will pull down my house.' The next day he was found lying dead on the floor in his London home, his throat cut with a razor.

'How could it ever enter into the scheme of providence,' wrote Lord Ossulston to Creevey the diarist, 'that a man like Whitbread, the best man in all the relations of life and the most valuable person, as well as the most esteemed in our time, should put an end to his immortal life?' It might have appeared less surprising to most people if Cochrane had been driven by persecution to cut his throat, unless they had reflected that in contrast to Whitbread he was no pacifist. He left prison fiercely determined to shoulder the causes Whitbread had left behind him as well as to pursue his personal vendetta against all who had wronged him. He was now nearly 40 years old but the longer span of life still lay before him and he did not waste it.

CHAPTER EIGHT

Rebel with a Cause

While Cochrane was serving his sentence in the prison of the King's Bench, a Bill was introduced in the House of Commons to protect the price of corn. It provided that corn could be imported from abroad only when the home price rose to eighty shillings a quarter. By maintaining the price of grain in this way a Parliament dominated by landowners through their control of the rotten boroughs was ensuring the level of their rents.

It was also raising the price of bread at a time of mounting distress amongst the industrial poor. While the Bill was being discussed these expressed their exasperation at scattered points throughout the country, while its supporters had their windows smashed in London. The riots were especially violent during the days immediately following Cochrane's escape from prison on 6 March, but it was not only the metropolis which faced the horrid spectre of attacks on property. This had begun in the eastern counties, where the troops were called out, two rioters were killed, and twenty-eight labourers condemned to death at the assizes. Five of them were hanged as a warning to the remainder but the example did not prevent demonstrations elsewhere over the high price of bread. The unemployed made senseless attacks on machinery, which they mistakenly supposed to be the source of their miseries.

The victory of Waterloo swelled the ranks of the unemployed with discharged soldiers and seamen. Perhaps the most unfortunate of these were the Highland Scots who had served with outstanding distinction in the army and now trudged home from the south coast ports to discover that their homes had been burned down, their families scattered. The Highland landlords had discovered how much more profitable it was to introduce mammoth sheep farming in place of subsistence farming, and since their clansmen were merely tenants at will, it had been a fairly simple matter to evict them in favour of a handful of shepherds with their dogs.

The most inhumane and sweeping of these human clearances were already being carried out in the far north of Scotland, which had been for so long a fertile recruiting ground of the British army. But the

Cochranes were not a Highland family and it would be many years before the horrors of the Sutherland evictions would penetrate to the Parliament and press of distant London. Meanwhile, there were causes enough for Cochrane to espouse. When he left prison it must have given him particular satisfaction to go straight to the House of Commons that very day, in time to secure the defeat of the government in a division by a majority of one. Two days later he gave notice that he would move for an enquiry into the conduct of Lord Ellenborough with a view to his impeachment.

Had Samuel Whitbread remained alive, he might have succeeded in dissuading him from such a course; alternatively he could have given Cochrane valuable advice in drawing up his articles of impeachment, since he had conducted the prosecution at the impeachment of Lord Melville in a manner that earned him universal respect. Neither firebrand Cobbett nor the feather-headed Burdett were well-qualified counsellors for a man naturally generous and constructive, now infected by the destructive spirit of hatred and revenge.

In the new session of 1816 Cochrane rose in the House of Commons to tabulate thirteen charges against Lord Ellenborough which he took 4 hours to expound to the few Members of a hostile Chamber who bothered to listen. Burdett supported him loyally as usual, but when they acted as tellers for the Motion, not a single Member entered their division lobby as a supporter. Cochrane exclaimed angrily: 'So long as I have a seat in this House I will continue to bring these charges forward, year by year and time after time, until I am allowed the opportunity of establishing the truth of my allegations.'

He did succeed in securing the prosecution of one of the witnesses at his trial on a charge of perjury. His name was Launcelot Davidson and his evidence, like that of the degenerate youth Crane, had been concerned with de Berenger's movements and with the clothes he wore. While it would have been impossible to establish that Crane had been lying on oath (and there is no evidence that he did so), Cochrane was able to establish that Davidson had at least been guilty of a misstatement of fact, for which he was tried in the court of the King's Bench on 20 July 1816. The judge was Mr Justice Abbott, who succeeded Lord Ellenborough as Chief Justice, and it was he who instructed the jury that the question 'supposing that you are satisfied that the defendant swore untruly, is whether he swore corruptly, whether it was the act of a wilful and corrupt mind desirous to cause the defendants to be convicted against the due course of law and justice'. To this charge the jury returned a verdict of Not Guilty, and both the judge's direction to them and their decision appear sound. But Cochrane had made his point; so that it is pitiful to find his unsleeping animosities still directed against Abbott's conduct of the case in his autobiography.

Nine days after Davidson's acquittal Cochrane caused far graver embarrassment to the authorities. William Wilberforce was active among the high Tories who wished to alleviate the hardships of the poor by means of charity, and to achieve this he attempted to revive the Association for the Relief of the Manufacturing and Labouring poor. On 29 July a public meeting was held under the Association's patronage with the royal Duke of York in the chair, his brothers the Dukes of Kent and Cambridge in attendance, the Archbishop of Canterbury and Wilberforce prominent among all those distinguished sympathisers with the distressed.

The last thing they wanted to hear was that philanthropy was a mere smoke-screen for the nation's ills, that the repeal of the Corn Law was the most urgent remedy; then the reform of Parliament, so that industrial towns such as Birmingham and Manchester would be represented there in place of the pocket boroughs whose owners had enacted the law in the first place. To the London Tavern came Cochrane with a large following of constituents and others who shared these views, to which their Member gave expression in a manner which caused deep distress to all those royal Dukes, the Archbishop and the devout Wilberforce. About a fortnight later, in mid-August, Cochrane was hailed before the Guildford assize on a charge of having escaped from the King's Bench prison in March of the previous year.

The attempt to impeach Ellenborough, the prosecution of Davidson, the demonstration at the London Tavern, all of these must have exasperated the government, and Cochrane later maintained that his belated prosecution was a deliberate reprisal. His son, the eleventh Earl, went farther and asserted: 'At the special instigation of Lord Ellenborough, as it was averred, the prosecution had been renewed in May 1816, almost immediately after the rejection by the House of Commons of Lord Cochrane's charges against the vindictive and unprincipled Judge.' Personal motive is generally a matter of surmise. All that can be said is that the record both of the government and of the Judge invited such imputations, and that in indicting Cochrane so long after his escape they were merely tarnishing their reputations further. The jury returned the verdict: 'We are of opinion that Lord Cochrane is guilty of escaping from prison, but we recommend mercy, because we think his subsequent punishment fully adequate to the offence of which he was guilty.'

The Judge however deemed otherwise in fining Cochrane a further

£100, which he refused to pay. Judgment was delayed until November, after the long vacation, so that Cochrane was threatened with another winter in prison for his recalcitrance; but once again the electors of Westminster stood by him, this time by raising the amount of his fine and a great deal more besides by public subscription. It was one more ominous reminder to all the officials who lived in that neighbourhood of the unshakable popularity of the man they had tried to discredit by every means in their power.

Now that Cochrane had abandoned any immediate hope of further service in the British Navy and had resumed the life of a politician, he left the house in Green Street for the convenience of a London home at number 7 Palace Yard, a mere stone's throw from the House of Commons. Here, as Christmas and his forty-first birthday approached, he collaborated with William Cobbett in launching a new journal called *Cobbett's Political Register*. Drama filled its pages from the very outset.

On 15 November a mammoth open-air meeting was held in Londdon's Spa Fields, at which Sir Francis Burdett was elected in company with the demagogue known as 'Orator' Hunt to present a petition for reform to the Prince Regent; but this was one of those occasions when Burdett lost his nerve at the eleventh hour, so that Hunt was left to carry the petition on his own. When he was refused access to the Prince public fury was inflamed by what was regarded as a contemptuous dismissal of his subjects' distresses. A second meeting was called in Spa Fields on 2 December and this time there was a riot. The shops of gunsmiths were raided for arms: many were injured before the tumult was suppressed; the ringleader escaped to America, a seaman was hanged for his part in it on 17 March.

The government interpreted this as a threat of immediate revolution and the docility of delegates from provincial Hampden Clubs at the Crown and Anchor Tavern on 22 January 1817 did nothing to calm its fears. Indeed the restraint and discipline of these representatives of the lower orders seemed more sinister than the outrages at Spa Fields. Sir Francis Burdett was chairman of the London Hampden Club but he was still suffering from loss of nerve and absented himself, while Cochrane attended to collect the petitions for reform with their half a million signatures. He brought them to the House of Commons a week later when Parliament reopened. The atmosphere was more stormy than ever, and the government's alarm increased when the glass of the Regent's coach was shattered as he drove to open Parliament. At the centre of this storm stood the man the government had failed either to intimidate or to destroy, the only man in the realm who might be a match for the Duke of Wellington if it came to revolution—Lord Cochrane with his monster petitions.

Amongst the delegates who had travelled to London from every part of the country was Samuel Bamford, the young Lancashire weaver who left such a graphic description of the scene he witnessed from the spectators' gallery in the House of Commons. 'A number of the delegates met Hunt at Charing Cross,' Bamford recorded, 'and from thence went with him in procession to the residence of Lord Cochrane in Palace Yard, where a large petition from Bristol and most of those from the north of England were placed in his Lordship's hands. There had been a tumult in the morning; the Prince Regent had been insulted on his way to the House. We were crowded around and accompanied by a great multitude, which at intervals rent the air with shouts. Now it was that I beheld Hunt in his element. He unrolled the petition, which was many yards in length, and it was carried on the heads of the crowd, perfectly unharmed. When questions were asked: "Who is he? What are they about?", and the reply was "Hunt, Hunt, huzza!", his gratification was expressed by a stern smile.'

Samuel Bamford wrote these reminiscences years later, after much of his revolutionary ardour had cooled, though not a detail of his lively memories. He had grown critical of that egotistical demagogue Orator Hunt, while his admiration for Cochrane remained undiminished. 'On arriving at Palace Yard we were shewn into a room below stairs, and whilst Lord Cochrane and Hunt conversed above, a slight and elegant young lady, dressed in white and very interesting, served us with wine. She is, if I am not misinformed, now Lady Dundonald. At length his Lordship came to us. He was a tall young man, cordial and unaffected in his manner. His face was rather oval; fair naturally, but now tanned and sun-freckled. He took charge of our petitions, and being seated in an armchair, we lifted him up and bore him on our shoulders across Palace Yard to the door of Westminster Hall; the old rafters of which rang with the shouts of the vast multitude outside.'

Like Mary Mitford, Samuel Bamford the weaver was a great deal younger than Cochrane, who was now over 40 years old. So it is equally remarkable that he too should have remembered Cochrane as a young man at this time and it suggests that Cochrane must have retained the vitality and the manners which sometimes invest people with the appearance of youth after they have in fact reached middle age. Bamford's exact observation also reveals that Cochrane was of the red or ginger-haired stock still frequently seen in eastern Scotland whose skin becomes freckled in the sun.

The government responded to the demonstration in which he played such an alarming part by suspending Habeas Corpus on 26 February 1817, thus enabling themselves to hold people in prison without trial. Other measures were rushed through Parliament to stamp out seditious meetings and literature 'of an irreligious, immoral or seditious tendency'. *Cobbett's Political Register* was an obvious target and its editor, disliking the prospect of another term in prison, fled to America in March. As spring came to Hampshire it must have been sad for Cochrane, by the Hamble River, that he could no longer ride over to Botley to visit William Cobbett. He suffered another vexation in April. He had refused to pay the extortionate bill for the entertainment of the inhabitants of Honiton after his election there in 1806. Wellington had sent a similar bill for £1200 to the proper authorities when it was presented to him and heard no more of it: a course that was only open to someone who stood on the right side of the authorities. Cochrane's creditors obtained an order to put an execution into his home.

He extracted what amusement he could from the situation by testing the limits of human credulity, as he so often did in warfare, as he had tried to do during the siege of Burdett's house in London. He stacked bags of powdered charcoal against the doors and windows of his home which so intimidated the sheriff of Hampshire and his men that for over 6 weeks they did not dare to force an entry. 'I still hold out,' Cochrane wrote to his secretary at Westminster, 'though the castle has several times been threatened in great force. The trumpeter is now blowing for a parley, but no one appears on the ramparts. Explosion bags are set in the lower embrasures and all the garrison is under arms.'

Finally an officer braver than the rest leapt through an open window, to receive the congratulations of Cochrane as he sat quietly eating his breakfast. He was compelled to pay up and by 20 May he was back in the House of Commons to speak with the effectiveness he could so often command when he was not complaining of his personal wrongs, in favour of Burdett's motion for the reform of Parliament. Fifteen years before the enactment of the Great Reform Bill the two Members for Westminster were the only two men in the entire chamber to speak in favour of such a measure.

By this time Byron had joined Cobbett in exile; Shelley in Rome fulminated against the rottenness of Britain's régime. Cochrane too was offered a way out when the government of Spain offered him the command of their navy. It was a great temptation, but the régime which the allies had restored to Spain did not consist of the patriots whom Cochrane had aided in the *Impérieuse*, the gallant guerillas who had rendered Wellington such essential service during the Peninsular war. These were being gradually eliminated by an administration as reactionary as the one which ruled Britain. Although Cochrane had reached middle age with his career lost and his financial future precarious, circumstances in which he might have snatched at any straw, he could not reconcile himself to supporting a government so similar to the one he attacked at home.

But he was now reconciled to abandoning his country as Cobbett, Byron, Shelley and so many others had done. 'My dearest Kate,' he wrote to his wife on one of those occasions when one of them was in Hampshire, the other in Westminster, 'I confess that my opinion of the Government here is such that I have nothing to expect from them—no, not even my just right. But then there are other countries, and I have in my head enough to make me useful in any part of the world.' His mind was already prepared for the prospect of emigration by the time he received his next offer.

In April 1817 Don José Alvarez arrived in Britain from Chile, seeking support for his country's revolt against the colonial government of Spain. It was naturally impossible for Cochrane to assess his appeal in the light of the subsequent 150 years of South American history, or in the light of what is now known about Spain's colonial record. It would not have been easy for him to reflect that whereas the democratic, freedom-loving Protestants of North America almost entirely extirpated the indigenous native peoples, the descendants of the Aztec, Maya, Inca and other native societies in the southern half of the continent survived in relatively large numbers, and that this was initially due to the protection afforded to them by the Catholic, paternalistic, but all-too-distant power of Spain. The revolutionary movement in South America was an essentially aristocratic one, designed to rid the colonial magnates of these shackles and the native peoples of what little protection they had hitherto enjoyed. In Cochrane's eyes it was a bid for freedom from an odious tyranny which might offer him an opportunity to start life afresh in a new world. When Alvarez offered him the post of Admiral of the Chilean Navy it must have appeared to him as a sign from the very finger of providence that his destiny was to be fulfilled at last.

Events in his own country during 1817 added their negative argument. There were no less than twenty-six prosecutions for seditious and blasphemous libel during that panicky year and in June James Watson was indicted before Lord Ellenborough on a charge of treason for his part at Spa Fields. A paper had been discovered in his pocket when he was arrested, containing the names of a Committee of

Public Safety, and they included those of Lord Cochrane and Sir Francis Burdett.

Ellenborough commented: 'This, one should suppose, was an intended committee, or more probably names put down to hold out the appearance to others of its being appointed.' As Cochrane had been incarcerated in the King's Bench prison at the time of the Spa Fields riot, following his conviction at the Guildford assizes, and Burdett had avoided involvement, the Lord Chief Justice could scarcely have commented otherwise.

In his long summing-up Ellenborough concentrated upon the primary objective of securing Watson's conviction; the jury responded by pronouncing him Not Guilty. 'Remember to pray in earnest,' Wilberforce confided to his diary, 'against sedition, privy conspiracy, and rebellion.' If any Christian had earned his right to be heard at the throne of God it was Wilberforce, but he had apparently overlooked the question of what he was praying for, whereas the jurors of Britain had not. Since the conviction of Cochrane they had turned an increasingly deaf ear to the arguments that Wilberforce uttered on his knees and the Lord Chief Justice on the bench.

The most sensational case was that of William Hone, since his offence was very real blasphemy within the definition of recent statute, and in a land in which Byron was soon to be denied the protection of the law of copyright on the grounds that his poetry was blasphemous Hone ought not to have stood a chance. He was prosecuted no less than three times, first for lampoons based on the catechism, the Lord's prayer and the ten commandments: next for blaspheming the litany: finally for his Sinecurist's Creed, which blasphemed the Athanasian Creed used by the Church of England. When juries had twice acquitted him and the prayers of Wilberforce had been answered by no thunderbolt from Heaven, Ellenborough sat in judgment on him on 20 December and ordered the jury to convict.

In ordinary circumstances such a conventional assembly of freeholders might have been glad to do so, for Hone stood like Samson in court, shaking those twin pillars on which their society rested, religion and the law. But Christianity itself had now become compromised by the character of the man who sat robed in its defence, and when Hone read out the parodies of others to show they were no less seditious or blasphemous than his own, he evoked convulsions of laughter among men who would normally have been shocked by such obscenities. The jury once again brought in a verdict of Not Guilty, which was widely believed to have upset Lord Ellenborough so much that it hastened his death, inasmuch as he died within the year.

A few days after Hone's acquittal, on 29 December 1817, a public meeting was held at the City of London Tavern to raise a subscription for his expenses 'in so nobly and successfully struggling against Ministerial persecution'. Cochrane made a rousing speech on the occasion in which he described how his constituents had raised the amount of his fine a year earlier. 'That money I now wish to return, and with feelings of heartfelt thankfulness to Mr Hone for his manly and able exertions in defence of the liberties of the people, I will now lay down the one hundred pounds which I hold in my hands, in addition to the sums already subscribed.' His closing words were drowned in applause.

But Cochrane never at any time contemplated the promotion of revolution in his own country, whatever the government's fears. On the contrary, he counselled it continuously over a period of years to adopt the reforms that would end the dangers of revolution. All of these reforms were realised during Cochrane's lifetime, but as the year 1818 opened he could perceive only that he had sacrificed his naval career for a political one that had achieved nothing. His wife was expecting a second child in March, and together they decided that as soon as she was fit to travel they would sail away with their family to Chile.

Don José Alvarez was able to inform his government in February: 'I have extreme satisfaction in informing you that Lord Cochrane, one of the most eminent and valiant seamen of Great Britain, has undertaken to proceed to Chile to direct our navy. He is a person highly commendable, not only on account of the liberal principles with which he has always upheld the cause of the English people in their Parliament, but also because he bears a character altogether superior to ambitious self-seeking.' Such was the public image of Cochrane which Don José encountered on his visit to London and it is scarcely surprising that the generality of mankind who had witnessed his career during the past 10 years should have reached such a verdict.

As soon as Cochrane had made his decision he turned his mind to the disparity between the naval forces of Chile and the strength of the Spanish fleet which it would be his task to sweep from the Pacific. His immediate solution was to commission the construction of a steam ship: the type of vessel which, he predicted, would soon sweep sailing ships from the seven seas. Since he could not possibly wait in Britain until she was built, he decided to invite one of his brothers to sail her across the Atlantic once she was ready, and the obvious candidate was Archibald who had served his apprenticeship with his eldest brother in the Mediterranean. But for some reason that has not been recorded it was not Archibald who undertood this task: it was Major William Cochrane whose health had given his family so much anxiety during the Peninsular war.

On 8 March Cochrane's second son was born and baptised William Horatio Bernardo, the last name being that of the man who had been established for the past few months as the first ruler of an independent republic of Chile. Cochrane now moved his family to a cottage at Tunbridge Wells while he disposed of their property and arranged for the transfer of their assets to Chile. The most substantial of these would arrive only after considerable delay, for Cochrane was building his steam vessel entirely at his own expense in the expectation that the Chilean government would be glad to acquire (and pay for) the first steamship ever to enter the Pacific.

Since he was bound for a Catholic country in which he might settle for the remainder of his life, Cochrane decided to celebrate his marriage to Kitty while he was in Kent, according to the forms of the Anglo-Catholic Church. It obviously did not occur to him that this act might be construed as an admission that the hand-fast ceremony at Annan under which his two eldest sons had been born was of doubtful validity.

At last the time arrived for Cochrane to make his farewell speech in the House of Commons, which he did on 2 June in support of Sir Francis Burdett's latest Motion in favour of Parliamentary reform. The futility of his years in Parliament swept over him as he addressed the sparsely occupied benches opposite, infusing the restrained contempt with which he spoke. 'As it it probably the last time I shall ever have the honour of addressing the House on any subject, I am anxious to tell its Members what I think of their conduct. It is now nearly eleven years since I have had the honour of a seat in this House, and since then there have been very few measures in which I could agree with the opinions of the majority.'

He did not expect that this majority would willingly reform the abuses on which their own power rested, but he warned that others might do it for them. 'I will say, as has been said before by the great Chatham, the father of Mr Pitt, that if the House does not reform itself from within, it will be reformed with a vengeance from without. The people will take up the subject and a reform will take place which will make many Members regret their apathy in now refusing that reform which might be rendered efficient and permanent . . . The gentlemen who now sit on the benches opposite with such triumphant feelings will one day repent their conduct. The commotions to which that conduct will inevitably give rise will shake not only this House, but the whole framework of government and society to its foundations. I have been actuated by the wish to prevent this, and I have had no other intention.' His enemies had reason to be thankful for that.

Hardly a hundred Members were present to hear the final words which Cochrane uttered with uncharacteristic emotion. 'I shall not trespass longer on your time. The situation I have held for eleven years in this House I owe to the favour of the electors of Westminster. The feelings of my heart are gratified by the manner in which they have acted towards me. They have rescued me from a wicked conspiracy which has nearly involved me in total ruin. I forgive those who have so done; and I hope when they depart to their graves they will be equally able to forgive themselves. All this is foreign to the subject before the House, but I trust you will forgive me. I shall not trespass on your time longer now—perhaps never again on any subject. I hope His Majesty's ministers will take into their serious consideration what I now say. I do not utter it with any feelings of hostility—such feelings have now left me—but I trust that they will take my warning, and save the country by abandoning the present system before it is too late.'

It might be thought that the government would have looked on the imminent departure of Cochrane with vast relief. Instead the authorities plotted to prevent his departure with a vindictive obtuseness that still astounds, by bringing a Bill before Parliament prohibiting British subjects from enlisting in the service of a foreign power. Their malice was only matched by their inefficiency. Cochrane sailed for Chile with his wife and children in August 1818; the Foreign Enlistment Bill was not enacted until 11 months later, so that its only effect was to make Cochrane an outlaw.

For this final insult he extracted a hilarious revenge. Returning to his native land as the Grand Admiral of a foreign power he demanded and received a full salute of guns; then he landed. Nobody then or ever thereafter dared to lay a finger on him.

CHAPTER NINE

The Liberation of Chile

Throughout the vast Spanish and Portuguese territories of South America the war of independence in the north, begun in 1775 and ended by a treaty of peace between Britain and the United States in 1783, exercised its disturbing influence. The nearest Spanish colonists, those who lived in the lands that were eventually to be divided between the republics of Colombia and Venezuela, were the first to feel this influence. Here Francisco Miranda was born in the future Venezuelan capital of Caracas, and he had scarcely attained his majority before he sailed north across the Caribbean to join the war against British colonial rule. Miranda next crossed the Atlantic to fight in the revolutionary armies of France, and at the same time he tried to interest the nations of Europe in the cause of Latin American independence. He won over some individuals to adopt his own career as freelance freedom fighters: the most remarkable of these was Gregor MacGregor, late of the Black Watch, who became a General in the Venezuelan war and a member of Simón Bolívar's Order of Liberators. But Miranda failed to persuade any European government to strike a blow at Spain through her American colonies, and therefore returned home to see what he could achieve without foreign aid.

Here he received assistance from another Scot. Rear Admiral Sir Alexander Cochrane was in command of the West Indian station during that crucial year of 1805, in which Spain joined the enemies of Britain in the Napoleonic war, and Nelson died at Trafalgar. When Miranda acquired and equipped a ship in which to raise the standard of revolt in his native land, Admiral Cochrane used British ships to support his landing there. In 1806 Miranda proclaimed the foundation of a republic of Colombia near Caracas and lit the fire at which he had already warmed his hands in North America and in France. It was the year in which Admiral Cochrane's nephew returned home in the golden *Pallas* rich with the booty of colonial Spain, to take his seat for the first time in Parliament.

In 1810 another native of Caracas joined the forces of revolt, the great Simón Bolívar himself, and in the following year their republic of Venezuela became the first in the southern continent to proclaim her independence. But for Miranda, the pioneer, it was the end of the road. In 1812 he was utterly defeated by the army of imperial Spain and although he capitulated on terms, these were instantly repudiated. He was carried back to the mother country where he was dragged from dungeon to dungeon until he died at Cadiz in 1816, collared and chained to a prison wall.

The rebellion spread, however, assisted indirectly by Napoleon's invasion of Spain; and during Miranda's captivity a luckier general emerged to join Bolívar in his task. His name was José de San Martín, and he had been born much farther south, by the river Uruguay. The son of a Spanish army officer, San Martín went to Spain to train for a similar career, fought against the army of Napoleon there, and then returned to Buenos Aires in the year of Miranda's surrender to offer his services to the revolutionary movement that had by now taken the field in Argentina also. In 1814 San Martín was appointed to command the freedom army of upper Peru, soon to become the republic of Bolivia. The Spanish government, fighting for survival against Napoleon with the victorious help of Wellington, was faced in its overseas possessions by two outstanding generals from opposite ends of the South American continent, Bolívar and San Martín. Soon they were joined by a man of very different stock from their own.

For centuries Spain had been a place of refuge for the Catholic Irish, fleeing from English persecution, and it was natural that some of these should have found their way to the Spanish colonial possessions across the Atlantic. Among them was Ambrose O'Higgins, a man of outstanding administrative ability, who was appointed Governor of Chile from 1788 until 1796. O'Higgins had a son by a native girl whom he named Bernardo, and whom he sent (odd as it may seem) to England for his education. There he spent 5 years in the academy of a Mr Hill at Richmond in Surrey where (even odder as it may seem) he is thought by some writers to have developed an admiration for British forms of government, although he never attempted to introduce them in his native country when he had the opportunity to do so.

From England Don Bernardo O'Higgins travelled to Spain and then returned to live on his family estate in Chile until the revolution broke out. Immediately he joined the patriots and fought with such gallantry that in 1813 he was placed in command of the Chilean army of freedom. It was while he occupied this position that San Martín in upper Peru made a decision of far-reaching consequence to Chile, as he pondered on the basic problems of a war that had by now extended over a gigantic area. He realised that the forces of revolt did not yet possess the resources to assault the central power at the seat of the Spanish Viceroyalty in

Peru. It would be necessary first to secure the southern end of the continent, Argentina and Chile, in order to strike north from a firm base. He therefore resigned his command in what is now Bolivia, travelled south along the passes of the Andes to Mendoza, and there assembled an army for the invasion of Chile. He was making his preparations when O'Higgins was defeated in 1814 and fled across the Andes to join him.

So the two men with whom Cochrane was to be most closely associated in Chile began their partnership in the year in which he was flung into prison in London. O'Higgins offered to serve under San Martín and in 1817 the two men performed the feat which had all the drama of, and a greater ultimate triumph than, Hannibal's crossing of the Alps. They transported 3000 foot soldiers and 1000 cavalry, well supported by artillery and baggage trains, over passes of extraordinary difficulty 13,000 feet above sea level, and they performed this with breathless speed to inflict the first of their hammer blows upon Spanish power in Chile. On 12 February Bernardo O'Higgins became head of the new independent government in Santiago, the capital in which his father had formerly held authority as colonial governor. San Martín continued to command the armed forces, which inflicted another crushing defeat on the Spaniards in 1818.

But these successes only served to bring into sharper focus a particular difficulty of the task that still lay before them. Both Peru and Chile are relatively narrow countries with immensely long coastlines, that of Chile containing innumerable fjords and islands which are especially vulnerable from the sea. However often the Spaniards were defeated on land, neither country would achieve its freedom until Spanish naval power in the Pacific was destroyed. Hence the urgent plea to Cochrane, the man who had both preached and demonstrated that wars could be won from the sea, to undertake the command of the Chilean Navy—such as it was.

When he sailed into Valparaiso Bay in the *Rose* on 28 November 1818 he was greeted with rapturous enthusiasm. Bernardo O'Higgins rode the 90 miles from Santiago, down the road his father had constructed to connect the capital to its chief port, and there the governor of Valparaiso gave a grand dinner in Cochrane's honour at which the Admiral of Chile invited his new colleagues to a dinner on St Andrew's Night.

Great was the astonishment and admiration when this tall and imposing man presided at it in the full dress of a Highland Chief. Of course the Cochranes were not a Highland clan in Scotland, but Cochrane had left his native land just when its central myth was being expounded in its latest and most colourful form. Ever since its diverse peoples had opted to be 'Scots', they had borrowed from the history (though not the Gaelic language) of the minority of Scottish settlers from Ireland. Mediaeval Scottish Kings who spoke French listened with uncomprehending satisfaction at their coronations to the bogus Irish pedigree recited by a shenachie, and now Sir Walter Scott was waving the magic wand which would marshal even the inhabitants of the border country into clans with kilts and tartans. Today the Cochranes generally wear a sett of the Strathearn tartan, but in fact the Chief of their name had anticipated the modern myth. Charles II had bestowed upon an Earl of Dundonald and his descendants the right to wear the royal Stewart tartan, and so it was probably in this gorgeous scarlet sett that Cochrane appeared on St Andrew's night.

'Extraordinary good cheer was followed by toasts,' one of the guests recalled, 'drunk with uncommon enthusiasm in extraordinary good wine. No one escaped its enlivening influence. Saint Andrew was voted the patron saint of champagne, and many curious adventures of that night have furnished the subject of still remembered anecdotes.' The guest who cut short his reminiscences in this rather discreet way was the 23-year-old Major of Marines who was to become the right-hand man of Cochrane's commando operations. William Miller came from Kent. He was tall, like Cochrane, possessed the same fantastic courage, and combined with it the same humanity in war. Just as Marryat the Midshipman had fallen under Cochrane's spell in the *Impérieuse* and celebrated his hero in novels of the sea, so Miller did the same in memoirs that contain the best account of the war they won together. These memoirs were assembled for publication by his brother John Miller 10 years later, but his claim that he was merely editing his busy brother's raw material has been generally accepted.

William Miller was an outstanding example of the enterprising young men of British extraction who were now flocking to this land of opportunity. They came as merchants and traders, soldiers and sailors, and several of them would soon be feeding the appetite of the British reading public for all that concerned this burgeoning continent, with the tale of Cochrane's achievements. A handful of them would criticise him savagely, for it is the lot of men who possess such a dominant personality and such superlative talents that they move others to extremes of admiration, jealousy and hatred.

For his own part the 43-year-old Admiral, restored to a quarterdeck at last, faced for the first time in his life an administration and a society composed of men of entirely different backgrounds, speaking a foreign language. His difficulties were lightened by the fact that their leader Bernardo O'Higgins did not belong to the Spanish colonial aristocracy which was conducting the revolution, but was half-Irish and educated at Richmond. This stout, round-faced man with a slightly uptilted nose and a wide, determined mouth evoked a respect in Cochrane which he never lost. He was soon describing O'Higgins in a letter to his brother William as 'our excellent and truly worthy Director': and long after O'Higgins had fallen from power, Cochrane remained loyal to his memory.

The new Admiral's relations with General San Martín were to be tragically different. Like O'Higgins, San Martín was three years Cochrane's junior and like his companion in arms he was never again to match the achievement of his victorious march across the Andes. But this has sufficed to earn him his place among the folk-heroes of the world, and a host of monuments throughout the southern half of the continent of Latin America. In Britain the Admiralty's last and crowning insult to Cochrane's memory has been to name only a concrete ship at Rosyth after him. Young sailors with HMS *Cochrane* emblazoned on their cap ribbons do not know whom the name stands for, while Henry Cecil's lamentable book about him did not fail to find a publisher. Throughout South America every child of the race of San Martín could tell his story, while criticism of him at home would be consigned to the bonfire; abroad, would probably be the subject of ambassadorial protest.

It is therefore difficult to pass beyond the two contrasting worlds of legend in which both men now live in human memory, and to re-enter that actual society of Valparaiso late in 1818 in which they first encountered one another. Each possessed the defect of character that did the greatest damage to the careers of both at times when they were not associated with each other. When Lady Cochrane wrote to her husband 10 years later out of her ample experience, 'you have always had the misfortune to befriend rogues', it might with equal justice have been San Martín's wife saying the same to her own husband. The tragic conflict between these two great men is that while each had an unenviable record for befriending rogues, both took the other for the rogue that he was not.

This would perhaps be understandable in San Martín's case if he knew of Cochrane's conviction over 4 years earlier, and accepted it as evidence of the Admiral's guilt. But the Chilean envoy had written more recently that Cochrane 'bears a character altogether superior to ambitious self-seeking', a judgment which he was to justify throughout his Chilean service. If San Martín had disagreed, he would presumably have opposed the appointment of Cochrane.

But amongst the entourage of San Martín were Englishmen whose part in poisoning the relations between the two leaders is perniciously clear. One of these was the son of a schoolmaster at Barking in Essex who had sailed for South America 12 years earlier when he was 21 years old, and who possessed the Huguenot name of James Paroissien. He would rise to the rank of General without any achievement to justify his rank, embezzle funds as Peruvian envoy to Britain, and die at the age of 43 after failing in a gigantic mining speculation in Bolivia. It is not an edifying career, but Paroissien had fought in the Chilean war of liberation and had even dressed the wounds of O'Higgins when the Director was wounded in action. Here was one whose future financial dealings, as well as his vicious comments during Cochrane's Chilean service, proclaim the jealousy with which he regarded the much fêted Admiral from Britain. Nobody in Britain or abroad ever tried to denigrate Cochrane's naval feats with such childish stupidity as Paroissien did, and the question remains whether he attributed to Cochrane the ambitions that certainly dominated his own thoughts, and influenced San Martín to call the Admiral 'el metalico Lord'.

To some extent these thoughts were general among people of every race and calling, for this was the land of El Dorado, the great undeveloped continent in which anyone might legitimately seek his fortune. Cochrane himself wrote to his brother William in London: 'I have every prospect of making the largest fortune which has been made in our days, save that of the Duke of Wellington.' The means by which he would seek to achieve this before he left Chile, poorer than when he arrived, prove that he might have enriched Chile rather more than himself.

Two Englishmen who had more immediate cause for jealousy than any others were Captain Guise and Captain Spry, free-lance sailors whose prospects of obtaining supreme command had been dashed by Cochrane's appointment. Their Admiral, Blanco Encelada, set them an example of unselfish patriotism as soon as Cochrane arrived. He had just captured a Spanish frigate of forty-eight guns which was renamed the *O'Higgins*. It was an unimpressive feat. The vessel had arrived from Spain on convoy duty in a fleet undermined by mutiny and sickness, and it required little effort to remove her from the bay in which she lay under the guns of a few feeble forts. But since the Chilean fleet consisted merely of two East Indiamen and four little brigs like the *Speedy*, any such offensive action was virtually a wind-fall, and the capture of a frigate fit to be an Admiral's flagship especially timely. The prestige of his success might have enabled Admiral Blanco to hold out for an independent command as his officers pressed him to do, but instead he offered to serve under Cochrane.

T.S.W.—N

So the undercurrents which were to grow into whirlpools of strife hardly rippled the surface of that merry evening when Cochrane presided in full Highland dress amongst his new acquaintances and colleagues. An abstemious man, he continued to drink toasts while he took his uncertain measure of those about him: the bulky Supreme Director O'Higgins; the long-visaged rather melancholy-looking General San Martín; the self-effacing Admiral Blanco Encelada; and all those ambitious fellow-countrymen of the new Admiral who had crossed the Atlantic before him. Finally he suggested that the celebrations should be suspended until the war had been won and hoisted his flag aboard the *O'Higgins*, to put to sea with his little fleet of seven ships. It was the first time he had ever commanded a fleet, the first time for nearly 10 years that his long legs had walked a deck except as a passenger. No Chilean patriot could have been fired with a stronger sense of urgency than this seaman who had been stranded ashore during the most active years of his maturity.

For once Cochrane made a wise choice of personal secretary and interpreter. William Bennet Stevenson had lived in South America for even longer than Paroissien and the experience and quality of mind that he was able to place at his Admiral's disposal are attested by the three volumes of *A Historical and Descriptive Narrative of Twenty Years' Residence in South America* which he published 6 years later, and dedicated to Cochrane. His exactness is well illustrated by his description of Valparaiso as the Cochranes first set eyes on it. 'The Bay is of a semi-circular form, surrounded by very steep hills, which arise abruptly almost from the edge of the water . . . During the winter season they are covered with grass, with stunted trees and bushes . . . but the soil being of red clay, the verdure soon disappears when the summer sun begins to shine on them and the rain ceases to fall.' Stevenson preserves an antique picture of the 'town built between cliffs and sea, a row of houses or rather shops, a few good houses also in the narrow street. The suburbs stand in a kind of recess in the hills on a sandy plain: a fort on the south side of the harbour and a citadel on the hill behind the governor's palace.' He tells how the road which O'Higgins' father had built to Santiago crossed a range of mountains and a bare plain with a view of the distant snow-capped Andes, and adds that previously everything had been carried by mule, now by carts drawn by oxen. The first coach service was introduced in 1820. Stevenson possessed a mind akin to Cochrane's.

The Admiral weighed anchor on 16 January 1819, after his wife had come aboard to say good-bye and been rowed ashore again. She had never been parted from her sailor husband like this before, and evidently the experience took her mind off her children. William Horatio Bernardo, the younger (known to his family as Horace), was a mere baby, doubtless safely in the care of a nurse. But Thomas was a boy of 5, and for him it was also a new and exciting experience. Escaping from his home he made his way through the crowds to where the last of the sailors were embarking in the ship's boats. He found a man whom he recognised, the Flag-Lieutenant, and begged to be taken to his father. The officer lifted him on his shoulder, where Thomas waved his cap with glee, calling out 'Viva la Patria'—so quickly do children learn a foreign language. By the time his mother spotted him he was a tiny gesticulating figure suspended above the cheering crowd on the beach, and before she could reach him he was being rowed in one of the boats to the flagship, already under weigh.

His father was not the man to delay his departure in order to send his son ashore, and so the 600 sailors in the *O'Higgins* found themselves favoured with this strange mascot, whom they fitted out in a miniature midshipman's uniform with their own rough hands.

Cochrane decided to sail north to Callao, the port of Lima, seat of the Spanish viceroyalty, 1500 land miles to the north across the Tropic of Capricorn. This gave him a long sea voyage in which to introduce his exacting standards of discipline to the heterogeneous members of his fleet under their largely British complement of officers; Captains Crosbie and Foster who acted as flag captain by turns; Captain Wilkinson who had sold the two East Indiamen to the government; William Cobbett's nephew Henry who had once been a terror to Frederick Marryat in the *Impérieuse*; and Guise and Spry, the two Captains who wished the Chilean Navy to contain two Commodores and no Cochrane.

On the journey a mutiny broke out which compelled him to turn aside and land the offenders. Then he received news that a Spanish treasure ship was due to leave Callao for Cadiz and he cruised out of sight of land for a space in an unsuccessful effort to intercept her. He had prepared the first of the proclamations which appear to owe so much to the literary influence of Cobbett and his own past experience of Westminster politics. 'Doubt not,' he told the Peruvians, 'of the near approach of that great day on which, together with the dominion of tyranny, the degrading condition of Spanish colonies which now disgraces you will be at an end; and you will occupy among the nations that noble place to which you are called by your population, your riches, your geographical position and the course of circumstances.' It was a form of composition that he evidently enjoyed, and in which he improved considerably with practice.

He found the greater part of the Spanish fleet lying in Callao harbour when eventually he arrived there: three frigates, three brigs, a corvette and a schooner, six heavily armed merchantmen and twenty-seven gunboats. They mounted 350 guns between them and were protected by batteries that possessed another 160 guns. To make an attack on such an armament was out of the question, so Cochrane decided to attempt cutting out the frigates at the festive climax of the carnival, using every subterfuge he could contrive.

He planned first to sail the *O'Higgins* into Callao harbour with one other vessel under the flag of the United States, then to send a boat ashore on the pretext of landing despatches, and lastly to make a dash at one of the frigates. But he was defeated by the fog which is such a distressing feature of that coast. It came down in a blanket and outlasted the festival. The flagship engaged the batteries for 2 hours without harm, her companion vessel became separated from the remainder of the squadron, its other ships believed that Cochrane and his companion had sailed into action, and moved closer to land. Momentarily the fog lifted, disclosing the Chilean fleet huddled together with a Spanish gunboat in its midst. After her capture the Spanish Lieutenant informed Cochrane that the enemy firing had begun as a salute to the Viceroy on his visit to inspect the fortifications of Callao.

Down came the fog again, while Cochrane reflected that the visit of the Viceroy from Lima might be causing just as much distraction ashore as the carnival had done, and that he might yet cut out the frigates by using his feint under American colours. But the lookouts ashore had not been too preoccupied by the Viceregal presence to notice the capture of the gunboat during the brief interval in which the fog had lifted. This dignitary was given an opportunity to inspect his shore defences in a gun-fight with the hostile fleet, in which Cochrane's ships had to contend with shoals, fog and intermittent lack of wind as well as the fire of over 300 guns which bombarded them from ship and shore.

It provided a baptism of fire for the ship's mascot, as his father never forgot. 'When the firing commenced I had placed the boy in my after-cabin, locking the door upon him; but not liking the restriction, he contrived to get through the quarter gallery window, and joined me on deck, refusing to go down again. As I could not attend to him, he was permitted to remain and, in a miniature midshipman's uniform which the seamen had made for him, was busying himself in handing powder to the gunners. Whilst thus employed, a round-shot took off the head of a marine close to him, scattering the unlucky man's brains in his face. Instantly recovering his self-possession, to my great relief—for, believing him to be killed I was spell-bound with agony—he ran up to me exclaiming, "I am not hurt Papa. The shot did not touch me. Jack says the ball is not made that can kill Mama's boy."'

He was not only Mama's boy, but also his father's son. William Miller the Commandant of Marines was there, and he published his description of the incident decades before Cochrane did. 'The shot,' he recalled, 'scattered the brains of the marine in the child's face. He ran up to his father and, with an air of hereditary self-possession and unconcern, called out "Indeed Papa, the shot did not touch me; indeed I am not hurt."' Perhaps it is not surprising that Miller should have given Tom's age as 10 when in fact he was 5.

Cochrane's triumphs in the *Speedy* and the *Impérieuse* had been won by crews trained and inspired by his leadership to a superlative level of efficiency. Was he over-sanguine in supposing he might repeat them with the relatively unpractised seamen so recently assembled under his command? He had gambled on the element of surprise only to be defeated by the weather. Now the element of surprise was lost because the Spaniards had recognised the *O'Higgins* as their captured frigate and knew that the Sea Wolf had arrived in their midst. They gave him a new name—El Diablo, The Devil—and set about dismantling their ships to construct a protective boom across the entrance to their anchorage. Cochrane cast about for a base from which to blockade the port and decided upon the island of San Lorenzo three miles away, which he captured without difficulty. Here his seamen were able to receive the training they lacked while Miller constructed an explosion vessel like the one with which Cochrane had burst the boom at Rochefort.

At San Lorenzo island they found thirty-seven Chilean soldiers who had been taken prisoner 8 years before. 'The unhappy men,' Cochrane recorded, 'had ever since been forced to work in chains under the supervision of a military guard—now prisoners in turn; their sleeping place during the whole of this period being a filthy shed, in which they were every night chained by one leg to an iron bar. The joy of the poor fellows at their deliverance, after all hope had fled, can scarcely be conceived.' Cochrane learnt that there were other prisoners in Lima 'whose condition was even more deplorable than their own, the fetters on their legs having worn their ankles to the bone whilst their commander, by a refinement of cruelty, had for more than a year been lying under sentence of death as a rebel'.

Cochrane thereupon sent a deputation to the Spanish Viceroy under a flag of truce, suggesting a general exchange of prisoners. With little sense of his impending doom he snubbed Cochrane with this lofty reproof: 'The regulating principles of the proceedings of the Viceroy shall always be those of such gentleness and condescension as shall not derogate from the dignity of his official situation; and he will not now comment on the occupation of a nobleman of Great Britain, a country in alliance with the Spanish people, employing himself in commanding the naval forces of a government hitherto unacknowledged by any nation on the globe.'

The Viceroy may have been unaware that he was dealing with a man who delighted in such exchanges of paper shot, and who had acquired considerable skill in putting them to a propagandist use. Cochrane replied, and we may be sure his reply was widely circulated: 'His Excellency the Viceroy does well not to make any comment on the employment of a British nobleman in the great cause of Southern America. A British nobleman is a free man, capable of judging between right and wrong, and at liberty to adopt a country and a cause which aim at restoring the rights of oppressed human nature.' (Cochrane was exaggerating his liberties: he had been declared an outlaw in his own country for doing this.) 'Without failing in his duty, and without incurring any species of responsibility, Lord Cochrane was honourably competent to adopt the cause of Chile with the same freedom with which he refused the offered station of high admiral of Spain which was made to him by the Spanish ambassador in London.'

On the island of San Lorenzo an accident occurred in which inexperience probably played its part. Major Miller and ten of his marines were involved in an accidental explosion as they worked on their torpedo, and dreadfully burned. Miller's injury was so severe that his face swelled to twice its natural size, his features became unrecognisable, and he had to be fed through a sort of plaster mask. For days he was blind and delirious with pain, and he could not leave the cabin in which he was nursed for 6 weeks. Cochrane himself attended to the explosion vessel while his indispensable partner made his gradual recovery.

On 22 March 1819 it was ready and the little fleet sailed the 3 miles to Callao to engage its shore batteries while the explosion vessel was launched towards the Spanish frigates. In vain: it was sunk by gunfire. Cochrane did not possess the materials to construct another, and so the Viceroy in his fool's paradise at Lima was left laughing at the Devil's luck while the Chilean squadron sailed away on other business.

First, Cochrane must supply his ships with arms and ammunition by raiding the stores of enemy shore bases; next, he instituted a system of intelligence through patriots ashore, such as had served him so well in the Mediterranean. Thirdly, he sought and pounced upon vessels carrying money and bullion, for the government in Santiago possessed scant resources to pay his men. Once however, a landing party brought back the treasures of a church and Cochrane had the tact, as a Protestant serving a Catholic nation, to return it with an apology and a sum of money in compensation for the damage his men had done.

It was easier for him to exploit the weapon of propaganda than it had been in the days when he designed kites to drop leaflets over France, since so many of the literate population were favourable to his cause and might be spurred into activity merely by his encouragement and his heartening presence. 'Compatriots!' he assured them, 'the repeated echoes of liberty in South America have been heard with pleasure in every part of enlightened Europe, more especially in Great Britain where I, unable to resist the desire of joining such a cause, determined to take part in it. The Republic of Chile has confided to me the command of her naval forces. To these must the dominion of the Pacific be consigned. By their co-operation must your chains be broken.' As usual he was exaggerating the enlightenment that prevailed in his own country: this was the year of Lord Liverpool's repressive rule, in which the Peterloo Massacre is the best remembered outrage. The Duke of Wellington, who was such a pillar of support to the panicky government, declared his opposition to showing any favour to the South American liberation movement lest the oppressed Irish should be encouraged to follow so dangerous an example. 'Considering what is passing in Ireland,' declared Wellington in words that the Viceroy in Lima could not have improved upon, 'and what all expect will occur in that country before long, the bad with hope, the good with apprehension and dread, we must take care not to give additional examples these times of the encouragement of insurrection.'

In mid-May Cochrane returned to his wife and children at Valparaiso, to be greeted again with rapturous enthusiasm. Among other compliments a public panegyric was pronounced upon his achievements at the National Institute of Santiago, which described his first assault on the Spanish fleet like this: 'He arrives at Callao: that port is defended by the strongest forts of the Pacific, and crowned with batteries. Ten ships of war and a number of gunboats present a formidable barrier. The gallant Admiral seizes on the island of San Lorenzo, anchors his squadron there, undertakes to force an entry into the port, and goes forward with the *O'Higgins* and *Lautero*: three hundred pieces of artillery vomit death around him. From three sides the shots come to destroy his ships: but he advances unalterable, at a steady pace through these torrents of fire: he strikes terror into the enemy, he spreads around horror and death, he fires into their ships . . . After having harassed them severely, he returns serenely victorious to the rest of the squadron.'

Doubtless this was gratifying, like the enthusiasm which had greeted his first arrival in Chile. But he had not been serenely victorious and he knew it: the opportunity to strike a decisive blow had eluded him.

Don Bernardo the Supreme Director visited Valparaiso from his capital to review the fleet. Grappling with the problems of administering a new Republic and raising public money, O'Higgins told Cochrane that funds would not permit a resumption of naval operations. The Admiral offered his share of the prize money for the manufacture of Congreve's rockets, and O'Higgins agreed to the rockets but insisted that their cost should be borne by the government.

Early in August Cochrane travelled to Santiago, leaving his family by the sea, and there wrote to his brother William in a mood of hope tinged with nostalgia. 'Although all around is delightful, yet the recollection of friends left behind and scenes that are past throw a damp on the spirits which it is not easy to wipe off. All is doing admirably—the Rockets, which are the first ever made, are nearly ready in sufficient numbers to annihilate the Enemy's force at Callao; on which enterprise I shall proceed in about eight days, and having succeed, of which there is not a shadow of doubt, I shall prosecute further operations which I cannot detail at length . . .'

He asked his brother to seek the advice of Francis Place the radical tailor about supplies of naval uniform material. 'Pray send me out by the first opportunity—and Place can put you in the way (the learned tailor of Charing Cross)—two pieces of superfine blue navy cloth, and a gross of admiral's buttons *without the Crowns*—which are to be got for 3$^{s.}$ 6$^{d.}$ per dozen.' He also mentioned that Captain Foster had recently married a girl of their acquaintance, and suggested that William should tell a friend of theirs 'that I would undertake to get one or two of his daughters off hand *creditably* if he liked to send them out'. Evidently the young British officers in his wardroom did not take kindly to the years of celibacy on distant service which Cochrane had so cheerfully endured, and found little prospect of marriage in the Catholic Spanish society of South America.

William had reached the rank of Major in an army now swollen with officers for whom there was little future prospect since the return of peace, and Cochrane urged him to seek a new career in Chile. 'I could make your fortune here just now—Do take the difference got on half pay and I will undertake to settle the rest.' It was the attitude of all loyal and close-knit families, especially those which, like the houses of Wellesley and Cochrane, had lost the capital asset which launched each fresh generation into life. Cochrane ended his letter with a warmth which leapt over the convention of his time and class. 'Lady Cochrane is at Valparaiso the sea port to which I return tomorrow having finished my business here but she has commissioned me always to remember her affectionately to you—My love to Archibald and my sister and believe me ever my dear Brother affectionately yours Cochrane.'

Alas for his confidence in Congreve's rockets. Their manufacture was placed in the hands of Spanish prisoners of war, who filled them with rubbish so that they proved to be useless. But Cochrane could not foresee this as he made the long return journey to Callao in September. He had arranged to collect one thousand troops on the way, but when he reached their place of embarkation he found only ninety men waiting for him, and these were riddled with disease and dressed in rags. He sailed on to Callao Roads, where he constructed rafts for the rockets and another explosion vessel. On 2 October he delivered his grand assault with a precision that repaid the trouble he had taken to improve the discipline of his fleet.

Once again Cochrane tasted the bitter fruit of failure. His rockets, filled with sand, sawdust and manure, proved harmless. When his explosion vessel was launched against the boom on the following day the wind dropped at the vital moment and it had to be abandoned where it lay, a sitting target. Finally it blew up without causing the slightest damage to the enemy. Worst of all, Major Miller was once again seriously wounded while his superior officer Colonel Charles was killed. An epidemic of disease broke out in the fleet and there were symptoms of mutiny.

It was as well that Cochrane did not know what little Kitty was enduring at precisely this moment. In Valparaiso she had busied herself with such proper activities for an Admiral's wife as the promotion of welfare organisations for the navy, but after the squadron's departure she removed with her children to a country house at Quillota, and it was here that she was menaced by an agent of the Spanish régime. He found his way without being observed into her private apartment and threatened to kill her if she refused to tell him what secret orders her husband had received. Kitty dived to rescue a paper that was lying on her table and there was a struggle. By the time her attendants arrived in response to her screams she had received a severe cut from a stiletto. The culprit was taken into custody, condemned to death, and ordered to be executed, as a dreadful punishment, without the last rites of the Catholic religion.

On the night before the execution she was awakened by loud lamentations beneath her window. She summoned a servant to find out the cause of this disturbance, who brought the wife of the condemned man into her presence. She besought Kitty to obtain for him the con-consolations of confession and absolution before he died. She did rather more. On the following day she travelled to interview the authorities, and prevailed on them to commute his punishment to banishment for life.

Unaware of the danger from which his wife had escaped, Cochrane lay off Callao surveying the wreck of his hopes. During the centuries since King Robert Bruce had created his nation of Scotland, it had reared just two men of the same calibre, that great soldier the Marquess of Montrose and himself, men who found their transcendant greatness in the extremities of difficulty and misfortune. The time had come for him to give effect to the words of the Scotsman who is his closest kindred spirit.

> He either fears his fate too much
> Or his deserts are small
> Who dares not put it to the touch
> To gain or lose it all.

Abandoning Callao, Cochrane dispersed his ships to various stations and sailed south alone in the *O'Higgins* for nearly 2000 miles. It was his intention to return to the form of the single-ship action which he had perfected in the *Impérieuse*, having still only one frigate at his command. His target was to be the other great Spanish arsenal on the Pacific, which lay hundreds of miles south of Valparaiso.

Valdivia has been described as the Gibraltar of that hemisphere, and it was reputed to be impregnable. He arrived in its waters on 18 January 1820 and William Miller, who accompanied him, recorded his words there. 'Well Major, Valdivia we must take. Sooner than put back it would be better that we all went to the bottom. Cool calculation would make it appear that an attempt to take the town is madness. There is one reason why the Spaniards will hardly believe us in earnest, and you will see that a bold onset, and a little perseverance afterwards, will give a complete triumph. For operations unsuspected by the enemy are, when well executed, certain to succeed whatever the odds.' With such words as these Montrose had led his cold, weary and hungry men out of wintry Scottish mountains to rout the great army which lay encamped below them on the day of Inverlochy.

Major Miller had not been on deck since he was so severely wounded 11 weeks before, but he now joined his Admiral on the quarterdeck to survey the target which lay before them. The spectacle was very different from that of tropical Callao and Miller left a vivid description of it. 'The country is beautiful, and clothed in perpetual verdure, rains being frequent and heavy ten months out of the twelve. The soil is rich, and produces potatoes of superior quality; apples are also very abundant. The banks of the river are bold and covered with majestic cedars and other forest trees.' Up the river lay the port of Valdivia, guarded on either side by forts as the estuary widened for fifteen miles to its mile-wide entrance into the Pacific.

Up the estuary sailed Cochrane under Spanish colours, and signalled for the services of a pilot as soon as he came within range of Valdivia. There his ship was mistaken for a Spanish vessel whose arrival was overdue, and an officer was sent aboard with four soldiers. The pilot obligingly directed the *O'Higgins* through the channels which led to the town's forts, whilst all the captives supplied Cochrane with a variety of useful information. Not least was the news that a brig of war bringing money for the payment of the garrison was expected, since Cochrane was once more bedevilled by the arrears of his own men's pay.

The peaceful reconnaissance was ended abruptly by a heavy bombardment from the forts. Their garrison commander had become suspicious of the flagship's movements; and the continued detention of the pilot's party at last convinced him that he had been the victim of treachery. But Cochrane had learned what he needed by the time he was forced to retire out of range and complete his survey from a greater distance. He hovered there until on the third day the pay ship came in sight.

She sailed on without the slightest suspicion that the frigate flying Spanish colours might contain El Diablo himself, alone in the mouth of Spain's strongest Pacific base. Cochrane captured her without firing a shot and took out of her $20,000 and some helpful despatches. Then he sailed away in search of a detachment of soldiers, for the enterprise he had planned would require a larger force than the 600 men aboard the *O'Higgins*.

Some 200 miles north of Valdivia lay the nearest garrison of the republican army of Chile, commanded by General Freire, a soldier of French extraction who had fought under San Martín in the crossing of the Andes with the rank of Colonel and now occupied the post of Governor of Concepción. It was Freire's difficult task to subdue the Indian tribes whom the Spaniards had encouraged to rise against the colonial aristocracy which was conducting the independence movement. Many of them did so with the utmost enthusiasm, in the hope that they would find release from servitude, and the atrocities they committed helped further to obscure Cochrane's understanding of the real issues of human freedom in this hemisphere. Although Freire could ill spare any of the troops under his command he was easily persuaded that the capture of Valdivia would virtually decide the issue of the war in this area, and he lent Cochrane 250 of his men.

Remembering the appalling standards of British security during the Napoleonic war, Cochrane asked Freire not to inform the government in Santiago of the loan of his troops lest he should forfeit any of the advantages of secrecy, and the General generously agreed although this might expose him to grave censure. Before the men were embarked in a brig and a schooner they were given a false story of the aim of the expedition, so that if any of them should happen to be captured their information would positively deceive the enemy.

But there was one defect in Cochrane's resources that could not be remedied. He had felt obliged to leave his most efficient officers in command of the other ships in his fleet, so that the *O'Higgins* contained only two other officers of whom one was by now under arrest for disobedience to orders, while the other had proved totally incompetent to carry out the duties of a Lieutenant. On the other hand, William Miller had recovered sufficiently from his injuries to resume his duties. On January 1820 the tiny armada sailed for Valdivia, and as soon as they were at sea Cochrane briefed the officers of the borrowed soldiers, since they had an extremely short time in which to prepare for an operation which would depend to such an extent on mutual confidence and careful training. During the entire journey south Cochrane combined the duties of Admiral, Captain of the flagship and First Lieutenant, which involved remaining constantly on watch.

As he confessed, the ordeal proved too much for him. 'On the night of the 29th we were off the island of Quiriquina in a dead calm. From excessive fatigue in the execution of subordinate duties I had laid down to rest, leaving the ship in charge of the Lieutenant, who took advantage of my absence to retire also, surrendering the watch to the care of a midshipman, who fell asleep. Knowing our dangerous position, I had left strict orders to be called the moment a breeze sprang up; but these orders were neglected, and a sudden wind taking the ship unawares, the midshipman, in attempting to bring her round, ran her upon the sharp edge of a rock where she lay beating, suspended as it were upon her keel; and had the swell increased she must inevitably have gone to pieces.' They were 40 miles from the mainland; the brig and the schooner were not in sight.

Cochrane was awakened out of his sleep by the movement of the vessel and the clamour of 600 men attempting to abandon ship in boats that would not have held more than 150 of them. Never was the adamant personality of Cochrane faced with a more stupendous task than that stampede of panicking seamen presented to him, shouting to each other in a foreign language as he hurried on deck in the darkness. Somehow he managed to persuade them that torture and death at the hands of savage tribes was all those could expect who succeeded in reaching the majestic forests of the distant coast. Somehow he convinced them that they must and could save their ship.

He had scant grounds for conviction himself. 'The first sounding gave five feet of water in the hold, and the pumps were entirely out of order. Our carpenter, who was only one by name, was incompetent to repair them; but having myself some skill in carpentry, I took off my coat and by midnight got them into working order, the water meanwhile gaining on us though the whole crew were engaged in bailing it out with buckets.' Once again his early training under Jack Larmour had paid off. Miller witnessed the double feat which Cochrane performed that night and described it to his countrymen with this comment: 'By his indefatigable activity and skill the frigate was prevented from sinking, and by the serenity and firmness of his conduct he checked a general disposition to abandon the ship.' In fiction such a feat would not seem credible.

As soon as the pumps started working the tide began to turn for them. 'To our great delight,' wrote Cochrane, 'the leak did not increase, upon which I got out the stream anchor and commenced heaving off the ship, the officers clamouring to ascertain first the extent of the leak. This I expressly forbade as calculated to damp the energy of the men, whilst as we now gained on the leak, there was no doubt the ship would swim as far as Valdivia, which was the chief point to be regarded; the capture of the fortress being my object, after which the ship might be repaired at leisure.' What other commander would have clung to his objective in such circumstances, particularly after discovering that the entire stock of ammunition had been destroyed by flooding except the small supply in cartouche boxes that were stored on deck? This last disaster Cochrane dismissed with the comment: 'About this I cared little as it involved the necessity of using the bayonet in our anticipated attack and to facing this weapon the Spaniards had, in every case, evinced a rooted aversion.'

The rising wind brought a heavy swell, in which Cochrane transferred Miller and his marines the next day to the brig and the schooner which held the troops. Since the garrison of Valdivia could now recognise the *O'Higgins* as an enemy vessel, he left her at anchor out of sight of the shore in command of the incompetent but chastened Lieutenant, while he shifted his flag to the brig. With his two small transports he approached the nearest forts, hoping to take the Spaniards by surprise as evening fell. But the wind which played the part of the

Homeric gods in the days of sail, deserted them and frustrated the plan.

The transports had reached the lethal waters of a channel three-quarters of a mile wide in which no ship could escape the cross-fire from the forts on either bank. Beyond lay the anchorage and the river leading to the town of Valdivia. Except for one small landing place beneath a fort, the shore was made impregnable by the pounding surf. Cochrane's only possible course was to gain access to that single landing place and march his men in single file up the precipitous path which led to the fort above. His brig and schooner flew Spanish colours; his troops were huddled out of sight below; the two launches and the gig which they had brought surreptitiously with them were secured on the far side of each vessel, out of sight of the fort above the landing place. Cochrane signalled for a pilot and was ordered to send a boat for him. He replied that he had just arrived from Cadiz, and that his boats had been washed away in the passage round Cape Horn.

To the consternation of those who kept watch in the little transports, they saw troops filing down the steep path to the landing place, while alarm guns signalled to the other forts to send reinforcements. Then the fatal accident occurred. One of the launches concealed under the lee of its transport drifted astern in the swell, revealing Cochrane's deception to the shore garrison. At once the fort above the landing place opened fire and two men aboard were killed. The moment for attempting the impossible could no longer be delayed.

The gallant young Miller pushed off in the first launch with forty-four marines, and when his coxswain was wounded he seized the helm himself. A bullet struck his hat but only grazed the crown of his head. They beached in the surf and rushed through it with bayonets fixed, and as Cochrane had predicted the Spaniards retreated before them. The Admiral had already entered the gig to direct operations and he now ordered the other launch to land its men. In less than an hour 300 soldiers and marines had made good their footing on the narrow landing place. Above their heads they could see the Spanish troops climbing by ladder up the wall of their fort and then drawing the ladders after them. It appeared that this was the only mode of entry.

Cochrane waited for darkness to fall and then divided his troops into two parties. The first climbed up the narrow path under the guidance of one of the Spanish prisoners and made their way in total silence to the far side of the fort, which they found to be protected by a ditch. While they were taking up their position here the second party moved forward, shouting threats, and the din they made was increased by an answering fire from the fort, from which the Spaniards poured the ammunition of their muskets and artillery into empty darkness. Such was the noise that the first party was not heard tearing up pallisades to bridge the ditch. Once within it, the men fired a sudden volley of their scant ammunition and it filled the Spaniards with such terror that they fled from their fort into the arms of a column of 300 of their comrades, who had arrived in answer to the summons for assistance. In the ensuing confusion these became infected with the same panic and all retreated helter-skelter to the next fort, chased at the point of the bayonet by a force of less than half their strength, armed with nothing but cold steel.

Darkness and fear proved to be more effective weapons than the ruined powder could have provided. Cochrane's men reached the second fort as quickly as those they pursued, and when it was opened to receive the Spaniards they rushed in behind, killing and wounding their enemy by dozens. So it continued until the stampede reached the innermost stronghold of all, the Castle of Corral. This at least it should have been possible to hold. But by now the Spaniards were so utterly demoralised that they allowed it to be stormed as well. While some escaped by boat to Valdivia, others sought safety in the surrounding forests. By dawn Cochrane saw from his gig the flag of Chile flying from the citadel of Corral; so did the troops in the forts on the north shore of the estuary, and it was a signal to them to abandon their own. With a couple of small transports, no ammunition and a sinking frigate beyond the horizon, Cochrane had captured the Gibraltar of the Pacific. He had done it with the loss of seven men killed and nineteen wounded. About a hundred of the enemy had been captured and as many again bayoneted.

Wasting no time in sleep, Cochrane returned to the *O'Higgins* and sailed her into Valdivia harbour. At the very sight of her the troops on the north bank fled from their forts though they might, had they stayed to look, have seen the Admiral's flagship laid on a mud bank to prevent her from sinking. One of the transports grounded accidentally on another mud bank and became a total wreck. The other was thus the last surviving ship in the fleet of the Admiral of Chile in which to sail to take possession of his prize. But a flag of truce came out to meet him in his way, with information of the flight of the Governor, of the plundering and disorder that had followed the Spanish retreat, of the wholesale flight of the inhabitants, and of the terror of those who remained. For the first time Cochrane adopted the role that was to be a recurrent feature of his service in South America. He moved in to restore order and establish a new civil government in place of the one he had dethroned.

On 6 February 1820 he was able to write from Valdivia to Santiago:

'We at least have the happiness to know that we have omitted nothing that might protect the people who, distinguishing between friends and oppressors, have assisted in the maintenance of good order. Those who had fled from their houses are beginning to return.' His report reflects the constructive approach which he adopted when he found himself with virtually untrammelled powers on sea and land. 'At first it was my intention to have destroyed the fortifications, and to have taken the artillery and stores on board; but I could not resolve to leave without defence the safest and most beautiful harbour I have seen in the Pacific, and whose fortifications must have cost more than a million dollars.'

The news that Cochrane had once more accomplished a feat without precedent in naval warfare was carried across the Atlantic to all those who had played a part in removing him from the British service. The busy, obsequious Croker remained Secretary to the Admiralty while administrations came and went. Admiral the Earl of St Vincent was still alive at the age of 85 to recall the young seaman who had once treated him with such impertinence, and whom he had rewarded with an old converted collier. Admiral Gambier was still in his early sixties, though it was years since he had been offered employment, and then it had been merely to act in a civil capacity as commissioner for a peace treaty. Lord Chief Justice Ellenborough had followed his reputation to the grave. The Prince Regent had just succeeded as King George IV, the most detested sovereign in British history. If Cochrane had time to reflect on the arrival of the news amongst the men who had humbled and insulted him, his thoughts must have been balm to his wounded pride.

An inventory of the captured stores was drawn up. There was upwards of 1,000 hundredweight of gunpowder to compensate for what had been lost in the *O'Higgins*, 128 guns, almost half of them cast in brass, 10,000 cannon shot and 170,000 cartridges, a corresponding number of small arms; and greatest prize of all for one in Cochrane's plight, the good ship *Dolores*. With such resources at his disposal Cochrane decided to attempt an assault on the Spanish garrison which occupied Chiloé, an island over 150 miles in length which guarded the approach to that majestic, relatively untrodden region of southern Chile which is so largely compounded of mountain and glacier, fjord and island. But unfortunately for his expedition the enemy were thoroughly prepared, and not even the courage of Miller as he led the assault could prevail against the hail of fire that greeted them. When he fell with a grape shot through his thigh and his right foot crushed by round shot, his marines showed their devotion to him. Risking their lives at every move, they ran to lift him where he lay and carried him to the beach and the boats that waited to carry the men back to their ship.

Cochrane never forgot what they had done and commemorated their courage nearly 40 years later in these words. 'The marines who, with affectionate fidelity, had borne off Major Miller had been careful to protect him from fire, though two out of the three who carried him were wounded in the act; and when, on arrival at the beach, they were invited by him to enter the boat, one of them, a gallant fellow named Roxas of whom I had spoken highly in my despatches from Valdivia on account of his distinguished bravery, refused saying, "No Sir, I was the first to land and I mean to be the last to go on board." He kept his word; for on his Commander being placed in safety he hastened back to the little band, now nearly cut up, and took his share in the retreat, being the last to get into the boats. Such were the Chilenos.'

These despatches from Valdivia were addressed to the Minister of Marine, José Ignacio Zenteno, and they caused him some embarrassment, for he had made the very mistake which Admiral Blanco Encelada had avoided, that of lending an ear to the arch-trouble-maker of the Chilean navy, Captain Spry. William Stevenson had been present to observe that even before Cochrane's arrival to take up his appointment Spry had declaimed against it, 'without alleging any other reason than that it was quite contrary to all republican principles to allow a nobleman to retain his title in the service'. Spry had been able to advance more specious criticism when Cochrane had sailed away on his secret mission to Valdivia, especially when he had profited by the experience of the Scheldt fiasco by withholding information about his plans which might have fallen into the hands of the enemy. By the time the news of Valdivia's capture reached Zenteno he had unfortunately identified himself with the strictures of Spry, and he would only have been human if he had shared some of the jealousy of the mischievous Englishman when he learned of an achievement which he had done nothing as Minister of Marine to promote.

Nevertheless Zenteno replied to Cochrane in handsome terms. 'My Lord, if victories over an enemy are to be estimated according to the resistance offered, or the national advantages obtained, the conquest of Valdivia is, in both senses, inestimable; encountering as you did the national and artificial strength of that impregnable fortress which, till now, had obstinately defended itself by means of those combined advantages. The memory of that glorious day will occupy the first pages of Chilean history, and the name of Your Excellency will be transmitted from generation to generation by the gratitude of our descendants.' This prediction was to be amply fulfilled.

Zenteno introduced a sour note however when Cochrane made his triumphal return to Valparaiso on 27 February. The Minister of Marine told his Admiral that he had acted like a madman, that he deserved to have lost his life in the attempt, and that he now deserved to lose his head for risking the safety of the forces under his command in such a manner without instructions. In fairness to Zenteno it must be recalled that this charge was made against Cochrane repeatedly on both sides of the world throughout his long life, even after each of his daring strategems had been crowned with ever more dazzling success. Nor would the motive of jealousy on Zenteno's part be hard to understand. Throughout South America men were elbowing one another in a scramble for the reins of power that were slipping from Spanish hands. The immediate enemy was only the representative of Spain until the moment of his defeat: then the man who had won the victory might easily become the next target, especially if he were a foreigner. Cochrane became an object of jealousy and suspicion to more powerful men than Spry as soon as he had demonstrated his full capacity, particularly because he possessed no rival at sea (as the generals did on land) although this was such a crucial theatre of the war.

Cochrane received his first serious intimations of this soon after he had taken the injured William Miller to stay in the house he had acquired in Santiago. The emergency took him to Valparaiso, when Miller was invited to complete his convalescence in the home of a Chilean officer. The gallant commander of Marines paid tribute to all this care and kindness in words that only had to wait 8 years for publication. 'The national character does not perhaps display a more amiable trait than the unceasing care with which people of every class watch over the stranger whom sickness overtakes and places at their threshold. Without distinction of rank or party, the palace or the hut is alike open to the invalid, for whom the liveliest sympathy is evinced by every individual of the family.'

The crisis which faced Cochrane was caused by a repeated failure to pay his seamen their arrears of wages. The finances of the new nation were indeed in a precarious condition, though Cochrane's victory had given it sufficient credit abroad to enable it to obtain a loan of a million pounds from Britain. Cochrane began to suspect that men who feared his rivalry were deliberately undermining the morale of the fleet on which his power depended, though he might have reflected that the firmly established British government had treated its own sailors in very much the same way. He had inveighed against it in his own country, and now that he possessed the authority of an Admiral he was determined to ensure that the men who had served him with such courage and fidelity should receive their just deserts.

Lady Cochrane's pregnancy was a further cause of anxiety until she gave birth to a daughter, whom they called Elizabeth Katherine. On 10 April 1820 Cochrane wrote to inform his brother William, in a somewhat hasty letter filled with high spirits. 'You will be glad to learn that I am doing famously here, and have prospects for the future better than the past, as we are now in earnest preparing for the *invasion* of *Peru* . . .' He appears to be well content with the land of his adoption, except that he has the prejudice from which a native of Calvinist Scotland could hardly have escaped. 'What a noble country this will be in a few years, especially if the cursed priests are put down, who are busy fomenting all kinds of illiberal prejudices in order to keep the people in the dark as to their knavery and humbug.'

But he was having second thoughts about his recommendation that his brothers should emigrate to Chile. 'I cannot make up my mind as to whether Archibald and you, if so inclined, would make yourselves tolerably comfortable here or not, as the society is so totally different from anything in Europe and the *military* service on shore is almost a guerilla, though it is tolerable afloat, the officers being almost all Englishmen.' However, he had an alternative to the profession of arms to offer his brothers. The Chilean government had rewarded him with the gift of an estate and already he was turning his mind to the crops that might be introduced into this country, and the agricultural machinery that could transform its farming methods. 'They have presented me with a farm of twenty thousand acres almost as big as the New Forest, and I am in treaty to purchase eighty thousand more of which you shall have a good slice when you can do nothing better.' The eldest brother's solicitude remained as strong as ever as he scribbled in his energetic hand 'Adieu my dear Brother. I have many other letters to send in haste. Ever yours most affectionately Cochrane.'

During the remaining months of preparation for the Peruvian expedition Cochrane was scarcely ever free of worry over the administration of the navy. A month after he had written that letter to his brother William the sailors had still not received their arrears of pay and as their hardships and murmurings increased he was driven to play his trump card. On 14 May he tendered his resignation to the Supreme Director. An attempt was made to suborn him with the offer of an estate confiscated from one of the adherents of the Spanish government, but he rejected it. 'The only hold upon the seamen,' he explained, 'was my personal influence with them, in consequence of my unyielding advocacy of their rights—a hold which I was not likely to forego for a grant to myself. In place, therefore, of accepting the estate, I returned the document conveying the grant with a request that it might be sold and the proceeds applied to the payment of the squadron; but the requisition was not complied with.'

The deadlock was broken by the arrival of General San Martín, who had been recruiting soldiers in his native Argentina for the invasion of Peru, and now required the Chilean fleet to escort it to its destination. On 13 July the seamen at last received a part of their arrears of wages, and when Cochrane held out for the whole the remainder was handed to them 3 days later.

But no sooner had this cause of discord been removed than a fresh one took its place. Captain Spry was appointed Flag Captain to the newly repaired *O'Higgins* without the Admiral being consulted. This man who proved to be nothing but a squalid nuisance in the Chilean Navy until the day he simply deserted it evidently possessed an extremely plausible personality. He succeeded in exercising his baneful influence on men as diverse as Captain Guise, an able naval officer who might otherwise have served Cochrane as well as all those other British sailors; General San Martín; and Zenteno the Minister of Marine. Cochrane threatened resignation again, and once more he won. The appointment of Spry was withdrawn and he was permitted to select his own Flag Captain.

But the trouble-maker turned his attention to the pliant Captain Guise as soon as he learnt that neither San Martín nor Zenteno had served his purpose, and stirred him to acts of direct disobedience to orders which compelled Cochrane to arrest him and ask the government for his court-martial. Zenteno refused, whereupon Cochrane despatched his resignation for the third time and informed the officers of his squadron that his command would cease from the moment of its arrival in the Minister's hands.

It was the signal for his loyal officers to express their solidarity in terms that could not be mistaken by the administration they served. 'My Lord,' they wrote to Cochrane from the *Independencia* on 18 July, 'the general discontent and anxiety which your Lordship's resignation has occasioned amongst the officers and others of the squadron afford a strong proof how much the ungrateful conduct of the Government is felt by those serving under your command.

'The officers whose names are subscribed to the enclosed resolutions, disdaining longer to serve under a Government which can so soon have forgotten the important services rendered to the State, beg leave to put in your hands their commissions, and to request you will be kind enough to forward them to the Minister of Marine.' The resolutions stated that the Chilean Navy depended entirely on the abilities of Cochrane, and they were signed by twenty-three officers.

Zenteno had already demonstrated the treacherous facility with which he could applaud his Admiral in public and intrigue behind his back. Faced with the alternative of a fleet commanded by the two would-be Commodores without a Cochrane, he once more employed his arts of blandishment. Two days after the ultimatum of the officers he wrote to Cochrane: 'My Lord, at a moment when the services of the naval forces of the State are of the highest importance and the personal services of your Lordship indispensable, the Supremacy with the most profound sentiments of regret has received your resignation which, it should be admitted, would involve the future operations of the army of liberty in the New World in certain ruin; and ultimately replace in Chile, your adopted home, that tyranny which your Lordship abhors, and to the annihilation of which your heroism has so greatly contributed.' No higher compliment could have been paid him than the assertion that in his hands alone lay the fate and destiny of South America, and it was endorsed both by San Martín and by O'Higgins, who each added their plea that he would not desert their cause.

Cochrane withdrew his resignation and reinstated Guise in the command of his ship, explaining 40 years later: 'I would not have done this but from a feeling of personal attachment to the Supreme Director General O'Higgins.' Cochrane was a man as inflexible in his loyalties as in his animosities.

Peace returned to the fleet, but it was a reconciliation soured by mistrust as Cochrane's next action reveals. He took the precaution of obtaining the signature of General San Martín, jointly with his own, to the following proclamation. 'On my entry into Lima, I will punctually pay to all foreign seamen who shall voluntarily enlist into the Chilean service the whole arrears of their pay, to which I will also add to each individual, according to his rank, one year's pay over and above his arrears as a premium or reward for his services if he continues to fulfil his duty to the day of the surrender of the city, and its occupation by the liberating forces.' With this formidable obligation he recovered the confidence of his men as they prepared for the long sea voyage to Peru.

It was still Cochrane's intention to settle permanently in Chile, and he had already selected the site of the home he intended to build there, the estate of Herradura which lay in the pleasant land-locked bay at Quintero, eight miles north of Valparaiso. Before the Peruvian armada sailed he wrote to Britain, ordering ploughs, harrows and spades, implements that were not yet manufactured in Chile and had never been imported before. He also placed orders for seeds of carrots and turnips, crops which he was the first to introduce to Chile, larch, beech and oak that had never been grown there hitherto. His preparations for war did not prevent him from laying his plans for the peace which would follow.

For the third time the government offered him an estate in recognition of his services. Zenteno wrote to inform him of the Supreme Director's decree on the subject on 20 August. 'The present deed shall serve as a sufficient title to the property in favour of the Vice Admiral,' he was assured by that slippery individual. On the same day he said farewell to his wife and three children and set off with San Martín on their joint enterprise.

CHAPTER TEN

The Liberation of Peru

The Christian tradition of European drama has commonly represented human conflict as a struggle between good and evil enacted by heroes and villains. The ancient Greeks often pursued their personal enmities with as much rancour as did Cochrane, but their dramatists usually found a deeper meaning in the conduct of the combative human species by dispensing with the myth that men are motivated exclusively by virtuous or wicked impulses. They found the true sources of tragedy in far more intricate and moving causes, which lifted the actors on the world's stage above the level of censure or praise.

Their detachment has touched few of the writers who have recounted the stories of Cochrane or San Martín, so that in the biographies of each they are forever exchanging the costumes of the hero and the villain, and a theme worthy of the pen of Euripides has never been treated by a great dramatist in such a manner as to rescue the two men from their charade. The people who witnessed and commented upon the conflict that was about to erupt between them were likewise confused by what they saw, so that their diverse evidence has helped to confuse as well as to enlighten posterity. From this evidence it is possible to compose a convincing portrait of either as the villain and either as the hero.

These witnesses, the chorus in the approaching tragedy, began their embarkation in Valparaiso bay on 18 August 1820 in the festive atmosphere of flags, crowds and military music which the Chileans knew so well how to enjoy. There were about 4,500 troops, Chileans for the most part but reinforced by veterans from Argentina, to sail to Peru in eighteen transports escorted by seven warships. Among the General's principal aides was the Englishman James Paroissien, who had recently abandoned his military career in favour of commercial speculations, but had returned to it a few weeks earlier at San Martín's invitation. Another was Juan García del Río, a native of the north who had travelled to England before he reached Chile and whose friendship with Paroissien was to play its part in Cochrane's story. But the most fateful appointment was that of Bernardo Monteagudo as Secretary of War, a man with whom Paroissien had formed a friendship 10 years

216 The Liberation of Peru

earlier, and who had since become Advocate-General of the army which San Martín led in the heroic march through the Andes. Even then Monteagudo had sullied his General's reputation by his brutal behaviour, just as he would do more than any other man in Peru to destroy it. If there was a stage villain among the men who embarked in that fleet it was Monteagudo.

Cochrane possessed the services of William Miller, raised to the rank of Colonel, and Stevenson as his secretary. Nearly all of his officers were still sailors of Britain or the United States, and the transports were commanded by Captain Paul Delano from Massachusetts. About a third of the sailors and marines were of the same foreign origins. As their fleet sailed out into a calm sea under clear skies, O'Higgins the Supreme Director declared that the destiny of America lay in the hands of those who travelled in it.

It would have been surprising if Cochrane had possessed as great an understanding of the country for which they were bound as San Martín. He had reached Chile after a republic had been established with the overwhelming support of the Spanish and creole population. When Cochrane wrote his letters to Britain they were carried through the Andes to Mendoza and thence to the capital of Argentina at Buenos Aires in the newly liberated United Provinces. Chile was not isolated in her independence but linked to another freed republic and to the world beyond.

Peru by contrast was the centre of Spanish power in South America, possessing in Lima its most magnificent city, its greatest centre of wealth, its most civilised and aristocratic society. While revolution ebbed and flowed round the perimeters, successive viceroys of Peru had crushed it with a strong hand, and many of the rich merchants with their links with Spain, the ecclesiastics and the courtiers, must have regarded Admiral Cochrane with as much alarm as their counterparts in London had done when he was Member of Parliament for Westminster. He certainly regarded them as the precise equivalents of the corrupt officials, jobbing politicians and courtiers fattening on gigantic sinecures whom he had attacked in Britain. He made this plain in the letter in which he told his brother of the impending invasion of Peru, 'where there will be glorious pickings from the Castlereaghs, Buckinghams, and other political and sinecure robbers of that land of slaves'.

This remark, of which such damaging use might have been made by his enemies if his letter had been intercepted, did not imply that he would embezzle public money as Paroissien did when the opportunity came his way, or indulge in the rapacious bestialities which finally led to the lynching of Monteagudo in the streets of Lima. The record of his acts entirely refutes such an imputation. But it does suggest that he was judging a society he did not know by one that was familiar to him, and sailed to Peru not so much a liberator as a conqueror, one who wished to destroy a system that he had attacked in vain the other side of the world.

What made the analogy between Britain and Peru such a false one was that the Spanish viceroyalty was, literally, a land of slaves. To destroy the régime of Castlereagh in Lima would not be to right the wrongs of Peruvians resembling the Lancashire weaver Samuel Bamford or London tailor Francis Place. Beneath the castes of Spanish aristocrats and wealthy creoles of mixed blood the overwhelming majority of negro slaves and native Indians lived in a state of subjection from which nobody was planning to liberate them. On the contrary, both sides in the struggle for independence lived with the same fear that they might seize the opportunity to liberate themselves, and Cochrane had seen something of one of these desperate and pathetic native offensives during his Valdivia expedition.

In Peru the different castes were divided not only by race and social status but also by the country's fantastic geography. Its million and a half people were divided between those who lived on the coastal plain, and the inhabitants of the high sierras, many of them remote and inaccessible. Spaniards were lured here only by the wealth of the silver mines: they rarely penetrated beyond the great range of mountains to the forest lands of the east which comprise the greater part of Peru. Most of them lived on the coast, or in their capital of 64,000 inhabitants with its cathedral and university, its walls 10 feet thick and its wonderful architecture. William Miller reckoned that they possessed 23,000 regular troops for their defence, of whom nearly 8,000 were stationed at Callao and Lima while the remainder were posted at the centres of disturbance in the north and south. No wonder Joaquín de la Pezuela, the Viceroy, had treated Cochrane with such contempt when the Admiral had asked for an exchange of prisoners. Even now he possessed almost twice as many soldiers on the spot as San Martín was bringing to Peru.

San Martín was by nature extremely cautious; he would never embark on any undertaking beyond the point at which the odds remained heavily in his own favour. But above all, it was San Martín's determination to enter Lima as a liberator, not as a conqueror, even though it was far from clear how the inhabitants could be persuaded by anything except force that they wished to be liberated.

The gulf between the Admiral and the General who led this expedition was thus complete, and every possible discrepancy of temperament, intention and method conspired to bring two men of more than ordinary stature into fatal collision. It might have been avoided if either or both of them had possessed the magic gift of human understanding in a higher degree. But the proud, touchy, impetuous Scottish nobleman stood as far beyond San Martín's focus as the dark, thoughtful creole was beyond Cochrane's limited comprehension of the subtleties of humankind, and both men were bedevilled by the agents of discord who increased their suspicions of one another.

They sailed north in separate ships, Cochrane in his flagship the *O'Higgins*, the General in the ship named after him *San Martín*. It was naturally Cochrane's expectation that they would make an immediate assault on Callao, so that he was horrified when San Martín ordered him instead to land the army at Pisco, a hundred miles to the south. The two men generally conversed with one another in French without using an interpreter. Either they were handicapped by language difficulties (though they were to exchange insults with sufficient clarity) or San Martín did not try hard enough to explain his strategy to Cochrane, or the Admiral refused to be persuaded. The latter explanation is probable enough, for San Martín was proposing to lie at Pisco while he tried the temper of the Peruvians by making landings up and down the coast and sending expeditions into the interior. Cochrane's considerable experience of war had taught him the truth of Nelson's axiom to dispense with such manoeuvres and go at them. Zenteno would certainly have prevented him from capturing Valdivia if he had not made his expedition in secrecy and without orders. If Cochrane could equate Viceregal Lima with Regency London, he could as easily mistake San Martín for another Lord Gambier, a superior from whose timidity there was no escape because he was directing operations on the spot. Whether he did so or not, it was at least apparent to him that if he were to repeat his feat at Valdivia he would probably have to contrive it without the co-operation of his General. Such a course would inevitably involve a further breakdown in communication between the two leaders.

The debate has not ended as to whether Cochrane could have made good his claim that the immediate capture of Lima was 'by no means difficult of execution, and certain of success'. Certainly Pezuela, the Viceroy, was in a far less confident mood when the news of San Martín's arrival at Pisco reached him than he had been when Cochrane had asked him for an exchange of prisoners. From Spain he learned that an army mutiny had forced the King to accept a liberal constitution which he had hitherto suppressed. In place of the troop reinforcements which the Viceroy was expecting to receive, he was instructed to suspend hostilities and negotiate with the rebels.

In the north Simón Bolívar had already proved himself a far more formidable menace than San Martín, by the victory he had won near Bogotá in the previous year. Pezuela sent an invitation to San Martín under a flag of truce which led, to Cochrane's consternation, to an armistice for 8 days being signed on 26 September. During the negotiations which occupied this time San Martín, according to Paroissien, 'proposed to the Viceroy to allow the Peruvians free and complete liberty to elect the form of Government they please, even if they should wish to crown a King of the Spanish Branch of the Bourbons, but he insists upon the seat of Government's being in America. This the Viceroy says he has no authority to agree to.' San Martín's apologists explain that he was playing for time, while the Peruvians were given an opportunity to generate their own sympathies in favour of the liberators. Cochrane soon had ample grounds for his contention that people would be unwilling to expose themselves to the penalties for treason unless they felt confident that the forces of liberation could offer them effective protection and that this required the winning of victories, not the signing of armistices.

The gulf between the two leaders was widened further by San Martín's proposals for the future government of Peru. His suggestion that an autonomous monarchy might be best suited to a country in which the majority were illiterate and lived in varying conditions of servitude was more realistic than the forms of republican democracy in which Cochrane believed. But although San Martín put forward this idea as a basis for discussion as soon as he had entered Peru, he also proclaimed others as positive undertakings that many besides Cochrane would expect him to honour. 'You shall be free and independent' he assured the Peruvians from Pisco. 'You shall choose your own government and laws by the spontaneous will of your representatives. No military or civil influence, direct or indirect, shall your brethren use to influence your social dispositions. You shall dismiss the armed force sent to your assistance the moment you judge proper.'

As though this were not binding enough, San Martín added a further assurance by proclamation before leaving Pisco to resume his journey northward. 'On the day when Peru shall freely pronounce as to the form of her institutions, be they whatever they may, my functions shall cease, and I shall have the glory of announcing to the Government of Chile, of which I am a subject, that their heroic efforts have at last received the consolation of giving liberty to Peru.' They had lain in Pisco for 6 weeks when Cochrane was ordered to contribute to these heroic efforts by transporting the army to Ancón, a few miles to the north of Lima, on 25 October 1820. A British merchant residing in Chile called John Miers was among those who commented with severity on the futility of the Pisco interlude. The delay at Pisco infuriated Cochrane, and it can have given little satisfaction to San Martín.

But at the General's camp there was Paroissien, the sole British aide, to fling reproofs on his own compatriot. 'It really is requisite,' he wrote on the 27th, 'to have more than the patience of an angel with Lord C. He is the most careless, unmethodical man I ever knew, promises everything and performs nothing. He appears only to be anxious about making money. Avarice and selfishness do certainly appear to form the groundwork of his character and from his speculative disposition he is often in great want of money to obtain which he is not so scrupulously exact in his word as every man ought to be, particularly a man of his rank and station. Not a day passes but brings some proof of this unfortunate selfish disposition and there is not a man in the fleet who does not lament his carelessness in keeping the convoy together, although we are within a few miles of the enemy's port.' Here is an indictment compounded of Cochrane's supposed guilt in the stock exchange hoax, of the steps he had taken to ensure that his seamen were paid, of the tittle-tattle of Guise and Spry, of the resentment of the Barking school-teacher's son at the way in which he was addressed by an angry Scottish peer. The portrait of a careless and unmethodical man who promised everything and performed nothing bore little resemblance to the hero of Valdivia, but it was the one which San Martín came to believe in, and it would be hard to acquit Paroissien of the responsibility for this.

In this poisonous atmosphere Cochrane decided that it was essential to attempt another of those fantastic feats of skill and courage which could achieve more than an army with banners. While San Martín's troops settled down in the wretched village of Ancón, surrounded by sand and barren hills, he brought his fleet into the bay of Callao to blockade the port, to the consternation of the people of Lima. It consisted only of his flagship, the *Independencia* and the *Lautaro* so that Spanish alarm was caused by the presence of El Diablo rather than the armament at his command, especially as they had enjoyed ample time by now to protect their naval arsenal. Their forty-gun flagship *Esmeralda* lay under the protection of the citadel's guns within a semi-circle of twenty-seven gunboats. It contained the most highly trained sailors and marines in the Spanish service; pieces of artillery supported them from the shore; a boom and guardships reinforced the gunboats to seaward. It would have seemed impossible that Cochrane could assault such a bastion with his three ships, and to make it appear more unthinkable still he despatched the *Independencia* and *Lautaro* to sea while he remained alone in Callao Roads in the *O'Higgins*.

Here he selected 160 seamen and 80 marines from those who stepped forward as volunteers, and trained them with infinite attention to detail for the execution of the plan he had devised. He selected Guy Fawkes Night for the attempt and composed an address to his men which William Stevenson translated for those who did not understand English.

'Marines and Seamen—This night we are going to give the enemy a mortal blow. Tomorrow you will present yourselves proudly before Callao, and all your comrades will envy your good fortune. One hour of courage and resolution is all that is required of you to triumph. Remember that you have conquered at Valdivia, and be not afraid of those who have hitherto fled from you.'

Stevenson kept a copy of the exact orders that were issued to complement this rousing manifesto. Fourteen of the ship's boats were to set off from the *O'Higgins* with muffled oars in the darkness at 10 o'clock, and make for the gap in the boom which guarded the enemy flagship. 'The boats will proceed, towing the launches in two lines parallel to each other, which lines are to be at the distance of three boats' lengths asunder. The second line will be under the charge of Captain Guise, the first under that of Captain Crosbie. Each boat will be under the charge of a commissioned officer, and the whole under the immediate command of the Admiral. The officers and men are all to be dressed in white jackets, frocks and shirts, and are to be armed with pistols, sabres, knives, tomahawks or pikes. Two boatkeepers are to be appointed to each boat who, under no pretence whatever, shall quit their respective boats, but are to remain with them therein and take care the boats do not get adrift. Each boat is to be provided with one or more axes, which are to be slung to the girdles of the boatkeepers. The frigate *Esmeralda* being the chief object of the expedition, the whole force is first to attack that ship which, when carried, is not to be cut adrift, but to remain in possession of the patriot seamen to ensure the capture of the rest.'

Cochrane intended to take every single ship in Callao with his handful of volunteers, just as he had taken every fort at Valdivia: and so he would have done but for Captain Guise. While he provided that his men should be able to recognise each other in the dark by their white costumes, he also found a means to confuse the enemy as to their identity. 'On securing the frigate the Chilean seamen and marines are not to cheer as if Chilenos; but in order to deceive the enemy, and give time for completing the work, they are to cheer "*Viva el Rey*".'

While Cochrane was leading his flotilla to the gap in the boom his launch stumbled on the Spanish guard-boat in the dark. A challenge rang out, then the sentry felt a pistol at his head and heard a whispered threat of death if he made another sound. Presently Cochrane's boats were clustering along the starboard side of the *Esmeralda* while the Admiral led the boarding party. But the next sentry he encountered made the first move without any challenge, toppling Cochrane back into his boat with a blow from his musket-butt. The Admiral landed on one of the thole pins, which entered his back near the spine, causing him excruciating pain. A doctor who examined him later said that the wound was a dreadful one, and Cochrane himself confessed that it caused him years of suffering.

But at the moment when the entire success of the operation hung in the balance he did not hesitate for a second, but immediately heaved himself back on deck where his men had all taken up their appointed stations with the utmost precision. 'We had not been on deck a minute when I hailed the foretop and was instantly answered by our own men, an equally prompt answer being returned from the frigate's maintop. No British man-of-war's crew could have excelled this minute attention to orders.' But beyond their discipline in executing what is held to be the most perfect cutting-out operation in all naval history, Cochrane never forgot his admiration for their courage. Neither, probably, did those Chilean seamen ever witness greater fortitude than their Admiral displayed that night. Almost as soon as he regained the deck he was shot through the right thigh above the knee. He caught the sentry who had wounded him by the heel and pitched him overboard, then bound his wound tightly with his handkerchief and sat on a pile of hammock-netting as he continued to bark out his orders.

The greater part of the unsuspecting crew of the *Esmeralda* was asleep below decks, where many of those on watch fled to join them while others scrambled overboard. The highly disciplined marines, however, held out on the quarterdeck until they were felled to a man. It was all over in no longer than a quarter of an hour. With the loss of eleven men killed and thirty wounded, Cochrane had captured the Spanish Admiral with all his officers in their flagship, 160 of whose seamen and marines had been cut down.

Hardly had this been accomplished when the shore batteries opened a devastating fire on the captured *Esmeralda* and her wretched Admiral and crew. Cochrane had foreseen this eventuality and had devised an alternative to sailing her out of range, which would have prevented him from capturing the remainder of the fleet. He had observed that the British and United States naval frigates which lay in Callao harbour had hoisted special identification lights to show the shore garrison where the neutral vessels lay in the dark. He had brought similiar lights with him, which he now displayed in the *Esmeralda*. Once again his simple trick worked. The shore garrison became confused as to which were the neutral ships. Their fire slackened: they fired in error on the neutral ships, which consequently cut their cables and sailed out of range, thereby confirming the suspicion that they were captured vessels.

The way was now open to complete the operation in accordance with the precise instructions which Cochrane had laid down in advance. 'The two brigs of war are to be fired on by the musketry from the *Esmeralda*, and are to be taken possession of by Lieutenants Esmond and Morgell in the boats they command; which being done, they are to cut adrift, run out, and anchor in the offing as quickly as possible. The boats of the *Independencia* are to turn adrift all the outward Spanish merchant ships; and the boats of the *O'Higgins* and *Lautaro*, under Lieutenants Bell and Robertson, are to set fire to one or more of the headmost hulks; but these are not to be cut adrift, so as to fall down upon the rest.' The Spanish flagship, free of annoyance from the shore batteries, was to be used as the means of securing the remainder of the fleet.

By now it was 3 o'clock in the morning and Cochrane was giddy with pain and loss of blood. Exercising a mistaken impartiality towards one who might afterwards have accused him of personal prejudice, he handed over the command to Captain Guise while he allowed himself to be rowed back to his flagship to have his wounds dressed. Guise thereupon abandoned the orders he had received for the capture of the other ships, cut the cables of the *Esmeralda*, and sailed her triumphantly out of Callao harbour. She was indeed ready for sea, with provisions aboard for 3 months and stores sufficient for 2 years. Cochrane's fury may be imagined when he awoke next morning to discover what Guise had done. He did not accept his slanderous excuse that his men had broken into the spirit room and were becoming incapacitated with drink, while others were disorganised by plundering. These were men whom Cochrane had trained and led until a few moments earlier. But since Guise had displayed a gallantry equal to theirs in the action he refrained from ordering a court-martial.

Among those who witnessed the incomparable achievements of that night was a British naval officer in the fleet of Captain Sir Thomas Hardy, Commander-in-Chief of the ships of His Britannic Majesty on the coast of South America. It was he who had served as Nelson's Flag-Captain at Trafalgar and listened to the dying whisper 'Kismet', or 'Kiss me'. In one of his ships, the *Conway*, Captain Basil Hall lay off

Callao Roads on the night of 5 November where he could observe Cochrane's 'matchless intrepidity and inexhaustible resources in war', as he was to describe them. Basil Hall had been appointed only recently to this station, and it was a most fortunate accident that an officer of such literary gifts and outstanding intelligence, one who turned his wardroom into a sort of floating academy, should have been present to chronicle these events. In the extracts from his Journal which he was shortly to publish, and which ran rapidly through several editions, he commented that the capture of the *Esmeralda* 'was a death-blow to the Spanish naval force in that quarter of the world; for, although there were still two Spanish frigates and some small vessels in the Pacific, they never afterwards ventured to show themselves, but left Lord Cochrane undisputed master of the coast'.

It would not have been surprising if these naval officers had adopted a severe attitude to the outlaw from their own country who was jeopardising the commercial interest of their compatriots and causing their ships to be fired upon; and so they would certainly have done if there had been any truth in Paroissien's slanders concerning Cochrane's depredations. So it is particularly significant that the British merchant John Miers should have quoted them like this in the account he was shortly to publish concerning these events. 'From Captain Hall I have heard the highest eulogium on Lord Cochrane's conduct . . . and I have repeatedly listened with pleasure to Commodore Sir Thomas Hardy, while expressing his respect for the character of his noble countryman generally, and his approbation of his conduct particularly in allusion to these transactions.' It is a melancholy reflection that of all the British subjects to whose opinion San Martín might have listened at this time, he had selected such a man as Paroissien as his aide-de-camp.

It was this man who stepped aboard the *Esmeralda* on the morrow of its capture, for he had been deputed by San Martín to organise an exchange of prisoners, a task vastly simplified for him by the capture of the Spanish Admiral and all his officers in the flagship. Paroissien arranged the removal of the wounded, who were handed over with his other prisoners to the Viceroy's representative, though Paroissien was not permitted to set foot on shore himself. 'What a pity,' he conceded to the Admiral, 'this man, who certainly does possess the elements of a hero, is so extremely avaricious.'

When the people of Callao awoke to discover that their flagship had been captured nothing could persuade them that Cochrane had achieved this without the assistance of the English frigate *Hyperion*, which was lying in the harbour after having returned to her moorings. Nor could they distinguish between its English-speaking crew and those of the

Archibald, 9th
Earl of
Dundonald
(1748–1831)
(*Collection:* The
Earl of
Dundonald)

Gold watch and
seal belonging
to 9th Earl.
They were given
to 10th Earl
when he went
to sea – his
father's only
contribution to
his scanty outfit.
(*Collection:* The
Earl of
Dundonald)

N. Pocock: Cochrane in
Speedy captures *El Gamo*
(National Maritime Museum)

Speedy beats off Spanish
gun-boats (National Maritime
Museum)

THE DESTRUCTION of the FRENCH BREST FLEET in BASQUE ROADS by the English LORD COCHRANE and

Basque Roads, 12 April 1809 (National
Maritime Museum)

The *Pallas* with the *Kingfisher* attempts to cut
out the French frigate *Minerve* (*Collection:*
The Earl of Dundonald)

GOD save the KING.

Doublons.

SPANISH
Dollar Bag
Consigned to Boney.

My LADS,
    The rest of the GALLEONS with the TREASURE from LA PLATA, are waiting half loaded at CARTAGENA, for the arrival of those from PERU at PANAMA, as soon as that takes place, they are to sail for PORTOVELO, to take in the rest of their Cargo, with Provisions and Water for the Voyage to EUROPE. They stay at PORTOVELO a few days only. Such a Chance perhaps will never occur again,

THE FLYING
PALLAS,
OF 36 GUNS,
At PLYMOUTH,

is a new and uncommonly fine Frigate. Built on purpose. And ready for an EXPEDITION, as soon as some more good Hands are on board;

Captain Lord Cochrane,

(who was not drowned in the ARAB as reported) Commands her. The sooner you are on board the better.

    None need apply, but SEAMEN, or Stout Hands, able to rouse about the Field Pieces, and carry an hundred weight of PEWTER, without stopping, at least three Miles.

COCHRANE.

To British Seamen.

BONEY's CORONATION
Is postponed for want of COBBS.

J. BARFIELD, Printer, Wardour-Street.

Rendezvous, at the White Flag.

Enlistment broadsheet (National Maritime Museum)

Drummond: Admiral Sir Alexander Cochrane, uncle of 10th Earl, with whom he went to sea for the first time as a midshipman (*Collection:* The Earl of Dundonald)

(*below*) James Gambier

(*below right*) Hoppner: John Jervis, Earl St Vincent (both National Maritime Museum)

Hayter: Thomas Cochrane, 10th Earl of
Dundonald (*Collection:* The Earl of
Dundonald)

W. Behnes: Captain Marryat,
1827 (National Maritime Museum)

H. Howard: Admiral
Collingwood (National
Portrait Gallery)

Lord Cochrane, half as naval officer, half in
dress he wore to the House of Commons,
21 March 1815 (Hamlyn Group Picture Library)

A. Buck: Sir Francis Burdett
(National Portrait Gallery)

THE SEVERE
SENTENCE
ON
LORD COCHRANE & OTHERS,
TO
STAND IN THE PILLORY,
IN THE FRONT OF THE
Royal-Exchange,
FOR
A CONSPIRACY,
TO RAISE, BY FALSE REPORTS, THE PRICE OF THE PUBLIC FUNDS;
As pronounced by Sir Simon Le Blanc,
IN THE COURT OF KING'S-BENCH,
ON TUESDAY, the 21st of JUNE, 1814.

" That you, Sir Thomas Cochrane, commonly called Lord Cochrane,* and that you, Richard Gathorne Butt, do pay a fine of one thousand pounds to the King; and that you, John Peter Holloway, having also benefited from this infamous conspiracy, do pay a fine of five hundred pounds to the King.

" That you, the six several Defendants, Sir Thomas, commonly called Lord, Cochrane, Richard Gathorne Butt, John Peter Holloway, Charles Random De Berenger, Henry Lyte, and Ralph Sandom, be severally imprisoned in the custody of the Marshal of the Marshalsea of this Court for the term of twelve calendar months, and that,

* Member of Parliament for the City of Westminster, and late Captain of his Majesty's Ship Imperieuse.

during that period, you, Charles Random De Berenger, you, Sir Thomas, commonly called Lord, Cochrane, and you, Richard Gathorne Butt, be set in and upon the pillory in the front of the Royal-Exchange, for the space of one hour, between the hours of twelve at noon and two in the afternoon.

" And that, you, Sir Thomas, commonly called Lord, Cochrane, Richard Gathorne Butt, and John Peter Holloway, be further imprisoned until your several fines be paid."

The other two persons found guilty of the said Conspiracy, namely, Andrew Cochrane Johnstone and Alexander M'Rea did not appear in Court, consequently judgment was not pronounced upon them.

Broadsheet against Lord Cochrane's sentence (Hamlyn Group Picture Library)

S. Drummond: Lord Ellenborough (National Portrait Gallery)

G. Cruikshank: cartoon of de Berenger, 21 May 1814 (Hamlyn Group Picture Library)

J. Holmes: Katherine Corbett Barnes, wife of Lord Cochrane (*Collection:* The Earl of Dundonald)

T. Lawrence: Maria Graham (National Portrait Gallery)

Drawings by Maria Graham
(Hamlyn Group Picture
Library)

View of the Chile coast (*above*)

Lord Cochrane's house at
Quintero

View of Valparaiso

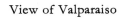

General Bernardo O'Higgins
(*Collection:* The Earl of
Dundonald)

General José de San Martín
(*Collection:* The Earl of Dundonald)

Simón Bolívar (Hamlyn Group
Picture Library)

Pedro I on his Coronation Day at
Rio de Janeiro (*Collection:* Rex Nan
Kivell, National Library of Australia)

Cutting out the *Esmeralda* from under the forts of Callao (National
Maritime Museum)

View of Rio de Janeiro, from a drawing by Maria Graham (Hamlyn
Group Picture Library)

The Rising Star
Built under the direction of
LORD COCHRANE, (Later Admiral the Tenth Earl of Dundonald).
For the War of Independence in Spanish South America, upon the Principle of Navigating either by Sails or by Steam; the
impelling Apparatus being placed in the Hold and caused to operate through Apertures in the bottom of the Vessel
NOTE.- The Rising Star was the first Steam-driven Vessel to traverse the
South Atlantic, and also the first Steam Vessel to enter the Pacific

The *Rising Star* (National Maritime Museum)

Maria Graham: Slave market in Rio de Janeiro (Hamlyn Group
Picture Library)

Maria Graham: View of Rio de Janeiro (Hamlyn Group Picture Library)

Hanover Lodge, Regent's Park, London (Photograph in the possession of the Earl of Dundonald)

H.M. Steam sloops *Rattler* and *Alecto* towing stern to stern to demonstrate the relative powers of the screw propeller and the paddle wheel (National Maritime Museum)

Model of the screw propeller of the *Rattler* (The Science Museum)

Thomas Cochrane, 10th Earl of Dundonald, photographed in his eighties (The Earl of Dundonald)

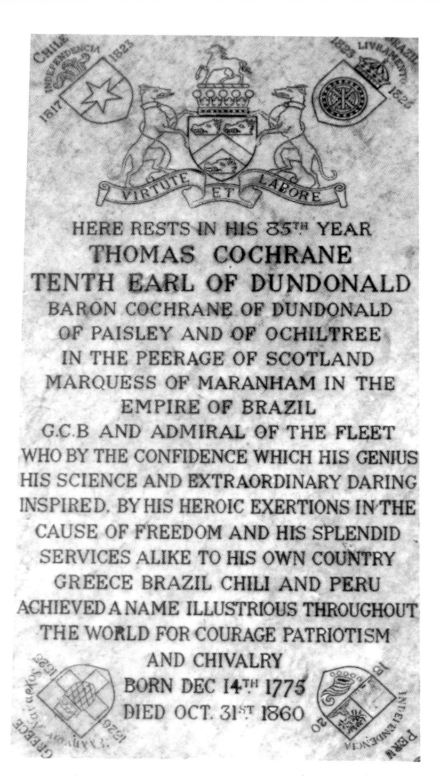

Memorial tablet in Westminster Abbey (The Dean and Chapter of Westminster)

American frigate *Macedonian*, whose identification lights had also served to confuse the Spanish gunners on the previous night. When a party rowed ashore from the ship of the United States on the morning of the 6th on their routine visit to the market-place to buy fresh beef and vegetables, an enraged mob of women set upon them and a large number were butchered.

General San Martín reported the action in handsome terms to Zenteno, the Minister of Marine. 'It is impossible for me to eulogise in proper language the daring enterprise of the 5th of November, by which Lord Cochrane has decided the superiority of our naval forces—augmented the splendour and power of Chile—and secured the success of this campaign. I doubt not that His Excellency the Supreme Director will render the justice due to the worthy chief, his officers and other individuals who have had a share in that successful action.'

Disabled as he was, Cochrane immediately sailed north to Ancón, taking his prize with him. Doubtless he hoped he might now succeed in persuading his General to seize the initiative which had been presented to him and march on Lima. San Martín proposed that the *Esmeralda* should be renamed after her captor, and when Cochrane demurred she was named the *Valdivia* instead and placed under the command of Captain Guise, who ought to have been silently grateful. But he had hoped she would be named the *Guise*, and fomented fresh discord over this petty issue by protesting that since her complement had not taken part in the capture of Valdivia, the name was inappropriate. But this was less vexatious to Cochrane than the discovery that San Martín would not alter his strategy. He had already decided to move his army north to Huacho, farther still from the Peruvian capital, and even the unexpected news of Cochrane's feat at Callao could not deflect him from his policy of waiting upon events. On 10 November 1820 his forces were convoyed by sea to their new camp seventy miles from the enemy port, where they remained ensconced for the next 6 months. On the 15th Cochrane returned to resume the blockade of Callao.

During this period Paroissien was bombarded with complaints from the British merchants, many of whom had close links with the commercial circles of Peru. 'I am almost at a stand,' wrote one in January, 'such an uncertainty appears to hang over your operations.' By May he declared roundly: 'The system your head man has adopted of procrastinating the war has not been attended with the great results expected.' Another merchant had warned Paroissien in March: 'If you don't do something very soon here we shall all assuredly be ruined.' There is no evidence whether Paroissien found this proof of avarice to equal Cochrane's when the Admiral wrote to the aide from Callao:

'Were the army here *now* we could drink our champagne this very night in your room over the great entrance of the Palacio.'

But nothing could deflect San Martín from his chosen course, and the dividends it yielded have satisfied many people of its wisdom from that day to this. A climate of revolt did begin to creep over the country, as San Martín desired, while the blockade of Lima gradually undermined resources and morale in the capital. As a neutral Captain Basil Hall could visit there freely, and he left this description of what he saw. 'From the highest to the lowest person in society, everyone felt the increasing evils that crowded round the sinking state. Actual want had already begun to pinch the poor; the loss of almost every comfort affected the next in rank; and luxuries of all kinds were discarded from the tables of the highest class. Military contributions were heavily exacted from the moneyed men; the merchants lost their commerce; the shopkeepers their wonted supplies.' In this atmosphere of gloom and frustration the Viceroy was deposed in February 1821 by a cabal of officers, and General La Serna took over his duties while the French General Canterac assumed command of the army.

Captain Hall recorded a conversation he held with San Martín in which the General explained his policy. 'People ask,' he told the British naval officer, 'why I don't march to Lima at once; so I might, and instantly would, were it suitable to my views—which it is not. I do not want military renown—I have no ambition to be the conqueror of Peru—I want solely to liberate the country from oppression. Of what use would Lima be to me if the inhabitants were hostile in political sentiment? How could the cause of independence be advanced by my holding Lima, or even the whole country, in military possession? Far different are my views. I wish to have all men thinking with me and do not choose to advance a step beyond the gradual march of public opinion.' Hall expressed his conviction that San Martín was absolutely sincere in what he said, although the weakness of his argument had been demonstrated by the time he published these words. For San Martín could not sit waiting for the march of public opinion for ever, while the men encamped at Huacho suffered more casualties by sickness than Cochrane ever lost in action. He would have to take a step forward in the end, and when he did so he fell flat on his face.

The ebbing of morale in court, counting-house and camp during this doldrum period was matched by a growing disaffection in the fleet. It spread from the *Valdivia*, commanded by the insubordinate Captain Guise, in which Cochrane was driven to order a court-martial which resulted in the dismissal of two of the ship's officers from the service. Cochrane sent the findings to San Martín with a request for replacements and planned an assault on the fortifications of Callao which would achieve the secondary object of keeping his men occupied constructively. While the sailors from other ships volunteered eagerly for the service, Captain Guise replied to the orders he received, refusing to take part unless the two officers under arrest were permitted to do so also. Past experience had taught Cochrane to suspect the hand of Spry in such cases, so he tested this officer's complicity by sending him an experimental order. Back came the reply that Captain Spry would not serve without Guise, 'under whose patronage he had left England'. Cochrane thereupon had him tried by court-martial and dismissed him from his ship on 2 March 1821. Guise returned with him to Huacho, where San Martín appointed Spry his naval aide-de-camp. He could scarcely have contrived an act more openly disloyal to his Admiral, more destructive of naval discipline, or more harmful to his personal credit. The part of Guise and Spry ought to have been as clear as the day to him, since they had never ceased to intrigue openly to oust Cochrane from his command since his arrival in Chile.

During this period in which the natural ebullience of Cochrane's character gave way to ever-increasing gloom he was at least consoled by the arrival of his wife and family. While he had been capturing the *Esmeralda* the previous November, Kitty had embarked on an adventure of her own. Taking her children with her, she set off on the journey through the Andes to Mendoza which the couriers made when they carried letters to Europe and Argentina. It involved crossing a 15,000-foot pass in which Kitty's party was for a time held up by snow and compelled to shelter in the bare building erected there against such emergencies. 'The absence of all comfort—there being no better couch than a dried bullock's hide—produced a degree of suffering which few ladies would be willing to encounter.' So her husband proudly recorded. Kitty was apparently as impervious to discomfort as to danger; which she faced again when a Spanish royalist met her party on a narrow and precipitous path beside a deep abyss, and threatened to block its passage. One of her attendants hurried forward and struck him before he could reach Lady Cochrane who, excellent horsewoman though she was, might have fared badly if her horse had become frightened and lost its footing.

She wrote her husband long accounts of these adventures which read like rather formal students' essays—in a clear careful hand which would become more masterful and fluent as her character matured. But in the letter she started 'in the high Andes', on 6 November 1820, there is already an open expression of her passionate nature. 'I can safely say that I never slept better except when in the arms of my beloved

Cochrane. Oh what would I give if you could just look in this room and see your little wife with her large family. They begin to make me look quite old.' Even before she was 25 years of age Kitty was revealing an anxiety that would grow with the passing years, a fear that the children she had borne so early in her life would make her appear old.

She also told her husband something that would depress him more than she realised, being ignorant of the extent of his vexations. She was coming to the conclusion that she ought to take her children home. 'If I go to England I am resolved to live at Tunbridge Wells in the identical cottage that I lived in before we left England. Pray my dearest Cochrane write often and let me hear your sorrows but God forbid you should have any more. You as well as myself have had our share of vexations in this world.'

Cochrane was aghast at the prospect of being left alone in this hemisphere while Kitty and the children returned to England and told her so plainly, to receive an equally plain reply. 'My dearest Husband from whom I have so frequently parted upon former occasions without ever witnessing the least tendency to that despair which is now so strongly depicted in your letters—' she could not know how many other pressures were helping to drive him to despair—'is it possible my dearest Cochrane that *you* who have left me a woman in this land of strangers and amongst villains as they have now turned out, and of the lowest stamp too, at a moment when I really want consolation can have lost that strength of mind which it was your pride to know you taught me?' It is hard to decide what villains Kitty is referring to, although Zenteno, the Minister of Marine, is a likely candidate, but her remark reveals the growing sense of insecurity which was undermining the spirits of this courageous little woman and making her nostalgic for her own country. 'You yourself,' she now wrote to her husband, 'determined that I ought to go home.'

She dropped her pen and spent a sleepless night before reaching the resolution to tell him she had made up her mind to go, particularly for the sake of the children. 'Keep your mind at rest my dearest and most beloved Cochrane,' she soothed him, 'and for my sake take care of yourself and remember that absence strengthens not diminishes love . . .' Having said that, she returned to the west coast where she succeeded in obtaining a passage with her children in the British vessel *Andromaque*, and was reunited with her husband at Callao in January 1821.

At the moment of her arrival General San Martín had just authorised Colonel Miller to make one of the small offensive expeditions with which he contributed to the blockade of Lima from the land and to the gradual change in public opinion. 600 infantry and 60 cavalry were placed under his command, to be transported by Cochrane to their secret landing-place. To Huacho Cochrane therefore sailed with his wife, and Miller recalled the effect of her presence on the troops who waited to embark in his fleet on 25 January. 'On the very day of his arrival there, and whilst he was inspecting the detachments in the Plaza, Lady Cochrane galloped on to the parade ground to speak to him. The sudden appearance of youth and beauty on a fiery horse, managed with skill and elegance, absolutely electrified the men, who had never before seen an English lady. "Que hermosa, que graciosa, que linda, que guapa, que airosa, es un angel del cielo!"' As the exclamations broke from the men, praising Kitty's beauty and grace, Colonel Miller turned to them and said: 'This is our lady-general.' At this, 'her Ladyship turned her sparkling eyes towards the line and bowed graciously'. The troops burst into cheers. 'Lady Cochrane smiled her acknowledgments and cantered off the ground with the grace of a fairy.'

A few days later Kitty played an even more curious part in Peruvian affairs. Returning with her husband to the blockade of Callao after Miller's expedition had been launched on its mission, she was in this neighbourhood in February when Pezuela the Viceroy was deposed, and applied to San Martín for a passport to enable him to return with his wife and family to Europe. The General refused it, overlooking the fact that it would be for Cochrane to decide whether or not they could sail from Callao. Donna Angela, the Vicereine, begged Lady Cochrane to intercede with her husband on their behalf, and as usual she did more, persuading the Captain of the *Andromaque* to carry the deposed Vicereine with her children back to Spain. A meeting took place aboard this ship between Donna Angela and Lord and Lady Cochrane, when the Vicereine could not conceal her surprise at finding El Diablo to be 'a gentleman and rational being, and not the ferocious brute she had been taught to consider me'.

There seems to be little doubt that the arrival of Kitty helped to transform Cochrane's relations with the Peruvian aristocracy, and that his cordiality for his opponents increased as fast as relations deteriorated between him and his General. Soon after the meeting between the Cochranes and the Vicereine, Lady Cochrane gladly left her lodgings in Callao to visit the Marchioness de la Pracer at Quilca, where she was able to enjoy the sunset splendour of viceregal life in rural Peru. She made the journey there on horseback, riding through deserts and across precipitous ravines, taking with her their youngest child Elizabeth. The idyll was disrupted by the baby's illness in a place where there was no doctor, but the Marquess de Torre-Tagle presented Lady Cochrane with a palanquin—a covered litter borne by men who carried its poles on their shoulders—to take Elizabeth back to the coast in comfort.

Kitty's departure was hastened by the intelligence that a Spanish army was approaching the neighbourhood, and that there was a plot to abduct both the mother and the child from Quilca and hold them as hostages. Kitty was informed during a ball and she responded with her usual presence of mind. Ordering the palanquin, she despatched Elizabeth in it in the care of her nurse under the protection of a guard, while she herself remained in the ballroom. Only when they had been given time to escape did she slip away from the party herself, change into riding clothes, and overtake her daughter's palanquin on horseback.

All night and the next day the fugitives continued their journey, until they were halted by one of the cane-rope bridges that hung above the deep ravines and raging torrents of that mountainous land. Lady Cochrane dismounted, snatched her child from its nurse and made her way across the bridge. But by the time she had reached its centre she had caused it to vibrate and sway so dizzily that she could only lie down and hold tight, clutching her baby to her breast. She was rescued by the same servant who had repulsed the royalist intruder on the road to Mendoza. He crept along the bridge on his hands and knees, took the child from her, and led her across the bridge. Once the party were all safely on the farther side they cut the ropes of the bridge behind them, not long before their pursuers reached it.

Immediately Kitty reached the coast she went aboard Cochrane's flagship, only to plunge into another adventure. 'Whilst she was on board,' he recorded, 'I received private information that a ship of war laden with treasure was about to make her escape in the night. There was no time to be lost, as the enemy's vessel was such an excellent sailor that, if once under weigh, beyond the reach of shot, there was not a chance of capturing her. I therefore determined to attack her, so that Lady Cochrane had only escaped one peril ashore to be exposed to another afloat. Having beaten to quarters we opened fire upon the treasure-ship and other hostile vessels in the anchorage, the batteries and gun-boats returning our fire, Lady Cochrane remaining on deck during the conflict. Seeing a gunner hesitate to fire his gun close to which she was standing, and imagining that his hesitation from her proximity might, if observed, expose him to punishment, she seized the man's arm and directing the match, fired the gun. The effort was, however, too much for her as she immediately fainted and was carried below.'

Once the treasure-ship had been crippled and the gun-boats were driven off, the *O'Higgins* returned to her former anchorage. Lady Cochrane returned on deck as the sails were being furled, and heard all the men in the tops and the crew on deck break out into their national anthem as soon as the operation was completed. But it was not the usual words that they sang: 'Some poet amongst them having extemporized an alteration of the words into a prayer for the blessing of Divine providence on me and my devoted wife; the effect of this unexpected mark of attachment from 500 manly voices being so overwhelming as to affect her Ladyship more than had the din of cannon.'

Despite the happiness that she had brought back into his life, Cochrane did not try to dissuade his wife any longer from returning to England. He must have appreciated by now that it was in the best interests of his children that they should go, especially when the immediate future was so dark with uncertainties. They would be able to sail in the frigate *Andromaque*, and Kitty would return after she had made arrangements for the children's welfare at home, provided Cochrane could tell her that the outlook was more auspicious.

So it was with an easier mind that Cochrane pursued his double task of blockading Callao and supporting stabbing raids up and down the coast. The spectacular culmination of these combined operations occurred in May 1821 when they returned to Pisco, re-occupied by the Spaniards after San Martín had evacuated the port the previous October. They discovered that those who had collaborated with the liberators had suffered severely, while the loyalist proprietors of the large estates had now returned with their livestock on the erroneous assumption that the emergency was over. Cochrane rounded up 500 head of cattle for the provision of his ships, and 300 horses for the Chilean army. Then he sailed south to Arica, now the northernmost province of Chile.

The region was to remain in dispute between the two countries for decades because of its wealth in gold and copper. The fertile lands beyond the town of Arica also yielded an immense quantity of red pepper, and only the scarcity of water presented a problem to the inhabitants. Through the skill and daring of Colonel Miller, supported by Cochrane with the greatest precision, this golden key to the entire border territory between Peru and Chile was in their hands after a campaign that lasted less than a fortnight. Upwards of a thousand soldiers of the Spanish army had been killed or captured by the time the remainder submitted. Cochrane was able to address La Serna, the acting Viceroy, with the warning: 'The richest and most opulent of our provinces has succumbed to the unopposable force of the enemy, and the remaining provinces are threatened with the same fate; whilst this suffering city of Lima is undergoing the horrible effects of a rigorous blockade, hunger, robberies and death.'

Cochrane and Miller were prevented from following up this threat by the 20-day armistice which San Martín signed with La Serna on 23 May. During the course of it the two men met, attended by the assiduous Paroissien, to discuss the constitutional future of Peru. San Martín remained in favour of an independent monarchy and suggested that while they waited for the approval of the King of Spain and the choice of a Prince of his house, they should erect a triple regency with La Serna as its President, and draft a constitution. But the two men could not agree on the terms for a peace and San Martín admitted later that he knew his proposals would not be accepted in Spain. While the discussions dragged on through two extensions of the armistice, until the end of June, he doubtless hoped that time would continue to work its own magic.

As usual, it was human action rather than the force of destiny which forced the issue. At the end of June Simón Bolívar re-entered his native Caracas after decisively defeating the forces of Spain in the north, and a week later General La Serna evacuated a capital which, largely through Cochrane's blockade, had been rendered untenable by famine. The disorders which followed the withdrawal of viceregal authority from Lima prompted Captain Basil Hall to offer the services of British sailors and marines to safeguard lives and property. But now at last San Martín was ready to move into the Peruvian capital as he had always wished to do, not as a conqueror but as a liberator, and on 10 July 1821 he made his unobtrusive entry. Within the week he had assumed the title of Protector with absolute powers, both civil and military.

It naturally seemed to Cochrane the final evidence of his bad faith that despite the promises he had made to the Peruvians in his proclamations from Pisco, despite his protestations that he came only as a liberator, he should have planted himself immediately in the seat of the Viceroy that others had won for him. Another British opinion, published only 4 years later, contains the same censure. 'Although he had passed the time since his arrival on the coast of Peru in total inactivity, and although the capital had been reduced by famine, yet he takes on himself the style and title of conqueror, and to read his official papers, one might think he had won the city by hard fighting.' The author had enjoyed an opportunity to study his reports to Chile but had not witnessed events on the spot in Peru.

Captain Basil Hall had been able to do this, and he was able to judge both San Martín and Cochrane better than either man succeeded in assessing one another. He could see that this was not the time or the place for San Martín to attempt experiments in Cochrane's forms of liberal democracy, despite the unfortunate promises contained in his Pisco proclamations. 'Under whatever name he might have chosen to mask his authority, he must still have been the prime mover of everything.' Captain Hall found San Martín's latest action further evidence of his integrity, rather than the opposite. 'It was more creditable to assume the full authority in a manly and open manner, than to mock the people with the semblance of a Republic, and at the same time to visit them with the reality of a despotism.'

But he had not played the conventional part of a hero—he had frequently protested that he did not seek such a rôle—and on the evening of 28 July 1821 when the independence of Peru was solemnly proclaimed, the hero's palm was withheld from him. 'Being at the theatre with Lord Cochrane, the people received them with the loudest acclamations: they gave San Martín all the titles and epithets that could gratify him except that of BRAVE, which they coupled with Lord Cochrane's name.' It was the same in Europe when the news reached there. Lord Byron, who admired courage above all other human qualities, wrote 'there is no man I envy so much as Lord Cochrane. His entry into Lima, which I see announced in today's paper, is one of the great events of the day.'

Courage is a virtue that people can most readily applaud since in the majority of human beings it is relative to the degree of fear and pain which it is called upon to face. Inflexible consistency of purpose, whether soundly based or not, is a merit which calls for greater perception to recognise, the capacity which Basil Hall possessed and Cochrane did not. Posterity has done ample justice to San Martín's adamant consistency, but he may have been weighed down by a feeling that it was not sufficiently recognised when he shouldered the responsibilities of Protector of Peru. Considering some of the men he had chosen as his lieutenants this is hardly surprising, but it may have been as a man aware that he was skating on thin ice that he composed his rather inflated despatches to his old colleague the Supreme Director of Chile.

Certainly it was not *folie de grandeur* or a deep-seated ambition that motivated him, as Cochrane supposed. Of his assumption of absolute power by proclamation on 4 August a critic wrote: 'In direct violation of his former promises he tells the Peruvians that his ten years' experience of revolutions had proved to him the danger of assembling congresses while the enemy still had footing in the country; and that therefore, till the Spanish forces were entirely driven out, he should direct the affairs of Peru, though he sighed for a private station.' While

San Martín sighed, Simón Bolívar in Caracas was helping to work out the new constitution that would be ready at the end of the month. But to demonstrate that San Martín was not a Bolívar, either in the field or in the conference room, is not to bring evidence for the prosecution: anyway Caracas was not Lima.

By an intolerable discourtesy, Cochrane was not even informed, let alone consulted, about San Martín's investiture as Protector of Peru. Since he insisted that he had given orders for the Admiral of Chile to be told that his superior officer had become the head of another state, it follows that members of San Martín's staff were responsible for so mischievously leaving Cochrane in the dark. Consequently Cochrane was ignorant that he was now the senior representative of Chile when he went ashore to discuss with San Martín the fulfilment of the pledge they had both signed in Valparaiso concerning his seamen's pay. The interview occurred on the very day of San Martín's inauguration, and Cochrane's secretary William Stevenson was present to keep a record of it.

It was now all but a year since the men of the Chilean navy had sailed from Valparaiso upon a specific undertaking that they would receive their pay and a bounty on the fall of Lima, and Cochrane asked San Martín to honour the promise which both men had then given. 'To this,' Stevenson related, 'San Martín answered that "he would never pay the Chilean squadron unless it was sold to Peru, and then the payment should be considered part of the purchase money". To this Cochrane replied that "by such a transaction the squadron of Chile would be transferred to Peru by merely paying what was due to the officers and crews for services done to the state."' This double act of treachery, to the state of Chile of which San Martín had been a servant, and to the men of its navy to whom he had made a solemn promise, is faced by defenders of South America's folk hero in one of two ways. Either they leave it out of his story, or they mention in passing that Stevenson was Cochrane's secretary, as though his report may therefore be discounted. But it was published only 4 years later in three volumes of wholly trustworthy narrative, and there is overwhelming corroborative evidence that what he wrote was true.

San Martín knit his brows at Cochrane's remark, and then turned to his two companions and asked them to retire. One was his aide García del Río, whom he was about to appoint Foreign Minister; the other, Bernardo Monteagudo, was to be Minister for War. Cochrane objected, saying that 'as he was not master of the Spanish language, he wished them to remain as interpreters, fearful that some expression, not rightly understood, might be considered offensive'. Evidently he was by now able to converse in Spanish after a fashion, though he had not yet mastered that rich and subtle language. San Martín turned round to the Admiral and said:

'Are you aware, My Lord, that I am Protector of Peru?'

'No,' Cochrane replied.

'I ordered my secretaries to inform you of it,' said San Martín.

'That is now unnecessary, for you have personally informed me. I hope the friendship which has existed between San Martín and myself will continue to exist between the Protector of Peru and myself.'

'I have only to say,' said San Martín, rubbing his hands, 'that I am Protector of Peru.' The manner of his speech provoked Cochrane.

'Then it becomes me,' he replied, advancing a step towards the Protector, 'as senior officer of Chile and consequently representative of that nation, to request the fulfilment of all the promises made to Chile and the squadron: but first and principally the squadron.'

'Chile! Chile!' said San Martín. 'I will never pay a single *real* to Chile. As to the squadron, you may take it where you please, and go where you choose. A couple of schooners are quite enough for me.' But he quickly regretted this outburst, and after pacing the room a short space came up to Cochrane and said: 'Forget, my Lord, what is past.'

'I will when I can,' Cochrane replied grimly and immediately left the new Protector's palace.

Back aboard his flagship, he composed an appeal to San Martín with considerable care, and despatched it to him on 7 August. He spoke candidly of the quality of some of the advisers who surrounded the new Protector. 'So far you have succeeded and, thank God, it is in your power to succeed yet farther. Flatterers are more dangerous than the most venomous serpents, and next to them are men of knowledge—if they have not the integrity or courage to oppose bad measures, when formally discussed or even when casually spoken of.' This was a plain allusion to García del Río and Monteagudo who had witnessed their recent interview, if not also to Guise and Spry and Paroissien. Cochrane ended with a striking metaphor. 'No man has yet arisen, save yourself, capable of soaring aloft with eagle eye embracing the expanse of the political horizon. But if, in your flight, like Icarus you trust to waxen wings, your descent may crush the rising liberties of Peru and involve all South America in anarchy, civil war and political despotism.'

'I know, my Lord,' San Martín replied, 'that one cannot fly with waxen wings. I perceive the course I ought to pursue, and that however great the advantages already gained, there are rocks which without the aid of prudence and good faith, must be encountered.' He sent Cochrane a formal letter from the Protector to the Admiral, and this private letter, dated 13 August, in which he pressed Cochrane to become Grand Admiral of Peru on the terms he had already laid down.

'My Lord, in my official letter addressed to you on the disagreeable business of paying the squadron, which causes us so much uneasiness, I have told you that it is impossible to do as we wish. I have nothing to add, unless my previous declaration, that I shall never view with in-difference anything that interests you. I told you in Valparaiso that "your lot should be equal to mine", and I believe myself to have proved that my intentions have not varied—nor can vary, because every day renders my actions more important.' Had Cochrane been motivated entirely by avarice as Paroissien believed, he would have secured his seamen's pay and his own fortune by exchanging his Chilean commission for the promises of San Martín and the 'glorious pickings' of Peru. Once again he rejected the overture.

San Martín therefore issued a proclamation on 17 August inviting Cochrane's officers to defect from their service as the price of their pay.

'The State of Peru acknowledges as a national debt the arrears of the Army and Squadron, as well as the promises made by me to both.

'All the officers of the Army and Squadron who sailed with the liberating expedition, and now remain in them, are acknowledged as officers of Peru.' The proclamation made no mention of the rights of those who might remain loyal to their Chilean commissions.

Cochrane had been placed by the actions of San Martín in the position of senior representative of the government of Chile in this theatre, responsible both for continuing to implement the orders under which he had sailed from Valparaiso, and for fulfilling its obligations to the men in its service. Although Lima had fallen, the fortress of Callao remained in Spanish hands, and he therefore took a step calculated to meet both the requirements that faced him. He made an offer to the Governor of Callao that if he would surrender the fort to the Chilean Admiral, he would be permitted to depart, taking with him two-thirds of the property it contained. San Martín learned of the negotiations and intervened to prevent the outcome at which Cochrane aimed; and he had hardly done so when General Canterac returned with his army to relieve the garrison of Callao, if not to recapture Lima also.

It was the natural consequence of San Martín's failure to attack the hungry and dispirited Spanish forces when they abandoned Lima. Since the liberation of Peru could never become a reality until the viceregal army was defeated, there was a general expectation that this time San Martín would fight at last. Stevenson related how Cochrane heard of the return of Canterac early in September 1821. 'On the morning of the 10th Lord Cochrane received on board the *O'Higgins* an official communication, informing him that the enemy was approaching Lima, and repeating the request that his Lordship would send to the army every kind of portable arms then on board the squadron, as well as the marines and all volunteers; because the Protector was "determined to bring the enemy to an action, and either conquer or remain buried in the ruins of what was Lima".'

By the time Cochrane arrived at the Protector's camp, his forces had taken up a strong position blocking the road to Lima and favourably placed to drive the army of Canterac to the sea. But despite the clamorous enthusiasm of his men, San Martín still withheld the order to deliver the long-delayed, decisive blow. At the sight of Cochrane even Guise and Spry exclaimed 'we shall have some fighting now the Admiral is come'; and General Las Heras cantered up to him, and begged him to persuade the Protector to give the command to attack. William Stevenson witnessed Cochrane's response as he 'rode up to San Martín, and taking him by the hand, in the most earnest manner entreated him to attack the enemy without losing a single moment'. But San Martín answered nothing except to remark cryptically:

'My resolutions are taken,' which he said in Spanish.

Soon afterwards San Martín dismounted and entered his house followed by Cochrane, who there spoke with him for the last time, asking why no attack was to be launched against the enemy. Once again San Martín made it clear that his mind was made up, without revealing what his intentions were.

'I alone am responsible for the liberties of Peru,' he said to the man whom he had summoned to the field with all his disposable forces, and had thus prevented from taking any independent action.

The Protector had indeed based his policy of inactivity on characteristically subtle considerations, as the immediate outcome proved. While his impatient troops stood to their arms all day without making a move, General Canterac altered course to make a rapid dash for Callao, 8 miles from Lima. As soon as the news was brought to San Martín he rubbed his hands in the manner Stevenson recalled on another occasion and exclaimed to General Las Heras: 'They are lost. Callao is ours. They haven't enough provisions for a fortnight and the reinforcements from the mountains will eat them all. Within a week they will be obliged to surrender or be spitted on our bayonets.' His prophecy was fulfilled to the day and has earned the admiration of posterity, but it did not impress those who witnessed the event, especially when Canterac was permitted to retire, still undefeated, with a great load of booty. They interpreted the triumph as Stevenson did. 'General Canterac with 3000. men passed to the southward of Lima—within half-musket shot of the protecting army of Peru, composed of 12,000—entered the castle of Callao with a convoy of cattle and provisions, where he refreshed and rested his troops for six days, and then retired on the 15th, taking with him the whole of the vast treasure deposited therein by the Limenos, and leisurely retreating on the north side of Lima.'

Stevenson's military estimates have been questioned, and it is emphasised that many of San Martín's troops were neither well armed nor adequately trained. Certainly soldiers who had been fighting an armchair war for a year were unlikely to have been improved by the experience. But whether or not San Martín scored a greater success on this occasion by not fighting, he had once again left the Spanish army intact, and this time he had totally destroyed his credibility as a Protector in the military sense. Whether or not it was really preferable that Canterac should have taken possession of the entire treasure of Callao, rather than that Cochrane should have acquired a third of it for the payment of his fleet, San Martín's failure to safeguard it did nothing to redeem his ebbing prestige. His failure to take Cochrane into his confidence is one of the most significant and distressing features of the whole episode, though it could scarcely have done further harm at this stage in their relations. It was his association with General Las Heras which suffered, for while San Martín issued a proclamation asserting that the enemy had fled before him, Las Heras resigned the service in disgust, and returned to Chile saying he would never again wear the habit of that disgraceful day.

While Canterac still lay at Callao, the condition of the Chilean fleet was becoming critical. It had been at sea for over a year without proper facilities for refitting, opportunity for rest ashore or payment of its wages. A pathetic appeal composed by the ship's company of the *O'Higgins* illustrates the feeling of the sailors who had served Cochrane so faithfully. 'It is the Sole thought of us all that if San Martín had any Honure he would not breck his promises wish out to have been fulfilled Long a go.' Naturally the crew of the *Valdivia*, inheriting the mutinous tradition planted in her by Captain Guise, expressed themselves more vigorously than this. 'We are disatisfied on account of our pay and prize money, and likewise the promises made to us on leaving Valparaiso, it is likewise our Determination not to weigh the anchor of the *Valdivia* until we get the whole of our wages and prize money.'

Cochrane acted with the speed and decisiveness that were habitual whenever he faced an emergency. He had learned that San Martín had carried to Ancón a quantity of treasure which belonged partly to the government of Peru and partly to private individuals, and had placed it for safety in a number of vessels there. On 14 September he sailed to

Ancón and took possession of it. So far as the integrity of the Chilean fleet was concerned, he had acted only just in time. On 19 September Crosbie, his Flag Captain, notified him: 'My Lord, it is with the utmost regret I have to inform your Lordship that being ready for sea early this morning, the foreigners refused heaving up the anchor in consequence of arrears of pay and prize-money, and to my great surprise many of the natives also came aft. I endeavoured by persuasive means to induce them to return quietly and willingly to their duty, which had no effect. Knowing well, had I commenced hostile measures to enforce these orders the consequence might have been serious, I refrained therefrom, being aware of your Lordship's wish to conduct everything as peaceably as possible.'

Cochrane issued a proclamation to the Peruvians inviting all who could show a title to their sequestered property to come and recover it. With the remainder he paid one year's arrears of wages to every member of his fleet and reserved a small surplus for the most pressing needs of his ships. Detailed accounts and receipts were sent to the government of Chile, which in due course endorsed his action.

San Martín and his ministers cajoled and threatened. 'My Lord,' wrote Monteagudo from Lima on 26 September, 'your note of yesterday, in which you explain the motives which induced you to decline complying with the positive orders of the Protector, *temporarily* to restore the money which you forcibly took at Ancón, has frustrated the hopes which the Government entertained of a happy termination to this most disagreeable of all affairs which have occurred during the expedition.'

Cochrane replied on the 28th in his most swingeing manner. 'You address your argumentative letters to me as if I required to be convinced of your good intentions. No Sir, it is the seamen who are to be persuaded; it is they who give no faith to professions after they have been disappointed . . . They are men of few words, but decisive acts; they say that for their labour they have a right to pay and food, and that they will work no longer than while they are paid and fed.' He reminded the men who had listened to the words of San Martín on the day when he had been installed as Protector: 'I assure you that no abatement of his Excellency the Protector's service took place until the 5th day of August, the day on which I was made acquainted with his Excellency's installation, when he uttered sentiments in your presence that struck a thrill through my frame . . . Well do I remember the fatal words he spoke . . . that he never would pay the debt to Chile, nor the dues to the Navy, unless Chile would sell the squadron to Peru. What would you have thought of me as an officer, sworn to be faithful to the service of Chile, had I listened to such language in cold calculating silence?'

Discovering that he could whistle for his treasure, San Martín ordered Cochrane to leave Peruvian waters. 'You will *immediately* sail from this port to Chile, with the whole squadron under your command, and there deliver up the money which you have seized, and which you possess without any pretext to hold it.' It is possible that San Martín, fed on Paroissien's picture of a man entirely consumed by avarice, believed that Cochrane intended to hoard the entire treasure for himself.

In fact the conduct of San Martín's own administration suggests that the Ancón treasure had passed into Cochrane's safe-keeping only just in time to prevent its embezzlement. John Miers, who enjoyed such intimate links with the merchants of Peru, asserted that the new administration was more corrupt than any which the people of Lima had suffered during the viceroyalty, and it moved with a speed that only Cochrane had succeeded in outpacing. His evidence is confirmed by that of Colonel Miller, and their combined testimony makes very clear that San Martín's capacity as a civilian head of state crumbled as fast as his military reputation. Meanwhile Monteagudo, who had arrived penniless in Peru, quickly amassed a colossal fortune. No one has ever suggested that San Martín suffered from the same weakness, but he had appointed the régime which was to become so hateful to those he had liberated.

Its immediate victims were the Spaniards from the mother country residing at this time in Peru. As in all empires, a variety of activities brought them here and they were among the richest members of the community. To them San Martín issued a proclamation soon after he had taken office, promising them his protection if they wished to remain in the state, provided they took an oath of allegiance. Those who wished to leave were assured that they would be able to take their property with them. If they had been able to study the value of San Martín's promises to the Chilean navy in Valparaiso and to the Peruvian people from Pisco, they might have treated his latest ones with greater caution. But they were lulled into a false sense of security and it was only after the surrender of Callao that anything like a mass exodus of Spaniards began. Even then they were deceived by another proclamation which promised safety to all who elected to stay in Peru, and many postponed their departure.

Soon afterwards they were ordered to leave, forfeiting half their property to the state—a euphemism for Monteagudo and his accomplices. John Miers described how these Spanish families were then herded into an old vessel while the remainder of their property was seized also, and carried off to Chile. Many of them had died of hardship and grief before they even reached Valparaiso.

Cochrane had naturally disregarded San Martín's order to return to Chile himself since, as head of the Peruvian state, San Martín was no longer competent to issue orders to the Chilean Admiral. He was consequently able to render assistance to the aged Archbishop of Lima when he was persecuted for his attempt to halt these iniquitous proceedings. It may appear bizarre that a man who had opposed Catholic emancipation in his own country, and had expressed himself with such extravagance concerning the Catholic priesthood in South America, should nevertheless have adopted this rôle. But in fact it was characteristic of him to warm with sympathy to misfortune and forget his prejudices in the process. 'My Dear Lord,' wrote the Archbishop when he was finally driven from the country, 'the time is arrived for my return to Spain, the Protector having granted me the necessary passport. The polite attention which I owe to your Excellency, and the peculiar qualifications which distinguish you, oblige me to manifest to you my sincere regard and esteem. In Spain, if God grant that I arrive in safety, I request that you will deign to command me . . .' The Archbishop was not only a Catholic but also an ardent royalist. It is one of the paradoxes of Cochrane's career that he was so often respected more by his enemies than by his colleagues, and this is the oddest instance of all.

But whether San Martín retained any respect for Cochrane's character or not, he knew his value as a sailor and made a final attempt to lure him into the Peruvian service. It was an embarrassing mission for which he selected Paroissien—a man who, it may be supposed, was not easily embarrassed. Paroissien used the arguments that came naturally to him, and that he consequently expected to weigh with Cochrane, 'telling me how much better it would be for me to be First Admiral of a rich country like Peru, than Vice Admiral of a poor province like Chile'. Cochrane had the satisfaction of snubbing him.

After this Paroissien made the same offer to other officers in the Chilean fleet, as a result of which twenty-three officers left Cochrane's fleet and a number of the foreign sailors on the lower deck followed them. In this predicament Cochrane left Peru on 6 October. 'Many of the officers had gone over to the service of Peru,' he later explained, 'and the foreign seamen had been kept on shore in such numbers that there were not sufficient left to perform the duties of reefing and steering. I therefore resolved on sending part of the squadron to Chile, and with the remainder to proceed to Guayaquil, in order to repair and

T.S.W.—Q

refit for a cruise on the coast of Mexico in search of the Spanish frigates.'

There were still two of these at large, since the capture of the *Esmeralda*.

Guayaquil, now the principal port of the republic of Ecuador, lies close to the Equator. It was part of the northern viceroyalty of New Granada which Simón Bolívar hoped to transform into a single independent country, although it is now divided into Venezuela, Colombia and Ecuador. The province of Guayaquil had proclaimed its independence soon after San Martín's arrival in Peru, and when Bolívar was elected President of a state of Colombia which then included Venezuela, Ecuador and its province of Guayaquil still lay beyond the bounds of the new polity. It was possible indeed that Guayaquil might become instead a part of the new nation of Peru, with which its proximity gave it strong links, and as Bolívar pursued his offensive, San Martín sent agents there, warning the inhabitants against Bolívar and promising them a golden future under his rule. But when Cochrane sailed into the port an army sent by Bolívar was expected to arrive in the near future, over the mountains to the north. The Chilean Admiral was given an enthusiastic welcome and the newly formed local government offered him all possible assistance during the 6 weeks he spent in repairing and refitting his ships. At his departure he was honoured with a public address, to which he replied with a lengthy panegyric on freedom, and particularly on the virtues of free trade.

'Tell the monopolist that the true method of acquiring general riches, political power, and even his own private advantage, is to sell his country's produce as high and foreign goods as low as possible—and that public competition can alone accomplish this. Let foreign merchants who bring capital, and those who practice any art or handicraft, be permitted to settle freely; and thus a competition will be formed from which all must reap advantage.' Cochrane delivered his address in Spanish, though it was soon to be published in this English translation.

He was one of the few, fortunate theorists who was in a position to promote his ideas in practice and who had the satisfaction of reading encomiums on the success with which he did it. Besides those of John Miers the merchant and Basil Hall the naval officer there came the praises of a fellow Scot, in such terms that all Cochrane's disappointments and resentments must have melted as he read them. 'Commerce has been gallantly protected by that extraordinary man who was once a British officer, who once filled a distinguished post in the British Navy at the brightest period of its annals. I mention this circumstance with struggling and mingled emotions—emotions of pride that the individual I speak of is a Briton, emotions of regret that he is no longer a British officer.' Perhaps the most touching words that Mackintosh wrote, at least in the eyes of Cochrane, were these: 'What native of this country can help wishing that such a man were again amongst us?'

For the present he sailed on into ever more distant waters, crossing the Line on 3 December 1821 to enter the northern Pacific for the first time. While he searched here for the remaining Spanish frigates, Simón Bolívar joined General Sucre in the struggle with the royalists that had now reached the neighbourhood of Quito, the future capital of Ecuador. In Peru San Martín had been faced by a conspiracy to overthrow him: he overcame it but his prestige continued to ebb.

When Cochrane reached Mexico the revolutionary General there, Augustín de Iturbe, had recently embarked on his short-lived career as Emperor. The reception which the Mexican authorities gave to the Admiral of Chile was bedevilled at the outset by false reports spread by two former officers in the Chilean service, General Wavell and Colonel O'Reilly, but Cochrane had established cordial relations with Augustín by the time intelligence of the whereabouts of the two Spanish frigates sent him hurrying to sea again. His ships were still extremely unseaworthy after their long service in Callao Roads, and by the time he caught up with his quarry they had taken refuge in Guayaquil. Here agents of San Martín had arrived since Cochrane's departure, who persuaded the Spanish officers to surrender their ships to Peru by promising them their arrears of pay and threatening them with the alternative of capture by Cochrane. Thus the Admiral deprived Spain of her last two frigates in the Pacific and presented to Peru her first two warships—although this was not precisely what he had in mind.

On 25 April 1822 he anchored once more off Callao, to discover that no less than five different Peruvian flags flew on shore while terrorism reigned in Lima. A servile press addressed San Martín as Emperor, and many believed that he desired to wear a crown like Augustín de Iturbe in Mexico. In fact he remained convinced that a constitutional monarchy would best suit Peru, but had no ambitions for himself: so that the accusation reflects the same failure in communication that had marked his relations with Cochrane. The protector had instituted a new Order of the Sun with which to reward service to the state, just as Bolívar created his Order of Liberators, and this also gave rise to taunts that he was playing the sovereign and erecting a new nobility round him. More ineptly still, he now tried to secure Cochrane's services for the last time with the offer of an estate and the Order of the Sun set in diamonds. Cochrane dismissed the vulgar olive branch with an icy comment: 'I

will not accept either honours or rewards from a Government constituted in defiance of solemn pledges; nor will I set foot in a country
governed not only without law, but contrary to law.'

On 25 May Bolívar and Sucre gained the decisive victory over Spain
which enabled him at last to descend to Guayaquil and incorporate that
province in his republic of Colombia. The only hope that remained for
San Martín was to travel to Guayaquil and persuade Bolívar to join
him in an assault on the royalist forces which he had left undefeated in
Peru. He arrived there, to the astonishment of Bolívar, on 25 July, and
the leaders of the revolution which had spread from either end of the
continent met for the first and last time. Unfortunately much of their
conversation took place without any witnesses, so that rivers of ink
have since flowed in speculation about what took place between them.

During the discussions, word was brought to Bolívar that Monteagudo had been driven from Peru. When he told the Protector, San
Martín said that if it were true, he would resign himself. He returned
from Guayaquil having failed to obtain from Bolívar the promise of
help that he sought, and wrote to O'Higgins: 'The Liberator is not
what we thought.' By this time Cochrane had brought his Peruvian
mission to a close, and sailed into Valparaiso harbour on 13 June 1822
after an absence of one year and nine months.

Here he discovered that San Martín's former aide and Foreign
Minister, Paroissien and García del Río, had passed on their way to
Europe to find a sovereign for Peru, and had spread injurious slanders
concerning his conduct during their residence. Paroissien himself was
emblazoned with the Order of the Sun and also enjoyed the rank of a
Brigadier General without having had to expose himself to fire in order
to earn it. He possessed the colossal salary of £3000, and a year's salary
in advance as well, together with the expenses of his journey and a
share in a Peruvian estate from which, however, he received nothing.
In London he would find a new forum for his slanders against Cochrane,
and a Peruvian loan to embezzle.

Back in Peru San Martín faced the wreck of his dreams. 'I am tired of
them calling me a tyrant and saying I want to be king, emperor and
even the devil himself,' he told a friend. 'What is more, my health is
much deteriorated. The climate of this country is sending me to the
grave.' On 20 September he called the Constituent Congress to meet
for the first time, and presented his resignation to its members. 'There
isn't room for Bolívar and me in Peru,' he explained. 'Let him come if
he can, taking advantage of my absence. If he succeeds in consolidating
what we have won in Peru and a little more, I shall be quite satisfied.'
Bolívar was to accomplish just that, though it would take him

more than another two years to drive General Canterac to surrender.

Only a week after the Congress had been invested with sovereign power it moved its resolution of gratitude to the Chilean Admiral.

'The Sovereign Constituent Congress of Peru in consideration of the services rendered to Peruvian freedom by the Right Honourable Lord Cochrane—owing to whose genius, worth, and bravery the Pacific is freed from the insults of enemies, and the standard of freedom is planted on the shores of the South—Resolves that the Supreme Junta shall, in the name of the nation, offer to Lord Cochrane, Admiral of the Chilean squadron, its most sincere acknowledgments of gratitude for his achievements in favour of the people of Peru.'

CHAPTER ELEVEN

The Parting of the Ways

In April 1822 Captain Thomas Graham died off Cape Horn while he was sailing HMS *Doris* into the Pacific. His 37 year-old widow Maria, who had been travelling with him, was rowed ashore at Valparaiso.

Maria Graham was the daughter of Admiral Sir George Dundas, and owing to her father's frequent absence on naval service she had spent long periods during her youth at the home of her uncle Sir David Dundas, where she enjoyed the society of poets, philosophers and artists. Her portrait was painted by Thomas Lawrence during a visit to Rome and in London she attended the famous drawing-room of Byron's publisher, John Murray, which is still preserved, practically unaltered, in Albemarle Street. Some years later she would marry Augustus Callcott the artist, and it is as Lady Callcott that she is remembered as the author of *Little Arthur's History of England*, the only book of its kind for children that has remained in print for nearly a century and a half.

This beautiful talented widow with the Grecian nose and brow was the latest recorder of Cochrane's Pacific exploits to arrive on the scene, but the first to publish her account of them. Her *Journal of a Residence in Chile*, sumptuously produced with her own illustrations, was issued in 1824, while William Stevenson's *Narrative* was published in 1825, John Miers' *Travels* in 1826, Miller's *Memoirs* in 1828 and Basil Hall's *Voyages and Travels* in 1831. Unlike these men, Maria Graham had not been present in this hemisphere during the period of Cochrane's war service and she possessed no personal connections with Peru where his disastrous quarrel with San Martín was enacted. Her *Journal* nevertheless has its own particular value: many of its pages contain eye-witness descriptions written from day to day and published without alteration, and her sharp eyes and fluent pen have preserved a most graphic picture. When she described events which she had not witnessed, she took care to quote extensively from documents, so that her *Journal* is the earliest published source of much historical evidence concerning the new republics of the Pacific.

But it is also by far the most severe in its interpretation of San Martín's career. Arriving in Valparaiso over a month before Cochrane's return, she was exposed to the comment of Chileans some time before he could say anything that might influence her, and what these comments were can be guessed from John Miers' record of the climate of opinion there.

'The aristocratical interests of Chile expected that the capture of Lima by the forces, and the money raised in their country, would ensure to them not only a commanding influence in the political management of Peru, but that the outlet it would afford for the sale of produce would meet with success proportionate to their extravagant imagination. These expectations were wholly disappointed and this was attributed by them to the conduct of San Martín who, besides having betrayed his trust to Chile, had thrown many impediments in the way of its commerce and levied heavy duties upon the introduction of its produce into Peru.' When envoys from Chile travelled to Lima to seek compensation for the expense of fitting out the liberating expedition they were treated by the new Peruvian Foreign Minister, that beast Monteagudo, in a manner that fed the flames of this antagonism. It would have seemed almost inconceivable that San Martín could have made such an unsuitable appointment after the departure of García del Río.

Paroissien's attempt to redeem his master's reputation by attacking that of Cochrane appears as ridiculous now as it must have done then. The military record of the newly promoted General during the Peruvian expedition was hardly one to lend weight to an indictment of the greatest sailor afloat, the man who had captured Valdivia and the *Esmeralda*. In addition, the mission of the two Peruvian envoys to seek a sovereign in Europe for their half-liberated country did not appeal to Bernardo O'Higgins. They left Santiago on 23 March to take the road to Mendoza, having done little to improve San Martín's image in Chile, the republic which his heroism had created.

But allowing for all the other influences that contributed to Maria Graham's hostile portrait of San Martín, that of Cochrane himself after his return in June must take pride of place—except that it was no matter for pride. It is this that gives Maria's *Journal* yet another claim to interest, because it preserves accusations against San Martín that appear to stem from Cochrane, and that are no less extravagant than those made against himself by the opposite faction.

For instance, Maria described Cochrane's rejection of a diamond Order of the Sun, and commented on this final exchange between the two men before Cochrane sailed away from Peru: 'It sets the character of San Martín in a light so odious as to gain full credit to the idea that he was the instigator of two attempts to assassinate the Admiral about this time, made by persons who contrived to get on board the ship by stealth.' Monteagudo made a practice of this sort of behaviour, and

Mrs Graham may be forgiven for joining the ranks of those who identified San Martín with the actions of the man to whom he had handed power in Lima. But they were as wrong as those who believed that San Martín shared Monteagudo's personal greed, and Cochrane should have known they were wrong. He had been identified himself with the villainies of Andrew Cochrane Johnstone and Richard Butt because they were his associates, which might have taught him a useful lesson, had he reflected upon it.

When Cochrane sailed into Valparaiso bay José Ignacio Zenteno had exchanged his former office for Governor and Port Admiral there, so that it was a less hostile Minister of Marine who welcomed him with these words: 'Most Excellent Sir, the arrival of your Excellency at Valparaiso with the squadron under your command has given the greatest pleasure to his Excellency the Supreme Director. In these feelings of gratitude which the glory acquired by your Excellency during the late campaign has excited, you will find the proof of that high consideration which your heroic service so justly deserves.'

Maria Graham summarised these services as they appeared to the country in which he stepped ashore that day. 'Lord Cochrane had now been two years and a half at the head of the naval force of Chile; he had taken, destroyed or forced to surrender every Spanish vessel in the Pacific; he had cleared the western coast of South America of pirates. He had reduced the most important fortresses of the common enemy of the patriots, either by storm or by blockade; he had protected the commerce, both of the native and neutral powers; and he had added lustre even to the cause of independence, by exploits worthy of his own great name, and a firmness and humanity which had as yet been wanting in the noble struggle for freedom.' It was a picture rather different from the one which Paroissien had been circulating, and the one which was generally accepted as true. O'Higgins the Supreme Director ordered a medal to be struck in honour of the officers and crews of the Chilean Navy.

As soon as Cochrane was able to take shore leave he hurried north to his estate beside the bay at Quintero. His seeds and agricultural implements had arrived and he was in a hurry to sow his crops, plant his trees and build a home in the local style of Spanish colonial architecture before his wife's return. There were many other enterprises, which he had discussed and helped to promote with John Miers before his departure for Peru, including the manufacture of flour and the rolling of copper by machinery. This may be the apparatus to which Miers referred when he wrote to Cochrane during that November of 1820 in which the *Esmeralda* was captured: 'Doubtless you will be gratified to hear that other parts of our Machinery have arrived in safety from England.' Perhaps it was his proposal in favour of a copper coinage to which he referred when he told Cochrane that 'Lady Cochrane was almost wild for the completion of this scheme and urged me strongly to undertake it without consulting you as she would be answerable for my so doing: but this I have not thought prudent to do and shall await your opinion and advice.' In that same month Kitty had set off for Peru, while Miers reported to Cochrane from Valparaiso on 26 May 1821: 'Yesterday the Adjutant of the Government of this place brought me the documents and papers that have been passing between the wiseheads relative to the Copper Coinage. The Master of the Mint offers all possible objections, but the Government generally seems anxious for me to undertake it. I have made no reply whatever to the opinions and statements of the several parties.' John Miers was evidently a discreet man.

But the machinery which Cochrane was probably most delighted to receive from home was a lithographic printing press of a kind never seen before in Chile, on which he would be able to reproduce his naval orders, addresses and public letters. He divided his time between the requirements of his fleet and of his estate of Herradura, eight miles to the north, and when he was in Valparaiso he made the acquaintance of Mrs Graham.

Although he never showed any snobbish predilection for members of his own class, the fact that she belonged to the same small circle of the Scottish aristocracy can only have increased their mutual understanding. Her family associations with the British Navy and her residence in parts of Scotland that were familiar to Cochrane were bound to have a magnetic influence on the two exiles. Most of all, Maria's intellectual gifts, her close association with the artistic and literary society of London, must have exercised a powerful attraction on the man who spent his entire life trying to remedy his lack of education in youth. Besides, the two were lonely and bereft and it was no less consoling for Maria to be admired by the naval hero of Chile than for Cochrane to bask in the esteem of such a clever and beautiful woman.

In the circumstances it would not have been surprising if they had fallen violently in love, he approaching the age of 47, she 10 years younger. But not a hint of scandal survives from that small and observant society in which their friendship was formed, and such a liaison would have been quite contrary to the behaviour-pattern of both their lives. Besides, Maria Graham was soon to publish the journal in which she described their friendship with a candour which appears to have nothing to hide. Her portrait of Cochrane is an idealised one in that it never mentions a fault, but it is also a perceptive one because the virtues it extols were real. For instance, in publishing the address on free trade which Cochrane had delivered at Guayaquil, she observed: 'I have translated this paper to show the spirit in which Lord Cochrane dealt with the South American provinces. No petty intrigues, or bargaining for power . . .' These are virtues, but not political assets.

Gradually the house at Quintero arose from its foundations, until Mrs Graham and the Miers family could join the guests whom Cochrane invited to visit him there. But still the idyll was marred by the repercussions of his quarrel with San Martín. Paroissien's accusations fell into Cochrane's hands, and instead of ignoring them he composed a violent refutation filled with counter-charges against San Martín. His honour had been impugned in the past, the spirit of rancour in his nature had been intensified, the strident gifts of the controversialist had been bred in him before he reached Chile. Neither success and its recognition nor the mellowing influence of time had robed him in the dignity of detachment. When he heard that San Martín had returned to Chile on 12 October, an exile from Peru, he went so far as to write to the Supreme Director from his flagship:

'Most Excellent Sir, Don José de San Martín, late Commander-in-Chief of the Expeditionary forces from Chile for the liberation of Peru having this day arrived at Valparaiso, and being now within the jurisdiction of the laws of Chile, I lose no time in acquainting you that, if it be the pleasure of Government to institute an inquiry into the conduct of the said Don José de San Martín, I am ready to prove his forcible usurpation of the Supreme Authority of Peru, in violation of the solemn pledge given by his Excellency the Supreme Director of Chile; his attempts to seduce the navy of Chile; his receiving and rewarding deserters from the Chilean service; his unjustifiably placing the frigates *Prueba* and *Venganza* under the flag of Peru; with other demonstrations and acts of hostility towards the Republic of Chile.'

It was exactly the kind of inept move that Cochrane had made to his own detriment in the past. O'Higgins had ignored the accusations against Cochrane as the Admiral himself ought to have done: it was inconceivable that he would revive the dead controversy by prosecuting instead the man to whom his republic principally owed its foundation. When San Martín returned weak in health and bitterly disappointed, rejected by Bolívar, unsuccessful in Peru, Governor Zenteno received him in state at Valparaiso and sent him with sovereign honours to Santiago where O'Higgins offered him accommodation in his palace. Discredited as he now was, Cochrane could have afforded to be generous to him, had he not been so obsessed instead by the injury which

San Martín had done to his own reputation. As it was, O'Higgins begged him to drop his charges, and out of respect for the Supreme Director he acquiesced.

But the sacrifice lowered his spirits as Maria noted. 'The Admiral himself does not look very well, but that is not marvellous; the squadron is still unpaid. The charges preferred against him by San Martín, though never credited by the government, which possesses abundant documents in its own hands to refute them, have remained uncontradicted by him at the request of that government, in order to avoid party spirit.' The documents she mentioned were in particular the receipts for the Ancón treasure, proving that Cochrane had not embezzled it. To compensate him for his silence, he saw Paroissien's charges against him and his own reply published in Lima in the following year: 'negras e infames inposturas' as San Martín described Cochrane's indictment, forgetting who had started this slanging match.

But during the month of October 1822 in which San Martín sailed down from the north, William Cochrane at last arrived from the south in the *Rising Star*, having rounded Cape Horn in the first steam-assisted vessel ever to enter the Pacific. Cochrane invited Mrs Graham to make the 8 mile gala journey in her from Valparaiso to Quintero. 'The first thing I did was to visit the machinery,' wrote Maria, disclosing that she shared yet another of Cochrane's interests, 'which consists of two steam engines, each of 45 horse power, and the wheels covered so as not to show in the water from without.' The paddle wheels were only intended as auxiliaries to the sails and had rarely been used during the voyage. 'It was with no small delight,' Maria recorded, 'that I set my foot on the deck of the first steam vessel that ever navigated the Pacific, and I thought with exultation of the triumphs of man over the obstacles nature seems to have placed between him and the accomplishment of his imaginations.'

She was equally entranced by Cochrane's printing press, and as she helped him to operate it she speculated whether it might also be able to reproduce pictures. She saw its owner as he no doubt saw himself during this brief interlude of peace in 1822, as the enlightened benefactor who would spend the remainder of his life helping to build a new nation, its commerce and agriculture, its arts and its political institutions.

But gradually the dream crumbled. The return of San Martín was a temporary cause of acrimony, the government's neglect of the fleet a mounting aggravation. What would have become of it, if Cochrane had not paid its crews a year's arrears of wages out of the Ancón treasure, there is no saying. The O'Higgins administration had not yet succeeded in placing the country's finances on a sound basis and once the navy had completed its task its past claims and its future usefulness alike receded from the public mind. While Cochrane's sailors remained unpaid he could hardly expect the government to pay for the magnificent new vessel which he had constructed and sailed to Chile at his own expense in response to their original request. Once upon a time Cochrane had suggested that his brother William might like to settle permanently in Chile. Now that he had actually arrived his elder brother gave him no further encouragement, and William returned home immediately, while Cochrane himself began to consider abandoning the peaceful, constructive life on which he had set his heart, in favour of the means of escape which were presented to him.

The first of these arrived from Brazil on the other side of the continent. The Portuguese colonials in its vast realms had at last followed the example of the Spaniards and creoles of South America, after a delay which had been caused by the accident of political events. In 1808 the entire Portuguese royal family had fled from Napoleon's invasion with their treasure and their courtiers and had sailed for Brazil, escorted by British warships. Overnight Rio de Janeiro was transformed from a colonial viceroyalty into the capital of Portugal. It doubled in size and began rapidly to rival Lima itself as a South American metropolis, until in 1821 the King returned to the mother country taking most of the holdings of the Bank of Brazil with him, but leaving his son Dom Pedro as Regent.

It soon became evident to the Brazilians that they were to be reduced to their former colonial status and Rio de Janeiro to be stripped of her jurisdiction over the provinces of their gigantic country. But when the young Prince Pedro was ordered home he yielded to the solicitations of the people amongst whom he had grown to manhood and promised them: 'I will remain.' After that the belated revolution gathered speed. In June 1822 Pedro promised to summon a constituent assembly; on 1 July the independence of Brazil was proclaimed; on 12 October the Prince was declared constitutional Emperor; and within weeks the new administration was begging Cochrane to come to its assistance. 'My Lord,' it addressed him in French on 4 November, 'Brazil, a power of the first order, has become a new empire.'

This was something of an exaggeration: an area twice the size of Europe was still controlled by the forces of Portugal, protected by the mother country's command of the sea. Once again it was Cochrane's magic that was needed to make independence real and permanent. A more urgent plea, also in French, was despatched after the first. 'Come my Lord; honour invites you, glory calls you. Come; give to our naval forces this marvellous order and incomparable discipline of mighty Albion.'

It was not only from the new world that such invitations came. In Europe the Greeks had begun their struggle for freedom from Turkish rule, and this was a cause that fired the imaginations of all who remembered the glories of classical Greece. The Greek Committee sent a request for help which made as strong an appeal to Cochrane in Chile as it did to Byron in Italy.

For a few more days Mrs Graham was able to record the tranquil life of Quintero as Cochrane superintended the building of his new home, entertained his friends of the British community, and clung to his dream despite the increasing disaffection in his unpaid fleet, increasing political unrest in the country, and the song of the distant sirens. John Miers and his wife were among the Admiral's guests when Maria noted on 18 November: 'We tried to persuade Mrs Miers to remain with us, but in vain. She was anxious to return to her children, and accordingly left us in time to get home by daylight. I made a little sketch of the house; and having found a lithographic press here, I mean to draw it on stone, and so produce the first print of any kind that has been done in Chile.'

The next night the idyll ended for ever. Cochrane himself had returned to the fleet and lay in the *O'Higgins* in Valparaiso bay when a great earthquake struck the neighbourhood. As soon as he felt the tremors he went ashore in one of the ship's boats, which was swept far inland on a great tidal wave. For the remainder of the night he ferried such survivors as he encountered in the dark to the comparative safety of his ships. 'The morning of the 20th,' wrote Mrs Graham, 'exhibited a scene of greater distress. Only twenty houses and one church remained standing in that large town. All the ovens had been destroyed and there was no bread: the governor had fled and the people cried out that his sins had brought down the judgment.' But O'Higgins the Supreme Director happened to be staying in Valparaiso at this time, and he did not follow Zenteno's cowardly example.

By the first light of day Cochrane's weary sailors used their ships' canvas to erect tents on the shore for the homeless. Mrs Graham's house was among those destroyed, but she was instantly taken into a Chilean home in the hospitable manner that William Miller had experienced, and here she spent the remainder of her residence in Chile, acting as instructress to the children. As for Cochrane's newly completed home, 'the house is not habitable,' she noted. 'Some of its inmates were thrown down by the shock, and others by the falling of various articles of furniture upon them.'

On 21 November there was another tremendous shock, and this was when Cochrane was able to rescue the Supreme Director, for he arrived with his men just as Government House collapsed and erected a tent on the hillside behind for O'Higgins. By the 23rd the shocks appeared to be diminishing, and the following day the sailors who had rendered such untiring service were at last rewarded with their arrears of pay. It had taken this catastrophe to remind the authorities of their obligation.

It was in the midst of this disturbance that Cochrane received a letter tantamount to a fresh seismic shock. It was written to him by the Governor of Concepción, General Freire, on 20 November. 'The moment has arrived for action. Answer me with promptitude and frankness. Let us have the satisfaction of applying effective remedies to the evils which afflict the country, zealously and disinterestedly for the good of the Republic, and without personal views. I hold the residence of San Martín in any part of Chile as suspicious and dangerous. Let him be off to make some other quarter happy, where he can sell his protection to the ill-fated inhabitants. I hope my intentions meet your approbation, and will be seconded by the officers of the squadron.'

Cochrane was bound to Freire by feelings of respect, and by gratitude to the man whose assistance had enabled him to capture Valdivia. In addition he agreed with every word that the General had written about San Martín. So he would have had unimpeachable grounds for accepting an invitation that might well have made him Supreme Director of Chile and enabled him to spend the remainder of his life implementing all the schemes of which the printing press, the steam ship, the agricultural implements and the plantations of Quintero were but the first visible symbols. Had he accepted the invitation of San Martín in Peru it would have been possible to convict him of the improper motives which Paroissien attributed to him, but not if he had yielded to the persuasions of Freire. In rejecting them Cochrane demonstrated more conclusively than on any other occasion the fundamental integrity of his character and made a mockery of all those accusations which he drew on himself throughout his career by his extraordinary capacity for making enemies.

But when General Freire took the field in spite of him, Cochrane was placed in an intolerable position. For it was he who held the scales, and he was bound by his oath of allegiance to O'Higgins, which would compel him to take part in a civil war against his former companion in arms on behalf of a man he detested. He took the only way out.

On 29 November 1822 he accepted the invitation from Brazil. 'The war in the Pacific being happily terminated by the total destruction of the Spanish naval force, I am, of course, free for the crusade of liberty in any other quarter of the globe. I confess however that I had not hitherto directed my attention to the Brazils; considering that the struggle for the liberties of Greece—the most oppressed of modern states—afforded the fairest opportunity for enterprise and exertion. I have today tendered my ultimate resignation to the government of Chile . . .'

Maria Graham visited Cochrane in his flagship while he attempted to lay down his commission and leave the country in which he had believed until so recently that he might settle in peace. 'I went aboard the Admiral's ship soon after breakfast to call on some of my friends who, with their families, had taken refuge there on the night of the 19th, and to whom he had given up his cabin and lived himself in a tent on deck.'

The seismic shocks continued day after day, filling the stricken Chileans with alarm, as the sands ran out for the three men who had done most to secure the foundation of their republic. On 4 December O'Higgins threatened to resign in the face of Freire's relentless advance with his army from the south. But a fortnight later the Supreme Director was still refusing to accept Cochrane's resignation. 'I find,' wrote Maria Graham, 'that although Lord Cochrane has twice tendered his resignation to the government, it has not been accepted.' She had dined with him aboard the *O'Higgins*, and noted that his mind was made up, and concentrated upon the problems of his departure. 'Lord Cochrane came up to me where I stood and gently calling my attention, said that as he was going to sail away from this country, I should take a great uneasiness from his mind if I would go with him. He could not bear, he said, to leave the unprotected widow of a British officer thus on the beach, a castaway as it were in a ruined town, a country full of civil war.'

During that dismal Christmas season, so different from the festival he had planned in his new mansion at Herradura, he also pondered over the interests of the foreign merchants whose commerce he had protected, and of the Chileans whom he still regarded as his own fellow-countrymen. On 4 January 1823 he issued his addresses of farewell. The longest was written to the trading community, whose forgiveness he asked for his departure: 'I trust you will do me the justice to believe that I have not determined to withdraw myself from these seas while anything remained within my means to accomplish for your benefit and security.' To his adopted countrymen he said:

'Chileans—My Fellow Countrymen!

'The common enemy of America has fallen in Chile. Your tricoloured flag waves on the Pacific, secured by your sacrifices. Some internal commotions agitate Chile. It is not my business to investigate their causes, to accelerate or retard their effects; I can only wish that the result may be favourable to the national interest.

'Chileans! You have expelled from your country the enemies of your independence; do not sully the glorious act by encouraging discord and promoting anarchy—that greatest of all evils. Consult the dignity to which your heroism has raised you, and if you must take any step to secure your national liberty—judge for yourselves—act with prudence—and be guided by reason and justice.

'It is now four years since the sacred cause of your independence called me to Chile. I assisted you to gain it. I have seen it accomplished. It only remains to preserve it. I leave you for a time, in order not to involve myself in matters foreign to my duties, and for other reasons concerning which I now remain silent, that I may not encourage party spirit.

'Chileans! You know that independence is purchased at the point of the bayonet. Know also that liberty is founded on good faith, and on the laws of honour, and that those who infringe upon these are your only enemies, amongst whom you will never find COCHRANE.'

Behind the tactful generalities there peeps a new-found self-knowledge, an impulse to save others from some of the pitfalls of his own past career: and there is no need to doubt the sincerity of his statement that he still regarded Chile as his home and that he intended to return to it.

On 10 January, when General Freire was less than 6 days' march from Santiago, the brig *Colonel Allen* sailed into Quintero bay, where the Admiral's flag flew from the *Montezuma*. Immediately the ships' boats began to ply to and fro across the water, loading the possessions of all who would be sailing in the *Colonel Allen* to Brazil. A week later the last dispositions had been completed and Maria noted in her journal: 'This morning I walked with Lord Cochrane to the tops of most of the hills immediately between the house of the Herradura and the sea; perhaps it may be the last time he will ever tread these grounds for which he was doing so much.' Her prophecy was to prove correct. 'We gathered many seeds and roots, which I hope to see springing up in my own land.' By the following year one of these had flowered in Hammersmith, that pleasant village by the river west of London. In Chile the plant was called Mancaya, in England it was named Cyrtanthia Cochranea.

The Admiral did not spend his last night aboard his flagship, but in the *Colonel Allen*. 'Everybody slept on board last night; and this morning was spent in getting in food and water. At six o'clock Captain Crosbie went on board the *Montezuma* to haul down Lord Cochrane's flag, and thus formally to give up the naval command in Chile. One gun was fired, and the flag was brought on board the *Colonel Allen* to his Lordship, who was standing on the poop: he received it without apparent emotion, but desired it to be taken care of. Some of those around him appeared more touched than he was. Under that flag he had often led them to victory and always to honour.'

On that very day, 18 January 1823, on which Cochrane sailed away from Chile, San Martín returned over the victorious route across the Andes which led back to Mendoza. At its summit a Colonel who had served under him met him there, looking careworn and dejected on his chestnut mule. 'Perhaps,' said San Martín, 'it would be as well for us to go down now from these lofty heights where once America looked up to me.' He travelled on to Buenos Aires in his native Argentina, and here he endured the sorrow of his wife's death. Nor could he continue to live there in peace for Bernardo de Rivadavia, the ruler of Argentina was ill-disposed towards him. So he took ship for Europe with his small daughter.

Sailing away from Chile when she did, Maria Graham was unable to record the drama in Valparaiso when General Freire marched in and made Bernardo O'Higgins his prisoner. But John Miers witnessed that strange confrontation, when O'Higgins resigned with his characteristic grace and Freire accepted his office with apparent reluctance on 1 April. He did not hold it for so long as his predecessor nor display a greater aptitude for its responsibilities than O'Higgins had done.

O'Higgins was thus the last of the triumvirate to leave Chile. His administrative shortcomings had been compensated by outstanding gallantry in war, and it was perhaps his supreme achievement to have retained the respect both of San Martín and of Cochrane when these combative men were at each others' throats. He retired to an estate that was bestowed on him by the grateful Peruvians, and there he witnessed the campaign that brought Simón Bolívar to Lima in 1823 and the surrender of Canterac in the following year. He lived on to see William Miller become Commander-in-Chief in Peru and suppress the insurrection there in 1834, while Captain Martin Guise, free of the baneful influence of Spry, rose to the rank of Vice Admiral.

Miller remained a British patriot to the last, and in 1843, the year after Bernardo O'Higgins' death, he was appointed British Consul-General in the Pacific. When he lay dying in Callao in 1861 he asked to be carried aboard the British warship *Naiad* so that he would be able to leave the world as he had entered it, beneath the flag of his own nation.

T.S.W.—R

When the news of his death was carried ashore all the bells of Callao were tolled; the first time they had ever been rung at the passing of a Protestant.

John Miers left Chile in 1825 on the invitation of Rivadavia from Argentina to set up a national mint in Buenos Aires. This required his return to England to make the arrangements, and while he was there he left the account of his experiences in South America to be published. So his countrymen were able to read the reflections with which he had watched Cochrane sail out of the Pacific.

'Thus Chile lost the further services of the most brave, zealous, successful and meritorious officer it ever possessed; a man whose services they never repaid, whose merit they never were able to appreciate, and whose salutary advice was always treated with disrespect; whose splendid achievements had secured the independence of Chile, laid the foundations of the liberties of Peru, and wholly cleared the Pacific Ocean of every Spanish vessel.'

By the time these words appeared in print in 1826, Paroissien had returned to South America in a vain attempt to make his fortune in the silver mines of Potosí, while San Martín had retired in poverty to Brussels.

CHAPTER TWELVE

The Marquess of Maranhão

Maria Graham had already visited several parts of Brazil with her husband the Captain of the *Doris*, and her published journal reveals how much she was able to tell Cochrane about the land to which they sailed in the opening months of 1823. Unfortunately they reached Rio de Janeiro in March on 'one of the most windy and rainy days that I ever remember seeing in Brazil; so that the beautiful landscape of the harbour is entirely lost to the strangers from Chile'. A port officer was sent aboard the *Colonel Allen* who could speak English. 'First he mentioned the coronation of the Emperor,' Maria related, 'and then the war at Bahia; on which I questioned him very closely, on the ground of having formerly visited the place.' Her knowledge of this tropical province in the north which was still occupied by the forces of Portugal must have been of the greatest usefulness to Cochrane.

But anon 'the officer began to question me in my turn. Did I come from Chile? Did I know Lord Cochrane? Was he come to Rio? For all eyes were turned towards him. When he found that His Lordship was actually on board, he flew to his cabin door, and entreated to kiss his hands; then snatched his hat, and calling to the Captain to do as he would, and anchor where he pleased without ceremony, jumped over the side to be the first, if possible, to convey to the Emperor the joyful intelligence.' While he was doing this, two naval officers came aboard who had never previously served under Cochrane, Captain Taylor from England and the Brazilian Captain Garção: and they proved an auspicious contrast to Guise and Spry who had confronted him on his arrival in Chile. Maria had no such fortunate encounter that day. 'The weather cleared up in the afternoon and I went ashore to see if I could find any of my old friends, or hear any news; but all the English were gone to their country houses and the opera, the proper place for gossip, is shut because it is Lent.' But Cochrane went directly to present himself to the Emperor in company with Captain Crosbie, returning to his ship late at night.

The 24-year-old Prince of the house of Braganza from whom Cochrane parted that night with such evident satisfaction possessed a character which resembled his own in more respects than anyone else's whom he met in his life. Dom Pedro, heir to King John of Portugal, had the same autocratic temper in conflict with the same advanced liberal ideals. He too had been deprived of a disciplined education in his youth, for which he compensated himself all his life by taking a voracious interest in the arts and sciences with the same versatility of talent. He played the flute, violin, bassoon and trombone, composed music for the chapel and the parade ground, had one of his symphonies performed in Europe and became the friend of Rossini. A skilful carpenter, he carved the bust of himself for the figurehead of Cochrane's new flagship the *Pedro Primeiro*. Growing up in the egalitarian society of servants and stable-boys, he could shoe his own horses, ride with a skill and endurance that aroused repeated astonishment, and speak with a freedom for which he was not too proud to apologise when the descendant of absolutist kings wounded people whose feelings he found to be no less sensitive than his own. Above all, he possessed courage, and the capacity to act decisively at moments when the destiny of a great continent depended upon what he said and did. He had already been offered the crown of Greece, and invested with that of Brazil: he was later to be offered the crown of Spain. When he died of tuberculosis at the age of 36 he had renounced four crowns, and secured for two of his children the thrones of Portugal and Brazil.

King John had authorised Pedro in advance to place himself at the head of the movement for independence. 'If Brazil should decide on separation, let it be under your leadership, since you are bound to respect me, rather than under that of one of those adventurers.' The part which Pedro played achieved the very object which San Martín had hoped to achieve when he sought a constitutional sovereign for the throne of Lima, and helped to preserve Brazil as a single nation while Spanish America disintegrated into a host of separate republics with governments that survived only until the next *coup d'état*. But Brazil's most distinguished son made a contribution that some people consider even more formative than the Emperor's. José Bonifácio de Andrada was a distinguished scholar and mineralogist who belonged to half the learned societies of Europe and had been a Professor at Coimbra University before he returned to Brazil to become the Emperor's Chief Minister. He was one of three outstanding brothers, of whom Martin Francisco served ably as Minister of Finance while José Bonifácio guided the impetuous Dom Pedro through the complications that the declaration of independence gave rise to.

The third man to whom Brazil owes her integrity as a single nation was the one who in 6 months destroyed the remaining bastions of Portugal in the northern provinces and brought them into the Emperor's obedience, the sailor of legendary reputation who sailed into the harbour of Rio de Janeiro on 13 March 1823. The high expectations were marked by joyous festivities, an inspection of the fleet, and negotiations over the terms of service of Cochrane and the officers who had come to Brazil with him.

These were bedevilled by King John's removal from Brazil of such a large proportion of the country's public funds and as much jewellery as he could scoop into his hands from that land of gold and diamonds. He had spent over a million pounds on the marriage of Dom Pedro to an Austrian princess in a display which astounded even the Hapsburg court in Vienna. The task of the Andrada administration was not an easy one, but Cochrane had been short-changed too often in the past to allow himself to be made the victim of a government's need for economies. He had come with the promise that he would enjoy the same pay and rank as in the Chilean service (even though he had not received anything like the whole of his salary there) and when he was offered the considerably lower pay of a Portuguese Admiral he refused it. When his salary was conceded, it was calculated at an unfavourable exchange-rate at which he protested a second time, and he was next offered a junior Admiral's rank that might have subjected him to the orders of a senior.

But he had no need to play his trump card, the threat that he would sail on to Greece. The office of First Admiral of Brazil was created for him, a rank that none but he would ever hold. Cochrane told José Bonifácio, with a tactlessness that must have reminded the Chief Minister of his own Emperor's bluntness of speech, that it was a pity all these arrangements had not been made in the first place. Then he boarded the *Pedro Primeiro* to watch his flag being hoisted and to hear it saluted by twenty-one guns from the surrounding ships. Ashore, Maria heard both British and Brazilian criticisms that he had sold his services dear, and remarked that he had only demanded the rates that were allowed to a British Admiral. Brazil has since proclaimed that his achievements, the masterpiece of his career, were such that no gold could pay for and has found other ways of acknowledging the debt, while generations of sailors study his campaign at the Naval War College of Rio de Janeiro with the same attention that is paid to the career of Nelson in his own country.

The *Pedro Primeiro* was a prime frigate of 64 guns, already prepared for sea with four months' provisions on board. She must have given particular satisfaction to the Emperor Pedro who had carved her figurehead, and who also left a miniature ship, perfect in every detail, as a sample of his craftsmanship in wood. Besides the flagship Cochrane was pleased with the sight of the *Maria da Gloria*, a 32-gun clipper that had been built in North America and was captained by the valiant French Captain Beaurepaire, with a leavening of his own countrymen among the better trained members of his crew. There were six other vessels in various stages of completion, including another frigate, but this promising armada suffered from a dearth of competent seamen since the Portuguese Navy, and a mercantile marine bound in loyalty to the mother country by her trading monopoly, had absorbed the experienced sailors of this hemisphere. Herein lay Cochrane's ultimate problem.

In addition to the staunch Thomas Crosbie, who had accompanied him to Brazil as his Flag Captain, he enjoyed the services of Lieutenant Pascoe Grenfell, a future Admiral of the Brazilian Navy. Other officers who had once served in the British Navy had defied the embargo of the Foreign Enlistment Act to join this fleet. Cochrane's Brazilian log-book preserves the names of many of them, Scots and Englishmen: Lieutenants George Clarence, William Inglis, Francis Drummond, Thomas Poynton, Broom and McCreight, men who would take part in an adventure from which Captain Marryat might have distilled a whole fresh saga of sea stories had he been present to witness it. The Brazilian Captain Garção and the French Captain Beaurepaire were among his most valuable lieutenants.

But where to find crews who would be able to carry out such duties as Cochrane required of his men? The seamen were for the most part the scourings of the waterfront, and their wages were according to their worth. The 130 black marines were emancipated slaves who had abandoned any taste for servile duties with their shackles, and required to be waited on by the sailors. But a stroke of good fortune brought the merchant vessel *Lindsay* from England into Rio harbour on 29 March. Cochrane instantly ordered Captain Crosbie to offer an enhanced wage from his private purse to any North American or British seamen who would transfer to the Brazilian service, and in this way he succeeded in creating a nucleus of 160 reliable men in the *Pedro Primeiro*.

He was almost ready for sea when he heard the distressing news that his wife and baby daughter Elizabeth were on their way to Chile to rejoin him there, so that they would have to endure the rough passage round Cape Horn twice before he would be reunited with them. Maria Graham tried to calm his anxieties by pointing out that their ship would probably put into Rio de Janeiro on their journey and two days later, on 31 March, the Emperor and Empress paid a visit to his flagship, to give their blessing to his expedition to Bahia. Maria recorded how the Hapsburg Empress gave a remarkable demonstration of Germanic solidarity in this Latin world. 'On some Portuguese officers complaining that the English sailors had been drunk the day before, the Empress said "Oh 'tis the custom of the North, where brave men come from. The sailors are under my protection: I spread my mantle over them".' They probably needed stronger protection from their abstemious Admiral than from any Portuguese officer.

Without waiting another day, Cochrane put to sea on 1 April 1823 with the four ships that were by now ready to sail. Crosbie commanded the flagship with three Lieutenants who had accompanied them from Chile. David Jowett commanded the *Piranga* while Captains Garção and Beaurepaire commanded the other two vessels. The squadron made its thousand-mile journey north to blockade the port of Bahia, where it was joined on 1 May by a fifth vessel which had since been completed, the *Nitherohy* or *Niteroi* under Captain Taylor. When the Portuguese fleet sailed out of Bahia 3 days later Cochrane apparently possessed the means to fight the only fleet action he was ever able to attempt in any part of the world.

The odds were against him because the Portuguese Admiral had a warship of seventy-four guns, no less than five frigates, five corvettes, a brig and a schooner, thirteen vessels in all against Cochrane's five. But Cochrane went after them until he spotted a gap in the enemy line through which he sailed, detaching four Portuguese ships from the rest. Holding the remainder of the fleet at bay single-handed in the *Pedro Primeiro*, he signalled to his fleet to engage in a contest of four ships against four.

Not a single vessel of his squadron obeyed the signal. Even in the flagship itself Grenfell had to arrest two seamen who prevented the guns from being fired by seizing the powder-monkeys who were trying to supply them. Disconsolately Cochrane withdrew, and sat down in his cabin to write the most swingeing indictment of a fleet ever penned.

'I warned the Minister of Marine,' he thundered, 'that every native of Portugal put on board the squadron—with the exception of officers of known character—would prove prejudicial to the expedition, and yesterday we had clear proof of the fact.' The equipment had proved as useless as the crews. 'Our cartridges are all unfit for service, and I have been obliged to cut up every flag and ensign that could be spared to render them serviceable, so as to prevent the men's arms being blown off whilst working the guns.' The accusations spread far and wide. 'The bed of the mortar which I received on board this ship was crushed on the first fire—being entirely rotten; the fuses for the shells are formed of such wretched composition that it will not take fire with the discharge of the mortar, and are consequently unfit for use on board a ship where it is extremely dangerous to kindle the fuse other than by the explosion.' Having once again the task of creating an efficient navy out of extremely raw materials, his technical flair stood him in as good stead as ever.

'The sails of this ship are all rotten—the light and baffling airs on our way hither having beaten one set to pieces, and the others are hourly giving way to the slightest breeze of wind.' Racy and somewhat ungrammatical, this is very different from the ornate style of his proclamations, an expression of urgency and anger.

He sent a graphic description of the emancipated slaves aboard his flagship. 'The marines neither understand gun exercise, the use of small arms, nor the sword, and yet have so high an opinion of themselves that they will not assist to wash the decks or even to clean out their own berths, but sit and look on whilst these operations are being performed be seamen; being thus useless as marines, they are a hindrance to the seamen, who ought to be learning their duties in the tops, instead of being converted into sweepers and scavengers.' In this campaign he would be forced to do without any equivalent of William Miller's marines, who had been so indispensable to his victories in the Pacific.

Like Cromwell when he turned from his indictment of troops of decayed serving men to plan the creation of a new model army, Cochrane lost no time in finding his own remedy. 'One half of the squadron is necessary to watch over the other half,' he informed the Chief Minister. He found that he could fashion only two effective instruments of war out of his fleet of six. So the senior officers in the other four were transferred with as many of their crews as were properly trained to his own flagship and to Captain Beaurepaire's clipper the *Maria da Gloria*. The remainder were left out of harm's way in charge of more junior officers until they should be better instructed, with a responsibility for transforming captured vessels into fireships. The *Pedro Primeiro* and *Maria da Gloria* returned alone to blockade the port of Bahia.

In Rio de Janeiro Maria Graham was exploring the state of slavery from which Cochrane's marines had been freed. It was a theme that constantly troubled her conscience, and the sight of the slave market in Rio appalled her. 'I went and stood near them, and though certainly more disposed to weep, I forced myself to smile to them and look cheerfully, and kissed my hand to them, with all of which they seemed delighted, and jumped about and danced, as if returning my civilities.'

Apart from its wealth of gold and diamonds, the economy of Brazil was largely based on the great agricultural estates run by slave labour. 'I spent the day with Madame de Rio Seco. Her house is really a magnificent one; it has its ballroom and its music room, its grotto and fountains, besides extremely handsome apartments of every kind, both for family and public use, with rather more china and French clocks than we should think of displaying.' While Cochrane was lying off Bahia a conflict was gathering momentum in the capital which would draw him into its vortex. Andrada, the Chief Minister, was opposed to slavery and his somewhat authoritarian government was seen as a menace to the high-ranking Portuguese potentates who possessed the ear of a Portuguese Emperor. The administration waited with increasing anxiety for news from Bahia, as reports of increasing famine there failed to add any tidings of a decisive military or naval victory.

On 13 June the *Sesostris* sailed into the harbour with Lady Cochrane and her daughter Elizabeth on board. 'Thank God,' wrote Maria, 'by putting in here she has learned where Lord Cochrane is, and is thus spared the tedious voyage.' The following day the two women met for the first time when Kitty went to call on Maria, who was ill. This was the day on which news arrived of the fiasco of Cochrane's fleet action.

Kitty had crossed the Atlantic in considerable comfort. She had been entrusted by William Cochrane to the care of A. E. Robson, one of those South American merchants who remembered Cochrane 'with the greatest admiration and respect'. He had been conferring in London with William about the Chilean government's outstanding debt to the two brothers for the *Rising Star*, which was separate from its arrears of pay to Cochrane for his services as Admiral of Chile. Robson arranged to return to Valparaiso in the *Sesostris* which bore a cargo of 500 tons of naval stores purchased out of the Chilean loan that had been floated in London; a ship that he chose, 'having large and convenient cabins the whole of which was engaged by Captain Sheriff and myself for Lady Cochrane's use, excluding all other passengers', and for which her Ladyship paid the owners no less than £1000.

Her entourage consisted of four male and six female servants, and she was also attended by 'two young Gentlemen, Mr Sutton and Mr Barker'. She had brought a considerable quantity of furniture with her, expecting that she would be settling in the mansion which her husband had built on the estate of Herradura. All of these articles were unloaded at Rio 'excepting those that are particularly adapted for Chile'. Evidently both Robson and Kitty expected that the Cochranes would be returning there at the end of the Admiral's Brazilian engagement. The moment he reached harbour, Robson sat down to reassure him: 'I hasten to announce the safe arrival here this day of your amiable Lady and Child in the *Sesostris*, after a passage of 50 days from England, in excellent health and spirits, so much so that I never saw her Ladyship

look better during her residence in Chile. She is at present overcome
with the joy of being so near to your Lordship and the fortunate escape
of a prolonged absence round Cape Horn.' He told the Admiral how
sorry he was that his ship must continue its voyage before they could
meet, and offered to do all in his power to recover the immense sum of
money 'locked up in the *Rising Star*'.

But at the very moment when Robson was writing Cochrane all this
exhilarating news in his fluent, punctilious hand, the Admiral was
preparing the greatest sea-hunt of his life. As usual he had devised a
stratagem designed to demoralise his opponent and to give an impression of uncanny power.

The thirteen Portuguese men-of-war had returned to the beseiged
and starving port of Bahia where they lay, 9 miles up river under the
protection of shore batteries. Even when Cochrane returned to resume
the blockade with no more than two ships, the enemy did not move
from its safe anchorages to attack him. He allowed the news to leak into
Bahia that he was preparing fireships, and so the atmosphere of disquiet
was fanned by a fear that he would carry out at Bahia the devilish
assault which he had been prevented by Gambier from completing in
Aix Roads. When he judged that the demoralisation had simmered to
a sufficient temperature he revictualled and watered his ships for a long
period at sea, and then searched the calendar for a night on which the
people of Bahia might in some way be preoccupied. There was no Guy
Fawkes Night or church festival to serve his turn, but the intelligence
service which he always maintained ashore with such effectiveness
informed him of a ball which was to be held on 12 June.

He accordingly chose this night for an operation which would test
the carefully selected crew of the *Pedro Primeiro* to the uttermost, since
it would be a feat scarcely to be credited. Somehow he navigated the
9 miles of the river to Bahia in the darkness, although he had never
examined those channels by daylight and possessed only the guidance
of rudder and sail, manipulated with exact precision. When he reached
within hailing distance of the nearest Portuguese ship he was challenged
and replied that his was an English vessel. Then suddenly the wind
failed, as he lay in the midst of the Portuguese fleet, under its shore
batteries. But for this also Cochrane had provided. In the last resort he
possessed the advantage of an ebbing tide, as he had done when he
drifted stern-foremost in the *Impérieuse* down Aix Roads. He now
repeated that manoeuvre, anchor adrag, in an even greater feat of skill
which carried him like a ghost-ship out of range of the guns of Bahia,
through 9 miles of invisible shoals to the river mouth.

The Portuguese Admiral was sitting at dinner ashore with General

Ignacio Luiz Madeira de Melo when they heard a shot ring out at 10 o'clock, just as a messenger made his entry.

'What is it?' asked the General.

'It's Lord Cochrane's line-of-battleship in the very midst of our fleet,' the man replied.

'Impossible,' snorted the Admiral. 'No large ship can have come up with the ebb tide.'

The effect on the nerves of the General and the Admiral when they discovered that the impossible had occurred can be judged by their reactions. They permitted St John's Eve to pass while Cochrane lay in wait at the river mouth, that happy night of 22 June 'whereon', as Maria Graham observed, 'the maidens of Brazil practise some of the same rites as those of Scotland at Hallow-e'en, to ascertain the fate of their loves. They burn nuts together; they put their hands, blindfold, on a table with the letters of the alphabet; and practise many a simple conjuration.' Cochrane had performed his own conjuration, and by 29 June his intelligence were able to report the interpretation which the Portuguese High Command had placed upon it.

The General and the Admiral agreed that the only possible solution was to evacuate Bahia before Cochrane could tighten the blockade so as to make escape impossible.

'The crisis in which we find ourselves is perilous,' General Madeira de Melo informed the people under his protection, 'because the means of subsistence fail us, and we cannot secure the entrance of any provisions. My duty as a soldier and as Governor is to make any sacrifice in order to save the city; but it is equally my duty to prevent, in an extreme case, the sacrifice of the troops I command—of the squadron— and of yourselves.' After some soothing reassurances came the final blow. 'You may assure yourselves that the measures I am now taking are purely precautionary: but it is necessary to communicate them to you, because if it happens that we must abandon the city, many of you will leave it also.' They would indeed, as many as could find a ship to scramble aboard.

A Bahia newspaper described the consequences of that proclamation. 'In the last days we have witnessed in this city a most doleful spectacle that must touch the heart even of the most insensible. A panic terror has seized on all men's minds—the city will be left without protectors— and families whose fathers are obliged to fly will be left orphans.' As Cochrane preserved an unbroken record for conducting war with exceptional humanity, the inhabitants of Bahia were allowing themselves to become the dupes of the devilish epithet which had been bestowed on him for his skill, not for his barbarism. The belief that El Diablo was waiting to destroy families 'whose fathers are obliged to fly' was a fiction of their own invention.

However, he did not neglect to threaten Bahia with fire and brimstone, the devil's weapons, once he learnt that this might contribute to the panic. The news was allowed to leak into the city that the fireships were now ready to be launched against the Portuguese fleet, and on this occasion they achieved their object without the striking of a match. Immediately the Admiral was informed of this latest threat he ordered the embarkation of every soldier in Bahia aboard the waiting transports, which led to a stampede of civilians into the merchant vessels that lay in the harbour. The thirteen warships were ordered to convoy this fleet to the safety of the open sea, abandoning the port and province of Bahia to the Admiral of Brazil.

Once again Cochrane received instant intelligence of these plans for evacuation, and he prepared a salvo of paper shot to fire into the mêlée of soldiers, sailors and civilians who were scuttling about the harbour of Bahia, lest the hysteria should subside. He wrote separately to the ruling Junta, to the General and to the Admiral, warning them against precisely the course that he wished them to take without further delay. To the Junta he said:

'Gentlemen, understanding that it is in contemplation to abandon the town of Bahia, without any security being given not again to resume hostilities against the subjects and territories of His Imperial Majesty, and that you may not be aware of the difficulty of retiring—whilst hopes may have been held out to you that this is practicable—I must, for the sake of humanity, caution you against any attempt to remove yourselves by sea, unless I have a perfect understanding as to the future intentions of the naval forces which may accompany you, but to whom I have nothing to suggest.

'I tell you, however, that it is in my power to take advantages which may be fatal to your escape . . .' Thus the commander of a frigate and a schooner.

While the enemy armada prepared to sail in even greater haste and disorder as a result of these warnings, Cochrane issued the first of his masterly succession of orders to Captain Beaurepaire and his other officers on 1 July. Beaurepaire was to proceed to Bahia at the first opportunity and there exercise authority in Cochrane's absence. He was to leave Portuguese flags flying at the river mouth to deceive approaching ships as to who held the port. Transports and merchantmen which were captured in the open sea were to be dismasted, their stores and arms flung overboard, and their water casks stove in, so that they would have no alternative but to return to Bahia and there surrender themselves. For Cochrane was so short of officers and trained seamen that he could spare none as prize crews.

The timing of each move he made proved to be exact. On 2 July the fleet of over seventy ships appeared at the river mouth and the chase began. On the following day he was joined by the *Nitheroby* and the *Carolina*, summoned for the limited duties which Cochrane designed for them. He was also gladdened by the sight of the *Colonel Allen* which had transported him from Chile, and which had since been recruited into the Brazilian naval service. He renamed her the *Bahia*.

Like terriers these ships fell upon stragglers in the unwieldy convoy and sent them home, one after another, helpless cripples. Cochrane remained constantly on the convoy's tail, never delaying for longer than it took him to pounce upon an enemy vessel and leave her to the attention of one of his lesser ships. So the devastation continued, night and day, until 4 July when the Portuguese Admiral abandoned his position at the head of the convoy to sweep down upon the *Pedro Primeiro* with his force of thirteen warships. But even with such a preponderance of numbers he was no match for Cochrane and his disciplined crew. Out-sailed and out-manoeuvred, the Portuguese warships returned to lead their convoy in its headlong flight, and that night and the next day a lengthening line of dismasted vessels tottered home before the wind to Bahia.

On the evening of 5 July Cochrane observed that six large vessels detached themselves from the convoy without any encouragement from himself and began to make sail westwards. He had already learned at Bahia of a Portuguese intention to reinforce the garrison of the great equatorial province of Maranhão, whose northward-facing coast stretched towards the mouth of the Amazon. Unwilling to leave the main convoy himself, Cochrane ordered Grenfell to intercept this contingent, and Grenfell soon discovered that it was indeed bound for Maranhão. He at once set about disabling the transports, throwing arms and ammunition overboard, and placing the officers on parole not to fight against the government of Brazil. Thus a division of several thousand troops was wiped off the strength of Portugal without the firing of a shot.

Meanwhile Cochrane continued his pursuit of the principal quarry across the Equator until a haze hid its sails from view and there was not a breath of wind to stir them. The ships lay becalmed in the intense heat until the 16th, when a breeze sprang up, enabling Cochrane to resume the hunt. Crowding every inch of canvas, he sailed straight for the squadron at the head of the convoy and poured a broadside at close range into one of the frigates. But while the *Pedro Primeiro* tacked to repeat the manoeuvre there was a resounding crack as her main-mast split. After 15 days the chase was over.

By this time only thirteen ships remained in the convoy, and even these did not escape unscathed as they continued their panic-stricken flight across the Atlantic. Cochrane ordered Captain Taylor to hang on their tail in the *Nitherohy*, and so he did all the way to Lisbon, and there set fire to four of the transports under the very guns of a battleship in the mouth of the Tagus. So ended yet another adventure that has been hailed as 'a feat without parallel in the history of war'.

The news of it reached Rio too late to save the Andrada brothers, who were dismissed from the posts of Chief Minister and Minister of Finance during July. The length of time which it took letters to travel a thousand miles by sailing ship also resulted in the fact that Cochrane was still ignorant of his wife's arrival when he was preparing to set off on his hunt. He had heard only that Maria Graham was ill, and therefore wrote to her on 2 July: 'My dear Madam, I have been grieved to learn of your indisposition; but you must recover now that I tell you we have starved the enemy out of Bahia. The forts were abandoned this morning; and the men of war, 13 in number, with about 32 sail of transports and merchant vessels, are under sail. We shall follow (i.e. the *Maria da Gloria* and *Pedro Primeiro*) to the world's end. I say again expect good news. Ever believe me your sincere and respectful friend Cochrane.' He would give her the satisfaction of being first with the intelligence.

Lady Cochrane and her daughter Elizabeth had been left by the assiduous Robson in the care of William Young, a man whose hospitality she had enjoyed when her ship had called at Rio during her passage to England. Young was extremely vexed that he was unable to offer her accommodation and wrote to Cochrane to explain: 'I am now living at my own house, and as my eldest daughter arrived here in the Sandwich packet with her husband and child, I have at this moment my two sons-in-law with their wives and families in my house; otherwise I should have invited her Ladyship to the same homely fare which her Ladyship did me the honour to partake of on her last visit to this place.' Evidently William Young was by no means pleased to have been deprived of the opportunity to enjoy that honour a second time, now that Lady Cochrane had returned as the wife of the First Admiral of Brazil.

But he allowed himself the satisfaction of writing to tell Cochrane this from the mansion in which Maria had observed so many French clocks. 'Their Excellencies the Viscount and Viscountess of Rio Seco have kindly waited on her Ladyship and invited her to live with them for a few days, where she now is with her beautiful little girl Elizabeth;

and I have much satisfaction in acquainting your Lordship that the Judge of the Custom house has complimented her Ladyship with the loan of his house at Botasago elegantly furnished.' Cochrane was spared the slightest anxiety over his wife's accommodation during his absence. 'The Viscount of Rio Seco wanted her Ladyship very much to take their house at Matta Poreos but her Ladyship thought it too far from the water.' Young was obliged to add one disquieting detail, however, to explain why Cochrane received no word from Kitty herself. 'Am sorry that Lady Cochrane has got her hand all swelled from the sting of a waspish fly and says she cannot write your Lordship as she could wish.'

Exhilarated by the news of his wife's safe arrival, Cochrane prepared to follow up his victory at Bahia with the speed that he had always regarded as essential if it were to be exploited to the full. This was what he had been prevented from doing by Gambier at Aix Roads, and by Guise and San Martín in their several ways at Callao. There had been none to restrain him at Valdivia, and he was a totally free agent once again in northern Brazil. As soon as the main-mast of the *Pedro Primeiro* had been repaired he sailed her straight to Maranhão, whose river he entered under Portuguese colours on 26 July. He found that he had succeeded in moving fast enough to outstrip any enemy intelligence which might have spoiled his confidence trick.

In the port of Maranhão the Portuguese saw with delight the appearance of the reinforcements for which they had been waiting so eagerly. A brig put out to the Brazilian flagship with despatches and congratulations; her captain was made a prisoner as soon as he stepped aboard; and while Cochrane hastily read the enemy plans that had been placed unwittingly in his hands, his captive was told of the great fleet that was on its way to Maranhão, escorting a convoy of transports crammed with the troops of an army of liberation. This information was imparted to the startled officer obliquely, in the manner of careless talk, after which he was sent back in his brig with an ultimatum from Cochrane to deliver to the Junta of Maranhão.

'Of the flight of the Portuguese naval and military forces from Bahia you are aware. I have now to inform you of the capture of two-thirds of the transports and troops, with all their stores and ammunition.' If the Junta was able to swallow this part of Cochrane's message, which was true, it was possible for them to digest which followed, which was pure fantasy. 'I am anxious not to let loose the Imperial troops of Bahia upon Maranhão, exasperated as they were at the injuries and cruelties exercised towards themselves and their countrymen as well as by the plunder of the people and churches of Bahia. It is for you to decide whether the inhabitants of these countries shall be further exasperated by resistance which appears to me unavailing, and alike prejudicial to the best interests of Portugal and Brazil.'

Back to the flagship came proposals for the capitulation of the garrison, but they were merely conditional, and the success of Cochrane's hoax depended on an immediate and complete surrender before anyone on shore began to wonder why the great Brazilian armada had not materialised. Once again Cochrane executed a manoeuvre that was at the same time a daunting feat of seamanship and an act so reckless that nobody could doubt he had overwhelming reinforcements within call. He entered the Maranhão river, which had never before been navigated by a battleship, and anchored her directly beneath the guns of the fort. Instead of capturing the Admiral in his flagship, the Junta sent a deputation aboard under the protection of the local Bishop to offer the submission of Maranhão to the Brazilian Emperor, and to place their town with all its troops in the hands of his representative.

The most delicate task of all remained. Somehow those troops would have to be immobilised before they realised that nothing more than the *Pedro Primeiro*, a sitting target, opposed them. Hastily Cochrane distributed his men behind the guns of every other armed vessel in the harbour. Ashore, he announced to a population of merchants and illiterate natives and half-castes that a new government was to be formed by democratic election, a proceeding unheard of in these regions. It is hard to decide at this point whether Cochrane had at last realised how inapplicable the political objectives of Francis Place and the British radicals were to such an environment, though he could still turn them to account as a weapon of war, or whether he went about his next task with the old, incurable optimism.

'Taking the necessary oaths and the election of civil government,' he announced solemnly, 'are acts which must be deliberately performed. Citizens, let us proceed gravely and methodically without tumult, haste, or confusion; and let the act be accomplished in a manner worthy of the approbation of his Imperial Majesty, and which shall give no cause for regret and leave no room for amendment.' It does look rather as though Cochrane hoped to kill two birds with one stone, the one for which he possessed an unerring eye, while he seldom hit the other.

Lest the voters should feel in any way intimidated by the Portuguese troops who had just surrendered to him, he ordered that these should be placed aboard their transports at once for shipment back to the mother country. Their embarkation began on 1 August, not a moment too soon. Exactly a week had passed since Cochrane had sailed up the Maranhão river to demand the surrender of the province, and still no Brazilian army or fleet had come into sight, even to be held on a leash.

As the soldiers marched to the harbour in their successive detachments to be ferried to their troopships, it began to dawn on them that they had been duped. Half-way through the operation the men who still remained in the town refused to be drawn into Cochrane's trap. But half of them were by now already in it, and on these Cochrane trained the guns of his ships, while patrols were sent ashore to round up the rest. Finally they were all safely locked up in the harbour under the guns of the Admiral of Brazil, and there they remained until 20 August to see that there was no army nor fleet at the disposal of El Diablo, only the genius of the man who had captured Valdivia. At the end of the month they sailed away to Lisbon.

To the west beyond Maranhão lay the most distant province of all from the central government, and the last that remained in Portuguese hands. Stretching his resources to the uttermost in the interests of speed and surprise, Cochrane sent his Flag Lieutenant Grenfell to repeat the hoax that had placed Maranhão in his lap. In nothing more impressive than a captured brig Grenfell sailed up the Pará river not far from the gigantic mouth of the Amazon, and delivered a summons from Cochrane to surrender, post-dated so that it would appear that the Admiral's fleet was in the offing. Once again the trick succeeded and the last great northern province of Brazil capitulated.

The only blood spilt was that of Grenfell, wounded when an unsuccessful attempt was made on his life, and the navy won a fine frigate named the *Imperatrice* which was then lying in Pará. But a hideous episode occurred soon after, when a group of partisans who called themselves the agents of the Emperor joined with a division of troops in an attempt to overthrow the provisional administration. As soon as Grenfell was asked for assistance he landed with a party of men who quelled the insurrection, took prisoners, and shot five ringleaders in the public square. After he had returned aboard the President of the acting Junta requested him to take charge of 200 prisoners, for which he selected a vessel of 600 tons. Instead of the number stipulated, 253 prisoners were despatched to the ship.

The difference in numbers does not appear remarkable, but crammed into the hold of a small ship in the stifling heat of the Equator it was sufficient to cause a tragedy more horrible than that of the black hole of Calcutta. Unable to breathe in their confinement, crowded together and increasingly desperate with thirst, the prisoners tried to force their way on deck. Here there were only fifteen Brazilian soldiers to guard their captives, who consequently acted with the different kind of panic induced by being outnumbered. They forced their prisoners back into the hold and battened it down by every means at their disposal.

T.S.W.—s

Throughout the night shrieks and ghastly sounds of turmoil could be heard from below deck, to which they eventually responded by hosing water to the struggling, dying mass of humanity beneath their feet. But it did not help. By daybreak it was discovered that only four men had survived that night of agony.

In Maranhão where he lay, the more enterprising spirits lost no time in turning the vicissitudes of life to practical advantage. 'On 26th of July 1823!' they wrote to the Emperor, 'Thrice happy day! Thou wilt be conspicuous in the annals of the province, as the sentiments of gratitude and respect inspired by the illustrious Admiral sent to our aid by the best and most amiable of monarchs will be deeply engraven on our hearts and those of our posterity. Yes, August Sire, the wisdom, prudence, the gentle manners of Lord Cochrane contributed more to the happy issue of our political difficulties than even the fear of his force.' If Cochrane had chosen this moment to look back over his career, he may well have wished that this compliment had been nearer the truth.

Although he knew by now that his wife was in Brazil, Cochrane still wrote with an easy conscience to Mrs Graham, informing her of the victories in the north and adding: 'Thus, my dear Madam, on my return I shall have the pleasure to acquaint his Imperial Majesty that between the extremities of his empire there exists no enemy either on shore or afloat.' Commodore Sir Thomas Hardy had meanwhile entered these waters to learn of the latest exploits of his countryman and to perform many acts of courtesy both to Lady Cochrane and to Mrs Graham. Maria had recovered by this time from her illness, and was at court when the Emperor celebrated the arrival of the news from the north by informing Lady Cochrane that she was now Marchioness of Maranhão. He made his announcement dramatically in the presence of a large assembly of people, so that Maria might be pardoned for digressing: 'I should do wrong not to mention the ladies of the court. My partial eyes preferred my pretty countrywoman the new Marchioness; but there were . . .'

Maria's entire Brazilian journal contains only three references to Lady Cochrane, of which the first barely mentions how Kitty called to see her for the first time when she was ill, and this is the last. The two women must have encountered one another repeatedly in the small social world of Rio, even if they did not seek each other's acquaintance, and Maria's second reference describes just such a meeting, at a ball given by the Baroness de Campos. 'There were only two English-women besides Lady Cochrane and myself, and these were the wives of the Consul and the Commissioner for the slave business. A foreign gentleman remarked that though we were but four we hardly conversed together. This was perfectly true: I like, when I am in foreign society, to talk to foreigners.' Clever Maria was already able to converse with some fluency in Portuguese. She also possessed considerable skill in writing between the lines in the journal, and one of the clearest footnotes she placed there was that she had little use for her pretty little countrywoman.

Poor Kitty was no match for all those highly cultivated, aristocratic people amongst whom the penniless widow of a mere naval captain moved with an unconscious and effortless sense of equality. Even in London she had enjoyed little opportunity to meet the distinguished people whom Maria had been accustomed to since childhood. Here in Rio Maria knew the brilliant José Bonifácio de Andrada as a matter of course, 'a small man with a thin lively countenance' as she described him, and a marvellous conversationalist. In other words, he enjoyed talking seriously with Maria. 'His lady,' she noted, 'is of Irish parentage, an O'Leary, a most amiable and kind woman, and truly appreciating the worth and talent of her husband.' In such a gallery as her journal contains it would have been most amiable and kind of Maria to have said more of Kitty than that she was pretty and that when Maria was thrown into the company of the Admiral's wife she preferred to talk to foreigners.

Of course it is possible that Kitty had snubbed her early in their acquaintance. It would be understandable if she had conceived a jealousy for this handsome and talented woman whom Cochrane had brought with him from Chile during her absence and with whom he obviously had such a close mutual understanding. In this case her greatest consolation (for Kitty was deeply conscious of age) was that Maria was a full 10 years older than she was, and approaching 40.

The Marchioness of Maranhão was next appointed a Lady in Waiting to the Empress in company with the Viscountess de Rio Seco, which enhanced still further her standing at the Brazilian court. The plump little Empress Leopoldina, with her unconcern for cosmetics and her passion for the natural sciences, had proved a disappointment to Dom Pedro from the first moment he set eyes on her. But she was every inch a Hapsburg Princess and she gradually won his fickle heart by her devotion to him, until in the end she awoke in him the virtue of remorse for his infidelities. Once again it was Maria Graham to whom the cultivated Empress was drawn by an affinity of interests. To Kitty went the rank and honours; to Maria the flattering invitation that she should undertake the duties of governess to the Emperor's daughter Maria da Gloria, the future Queen of Portugal.

Mrs Graham accepted the appointment, but was given permission to return to Britain before she entered on her employment as the Princess was still so young. On 19 October 1823 she and Leopoldina met for the last time. 'I saw the Empress, who is pleased to allow me to sail for England in the packet the day after tomorrow. I confess I am sorry to go before Lord Cochrane's return. I had set my heart on seeing my best friend in this country after his exertions and triumph.' So Kitty lost her rival and Cochrane lost his most vivid chronicler and Maria da Gloria lost her governess: for Mrs Graham returned to the world of writers and artists in which she met and married Augustus Callcott, and never returned to Brazil.

She missed Cochrane by only a few days after his 7-month absence. In the vast tropical regions which he had reduced to the Emperor's obedience increasing vexations had followed upon his triumphs, of exactly the same kind as those that convulsed so many of the other liberated lands of South America. The heroes of the 'thrice happy day' at Maranhão, the members of the new Junta voted into power by Cochrane's elections, lost no time in rewarding themselves for their new-found loyalty to the Emperor. They filled every post of profit with their friends and relatives and claimed all Portuguese property as their own. In doing this they infringed the Imperial decree which bestowed prizes of war on their captors and Cochrane, alert as ever to safeguard his pecuniary rights and those of his subordinates, took vigorous action. He despatched all the imperishable property to Rio for adjudication in such ships as were capable of making the long voyage. Over a hundred vessels remained and a quantity of perishable goods, all of which he offered to sell locally for two-thirds of their value. When this was agreed he undertook to make a loan to the Junta out of the proceeds for current expenses.

His attempt to safeguard the democratic institutions he had attempted to plant at a stroke in such alien soil was a more immediate failure than the measures by which he tried to protect the navy's financial rights. The new Junta raised what purported to be a police force, but which amounted to little less than a gang of bully-boys to intimidate the wealthy Portuguese merchants, now loyal subjects of the Brazilian Emperor. Unable to look beyond the institutions he had promoted as Member for Westminster, Cochrane ordered fresh elections, in which the vote was extended from the citizens of the town to the entire province of Maranhão, as though this would produce as if by magic an honest administration. He angered the Junta of his own creation by commanding them on 12 September to hold the new election during October. The only hope for its success would have been provided by the Admiral's presence, but by this time Cochrane was worn out by his phenomenal activities and responsibilities, his health undermined by a tropical climate that did not agree with his constitution. As soon as he had supervised the arrangements for the election he sailed in the *Pedro Primeiro* to Rio de Janeiro.

When the living legend returned to the capital he had visited so briefly in March, the Emperor and Empress came aboard his flagship to greet him. 'I must say for the people here,' Maria Graham had remarked before her departure, 'that they do seem sensible that in Lord Cochrane they have obtained a treasure. That there are some who find fault, and some who envy, is very true. But when was it otherwise?' In the days of adulation which followed his return he was invested with his rank of Marquess, introduced into the Imperial Order of the Cruzeiro and created a Privy Councillor. Above all, he was reunited on 9 November 1823 with the wife from whom he had parted at Callao over 2 years earlier.

But Cochrane returned to a political turmoil in the capital similar to one he had left behind him in Maranhão, and despite his weariness and the presence of his wife and daughter after such a long separation he could not resist taking part in the conflict. The three Andrada brothers had become the leaders of an anti-Portuguese party in the National Assembly after the dismissal of José Bonifácio and his brother from the offices of Chief Minister and Minister of Finance; and since September the legislature had been debating a new constitution in language which clearly threatened the Emperor's prerogatives and aimed its shafts at the Portuguese influences that surrounded him. On 11 November, two days after the arrival of Cochrane, the Emperor Pedro dissolved the Assembly on his own initiative and sent cavalry and artillery to enforce his action. The deputies filed out of their chamber between ranks of soldiers and the three Andrada brothers were sent into exile. Like Oliver Cromwell, Pedro had been carried to his throne by a revolution and invested with his powers by a legislative process. Like Cromwell, he had removed the legislature by force when it tried to circumscribe those powers.

But although Pedro possessed the heart of an autocrat, his head was filled with the most advanced political ideals. The Braganza prince would not tolerate dictation nor threats; the youth who had grown to manhood in Brazil and uttered the immortal words, 'I will remain' did not take kindly to the accusation that he was the head of a Portuguese fifth column. Having removed the Assembly, he appointed a Council of State composed of the most distinguished citizens and instructed it to prepare a new constitution under his personal direction. He would bestow liberty now that he had removed the menace of licence.

To Cochrane the Privy Councillor this was an irresistible opportunity to indulge his mania for political experiment. Within a week of his return he had composed a long memorandum for the Emperor in which he congratulated Pedro on having dissolved the Assembly with the warning: 'There are, however, individuals who will wickedly take advantage of the late proceedings to kindle the flames of discord, and throw the Empire into anarchy and confusion, unless timely prevented by the wisdom and energy of your Imperial Majesty.' Cochrane was as autocratic by nature as Pedro, and generally defined as the flames of discord those actions which were in opposition to his own will. The solution, he advised the Emperor, was to bestow on Brazil the blessings of the British constitution. 'As no monarch is more happy, or more truly powerful than the limited monarch of England, surrounded by a free people, enriched by that industry which the security of property by means of just laws never fails to create, if your Majesty were to decree that the English constitution . . . shall be the model for the Government of Brazil under Your Imperial Majesty, with power to the constituent assembly so to alter particular parts as local circumstances may render advisable, it would excite the sympathy of powerful states abroad, and the firm allegiance of the Brazilian people to Your Majesty's throne.'

Distance had lent enchantment to Cochrane's memories of the unreformed Parliament of Britain, of what justice he had received from her laws, of the testimony of such men as Samuel Bamford and Francis Place concerning her free and industrious people. And it was as well that this was so, for there *was* no better model in the world for Parliamentary government under a limited monarchy than the one which England had evolved over so many centuries. In some respects the constitution which Pedro imposed by decree in March 1824 was far in advance of Britain's. It guaranteed freedom of speech, for which so many had been imprisoned under British law; freedom of religion, when Catholic emancipation was still denied by Britain's Parliament; a second chamber whose members were appointed for life in the manner introduced in Britain a century and a half later. Pedro's constitution was to endure for 65 years, until the fall of the monarchy in 1889, and the part which Cochrane played in influencing those who framed it was a matter of lifelong pride to him.

But by intervening in a conflict that had engendered such widespread bitterness during his absence he naturally made himself a target for the animosities that filled the capital and particularly among those who, as

Maria Graham had observed, were the most disposed to envy and find fault with him. These consisted principally of the wealthy Portuguese, many of whom secretly yearned for a reunion with the mother country and did all they could to encourage Pedro's absolutist tendencies. They had almost certainly heard of Cochrane's radical career in the politics of Westminster, which must have caused them to view with alarm his influence with the Emperor. In addition, many of them were closely connected with the wealthy Portuguese communities of the north which had suffered from his conquests.

As usual, they found the means to hit Cochrane in his pocket. When the tribunal sat to adjudicate the prizes sent south in the course of the northern expedition, it was packed by men who blocked the payments due to the Admiral and his crews. When he protested, they were offered 3 months' pay which he indignantly refused.

It was a situation in which the Emperor might with honour have intervened, but while the rights of his seamen under their contract of service was clear beyond any ambiguity, the prizes to which these entitled them had been largely the property of people who now claimed to be his loyal subjects. They were Portuguese like himself, while those who demanded their just rewards for having 'liberated' them were for the most part foreigners. Pedro did not try to overturn the judgments of the prize tribunal, and it is doubtful whether he would have succeeded if he had attempted it.

Cochrane's health and spirits were not improved by the heat of a Rio summer and both his wife and his daughter were ailing as well. If Maria Graham had been there to fire them with her manifold interests—the orphanage and the hospital, the botanic gardens and the Protestant burial ground, 'one of the loveliest spots I ever beheld'—if they had travelled about the country as she had done with enquiring eyes, they might have found health and contentment. As it was, Cochrane's forty-eighth birthday passed in a mood of depression, and early in 1824 Lady Cochrane decided to leave her husband again after this brief, unhappy interlude with him and return to England. He wrote to his brother William:

'Lady Cochrane embarks this day 16th February for England for the recovery of her health, she having been ill ever since her arrival in this cursed hot place; and the little girl has only been saved by the utmost attention and great skill of a Dr Williams who is now going home with Lady Cochrane.' He did not add that his wife was again pregnant. She gave birth to her fourth child, Arthur, the following September. 'I am battling the watch here with the same kind of people I left on the other side—an ignorant obstinate narrow-minded gang; the Emperor

however is my friend, and I *shall*, indeed, I *have* beaten all the intriguers
who have attempted to annoy me; and I have a written memorandum
under the Emperor's own hand that he will cause justice to be done in
all things regarding me, and the prize affairs. My mind is therefore
comparatively easy, though I am greatly annoyed that I am obliged to
part with Lady Cochrane.' As usual, he was being over-sanguine
concerning his financial affairs. He had never learned how it was that
the Duke of Wellington had become the most richly rewarded public
servant in British history, simply by sitting back and allowing the
leaders of the establishments of Europe—and Brazil—to pour the
tokens of their gratitude into his lap. Cochrane by contrast was still
pursuing the fatal course of flouting the establishment and then
fighting a losing battle with it for his rights. Now he pinned his
faith on Pedro, having proposed to him a constitution which would
place the direction of naval affairs in the hands of a ministry and a
constituent Assembly.

In this letter to William, Cochrane was curiously defensive about his
wife. 'I am greatly indebted to Archibald and you for your kind feelings
towards her, and I am sure she will ever prove a credit to us from her
conduct; which to me has ever been most affectionate.' Evidently she
had spoken severely to Cochrane after her arrival in Brazil about her
treatment at the hands of other members of the family, because he told
William: 'I have forbid her ever speaking of, or having any connection
with the female Puritans of our family, who have heated (sic) her and
who have behaved so ill to me.'

Who these female Puritans were can only be surmised. The Earl had
taken a third wife in 1819, who must either have considered the rank
of Countess a sufficient recompense for considerable discomfort, or
have possessed a remarkable compassion for the eccentric, drunken,
poverty-stricken man whom she married. The wife of the Earl's
brother Basil was the widow of a clergyman, while his brother James
was the Vicar of Mansfield and married. Andrew Cochrane Johnstone,
needless to say, had married another heiress after the death of the Earl
of Hopetoun's daughter, her father being Baron de Clugny, Governor
of Guadaloupe. The only other brother was Admiral Sir Alexander;
and it is among the womenfolk of these men that there presumably
lurked the female Puritans who heated or hated Kitty Cochrane.
William and Archibald were both married, with children of their own,
but it is clear from Cochrane's words of gratitude to them that their
wives could not have been to blame. The question that naturally arises
is whether Lady Cochrane, who was evidently no woman's woman, was
in any degree to blame herself.

In his dark mood, Cochrane's mind reverted to the problems of Chile and he wrote to William with unusual sharpness: 'Packet after packet comes, and you say not one word about your claims on the Chilean government or what steps you are taking to get your money. If you have nothing to do why not come here and we will devise a way to obtain it?' In the unsettled state of the new republics of Spanish America it was scarcely possible for anybody to retain an estate and run it profitably without residing upon it, but Cochrane made no mention of Herradura, where he had so recently intended to make his permanent home. Presumably that dream had faded forever with his wife's desire to return to England and have done with South America. 'My dear Kate will tell you all the news of this place that I cannot detail in ten letters were I to try it. Pray do what you can to assist her in settling at Tunbridge Wells where she proposes to reside.' That had always been Kitty's kind of place.

Left alone once more, Cochrane offered his resignation from the office of First Admiral. Four days later, on 25 March 1824 Pedro I gave his oath to the constitution amid public rejoicing. The man who had done more than any to preserve Brazil from disintegration and had done all he could to promote the new system of government took no pleasure in the ceremonies in which he occupied so prominent a place. His attempt to resign was ignored, but he found himself designated by a variety of inferior titles such as Port Admiral of Rio de Janeiro and Commander-in-Chief for the duration of the war, pin-pricks that he had always been too touchy to ignore.

They formed the prelude to more serious humiliations. On 24 May Grenfell returned from distant Pará in the captured frigate *Imperatrice* and instead of being received with the highest honours, this future Admiral of Brazil was arrested and his papers and personal possessions seized from his ship. In the following month a similar outrage was planned with the First Admiral himself as its target, but he received a secret warning in his house on the very eve of the assault. Escaping in the night when his home was already surrounded by soldiers, he mounted a horse and rode straight to the Emperor's palace to which he enjoyed the privilege of access at all times. Here he was informed that Pedro had retired to bed.

'No matter,' he replied. 'In bed or out of bed, I must see him.' The Emperor heard the disturbance and emerged in his night clothes. He had acted with decision in many similar emergencies, and after listening to Cochrane's story he did so again.

The object of the plotters in both cases had been to remove from Grenfell's and Cochrane's ships any prize money or treasure from the northern provinces which might be found in them. It amounted to simple looting under the pretext of law enforcement, and Cochrane asked the Emperor to ensure that trustworthy persons should accompany any search party which should visit his flagship. Pedro did better than this. He intended to hold a review of troops on the morrow which he now assured Cochrane that he would cause to be cancelled on the pretext that he was ill, thus bringing all military movements to a halt. Cochrane returned to the palace in the morning to attend the royal levée and witness the outcome. As the Emperor announced his indisposition he caught the eye of his First Admiral and the two men laughed together, to the amazement of the courtiers who were present.

But the situation was no laughing matter. By the speed with which Pedro had introduced the new constitution he had saved Brazil as a united and independent nation and his throne with it. He had not saved his fleet, however, by protecting its Admiral from this latest insult. It was totally dependent on the foreign officers and seamen who had joined it upon specific promises of pay and prize money which had been dishonoured now that they had performed their duty, and as a result they began to desert. It was exactly what had occurred before in Chile and Peru.

As in Chile, it took an emergency to remind those Brazilians who had an interest in dismantling their navy that they were jeopardising the national interest. For the ink of the new constitution was hardly dry before the province of Pernambuco north of Bahia rejected it, and followed the example of Spanish America in setting itself up as an independent republic. The leader of this separatist movement was a Carmelite monk, Friar Caneca, whose motives were as high as his courage, and his province had already revolted against King John during his exile in Brazil, seeing little advantage in a monarchy and a distant capital from which it derived no benefits. The rebels appealed to the other northern provinces to join with them in a Confederation of the Equator, and although the response was disappointing, anxiety in Rio de Janeiro mounted as the months passed and no news arrived that the revolt had been suppressed. The solution, naturally, was Cochrane.

The Emperor himself promised his First Admiral the sum of $200,000 for his squadron, with which he was able to lure his seamen back to their ships. For himself he obtained a patent granting him a life-pension of half his pay when he should elect to leave the Brazilian service. So the fleet put to sea again on 2 August 1824, escorting the transports that contained 1200 troops. When they reached their destination the republican President of Pernambuco offered Cochrane a colossal bribe if he would defect to their cause, knowing that they were bound to win their independence with his support. But El metalico Lord rejected the overture and blockaded the port of Pernambuco until it was captured by the land forces in September. While Friar Caneca was captured and executed, the Admiral sailed on to the north for a tour of inspection of the remoter provinces. In November he arrived back at Maranhão, a little over a year since he had left the province on the eve of its election.

He was now its Marquess, titular owner of a vast, virgin property (which he never received). But if this quickened his paternal concern for the undeveloped equatorial region in which he had attempted to plant democratic institutions, the sight that met him there only made his disillusion the more bitter. At Westminster he had witnessed the shortcomings of a system that had evolved in that environment through centuries of inventive effort, and they had filled him with impatience; here, in his present mood, they drove him near to despair. The liberation of Maranhão, he confessed, had proved to be a curse rather than a blessing.

He found a civil war raging in which the President of the present Junta, who possessed the suggestive name of Bruce, had enlisted negroes in his conflict with the local Commanding Officer. There were in addition other combative groups, all claiming Imperial authority in their internecine feuds with each other. Like Pedro, when he was faced by such emergencies, Cochrane flung aside his liberalism and became the authoritarian once more. He rounded up Bruce's negroes and placed them under hatches in his ships. He despatched Bruce to Rio and installed a new administration without attempting any more democratic procedures. While the British and French Consuls brought him their complaints of the outrages committed by Brazilians against their nationals, he drew up his own to present to the new Junta on behalf of the fleet that had been short-changed during its liberating expedition to Maranhão. Having failed to secure justice for it in Rio, he determined to enforce it here.

On the first day of 1825 another of his fits of depression seized him, and he tendered his resignation, to have it ignored as usual. Then a fresh outbreak of disorder restored his energies, undermined by the sweltering equatorial heat. When he had restored peace he entered into his final negotiations with the Junta, and this eventually led to the payment of a first instalment of the debt to the fleet, which he distributed at once to his seamen. During these opening months of his fiftieth year the reports which he had sent to Rio were answered by endorsements of his actions unillumined by any further instructions.

From time to time he would go ashore to proclaim martial law or to enforce the peace in more summary fashion. On 18 May 1825—and it is a wonder that it did not happen sooner—the ageing, exhausted colossus reached his breaking-point. He transferred his flag to the *Piranga* and ordering the *Pedro Primeiro* to return to Rio, sailed away from Brazil forever with the gallant band of men who had served him with such ill-rewarded fidelity.

There has always been doubt over Cochrane's intentions at the time when he took this step. It need not be doubted that he sailed north into cooler latitudes in order to restore his own health and that of his crew. Even though he stated no intention to return as he had done so gracefully before he left Chile, this may well have been due to illness and irritability rather than a silence into which any significance can be read. Similarly, the episode which occurred off the Azores early in June is open to question. The *Piranga* ran into strong gales which proved that the main mast and several of the spars were unserviceable, while much of the rigging was too rotten to stand bad weather. In addition, the salt provisions shipped at Maranhão proved to be tainted, so that the ship had little more than a week's supply of edible food. A council of officers was held, which decided that since they could not put into a Spanish or Portuguese port, it would be best to sail for England, risking the penalties of the Foreign Enlistment Act.

Perhaps there was no more to it than that, or possibly Cochrane was influenced also by a home-sickness that grew in him as he sniffed once more the bracing air of the north Atlantic. Besides these factors, improved health and spirits were restoring to Cochrane a sense of initiative that appears to have ebbed from him utterly during those stagnant months at Maranhão. At some time during this expedition he discovered a further purpose for it, and the only question is when this admirable idea occured to him. He, Britain's disgraced outlaw, would return as First Admiral of Brazil and demand at gunpoint the first recognition of the Brazilian flag to be accorded to it by any European power. He knew the channels at Spithead better than those of Valdivia or Bahia and when he entered them on 26 June he did not come up in the dark. He enquired of the shore authorities whether his salute would be answered by an equal number of guns; back came an affirmative answer; and as he listened to the boom of the shore batteries, paying Britain's respects to the flag of Brazil and his own, it must have sounded to him like the music of the spheres.

Two months later Portugal also recognised the independent Empire of Brazil, and a peace treaty was signed between the two countries in November 1825. Cochrane was well entitled to boast later: 'Had the negotiations for peace been broken off, I had formed plans of attacking Portugal in her own waters, and I had no reasonable doubt of producing an impression there of no less forcible character than, with a single ship, I had two years before produced on the Portuguese fleet in Brazil.' In these words he recalled the final triumph of his Brazilain service.

Cochrane returned home 3 months after San Martín's latest visit to London in March, and instead of encountering one of his South American rivals there, San Martín almost literally crossed swords with another. For Rivadavia had recently come to Britain as Argentine Minister Plenipotentiary, and their mutual animosity remained so violent that San Martín was only restrained by his friends from challenging Rivadavia to a duel. He soon returned to Brussels to live as best he could on the interest from some Peruvian bonds and from his property in Argentina. Both he and Cochrane had accused one another of amassing a fortune in Peru, and both were wrong: like Cochrane, San Martín would not even receive the state pension he had been promised.

James Paroissien and García del Río, the envoys whom San Martín had sent from Peru to search for a King, were the two men who played a principal part in dissuading him from challenging Rivadavia to fight in the British capital. By this time they had been relieved of their official positions and in April the new administration of Peru ordered them to hand over the archives of their mission. Paroissien was thus deprived of any further opportunity to dip his fingers into the Peruvian loan, but by the time Cochrane sailed into Spithead he had arranged to make his fortune in the silver mines of Potosí instead. There is no evidence that he encountered the man whom he had been accusing of greed and avarice in two hemispheres before he sailed to failure and death on 28 September 1825. General Sucre, hero of the final victory over Canterac in Peru the previous December, wrote his epitaph:

'These English gentlemen must have been reading the history of El Dorado with a little more credulity than it deserves, if they imagined that the precious metals were to be obtained without labour and expense; for, although it is true that they abound in this country, they cannot be had for *nothing*.'

It was a curious paradox that the men who had been defaming Cochrane in London during his absence should have lost so much stature by the time of his return; while the outlaw, the former jailbird came home 'in the estimation of the Old World and the New, the greatest man afloat'. So Admiral Sir Henry Keppel proclaimed, while all could read the story of his achievements in the sumptuous volumes of Maria Graham's journals that John Murray had published, and in the three volumes of William Stevenson's narrative. Cochrane might well have caught his breath as he examined Maria Graham's portrait of the perfect gentle knight, without fear and without reproach. Greater and more impartial justice would be done in the end to the reputation of his rival San Martín, but he would not live to enjoy the consolation of returning in triumph to a native land which he had left under the shadow of failure. This balm to his injured spirits was given to Cochrane, while San Martín paid a disappointing visit to his home-land and then left to end his days in stoic exile.

But Cochrane's satisfaction was clouded by the news which reached him from Chile. There, as the sole reward for his services, he still enjoyed the estate of Rio Claro in the south, where he had left William Edwards as his manager. Nor had he neglected his property: when he was most preoccupied in Brazil, Edwards had been able to acknow-ledge the arrival of a box of filbert nuts to plant on his land. It was only after a long delay that the distressing report which Edwards wrote to him so laboriously on 31 August 1825 finally reached him in England.

'My Lord, I am sorrow to inform you that the Chile government has taken the Rio Claro estate from you and would not give any reason to me for there doing so. I went to Concepción to Reviro who is present governor. I asked him for documents to show your Lordship, he refused to give me any, he said that it was by order of the Supreme, and if I wished documents to show your Lordship I must get them from the Supreme for he would give me none. I went to Santiago and presen-ted a representation to the Supreme, but he was absent at the baths.' Edwards described how he was kept waiting for 6 days and then referred back to Concepción. When he tried to return to Rio Claro he was advised 'not to go to live on the estate for it was in the hands of the Indians' but he had the courage to explore for himself, and discovered that this was a lie. However, he was barred from any of the dwellings on Cochrane's property, and so went to spend 12 months at Concep-ción.

A Chilean, to his great credit, then took up the matter in Congress, but by this time Concepción had declared itself a province independent of the government of Santiago. Edwards tried once more to resume his occupation of Rio Claro, but he was evicted forcibly and it was given back to its former owner, 'and I am living here in your house without any employment whatever, and if God spares me I will remain till your lordship's arrival here'. Edwards had abandoned Chile, in fact, and travelled to Rio de Janeiro in the hope of telling his story to his master in person.

In fairness to the Chileans Cochrane might have recalled that they had granted him the forfeited estate in the belief that he intended to settle permanently amongst them, and since his departure they had invited him to return. A people recently freed from colonial rule is the least likely to look kindly on absentee landlords. On the other hand the Chileans might have taken steps to ensure that the news of what had occurred reached him in a more courteous manner, even if they did not elect to compensate him for his loss. Reading Edwards' report, Cochrane may well have wondered what would become of his house in the Brazilian capital and his estate of Maranhão if he did not return there soon.

Meanwhile, the adoring husband and devoted father was reuinited with his family for the first time since they had separated on his arrival in Chile. He discovered also that the government did not dare to bring forward the prosecution which it had prepared under the Foreign Enlistment Act, so that he was able to move about in freedom, revisiting his old friends. Prominent among these was Sir Francis Burdett, who was active among the members of the Greek Committee. Byron had died at Missolonghi, and these now renewed their invitation to Cochrane to adopt the cause for which the poet had given his life.

It was a colossal temptation. Cochrane had returned from South America no richer than he had left to find his fortune there. The glory in which he basked could no more support him than the long account of payments due to him. He approached the Brazilian legation in London, which disbursed 2 months' pay to his crew but protested that it did not possess the necessary funds to refit his ship. When Cochrane himself advanced £2000 for this purpose, the Brazilian Envoy Chevalier Gameiro set it against the money paid already, alleged an error in the Maranhão accounts, and informed the Admiral that he now owed the Legation twenty-five pounds. Gameiro was puzzled concerning the Admiral's intentions in remaining in Britain, as Cochrane perhaps was himself. He learnt that Cochrane had been offered the command of the Greek Navy, and enquired whether he proposed to accept it. Cochrane replied that while he commanded the Brazilian Navy he could not serve Greece, consequently he had neither refused nor accepted the invitation.

He had not yet returned to Scotland, the country in which his father had owned what had once been the finest unfortified mansion in the land, now a roofless ruin possessed by strangers. Hither he had brought his young bride to make her his wife, and here he came with her once more in the autumn of 1825. On Monday, 3 October, they attended the theatre in Edinburgh, where their presence was soon noticed. As a result an allusion to South America was inserted in the epilogue to the play. By the time it was delivered Cochrane had left his seat, so that it was Kitty alone who faced the barrage of applause from an audience which turned to acclaim the pair of them; and she, who was more affected by such a demonstration than by the din of cannon, fainted in the arms of her companions. Sir Walter Scott was present to witness this scene and it moved him to extemporise some verses which were published in *The Morning Post* on 19 October.

> I knew the Lady by that glorious eye,
> By that pure brow and those dark locks of thine,
> I knew thee for a soldier's bride and high
> My full heart bounded. For the golden mine
> Of Heavenly thought kindled at sight of thee
> Radiant with all the stars of memory.
>
> Thy name ask Brazil, for she knows it well,
> It is a name a Hero gave to thee.
> In every letter lurks there not a spell,
> The mighty spell of immortality?
> Ye sail together down time's glittering stream;
> Around your heads two kindred haloes gleam.
>
> Even now, as through the air the plaudits ring,
> I marked the smiles that in her features came.
> She caught the word that fell from every tongue
> And her eye brightened at her Cochrane's name,
> And brighter yet became the dark eyes' blaze—
> It was his Country and she felt the praise.
>
> May the Gods guard thee, Lady, wheresoe'er
> Thou wanderest in thy love and loveliness.
> For thee may every scene and sky be fair,
> Each hour instinct with more than happiness.
> May all thou valuest be good and great,
> And be thy wishes thy own future state.

These verses will not be found among Scott's collected poems, but they are an interesting illustration of his facility for spontaneous composition, and only the last verse arouses a suspicion of subsequent polishing. In the aftermath of her tears and vapours they must have given Lady Cochrane exquisite satisfaction.

At the end of October the Chevalier Gameiro sent Cochrane an order to return to Rio de Janeiro at once, to which the Admiral replied that he would do so. But on 3 November, when the formal announcement of peace between Portugal and Brazil was announced, Gameiro took a step which settled the question of Cochrane's future for him. He relieved the Admiral of his command, and ordered his crew to place themselves under the instructions of his legation. A week later, aboard his frigate, Cochrane handed to Captain Shepherd 'the key of the iron chest in which the prize lists and receipts for the disbursement of public monies have been kept during His Excellency's command; which key and chest I engage faithfully to deliver to the accountant-general of His Imperial Majesty's navy, or to the proper authority at Rio de Janeiro'. So the receipt is worded which Cochrane was so careful to preserve among his papers. On 30 December 1825 a letter was despatched to him from Rio dismissing him from the Brazilian service and in this unceremonious manner it was brought to an end.

The ceremony was to come later. On 28 June 1901 the Captain and officers of the Brazilian warship *Floriano* were received by King Edward VII at Marlborough House in company with the Brazilian Minister, Lord Lansdowne the British Foreign Minister, Major-General the Earl of Dundonald, Burdett's daughter Baroness Burdett-Coutts, and diplomatic representatives of Chile, Peru and Greece. The crew of the *Floriano* next paraded in Westminister Abbey bearing their arms, the only foreign troops ever to have been invited under arms into that sacred building. Twenty Brazilian sailors formed a guard of honour at the foot of the grave of Admiral Cochrane, Marquess of Maranhão, presented arms on orders issued in Portuguese, and then knelt at the burial-place of the man who had founded their navy. Dean Bradley was present, Chancellor of the Order of the Bath, the only honour Cochrane ever received from his own countrymen. To him and to Cochrane's grandson the Earl of Dundonald the Brazilian Minister said: 'Mr Dean, My Lord, we place these flowers on Lord Cochrane's tomb in the name of the Brazilian Navy which he created, and of the Brazilian Nation, to whose independence and unity he rendered incomparable services.'

The Minister turned to the men of the *Floriano* and said: 'Today London has seen the first pilgrimage from our continent to the tomb of the South American Lafayette. It is a course in which Brazil is proud to lead the way.' The ancient nave in which Cochrane lies, so near to to the tomb of the Unknown Soldier, echoed the anthems of Britain and Brazil.

Chile has followed the example of Brazil by holding annual ceremonies in the Abbey to comemmorate the founder of her navy, while Peru expressed her gratitude by issuing a set of stamps bearing Cochrane's portrait to mark the centenary of her independence in 1921.

CHAPTER THIRTEEN

The Liberation of Greece

Cochrane had reached the age of 50 in a blaze of celebrity, but without having achieved the stability of a settled home or a secure livelihood. Culross Abbey was in the hands of strangers, the house by the Hamble river was sold, the estate of Herradura lay neglected in the hands of agents, its depleted mansion untenanted. While Cochrane was in Brazil the administration of General Freire had begged him to return, and if he had done so he might have passed the remainder of his days prosperously in Chile to the lasting benefit of that country. Alternatively he might have made his career in Peru after the resignation of San Martín as William Miller did, assisting Bolívar and Sucre to consolidate the work of independence, for it is inconceivable that Guise would have been preferred as Admiral of Peru if Cochrane had been present to accept the appointment.

He had already abandoned Britain, Chile and Peru by the time the Brazilian envoy tried to persuade him to return to Rio de Janeiro in the summer of 1825. But instead of remaining to overcome obstacles with patience and build upon the foundations he had laid, it had become habitual in him to flounce off under stress and seek the solution for life's problems in a new environment and if possible in his native element, the sea.

But by the summer of 1825 Cochrane's behaviour pattern was showing signs that it had become fixed in a mould. He had left Britain because his naval career had been brought to an end here. He had sailed away from Peru despite San Martín's invitation to him to remain, because he disapproved of San Martín's course of action there. He had left Chile as a result of the civil war and of the invitation from Brazil. But the solicitations of the Greek Committee did not constitute comparable grounds for abandoning his post as First Admiral of Brazil, least of all, without sailing his Brazilian warship back to Rio de Janeiro. Nor did he ever favour the Brazilian legation with a distinct statement that it was his intention to do this; he simply prevaricated until the Chevalier Gameiro was placed in the embarrassing position of having to sack him. Had Cochrane returned to Brazil he might either have resigned with dignity or have continued to serve an Emperor who honoured him, and whom he admired. In this case he might have returned to Europe with Pedro after he had resigned the Brazilian crown to his son in 1831, and come to Portugal to secure its throne for Maria da Gloria his daughter. In that case Cochrane would have been able to fight the fleet action that was denied him throughout his life; when Admiral Sir Charles Napier instead commanded the Portuguese fleet which won the victory of Cape St Vincent in 1833. Not only did he forfeit this opportunity by defecting from the Brazilian service when he did, but he also imperilled his arrears of pay, and he ought to have known by this time that the man who wished to safeguard his property and emoluments in South America did well to remain on the spot.

The alternative which the Greek Committee dangled before his eyes was indeed a tempting one, especially for a man whose assets were largely tied up in another hemisphere. The sympathy for their cause engendered by Byron's death in the previous year had enabled them to raise a loan of £150,000 to which they presently added a further loan of no less than £2,000,000. They were able to pay Cochrane £37,000 on his acceptance of the office of Admiral of Greece, with the promise of another £20,000 after the achievement of Greek independence. By August 1825 Sir Francis Burdett was able to announce enthusiastically, 'Lord Cochrane is looking well after eight years of harassing and ungrateful service and, I trust, will be the liberator of Greece. What a glorious title!' Burdett ought not to have been in a position to write this while Gameiro remained wholly in the dark concerning the intentions of the Admiral of Brazil.

Cochrane's payment for his Greek services has exposed him to fresh charges of greed and avarice from that day to this, so that it is necessary to relate it to similar transactions of his time. On resigning his Greek commission he waived the second payment of £20,000, asking that it be devoted to the relief of the war wounded and of the relatives of the dead. So his salary amounted to a lump sum of £37,000, which may be compared to the £40,000 ultimately paid to Cochrane's family after his death by the government of Brazil in payment for his services there. Each of these sums represents his salary, not additional rewards such as the Duke of Wellington had received in recognition of his victories. These included a grant of £2000 a year which accompanied an earldom after one victory in Spain; £100,000, the rank of Marquess and the estate of Wellington after another; £400,000 and a dukedom after a third; and £200,000 after the victory of Waterloo. Even if the achievements of Wellington on land are held to overshadow those of Cochrane at sea, he does not appear as a hard bargainer in such a comparison as this.

No doubt the prospect of employment which would guarantee him a dependable salary at last influenced Cochrane to accept the post of Greek Admiral; so did the wave of philhellenic sentiment that was sweeping Europe; so did the restlessness of Ulysses the wanderer, the inventor of the wooden horse in search of yet another Troy. Yet he took the step untidily, with less than the old assurance, and during the ensuing months he exhibited extremes of elation and anxiety, the symptoms of manic depression. The bold leader of men was no longer confident that he had not lost his own way.

The men who gave their services, their money and their lives in the cause of Greek independence have generally been treated with ridicule. Cochrane's own biographer J. W. Fortescue wrote in 1895: 'Not one of the sentimentalists knew anything whatever about Greece. Their sympathies were with the ancient glory of Hellas and the treasures of art that lie hoarded in its soil; but with these they must needs confound a population of lawless savages who, because they occupied the fatherland of Homer and Plato, were therefore, against all evidence of history and commonsense, rated as lineal descendants of classical Athens.' Cochrane had been denied the classical education which most contemporaries of his class had received, and which had recently inspired the Earl of Elgin, his family's neighbour at Culross, to impoverish his estate for three generations to come, through the colossal expense of bringing the marbles of the Parthenon to Britain. To Cochrane the cause was one of human freedom, the rescue of Christians from Muslim domination, of a native people from a foreign tyranny. Whether they were lawless savages or not was immaterial: such conditions generally bred lawless savages. Characteristically he tried to remedy the defects of his education by studying about fifty books on Greece.

Several of the men with whom he was soon to be associated had no such illusions about the cause they served as Fortescue ridiculed, and yet did not abandon it. 'Whoever goes into Greece at present,' Byron had written, 'should do it as Mrs Fry went into Newgate—not in the expectation of meeting with any especial indication of existing probity, but in the hope that time and better treatment will reclaim the present burglarious and larcenous tendencies which have followed this General Gaol Delivery.' Prominent among those who agreed with these sentiments were two wealthy Scots who nevertheless devoted the remainder of their lives to Greece, long after the cause of independence had been won.

George Finlay was the son of a Captain of the Royal Engineers on whose death he was brought up by his uncle Kirkman Finlay, a Lord Provost of Glasgow who was one of the founders of his city's commercial prosperity. George gave up the study of law to visit Greece, where he met Byron in November 1823 in Cephalonia. 'You are young and enthusiastic,' Byron warned him, 'and therefore sure to be disappointed when you know the Greeks as well as I do.' But Finlay did not succumb to his disappointment any more than Byron did, and at Missolonghi the two men delighted one another with their conversation through the long evenings. After Byron's death Finlay returned to Scotland to complete his legal studies, but despite his first-hand experience of the venality and rapacity of the Greeks, he had lost his heart to their country.

His compatriot Thomas Gordon came from Aberdeenshire and it was a commission in the Scots Greys that he surrendered before joining the Greek leader Ipsilanti at the very outbreak of the war of independence in 1821. He too retired in disgust, but it was the wholesale massacre of Turks that filled him with horror over the behaviour of those whom he had come to assist. Nevertheless he stepped forward as an original member of the Greek Committee in London, one who could not be described like Burdett as an ignorant sentimentalist. Of the Greek executive that his committee was designed to help, Gordon said that they were 'with *perhaps* one exception, no better than public robbers'.

Of more immediate importance to Cochrane than either of these men was Finlay's friend Frank Abney Hastings, the man who lured him a second time from his legal studies to return to Greece. Hastings was the son of a General who had gone to sea at about the age of 11 and had served in the *Neptune* at Trafalgar. He had been expelled subsequently from the British Navy for challenging a superior officer to a duel, and on 3 April 1822 he reached Greece to serve in the war of independence both on sea and on land. Towards the end of 1824 he returned to England to promote the construction of a steamship for the Greek Navy, and offered to contribute £1000 to its cost if he were given the command. Hastings was almost 20 years younger than Cochrane and he possessed many characteristics and talents in common with him. Had Cochrane refused the invitation of the Greek Committee it is likely that the command of the Greek Navy would have been offered to Hastings, and it would have been very much better for everyone if this had occurred. But Hastings did not possess the magic of Cochrane's name, and nobody stopped to consider that the Foreign Enlistment Act would prevent the recruitment of British seamen to the Greek Navy. The essential equipment for the feats of the Sea Wolf had always been a devoted and highly disciplined crew, even if it were so small as the complement of the brig *Speedy*.

'Greece cannot obtain any decisive advantage over the Turks without a decided maritime superiority,' Hastings had written to Byron in 1823, and it was what Cochrane had said and demonstrated in so many other theatres of war. Hastings had also adopted Cochrane's axiom that steamships would sweep sailing vessels from the seas, long before the British Admiralty would entertain such a heresy. But as soon as it was known that Cochrane was to command the navy of Greece, the British government moved to deprive it of its essential supply of trained seamen. Even Cochrane himself felt that his safety was in danger after all these months of freedom in Britain, and wrote to Burdett on 8 November to inform him that he had decided to retire across the Channel with his wife. 'My life is rendered so inquiet by the constant fear of prosecution under the Foreign Enlistment Act which Brougham has given his opinion may be put in force against me, even for my services in Brazil, that I have resolved to place myself on the other side of the water without delay, and tomorrow morning I make the attempt by steamboat from the Tower.' When he reached Boulogne he found himself threatened with prosecution for the capture of a French brig in the Pacific, and so retired, as San Martín had done before him, to Brussels. Here he composed for the Greek Committee a memorandum on the fleet which it possessed such ample means to build. That body had at last accepted Hastings' recommendation in favour of a steamship when Cochrane told them categorically:

'Required:

'Six steam vessels having each two guns in the bow and perhaps two in the stern not less than 68-pounder long guns.

'The bottoms of two old 74-gun ships, upper decks cut off and heavy cannon mounted on the lower deck.

'These vessels well manned appear to be sufficient to destroy the whole Turkish Naval power.'

Admiral Viscount Exmouth had been engaged in effective service since the end of the Napoloenic war against Muslim warships in the Mediterranean, in the course of which he had freed many Christian slaves. When he saw Cochrane's specifications for a Greek Navy he is reported to have remarked: 'Why, it's not only the Turkish fleet, but all the navies in the world you will be able to conquer with such craft as these.' But this took for granted that they would be 'well-manned'.

It also assumed that they would be promptly and properly built and this was to be the second fatality in the operation. Alexander Galloway of Smithfield, the radical marine engineer, had already let Cochrane down over the steam engines of the *Rising Star*, and it was not Cochrane's fault that he was also commissioned to supply the equipment for the

Greek vessels. The contract had already been handed to him in March 1825 when the Greek Committee at last yielded to the advice of Hastings before Cochrane arrived at Spithead. A corvette of 400 tons was to be built at Deptford for which the steam machinery was to be made by Galloway. When the number of steamships was increased under Cochrane's direction, the arrangements for their construction were allowed to stand.

But by the spring of 1826 not even the original ship was ready for sea. In desperation Cochrane paid a furtive visit to Galloway's yards to inspect progress, and threatened to abandon the whole project if the vessels were not soon launched. There has always been doubt as to whether the delay was caused by technical difficulties, or whether Galloway was actually in league with Greece's enemies. Certainly Mehemet Ali of Egypt had commissioned him during the interval to build a steamship which would become the foe of Cochrane's fleet, and Galloway sent his son to Egypt at this time in the hope of obtaining for him the post of engineer to the principal maritime ally of Turkey. In due course the Galloways sent equipment to Egypt, which was intercepted with a correspondence which proved that the eloquent radical of Smithfield was swindling Islam and Christendom with complete impartiality.

Whether or not the sudden appearance of Cochrane at his workshop warned the devious Alexander Galloway not to push his luck too far, the first corvette was put through her trials on 18 May 1826. They were satisfactory, but this did not save the engineer's reputation. Hastings considered him to be 'the most impudent liar I ever met with'; while one of the partners in Messrs J. and S. Ricardo, the London bankers who had floated the £2,000,000 loan, expostulated, 'Galloway is the evil genius that pursues us everywhere; his presumption is only equalled by his incompetency, whatever he has to do with us is miserably deficient; we do not think his misconduct has been intentional.' It may be that Galloway was a good deal less incompetent in his own way than Ricardo suspected.

The guns of the new steamship were consigned to Greece by way of the United States in order to evade government intervention, while the unarmed vessel's papers stated that her destination was the Netherlands. These subterfuges enabled Hastings, to whom Cochrane had naturally conceded the command, to recruit British seamen in defiance of the Foreign Enlistment Act. So the *Karteria* (as she was to be named when she reached Greece) sailed out of the Thames to the relief of the Greek Committee and the delight of her Captain. But while the unfamilar sight of her tall funnel belching smoke was observed with wonder by spectators on the coasts of Kent and Sussex, her crew soon found themselves in difficulties. Her furnaces were found to require coal rather than wood to raise enough steam for the propulsion of her paddle wheels, which also proved to be too high in the water. Hastings had no sooner reached the Mediterranean despite his vessel's defects than her boilers burst and delayed him for 3 months while they were being mended. But this proved immaterial when it transpired that the guns of the *Karteria* had gone missing in the United States. It was not until December 1826 that the first armed steamship was ready for action in Greek waters.

Cochrane had been cruising expectantly off Ireland in a yacht after the departure of Hastings, waiting for the promised news that two more steamships were ready to sail. As soon as it reached him he sped to the Mediterranean to take command of his fleet, only to learn that the intelligence had been false. Once again it had been found that it was impossible to generate enough steam to turn the paddle wheels without exploding the boilers.

The effect of these seemingly endless mishaps on a man whose nerves were already stretched to breaking-point must have been extremely harmful. 'My undertaking will outdo the adventures of Quixote,' he had assured Burdett in one of his earlier moods of elation. 'Within a few weeks Lord Cochrane will be at Constantinople and will burn the Turkish vessels in the port,' Edward Ellice, Member of Parliament and of the Greek Committee, had assured a visiting delegation of Greek deputies. He had never failed in the past, whatever the odds, and nobody expected him to fail now. Yet when he said good-bye to his wife for the last time before his departure for Greece, after that visit to Galloway's yards, she found him 'more uneasy than I ever before knew him to be'. She had chided him for a similar mood of depression in Peru; but this was much worse, scant solace to the long-suffering family whose reunion and tranquillity had proved to be so shortlived.

Sailing disconsolately about the Mediterranean, Cochrane was tempted by an invitation from the Knights of Malta to fly their flag. But several people advised against it and meanwhile the Greek Committee in France stepped forward to supply the vessel for the Greek Admiral which the London Committee had failed to provide out of its huge resources. In October 1826 he had sailed into Marseilles in the hope of hearing news from England, where he could see the dockyards filled with the warships that were being built for the fleet of Mehemet Ali in Egypt. Byron's friend John Cam Hobhouse, another Member of Parliament and of the Greek Committee, came to meet him here and was able to assure him that even if the steamships failed to materialise he would soon be able to hoist his flag in a sailing ship of the conventional type. For his Committee had commissioned a firm in New York to build two frigates, and although there had been the usual delays, the same mysterious disappearance of vast sums of money, Cochrane would soon be receiving a fine new frigate for the price of two.

In Marseilles he also met Dr Louis-André Gosse, a Swiss member of the French Committee, who played the leading part in purchasing the brig *Sauveur* and equipping her for his immediate use. Gosse found Cochrane 'tall and bony-framed, strong and slim, though slightly corpulent: hair reddish, expression gentle though serious, pleasant and cultivated in his conversation'. Evidently he was a little out of condition since he never grew stout. Gosse's description agrees with that of Admiral Henry Keppel in recording how little Cochrane's figure or hair had altered in 50 years. 'He was tall and thin,' wrote Keppel, 'of powerful build, with close-cut red hair.'

Such was the appearance of the Admiral who sailed at last into Greek waters, a year and 3 months behind schedule, bringing with him a fleet consisting of a brig and two yachts. There he found his American frigate, named the *Hellas*, to which he shifted his flag; in December the guns of the *Karteria* were installed at last.

One of the first men whom Cochrane met in Greece was Thomas Gordon, whom the London Committee had succeeded in persuading to return there the previous May in an effort to promote unity and military discipline amongst the diverse leaders of the revolutionary movement. Gordon had done all in his power to pave the way for Cochrane's arrival, as he wrote impatiently on 7 June. 'During the fifteen days that I have acted as minister of war, minister of marine, commissary-general and inspector of fortifications, I have prepared everything for his arrival if he chooses to come.' There is a hint here that Gordon suspected Cochrane of dawdling, at a time of critical urgency, and it is confirmed by the accusation of George Finlay, his aide, that at this critical juncture of the war Cochrane had 'been wandering about the Mediterranean in a fine English yacht'. The exasperation of the two men is understandable, although they could hardly have chosen their scapegoat with less justice.

Finlay left an impressive picture of the man who had sailed to join them at last. 'He was tall and commanding in person, lively and winning in manner, prompt in counsel, and daring but cool in action. Endowed by nature both with strength of character and military genius, versed in naval science both by study and experience, and acquainted with seamen in every clime and country, nothing but an untimely restlessness of disposition, and a too strongly expressed contempt for mediocrity and conventional rules, prevented his becoming one of Britain's naval heroes.' Finlay's penetrating analysis unfortunately adds hearsay to personal observation. 'Accident, and his eagerness to gain some desired object, engaged him more than once in enterprises in which money rather than honour appeared to be the end he sought.' Finlay possessed at least this excuse for finding fault with another because he fought in Greece for money as well as honour, since he himself flung away most of his considerable fortune there.

By the time the new year of 1827 brought with it a promise of the long-awaited offensive by land and sea, the predicament of the Greek revolutionaries had become desperate. In April 1826 Missolonghi had fallen to the forces of Ibrahim, son of Mehemet Ali of Egypt. It was only a small, fever-haunted fishing town of no strategic importance, but it was the place where Byron had died, the symbol to all Europe of Greek freedom. After its sack the Sultan of Turkey was sent ten barrels of human ears preserved in salt while the Egyptian soldiers collected 3000 human heads and kept perhaps as many as 4000 women and boys as slaves. The Greeks had committed similar horrors against the Turks, but it caused a special sense of outrage that such atrocities should have occurred *where* they did. The Sultan of Turkey and the Pasha of Egypt hailed their victory with delight, unable to understand that while it had extinguished a local conflagration it had fanned the flames of distant fires.

Opposite Missolonghi lies the land-mass of the Peloponnese, joined by its narrow isthmus to the Greek mainland with its capital at Athens, and since Ibrahim had been invested with the control of the Peloponnese by the Sultan he did not attempt to carry his victorious arms further afield, but remained in this province throughout the summer. It was the Turks who advanced from the other direction, to repossess what little remained of free Greece between Athens and the isthmus, with the offshore islands in which rival Greek governments carried on their feuds with one another. The capital was occupied by a Greek warlord of such bestiality that when the Turkish army appeared it was hailed by the inhabitants as a deliverer, and from June 1826 only the Acropolis remained in the hands of the insurgents.

As Christmas approached, a French philhellene who had become increasingly disgusted by the Greeks whom he had come to succour gradually succumbed to the appeals made to him to relieve the citadel of European civilisation. On the night of 12 December Colonel Charles Fabvier landed at Phaleron with 570 men, each carrying a sack of gunpowder which they intended to deliver to the defenders and then retire. But an alarm was given as they approached the white rock on which the battered Parthenon stood in the moonlight. They were forced to charge with the bayonet and to seek safety in the Acropolis itself. With such an experienced soldier now accidentally committed to its defence, Colonel Thomas Gordon was asked to raise the siege of the last Greek citadel that had not yet fallen to the Turks or their Egyptian allies.

A fresh complication now arose to increase the discord between rival Greek factions and the motley collections of volunteers who had arrived from all parts of Europe to lend them aid. Sir Richard Church, a General who had seen as much service as Fabvier during the Napoleonic war, was invited by one of the rival Greek governments to command the land forces as Cochrane had been commissioned to command those of the sea. 'Come! Come! And take up arms for Greece, or assist her with your talents, your virtues, and your abilities that you may claim her eternal gratitude.' After 5 years of havering in his enthusiasm for the Greek cause Church accepted, and Gordon agreed unselfishly to conduct operations until his arrival. But he was to prove a poor substitute for the experienced Scotsman whom he supplanted, and the very first rumour of his appointment angered Fabvier in the Acropolis, in touch with the outside world through the use of carrier pigeons.

Such was the aspect of the field when Cochrane arrived at the island of Poros, south of Aegina, on 17 March 1827 in the *Sauveur* with his two yachts. The *Karteria* and the *Hellas* awaited him on the leash but the political and military arms of the independence movement were in total disarray while the strategic situation was at its nadir. He acted with all his old decisiveness. The war was to be won at sea and to Mehemet Ali, controller of the fleet at Navarino which supplied the land forces of Islam, he quoted a passage from Isaiah: 'Now the Egyptians are men and not God; and their horses flesh and not spirit. When the Lord shall stretch out his hand, both he that helpeth shall fall, and he that is helpen shall fall down, and they all shall fall together.' With his extraordinary foresight he recommended to the Pasha of Egypt in another manifesto that he should leave the Greeks alone and turn his attention instead to the building of a Suez canal.

The arrival of the Sea Wolf did have the effect which the London Committee had envisaged when they begged him to become the Admiral of Greece. Adolphus Slade the tourist wrote that 'the Turks imagined him to be a sort of half man, half devil—a sorcerer who needed not the agency of winds and currents, but who could rush to his object in spite of them. I really believe some of them thought he could sail his ships on land.' Charles Macfarlane, another traveller who visited Constantinople at this time, reported that Cochrane's enemies were so terrified of him that they would not venture out of port even if he appeared in a vessel no larger than a schooner. Cochrane's first objective was to augment this terror so far as he was able with his pen.

His second was to use his position to bludgeon the Greeks into some semblance of unity. In this discordant sphere also Cochrane's reputation had its effect, as George Finlay observed: 'His influence became suddenly unbounded, and faction for a moment was silenced'. Cochrane used it to compel the two principal governments on the islands of Aegina and Hermione to cease their attacks upon one another and join together in the common cause. To the overtures from Hermione, whence Sir Richard Church had also received his invitation, he replied with a quotation from the first Philippic of Demosthenes. 'If you will become your own masters, and cease each of you to expect to do nothing himself while his neighbour does everything for him, you will then with God's permission get back your own, recover what is lost, and punish your enemy.' When the National Assembly in Aegina sent him his Admiral's commission he rejected it, saying that unless the two political factions sank their differences forthwith he would quit the country.

The threat was effective. The Assembly met to elect a President, and chose a Greek who had never visited the country in his life, but one who possessed considerable diplomatic experience abroad since he had held the office of Russian Foreign Minister. The promotion of Count John Capo d'Istria as leader of the Greeks had been canvassed abroad as early as 1825, and he was now elected President for a term of 7 years without having so much as presented himself as a candidate. It was one of Cochrane's most substantial contributions to the Greek cause to have played this part in securing a leader who stood apart from any local faction, for Capo d'Istria remained the ruler of Greece until his assassination in 1831. Cochrane permitted himself to be sworn in as First Admiral on 18 April, 3 days after Sir Richard Church was formally appointed Commander-in-Chief, and immediately appealed for a spirit of unity throughout the country. 'To Arms! To Arms! One simultaneous effort, and Greece is free. Discord, the deadly foe you have had most to fear, is conquered.'

Cochrane's third and most immediate objective was the one which Colonel Thomas Gordon had already adopted, the relief of Fabvier in the Acropolis. He alluded to it in the characteristic terms in which he had so often succeeded in investing his aims with an aura of invincibility. 'The task that now remains is easy. The youth everywhere fly to arms. The fate of the Acropolis is no longer doubtful. The Turks surrounded, their supplies cut off, the passes occupied, and retreat impossible, you can ensure the freedom of the classic plains of Athens, again destined to become the seat of liberty, the sciences and the arts.' Cochrane was briefly infected with the philhellenic fervour that meant so little to the Greeks themselves, and that the Turks found so incomprehensible.

For one thing, he had just set eyes for the first time on the distant outline of the Parthenon, and who can resist its influence, whether or not he has prepared himself for the experience by studying fifty books? 'The Acropolis was beautiful,' he confided to his journal. 'Alas! What a change! What melancholy recollections crowd on the mind. There was the seat of science, of literature, and the arts. At this instant the barbarian Turk is actually demolishing by the shells that now are flying through the air, the scanty remains of the once magnificent temples of the Acropolis.' The Turks had threatened on one occasion to destroy its monuments, and on another had given the British an undertaking to preserve them from harm. The slight damage which the ruins sustained during the siege was due to innacurate firing rather than to either of these pronouncements.

To Fabvier in the Acropolis, Cochrane and Church sent reassuring messages, promising that they would make every effort to raise the siege. Despite the fact that the French commander, his thousand troops, and some 400 women and children were totally dependent on the newly appointed General and Admiral to save them from a fate as horrible as the defenders of Missolonghi had suffered, Fabvier replied with characteristic rudeness, sharpened by his antipathy to Sir Richard Church. He accused the Greeks of delaying their assistance out of cowardice, and with a mendacity that was to prove fatal in its consequences he warned that he only possessed the resources to hold out for a few more days. Cochrane possessed no means of checking the accuracy of this intelligence nor any reason to doubt it. He moved with feverish haste to avert catastrophe.

He adopted the plan which Colonel Gordon had attempted to carry out in February without success. First he despatched Captain Hastings in the *Karteria* to seize the Turkish victualling ships, which Hastings did with great gallantry and speed. Next he sailed in the *Hellas* to Phaleron with Sir Richard Church and 3000 soldiers, to reinforce the bridgehead nearest to the Acropolis and to the Turkish troops who were investing it. He had himself recruited a force of 1000 men from the island of Hydra, increasing the army of liberation to a total of about 10,000. Gordon already lay before Athens with 3000 men, while the Greek leader Karaiskakes commanded a force only slightly smaller on the other side of the Piraeus peninsula. Between them stood the monastery of Spiridion, a favourite saint of the Orthodox Church, manned by a Turkish garrison.

To the Greeks Cochrane displayed a device that had so often served its turn in the past. He displayed a huge flag showing an owl against a blue and white background, which he had brought from Marseilles, and announced through an interpreter that he would give 1000 dollars to the man who raised it on the Acropolis and 10,000 to be divided amongst those who accompanied him. Then he tried to persuade Karaiskakes either to attack the monastery of Spiridion in order to effect a union with the remainder of the Greek army, or to permit the fleet to transport his men into the fold by sea. When Karaiskakes remained entrenched in his position, refusing to agree to either course, Cochrane himself landed with a small Greek force beneath the monastery on 25 April.

The old magic flashed in this new setting. Turkish sentinels observed the enemy disembarking and a party came out to attack them. Cochrane signalled for reinforcements of his men from Hydra, which provoked the Turkish advance party to do the same, and so the offensive gained momentum. Cochrane himself was armed with nothing except a telescope, but brandishing this as he shouted encouragement to his Greeks he dashed towards the Turkish entrenchments where they quickly overran nine enemy redoubts and sent some 300 of the defenders scuttling into the monastery while others scattered in the direction of Athens. Cochrane sent a message to Karaiskakes urging an immediate assault, and when he still refused to move, the guns of the *Hellas* bombarded the monastery until, by the following morning, it lay in ruins. 'Henceforth commences a new era in the system of modern Greek warfare,' Cochrane wrote to the government, but three days later he discovered how wrong he was.

Surrounded in their wrecked monastery, the little garrison of Turks and Albanian Muslims surrendered to Karaiskakes on terms. Gordon and Finlay, his aide, had come aboard Cochrane's ship to confer and stood watching the ant-like movements ashore as the capitulation took place. Suddenly Finlay pointed to the column of men who were marching out of the monastery and said:

'All those men will be murdered.'

'Do you hear what he says?' Cochrane exclaimed in horror to Gordon, who stood on the other side of him.

'My Lord, I fear it is too true,' Gordon replied.

Karaiskakes did attempt to prevent the massacre which took place as the three men watched through their telescopes, and several Greeks were shot as order was restored. Nor was this atrocity comparable to the torture and murder of thousands of civilians, women and children, committed by both Greeks and Turks. But it was the final enormity which drove Gordon from the Greek cause in disgust. By July he was back in Scotland with letters of profuse gratitude from the Greeks in his pocket and the material for his admirable history of the Greek revolution in his head.

Cochrane himself threatened to abandon the Acropolis to its fate, and although he soon relented, he became henceforth as cynical and sarcastic as anyone else who had experienced the reality behind the philhellenic dream. To the soldiers whom he had recruited in Hydra he proclaimed: 'I was no party to the capitulation this day. Fearing that some outrage might be committed, I sent you an order to retire, and I glory in the consciousness that I have saved you as well as myself from being inculpated in the most horrid scene I ever beheld—a scene which freezes my blood, and which cannot be palliated by any barbarities which the Turks have committed on you. I send you the thousand dollars which I promised should be distributed, as a reward for your valour and for your obedience to my directions, which you will ever find to lead to the path of honour and humanity and the duty we owe to your country.'

The relief of the last mainland stronghold of free Greece had by now become virtually the sole responsibility of Cochrane, because Church, the Generalissimo, proved incapable of adapting his habits to the requirements of the command he had accepted. As though he were marshalling a European army of trained regular soldiers he lived in a yacht offshore with all the paraphernalia of a headquarters and staff, through which he would issue his orders in writing. What the undisciplined and disheartened Greeks needed was the inspiration of a Cochrane, waving them into action with his telescope. They soon came to believe that Church was too cowardly to step ashore.

The precious days which Fabvier had allowed for the relief of his garrison were trickling away. On 4 May Karaiskakes was wounded in a skirmish and asked to be carried, dying, aboard Cochrane's ship in order to thank the Admiral. He also left the final request to his officers that they should support Cochrane in an immediate offensive against the Turkish army of Athens, and Cochrane grasped at this straw. With Karaiskakes dead, Gordon gone and Sir Richard Church in his yacht, the sole initiative lay with him to make a final bid to relieve Fabvier and on 6 May he attempted it. He hoped that the spearhead of foreign volunteers and the little contingent of trained troops at his disposal would serve as an adequate leavening of the Greek force which he landed by moonlight near Phaleron, and that they would march directly on Athens from the south. But instead of supporting the advance party the irregulars tried to dig themselves in near the shore, so that when the Turkish cavalry came to investigate the matter in the morning they found only scattered groups of disorganised and terrified men to hack to pieces. Cochrane had gone ashore as usual, although it was General Church who ought to have been there, not the Admiral, but he could do nothing to stem such a panic as ensued. He was carried back to the beach in the general flight and only regained his boat by wading up to his neck out to sea. To the government he wrote: 'The use of the bayonet would have saved most of those who fell on this occasion and would have rendered unnecessary those redoubts which delay the progress of your arms.' But Fabvier's ultimatum had deprived him of even the shortest training period in which to prepare his men for their task, and so upwards of a thousand men perished and the morale of the remainder fell to new depths.

The very day after this fiasco had occurred, Cochrane took the only step that remained in his power to save the occupants of the Acropolis from the dreadful fate of the defenders of Missolonghi. He wrote in his capacity as First Admiral of Greece to the naval commanders of other nations who might, by their presence, be able to intervene to prevent such a catastrophe. It was the commander of the French naval squadron who played the most important part in the ensuing negotiations, which resulted in an agreement with the Turks that the Acropolis would be surrendered after all its inmates had been evacuated safely. The capitulation was endorsed on 5 June and implemented without mishap, when it was discovered that Fabvier still possessed provisions and ammunition sufficient to withstand a siege for another 4 months. As Cochrane helped to organise the embarkation of the men, women and children whom Fabvier had so wantonly betrayed amid the wholesale desertion of the Greek soldiery, he tasted for the first time in his career the bitterness of total defeat. He had prevented a massacre, but he had been unable to achieve a miraculous victory as of old with a negligible list of casualties.

Thomas Gordon later wrote critically of the inexperience of General Church and Admiral Cochrane in Greek matters, and there is much truth in his censure. It would probably have been better if Gordon and Hastings had filled these positions, since their proven capacity was matched by considerable past experience of war in this theatre. In particular they knew the limitations of the Greek as a soldier. But Gordon was a member of the Greek Committee in London which urged Cochrane to accept the post of Admiral when others sought to dissuade him, and Cochrane cannot be blamed for having attempted during the grave emergency of May an operation which Thomas

Gordon himself had tried without success to carry out in February.

After the fall of the Acropolis the attitude of the European powers was of paramount influence on the future of the forlorn Greek cause. The most hostile to it was the Hapsburg empire of Austria-Hungary, whose ruler Prince Metternich scoffed that there was no such thing as a Greek nation, the term being used 'indiscriminately to signify a territory, a race, a language, or even a religion'. Certainly nobody had been able to define what constituted Greek territory and most of the philhellenes were supporting rebellious Turkish subjects because they spoke a language resembling that of the classical Greek hero Epaminondas and belonged to the Orthodox Christian religion. The attitude of Russia was regarded with the greatest suspicion in the chancelleries of Europe, since the Tsar possessed a pretext for transferring Greece from the Turkish empire to his own on the grounds that Moscow was the centre of the Orthodox Church.

In 1825 Tsar Alexander had passed a secret message to the British Foreign Minister George Canning. 'My people demand war; my armies are full of ardour to make it, perhaps I could not long resist them. My Allies have abandoned me. Compare my conduct to theirs. Everybody has intrigued in Greece. I alone am pure. I have pushed scruples so far as not to have a single wretched agent in Greece . . .' Canning seized this prickly olive-branch and entered into an agreement with Russia to co-ordinate the policies of the two countries. He also despatched Admiral Sir Edward Codrington to Greece in that very month of December 1826 when the *Hellas* arrived from America and Hastings installed his guns in the *Karteria*. Codrington was ordered to employ the British fleet with the utmost discretion in preventing the supply of men and arms for use against the Greeks by Turkey or her Egyptian ally. But the British government preserved its purity like the Tsar as the First Lord revealed when he said that Codrington had been appointed because 'he is a person who I have no doubt will *stand up* to Lord Cochrane, and compel him to keep within proper bounds'.

Codrington's instructions gave him no latitude to intervene in the events which led to the surrender of the Acropolis, neither did he show the slightest inclination to do so. The descendant of the public servant after whom the beautiful Codrington Library in All Souls College at Oxford was named, he was one of those who did not pass through the cycle of enthusiasm followed by disillusion which afflicted most of his contemporaries when they became involved with Greece. 'I am no philanthropist, nor am I the least a philhellenist,' he told President Capo d'Istria after the Count had arrived to take up his appointment.

T.S.W.—U

'I set no particular value upon either Greeks or Turks, and I have no personal feeling towards either. I am guided solely by my duty as an English officer.' Canning would have approved this down-to-earth attitude. He had welcomed the message which the Tsar sent him 'because it has nothing to do with Epaminondas nor (with reverence be it spoken) with St Paul'. Codrington was so punctilious as to correspond with Cochrane exclusively through the Greek government, treating him with propriety as an officer in the service of that nation. In April 1827 Canning succeeded the effete Lord Liverpool as Prime Minister and a month after the Acropolis had fallen Russia, France and Britain signed the Treaty of London which simplified Codrington's task in that it laid down a common policy for the navies of the three countries in the Mediterranean. They were to propose an armistice, and enforce it if necessary. This amounted to intervention on behalf of the Greeks, since these were able to resume hostilities on land with impunity while Turkey and Egypt were prevented from supplying their forces from the sea. The strategy which Hastings had recommended to Byron, and Cochrane had come to Greece to implement, was at last being adopted by the allied powers.

It nevertheless remained Cochrane's responsibility as Admiral of Greece to play his own part with such resources as he possessed. Since the *Karteria* had been surmounting her teething troubles in the expert hands of Captain Hastings and was proving to be the most formidable small warship in this theatre, it was a great disappointment to learn that the second of the six promised steamships had burst her boiler in the English Channel and been towed into Plymouth for repairs. But Cochrane still possessed the excellent frigate *Hellas* and the brig *Sauveur* and he sought to augment his fleet with the Greek vessels of the islands of Poros, Hydra and Spetsae, hoping to lure them from their usual occupation of piracy into the service of their country. He sailed to the port of Poros where they had assembled for a review of his ships and here George Finlay was present to record the most ignominious episode in Cochrane's naval career.

When he signalled to his ships to get under way his order was ignored and a deputation instead rowed to his flagship to demand a month's pay in advance, insolently telling the Admiral that he had ample funds on board for the purpose. With surprising patience Cochrane replied that he had spent so much on the attempted relief of Athens that he would be unable to pay more than a fortnight's wages in advance. 'In vain,' wrote Finlay, 'the Grand Admiral urged the duty they owed to their country. No seaman could trust his country for a fortnight's wages.' Nor, he might have added, the naval commander who had done more to safeguard the rights of his seamen in two hemispheres than any other man of his age.

The deputation left the *Hellas* with Cochrane's answer and it was the signal for wholesale desertion. 'The afternoon was calm,' Finlay remembered, 'the sun was descending to the mountains of Argolis, and the shadows of the rocks of Methana already darkened the waters, when brig after brig passed in succession under the stern of the *Hellas*, from whose lofty mast the flag of the High Admiral of Greece floated, unconscious of the disgraceful stain it was receiving, and in whose cabin sat the noble admiral steadily watching the scene.' As Gordon had discovered earlier they were merely public robbers, and if they could not rob government funds they would return to the less hazardous perquisites of piracy. But for Cochrane there was a more embarrassing consequence than their loss to his service: unless he devoted all his energies to suppressing their depredations, he stood accused of neglecting his responsibilities, or even of being a party to their crimes. Yet he had not been appointed to Greece in order to take over the maritime police duties which the Turkish fleet was now prevented from fulfilling through the action of the allied powers. The position in which he was placed had become an almost impossible one.

The resilience of mind and spirit which he displayed in his predicament are truly remarkable. He set out with his wretched resources in a last desperate attempt to achieve another Rochefort coup, another triumph such as he had dragged from the very teeth of fate at Valdivia and Callao. At Alexandria Mehemet Ali was preparing another Egyptian fleet to bring to Greece. Cochrane succeeded in assembling fourteen Greek brigs and eight fireships to accompany the *Hellas* and the *Sauveur*, and on 15 June 1827 they arrived within sight of the enemy harbour. Only 10 days had passed since the capitulation of the Acropolis—Cochrane had not wasted his time. That night was spent in preparing an explosion vessel to add to the terror of the fireships and on the morrow Cochrane tried yet again to instil the spirit of Epaminondas into his men.

'Brave officers and seamen, one decisive blow and Greece is free. The port of Alexandria, the centre of all the evil that has befallen you, now contains within its narrow bounds numerous ships of war and a multitude of vessels laden with provisions, stores and troops intended to effect your total ruin. The wind is fair for us, and our enterprise is unsuspected. Brave fireship crews, resolve by one moment of active exertion to annihilate the power of the Satrap. Then shall the siege of Athens be raised in Egypt.'

For a short space it appeared that the old magic might work again.

Kanares, the Greek commander, was a brave and determined man and he succeeded in persuading the crews of two of the fireships to sail towards the enemy. Their success ought to have heartened the rest because they set fire to a small Egyptian warship and caused such alarm among the remainder that they began to weigh anchor and prepare to flee. But this was interpreted as a preparation to attack which so terrified the Greeks that they scattered headlong in all directions. Cochrane would have advanced upon the enemy singlehanded but that he could not even depend upon the seamen in his flagship. Instead of the victory that had appeared to be within his grasp he was left with the mortifying task of rounding up his miserable fleet. He found some of the ships still at sea but most of them had returned home and when the Admiral reached port also, even his own Greek seamen deserted from the flagship.

Cochrane described the behaviour of the only men who ever served under him without learning either discipline, courage or patriotism. Once he tried to keep them amused on board the *Hellas* by showing them pictures through his magic lantern. By accident he displayed a slide which showed a Greek running away from a Turk, and when he hastily substituted another, it proved to be a picture of a Turk cutting off a Greek's head. The sight terrified his audience so much that some fled into the hold, others jumped into the sea, and it was many hours before the hysteria subsided. On other occasions the Admiral had to use his own bare fists to compel his men to do their duty and he never left his cabin without a loaded pistol in his pocket.

He still refused to admit defeat. Gathering fresh seamen as fast as he could to replace the deserters, he sailed for Navarino on 28 July where the main Turkish fleet lay, immobilised by the embargo imposed by the allied powers under the terms of the Treaty of London. As he fluttered outside that capacious bay a corvette came out to give chase, accompanied by two brigs and two schooners, and somehow Cochrane was able to drive his crew to maintain the series of manoeuvres with which he outwitted his pursuers for a day and a night. By 1 August he had lured the corvette into position for the kill, and closed with her in an action which ended in her capture after nearly an hour's bombardment. 'The boys behaved pretty well,' Cochrane reported, 'but the oldest and ugliest and fiercest-looking bravos of Hydra ran to the other side of the deck, roaring like bulls.' It was the last naval action he ever fought in his life and the corvette was one of the only two vessels he captured during his Greek service. But even though this tiny success made not the slightest contribution to the cause of independence, it did enable Cochrane to rescue from the corvette 'the usual horde of Greek women and children'. In August Mehemet Ali's fleet at Alexandria was ready for sea, and sailed to join the Turkish fleet at Navarino, bringing the total of vessels there to upwards of a hundred.

Navarino lies on the south-western side of the Peloponnese landmass, which was occupied by the forces of Mehemet Ali's son Ibrahim. In concert with General Church and Captain Hastings, Cochrane now shifted his theatre of operations round the north shores of this province, past Missolonghi where he briefly contemplated the capture of a fort, into the gulf of Corinth. Church marched with his army, such as it was, from the other direction along the north coast of the Peloponnese, while Cochrane did his best to incite the local tribes on the other side of the gulf to raise in arms. The part which Hastings played demonstrated to all the world the effectiveness of his new type of warship. The *Karteria* carried a portable furnace which enabled her to fire red-hot shot and at the end of September Hastings sank no less than nine Turkish vessels in a succession of brilliant actions in the bay of Salona.

Admiral Codrington did what he could to enforce the armistice with impartiality. Instead of communicating with Cochrane through the Greek government, he sent a British warship to him directly under Commander Viscount Ingestrie, the most senior member of the peerage in his fleet if not the highest in naval rank. It was Ingestrie's diplomatic duty to deliver a stern warning to Cochrane to preserve the armistice and then to sail on through the Gulf of Corinth until he should find General Church, and place the same embargo on his movements.

Whether or not Ibrahim Pasha knew of these efforts to restrain the Greek commanders who happened to be British subjects, he was justifiably incensed by all this activity on the part of defeated rebels, made possible by the interposition of the allied fleets. He sent an emissary to Codrington to demand the freedom to sail against Cochrane, but Codrington refused his request. Then Ibrahim heard of the sinking of the nine Turkish ships in the bay of Salona and he decided that he had tolerated the armistice imposed by the Treaty of London—a treaty in which Turkey had not been invited to participate—for too long. On 1 October 1827 Codrington read a signal telling him that a squadron of the Turkish-Egyptian fleet was sailing out of the bay of Navarino, and he could not doubt that it was bound for the Gulf of Corinth and a confrontation with Cochrane. Hastily putting to sea, Codrington pursued the Turkish squadron and deduced from the skill with which it was handled that the French Captain Letellier was in command. During the night Codrington outsailed him, and lay by dawn in the entrance to the Gulf of Corinth. While his ships prepared for battle there was intensive parleying, before the Turkish squadron agreed to return peacefully to Navarino, escorted by Codrington.

It was at this point that the Russian fleet arrived in the area, commanded by Admiral Heiden and backed by the most anti-Turkish signatory of the Treaty of London. But Codrington's French colleague was also aggressive in mood, writing to his wife on 6 October 'all these hostilities without hostilities are too subtle for me'. And although Codrington's more dispassionate attitude was supported by Canning the British Prime Minister, Lord High Admiral the Duke of Clarence, brother of King George IV and heir to the throne, is believed to have sent very different advice. 'Go in, my dear Ned, and smash those bloody Turks.' Of all the protagonists it was Ibrahim who sounded the most cautious, in the reports he sent to Constantinople. 'The allied powers are on the side of the Greeks,' he warned, 'and if the imperial fleet is directed against the Greeks, war will be declared.' Just by being there, in the Gulf of Corinth, Cochrane was providing the irritant that would provoke others into fulfilling his prophecy: 'One decisive blow and Greece is free.'

While Ibrahim waited for orders from the Sublime Porte, telling whether he should risk battle with the combined allied fleets of Europe, he found relief for his frustration in a holocaust of brutality which caused it to be reported that he intended to wipe out the native population of the Peloponnese altogether and settle the land with Muslims. When he heard of these atrocities, Codrington sent Captain Gawen Hamilton of the *Cambrian* to 'put yourself in communication with the Greeks, and use your utmost endeavours not only to defend them against these barbarities but to drive back the army of Ibrahim Pasha within the lines of Navarin'. On 13 October the allied Admirals met to confer for the first time, and a week later their ships lay alongside those of Turkey and Egypt in the great basin of Navarino harbour. It was nobody's intention to fight, and when the French Admiral ordered his countrymen serving as officers in the enemy fleet to quit their ships, they did so. But many people had the premonition of the sailor who wrote home: 'Can't say if you'll get another letter from me; for we mean to go in tomorrow to Navarino Bay to beat the Turks, so, whether I'll be sent to Davy or not I cannot tell; but you must not fret, dear mother, if I should be called away tomorrow, for you know that death is a debt we must pay.'

He paid it the next day in an action that began by accident and ended when sixty enemy ships had been sunk and some 8000 men killed or drowned. None of the allied ships had been sunk and only 176 men had been lost. To Metternich in Vienna it was a 'frightful catastrophe';

to the Duke of Wellington an 'untoward event'; while Mehemet Ali in Egypt said 'I told them what would be the consequences. Did they think they had to deal with Greeks?' There was much satisfaction in France and Russia while the Sailor Duke of Clarence bestowed the order of Knight Grand Cross of the Bath on Codrington, forgetting in his enthusiasm to consult anyone. 'I have sent him the riband,' his brother King George said irritably, 'but it ought to be a halter.' In his Speech from the Throne on 29 January 1828 the King said: 'We lament that this conflict should have occurred with the naval force of an ancient ally.' Codrington had placed himself in the company of such men as Byron, Church, Hastings and Gordon, and in achieving the object for which Cochrane had come to Greece despite the official disapproval of his government, he soon found himself an object of censure.

In the eyes of the British government Cochrane remained as objectionable as ever. Faced with the problems of suppressing piracy in Greek waters, he was insulted and embarrassed by its announcement that the ships flying under his flag would be treated as pirate vessels. The second steamship had at last arrived during September 1827, to be renamed the *Epicheiresis*: but when Cochrane could not recruit dependable seamen even to man his flagship, it was not likely that he would succeed in finding hands competent to manage this new type of vessel. 'There are no naval officers in Greece,' he stated, 'who are acquainted with the discipline of regular ships of war, the seamen will submit to no restraint, they will not enlist for more than one month, they will do nothing without being paid in advance.' More bitterly still, he complained early in 1828: 'Though styled Commander-in-Chief of the Greek naval forces I have, since the 12th April last when I hoisted my flag, been in truth under the control of wild and frantic savages, whose acts are guided by momentary impulses or heedless avidity to grasp some immediate pecuniary or petty advantage, regardless of any future benefit, however great, to their country or to themselves.' Early in the new year of 1828 Cochrane sailed into Portsmouth in the yacht *Unicorn*, in order to lay this state of affairs before the members of the Greek Committee in London and Paris, and to discover whether he would be able to recruit British seamen in the present circumstances.

It was a disheartening experience, and even though Cochrane was able to visit his wife, living in Paris, it did not cure the mood of depression in which he returned to the Mediterranean. Kitty tried to lift his spirits in her characteristic way, telling him what there was to tell of her social life in Paris, and encouraging him to look on the bright side of life. When Cochrane sent a morose letter back to her criticising her plans to hold a dance for her friends, she could stand no more of it. She was a woman in her early thirties who had been dragged about the world in the wake of her husband, parted from her children, provided with no settled home, and the reply she wrote to her husband on 2 May 1828 indicates that her patience was not inexhaustible.

'I am sorry my dearest Cochrane to see by your letter that you are out of spirits and that you are annoyed at my giving the little dance, which is now gone too far to be recalled. If, my Ever, I had been in the habit of doing these sorts of things I should justly merit the hints you have given me, but surely few women after sixteen years of hardships and privations could have been more moderate than I: at least I think so; if I am wrong, pardon me.' She pleaded that it was her social obligation to return 'the extreme civilities of the people here. I might, it is true, have gone from Paris or have given up the world, but then some other motive would have been attributed to me.' As she worked herself up into this mood of self-pity over her husband's apparent distrust, old grievances began to rankle once more.

'You must recollect how few people could have got on as I have done; what an uphill journey have I had, neither Mother, Husband or friend to uphold me, but on the contrary I have had both tide and wind against me. But of one thing I am sure. Do what I will or leave undone what I may, I shall never give you happiness or satisfaction.' Remembering that it was her projected dance that had provoked Cochrane's cantankerous remarks, she added: 'From the bottom of my heart I shall be glad when the thing is over. It will be in the course of twenty-four hours and I hope it will be as many years before I give another. I think you might not have written me such a trite letter to mar my little anticipated pleasure.' She did not post these words immediately, but waited until she was in the mood to add to them more cheerfully. On the other hand she did send them on to her husband in the end, impervious to the fact that they were an ill medicine for his condition.

Her own anticipated pleasure does not appear to have been marred. 'My dearest Cochrane,' she wrote after the ball, 'I did not write to you last post day or by George Sutton for I was so tired after my dance that I hated the sight of a pen or in fact anything else that required the slightest consideration.' There was no other cause of her exhaustion, she hastened to reassure her husband. '*I do not* think I am in the way that ladies wish to be who love their Lords. I tell you this just by way of a little consolation for I am sure we have enough and I am by no means ambitious for a large family.' A few years later she would increase the total to five, all of them boys except Eliza, her mother's special love. 'Dearest Lizzy is blooming like the roses in the midst of which she lives, sweet happy baby. God preserve her to me; she is the happiness of my life; my heart is wrapt in her.' Evidently Tom, the oldest boy, was his father's favourite, and it may be that this was a subject of banter between the parents for Kitty next defended her daughter, saying, 'You need not fear her being spoiled, no no, my dearest Ever. I have suffered too much from over indulgence and I will profit by my dear bought expense.' She then added waggishly, 'I hope my dearest Ever while we are on the subject of spoiling, *you will* not be too indulgent to Tom.'

As for the objectionable ball, Kitty was rather gratified by its success, though she informed her husband of this in muted tones. 'I think the dance went off very well. Many came and many did not.' She had enjoyed little opportunity to enjoy the social life to which her husband's rank would have entitled her had she not married him on the eve of his disgrace. It was Castlereagh who had risen in the House of Commons to announce that he would be spared the pillory sentence; Castlereagh had cut his own throat in 1822, and now Kitty was enjoying the pleasure of entertaining his son in Paris and feeling that she was accepted as one should be who could sign herself 'K. Cochrane Maranhão'.

'You do not know how over polite Lord Londonderry was to me. I am sure if I were in London and could afford to live, and in any style give these big wigs a few dinners and a little flattery I might accomplish a great deal.' But alas, the prosperity she dreamed of was to remain a fiction of her husband's enemies. When Cochrane replied that they would probably have to remain in exile, Kitty replied on 19 May: 'As to our living abroad, it will be no punishment to us. We are much better treated from our own country than ever we have been in it.' She was in one of her bright, optimistic moods, looking forward to the day when she and her husband 'will be better able to feast the powerful and we shall be thought the nicest people in the world'. They were in financial difficulties again but 'everything will change for the better, I know'. It was partly that Paris had proved to be the city of her choice, a preference sharpened perhaps by the brief, lonely visit which she had paid to London during the previous November—not the most attractive month in the English metropolis.

'I hate London so very much and here I like and am liked, but all these are very minor considerations when put in competition to my affection and duty towards you.' She wanted to fly to him, she said, but unlike Chile, Peru or Brazil, Greece was not a suitable country for her to visit, with or without the children. 'I am content with the blessings God has been pleased to grant,' she wrote with resignation, 'without wishing for more. Yet I cannot help *informing you* that I am *not stone* and the sooner I find my little head on your bosom the sooner I shall be content. Do not however let the little wish alarm you, or believe that if I were a widow as many years as I have been days, that I should seek consolation elsewhere. You know, my Ever, nature will be nature and I am human and you know that little secret.'

While Kitty sought to amuse herself in Paris without allowing her husband's absence, his moods or his difficulties to depress her spirits, Cochrane himself suffered another bitter blow in Greece. In the aftermath of the battle of Navarino Captain Hastings had pursued the objectives agreed by the Admiral and General of Greece with the greatest devotion to duty. But gradually he became as disgusted with the negligence of the Greek administration as Cochrane himself, until he handed in his resignation. In May however he was persuaded to resume his operations in western Greece, and it was in the course of them that he was wounded in action aboard the *Karteria* on the 25th. The amputation of his left arm was considered necessary, and so his vessel steamed to the island of Zante where there was a surgeon competent to perform the operation. But on the journey Hastings developed tetanus and died in his ship. He was 34 years old, the most successful pioneer of warfare in a steam vessel in the records of the senior service, the hero of his friend George Finlay's history of the cause which he enobled. His loss to Cochrane was irreparable.

During 1828 the Turkish and Egyptian forces were evacuated from the Peloponnese, since the destruction of Turkey's maritime power had rendered these Greek territories untenable, and both Church and Fabvier pursued independently a policy of adding as much territory as possible to a free Greece. At least Cochrane could endeavour to ensure that her navy would be the first in the world to be founded upon a fleet of steamships. One day, perhaps, the Greeks would train disciplined crews to man them. Meanwhile, when he heard that a third steamship was ready for delivery he sailed to Marseilles to await her arrival. From there he wrote to Kitty on 4 September in a mood that was becoming ever more familiar to her. Bravely she did her best to soothe him: 'I regret to see that you are still in the same uneasy state of mind. Do not, my dear Cochrane, fancy such nonsense. Why are we not to be happy, at least why not as much as we have ever been? I cannot understand your state of mind or feeling; what can you dread? There is no fighting now in Greece. You surely cannot be well or such vile blue devils would not hold you so tight.' Of course she was right: her husband's condition was becoming manic. 'I would strongly advise you to look on the bright side and leave that sad train of thoughts,' she urged him. 'Try reading, writing, walking, in fact try anything but thinking. Give your poor head a holiday. You will addle your brains and you will look so old. Do not, my Ever, fidget. Your life is made miserable by such melancholy thoughts.' Katherine Cochrane Maranhão was certainly trying to do her best.

The steamship reached Marseilles in September and Cochrane sailed in her to Greece where she was named the *Hermes*. He donated £2000 of his own money in an attempt to speed the construction of a fourth, and she too reached Greece by the end of 1828. But by that time Cochrane had resigned his command, and there was no one to secure the completion of the remaining two steamships which had been ordered, so that they were left to rot in the Thames.

But now there were four steamships, even though there was no longer a Hastings to command any of them, and the excellent frigate *Hellas* and the brig *Sauveur*, to which Cochrane added as a gift his only two prizes, at the same time waiving the remaining £20,000 owed to him on completion of his service in a final gesture of generosity that he could ill afford. On 15 December he wrote to Louis-André Gosse, the Swiss philanthropist on the Greek commission who had promoted the equipment of the brig *Sauveur* when he was still waiting to command a fleet in Greek waters. 'Glad shall I be,' he said bitterly, 'when the tops of these mountains sink beneath the horizon, and when new and agreeable objects shall obliterate the names of Mavrogordato, Tombazi and such double dealing knaves from my recollection.' Five days later he struck his flag and wrote to Gosse: 'Thank God we are both clear of a country in which there is no hope of amelioration for half a century to come.'

George Finlay knew Greece better than Cochrane did and had suffered comparable disillusion, yet he bought an estate in Attica and remained in the land for which his friend Hastings had given his life, for the rest of his days. 'I lost my money and my labour,' he confessed, 'but I learned how the system of tenths has produced a society, and habits of cultivation, against which one man can do nothing. When I had wasted as much money as I possessed, I turned my attention to study.' Thomas Gordon too returned and built himself a house in Argos, after which he divided the remainder of his life between Scotland and Greece, where he held a succession of military appointments. But Cochrane had been no William Miller in Peru, no Grenfell in Brazil, and his attitude was equally different from that of his fellow Scots in Greece.

So, oft it chances in particular men . . .

Cochrane was now 53 years old and in his last supreme command he had outlived the legend which he created. But his very despondency helped to inspire him with the mania that was to obsess him for the remaining 30 years of his life.

His leave-taking contained the paradoxes of many an earlier one. Capo d'Istria thanked Cochrane for his services in handsome terms, but when he requested transport to carry him from the country, having donated his own vessels to the government, a miserable brig was placed at his disposal, commanded by one of the ruffians of the Alexandria expedition and manned by an insolent crew. It would have been impossible for Cochrane to have entrusted himself to such men, but his protest to President Capo d'Istria was cut short by the Russian Admiral Heiden. 'I am certain,' he wrote, 'that Lord Cochrane must have suffered greatly from the treatment to which he has been exposed. In proof of my esteem I beg that he will send back to their kennels the miserable causes of his annoyance and proceed to Malta, or to Zante if he wishes, in one of my corvettes, taking with him as large a suite as he likes. It cannot be too numerous. As regards his salute, I will receive him with the honours due to his rank, and with musical honours, and at his departure I will man yards.'

At Malta Cochrane was greeted by Admiral Sir Pultney Malcolm who had served with him in Aix Roads and spoken in his favour at the trial of Lord Gambier. Malcolm forwarded him with equal respect in a British warship to Naples, whence the Sea Wolf made the journey overland to be reunited with his wife in Paris.

CHAPTER FOURTEEN

Home from Sea

Just as he had been invited to Brazil before he had left the Chilean service, and to Greece before he had resigned from his command in Brazil, another urgent summons was on its way to the Sea Wolf long before he turned his back on the Aegean. As soon as the news of his visit to England in the new year of 1828 reached Rio de Janeiro, Captain Grenfell wrote to him from there: 'My dear Lord, we have just received the news of your return to England from Greece, and I cannot resist the inclination I feel to avail myself of the opportunity afforded by the departure of HMS *Ranger*, to offer you my best respects, and best wishes for your welfare.' He told Cochrane that he had written to him twice since he had last heard from his former Admiral in 1825, and suspected that their letters had been going astray; that he had visited England at the time of Lady Cochrane's brief return to London in the November of 1827, but 'did not hear of her ladyship's arrival in England until after her departure'.

However, the first two pages of Grenfell's letter were only a preamble to the invitation which it is clear that he was inspired by the Emperor Pedro to send without a day's delay. 'I am now awaiting the arrival of a corvette of 28 long 18 pounders, and *12 feet* draught of water, to the command of which the Emperor has appointed me: and in which I am in great hopes of doing something as she has the credit of being a very fast vessel. We have now a far finer squadron *as to ships* than when your lordship was here, and there are plenty of men to be had, but *we have no commanders*. I think if your lordship *would*, they would be glad to arrange with you, *with a handsome income, to rehoist your flag*. But the secret is this. *The Emperor wants an Independent Force on whom he can depend, let whatever party be in power, and with the Emperor alone your lordship should treat*. Your lordship will excuse the liberty I am taking, and if I am presuming in thus addressing you, I think you will set it down to the regard I still bear my late Noble Chief, and my desire to see him at our head. Adieu my dear Lord, and believe me to be with the greatest respect and gratitude your faithful friend and servant.'

But it was not the Cochrane of the old brave days who read that appeal. It was a man who could write: 'The mental fever I contracted in Greece has not yet subsided, nor will it probably for some months to come.' The blow of his brother Archibald's death on 6 August 1829 distressed him further. They had served in the navy together in their earliest days, and Cochrane had once suggested that Archibald might find a career in South America after he had retired with the rank of Captain. Archibald was not the first of his immediate family to die: his hospitable Uncle Basil had expired in 1826, leaving his illegitimate children to fight for his inheritance. But Archibald was the first casualty of Cochrane's own generation and he left a widow with young children to rear.

Sometime during that year, exactly when is uncertain, another appalling event occurred. Kitty suffered what her husband was to describe nearly 30 years later as 'dreadful puerperal convulsions' and a month later she was delivered of a full-grown dead child. The immediate effect on her can only be gauged by the fact that Cochrane was still attributing his wife's condition to this accident so long afterwards. In the circumstances it is hardly surprising that he did not respond to the invitation transmitted through his former companion-in-arms from the Emperor whose character was so akin to his own. For 6 months he drifted about without employment, without even returning to settle in his own country.

Officially he was still an outlaw from it, but the growing literature of his past career must have been as balm to his injured spirits. To the panegyric of Maria Graham and the sound, informative narrative of William Stevenson there had been added the account of John Miers the merchant, and the memoirs of William Miller followed in 1828, while in 1829 there appeared *Frank Mildmay*, the first of those novels in which Frederick Marryat immortalised Cochrane in the heroic days of the *Impérieuse*. The avidity with which all these books were read is illustrated by the request which Miller sent to him on 29 April 1829, that he should correct a new edition of his memoirs before its publication. 'You will find the second edition less surcharged with defects, but as there is still something wanting in many places to fill up the outline, I trust you will do me the favour to mark such inaccuracies or oversights as strike you in the perusal, and let me have the benefit of your criticisms in order to purify the narrative of blemishes as far as is possible. You will perceive that we do not shrink from speaking out, and I think you will give us credit for the wish to render the book conformable to what rigorous historical justice demands.' The gallant Major of Marines had never shrunk from anything, and from speaking out the hero of his narrative had never shrunk either. This was a request that Cochrane could accept, that possessed a greater therapeutic value than Miller could possibly have understood, reminding Cochrane as it did of the years in which he had still held destiny by a tight rein.

Miller wrote from London, but he told the man whom he addressed as 'an old shipmate' that he contemplated returning to Peru. 'Let me have the pleasure of hearing from you once more before I start, for I still think of returning, and I suppose I shall one day be as good as my word. But whether I go or remain be assured that you have my sincerest wishes for your welfare, and that not one of your many kind offices is unremembered.' All the people who expressed the deepest feelings for Cochrane, apart from two women and the members of his family, were men's men, and there is much to be read into the reticent phrases with which these were committed to paper.

Gordon and Finlay would remain in Greece, Miller in Peru, Grenfell in Brazil: where would the restless Cochrane find rest? On 25 June 1830 King George IV died, presaging the downfall of the long-entrenched Tory administration which depended finally on the great Duke of Wellington for its survival. Cochrane took his wife on a tour of Italy at this time, and it was in Florence that Charles Greville, that penetrating judge of men, encountered them. 'It is a pity he ever got into a scrape,' Greville observed. 'He is such a fine fellow, and so shrewd and good-humoured.' Evidently his old spirits were returning, stimulated by the prospect of change at home. Greville told him that 'I thought things would explode in England, which he concurred in, and seemed to like the idea of it; in which we differ, owing probably to the difference in our positions. He has nothing, and I everything, to lose by such an event.' Greville the sinecurist need not have worried, for men of all parties thought well of him and he earned no less a compliment than that he was 'always most a friend when friendship was most wanted'. Such people rarely lack friends themselves.

When Wellington's administration finally crashed in December 1830, it marked the opening of a new era for Cochrane, one in which his friend Brougham would become Lord Chancellor, and Samuel Whitbread's brother-in-law, Grey, Prime Minister, while the reforms for which Cochrane had fought at Westminster so long ago would sweep through Parliament despite the opposition of the Duke.

Cochrane's recovery from his prolonged nervous breakdown was manifested by brilliant mechanical invention. During the years since his disgrace and exile the most talented exponent of ideas resembling his had been a farmer's son from Normandy named Marc Isambard Brunel.

In 1814 Brunel had received treatment from the Admiralty which resembled Cochrane's. It had accepted Brunel's offer to demonstrate the utility of steam tugs for towing warships, promised to contribute towards the cost; then they condemned the idea as 'too chimerical to be seriously entertained' and left him to foot the bill. Brunel turned his attention to tunnelling, for which he drew up a patent in 1818, and when Cochrane returned from Brazil he had begun his attempt to bore a tunnel under the Thames between Wapping and Rotherhithe. By the time Cochrane left Greece, operations had been discontinued after the river had broken through the roof of the tunnel for the second time. With astonishing insight, Cochrane detected the weakness in Brunel's patented apparatus, 'a circular shield worked under ordinary atmospheric pressure'. As *The Times* explained, 'when Brunel was in difficulties from the influx of mud, a no less eminent inventor, Lord Cochrane, at once saw that compressed air afforded the remedy, and the compressed air arrangements at Blackwall are covered by Cochrane's patent of 1830'. This was written as long after Cochrane's death as 1894 when the Blackwall tunnel had been completed, and *The Times* proposed: 'It would be a graceful act on the part of the London County Council if medallion portraits of Brunel and Cochrane respectively were placed at each entrance of the Tunnel'.

Meanwhile Cochrane's invention had been used successfully to tunnel under the Hudson river in the United States, and when the Blackwall tunnel was opened, its Chief Engineer stated that both owed their existence to his discovery. 'The suggestion of using air pressure in tunnelling was due to Admiral Lord Cochrane . . . who in 1830 drew up a most complete patent embodying his ideas. It was first used by Mr Hoskin in the Hudson Tunnel in America.' Although Cochrane did not live to see the triumph of his 'Apparatus for Excavating, Sinking and Mining' or derive a penny's profit from it, this could not diminish his present well-being as he and Kitty settled at last in their own country.

His new-found vitality prompted him to re-enter politics. It would be hazardous to venture an analysis of his motives, whether these were based primarily on a desire to be in at the kill, now that the old order was to be swept away at last in spite of the Duke of Wellington, or whether personal redress was what he had most in mind. He was invited to stand by the electors of Southwark, and the immediate obstacle which led to his withdrawal was the discovery that Lord Chancellor Brougham's brother was also a candidate. It was as well that his natural generosity and loyalty to an old friend should have influenced him to do this, for his father died on 1 July 1831. Under the treaty of union concluded between Scotland and England in 1707, Scottish peers did not enjoy the same right as English lords to sit in the upper House, but could merely elect sixteen of their number to do so, an arrangement only recently abolished. At the same time Scottish peers were barred from sitting in the House of Commons, unlike Irish peers, so that Cochrane found a political career closed to him now that he was the tenth Earl of Dundonald, since he could hardly expect to be elected among the representative peers of a country with which his personal and family connections had for so long been severed.

An obituary of the ninth Earl began: 'It is impossible to contemplate the life of the noble subject of this memoir without pain. Like many other celebrated men, he greatly contributed to the progress of useful knowledge, and the benefit of his country, without the slightest advantage to himself. Indeed, he wholly expended his private fortune in speculations which have proved profitable only to others; and devoted to the public that time and those talents which, if they had been bestowed, or even partially bestowed, upon the management and improvement of his own estate, would have rendered him as opulent as he actually became necessitous.' He had died in Paris, and his heir learned the news at his new home, Hanover Lodge in Regent's Park. Invested with the prestige of his inherited earldom, restored to fighting fitness, settled at last in a London mansion of his own with his Countess, Cochrane was poised for his long, last battle.

There were four wrongs to be righted: he had been outlawed by the Foreign Enlistment Act; convicted of a criminal offence by the verdict of 1814; struck off the Navy List; and stripped of the Order of the Bath. During his Greek service he had made a submission to the government and it had been rejected. 'I apprehend,' said the second Viscount Melville, First Lord of the Admiralty, 'that nothing but a free pardon from the Crown can now do away with the effect of the verdict.' Melville lost his office with Wellington after King George IV's death, and so did John Croker, the Secretary to the Admiralty. This occupant of rotten boroughs swore that he would never sit in a reformed House of Commons and he never did. The establishment against which Cochrane had pitted his might in vain was in the process of dissolution when he came home from sea.

But the year 1831 was a critical one for Earl Grey, the new Prime Minister, as he faced the task of forcing his Reform Bill through the House of Lords. When Sir Francis Burdett wrote to him on Cochrane's behalf he replied: 'You may be assured that I have this matter at heart; but I am very unwilling to have it brought into public notice at a moment when the bitter and hostile spirit which prevails in the party most opposed to the Government would be likely to seize upon it as a good question for annoyance.' In the eyes of Grey, Cochrane might still raise a whirlwind.

Kitty, meanwhile, saw her elevation to the rank of Countess as a golden opportunity to exercise the influence she had dreamed of exerting when the Marquess of Londonderry had eaten out of her hand in Paris. She obtained an interview with King William at Brighton, where she implored him to intervene on her husband's behalf. William IV had his own problems by this time, since Grey's cabinet had decided that the only way to secure the passage of the Reform Bill through the House of Lords and thus avert revolution was to ask the King to create a sufficient number of peers to provide a majority in its favour. Yet it was precisely while he was enduring agonies of indecision over this request that he accepted the Countess of Dundonald's prayers. The Earl was a sailor, the Countess still young and beautiful; but above all, the King was being asked to exercise the royal prerogative in a case of almost sublime simplicity compared with that of swamping the House of Lords with peers in order to plant a revolutionary measure on the statute book. On 2 May 1832 the royal pardon was formally recorded by the Privy Council and Cochrane's name was consequently restored to the Navy List on the same day.

On 9 May, having held the rank of Admiral in Chile, Brazil and Greece, and been offered it in Peru, Cochrane attended his first royal levée as Rear Admiral Dundonald in the Royal Navy of the United Kingdom. On that very day King William rejected Grey's request to create peers in support of his measure of Parliamentary reform, and accepted the resignation of his government. Was it not enough for one day to have received the arch-radical into the bosom of the establishment? Cochrane arrived only just in time to maintain a continuity of his name in the office he held. In the following month Admiral Sir Alexander Cochrane died, after witnessing the belated triumph of the nephew whose career he had promoted, sometimes not wisely but too well.

King William hoped that the Duke of Wellington would be able to extricate him from his difficulties, but the Duke failed and William was forced to accept Grey's terms. Brougham even compelled him to give his undertaking in writing; and thus the measure for which Cochrane had fought as Member for Westminster, and recommended to the House of Commons in his farewell speech, passed into law at the very moment of his own reinstatement.

It was an ominous day for the Admiralty when the news of Cochrane's promotion was announced there. For although the long reign of Lord Melville and John Croker was over, its corridors were still the warrens in which bureaucrats scuttled and intrigued as they laid out its amenities for their own ease and profit. They had already embarked on their last-ditch defence of sail against steam, and as they mounted their stand, in favour of wooden ships against metal ones, of canvas against paddle wheels, of paddle wheels against screw propellers, they were faced at each redoubt by the awful figure of the man they thought they had destroyed—no querulous ghost, but an Admiral of flesh and blood.

One of Cochrane's principal preoccupations at this time, however, was his new home, the last in which he would ever attempt to settle with Kitty. It was evidently before his succession to the earldom that he had drawn up a memorandum showing how they would be able to live at Hanover Lodge at an expense of under £4000 a year, and it reveals that the fortune which he was suspected of having extracted from the countries he had served was a chimera. For he was forced to borrow and pay interest on the purchase price of the property while he waited for Chile and Brazil to honour their obligations to him.

Price of the house	£12,000	interest at 4%	£480	
Value of ground	£5,000		£200	
Ditto of taxes	£2,000		£80	
			£760	£760
Lady Cochrane's private expenses			£365	
Ditto of Lord Cochrane			£135	
Tom and Horace			£400	
			£900	£900
Household bills including coals and oil			£960	
Wine			£180	
Three menservants' wages			£120	
Lady Cochrane's maid and cook			£60	
Nursery maid, housemaid and scullerymaid			£60	
Governess			£60	
			£1,440	£1,440
Doctors' and Apothecaries' bills			£100	
Washing			£120	
Small items and expenses			£200	
Riding horses			£120	
Carriage horses			£240	
Repairs of carriages			£80	
			£860	£860
				£3,960

The total allowed nothing for 'travelling and amusements at home and abroad', an item for which he provided no estimate. But the list reveals Cochrane's determination to provide a home at last in which Kitty would be able to live in security and a degree of style. From the outset he was absent for much of the time, living at Weston Grove near Southampton where he conducted his latest experiments. From Hanover Lodge his agent John Hill sent him frequent reports on the progress of the improvements he had ordered for his new home. On 25 July 1822 Hill wrote about the final work of putting lead on the roof, completing the plastering inside and the external cementing. The Countess was on the spot, making suggestions, and Hill hoped that Cochrane would return soon 'as there are many minor things touching the finishing of the stables etc., as also the floor, water and roof of the addition to the house'.

He had already sent Cochrane a plan showing the relationship between the lodge, stables, and dwelling house and coach houses, with the roads linking them. The complex lay within the orbit of the buildings which Nash had designed to run from the park to Piccadilly, and by September Hill was informing Cochrane: 'The commissioners had referred the consideration of your lordship's intention in building the wing now in progress to Mr Nash, and to which there could be no possible objection: and from the explanation I gave him he said that he should report to them most favourably today.' Hill submitted his accounts in November 1832, from which it may be concluded that the improvements had been completed by then.

Now at last Kitty could play the part in British society that had been denied her so long, and in the following summer the press was able to report her triumph. 'The *fête champêtre* at Hanover lodge in the Regent's park on Saturday last, given by the Countess of Dundonald, is another proof how much this species of entertainment wins its way in the fashionable world. It [the house and grounds] unites, to a delightful situation, all the beauties of nature and art combined, surrounded by gardens, wherein are the most beautiful promenades. The interior of the villa is adorned with groups of the most classic busts and statues, both ancient and modern: added to which are paintings by the first masters of the gallant Admiral's achievements, by sea and land. The visitants began to arrive at three o'clock; at the hour of six the *déjeuner à la fourchette* commenced in a noble temporary room, communicating with a beautiful corridor or gallery; at eight o'clock dancing commenced: at nine the grounds were really an *illuminated garden*;—the effect was magical, and produced by an infinity of variegated lamps. All were delighted with the graceful manners of the accomplished hostess and her amiable daughters. The party did not break up until midnight.'

In fact the Countess possessed only her single daughter Lizzie who, being no older than about 15 at this time, may have been sent to her bed before the gaieties were over. Of the younger children, the 9-year-old Arthur was away at school in Winchester, from where he wrote to his mother in September asking for warmer clothes. Little Ernest, the youngest of all, must have been tucked up in bed. Cochrane's eldest son Tom was now in his twentieth year and like his younger brother Horace was being groomed for the army, supported by the handsome allowance that their father listed amongst his expenses. There is no evidence whether these two young men were present at the *fête champêtre* beside their 35-year-old mother, already sensitive about her grown-up children. But it is evident from the report that Cochrane himself was not present to act as host to the Prince of Canino, the Duke and Duchess of Padua, the Duke of Hamilton, the Marquess and Marchioness of Lansdowne, ten Earls and as many Countesses, peers and knights innumerable and what appears to have been most of the rest of London society. Recalling his reaction to the news of Kitty's ball in Paris, one can only speculate upon his attitude to this extravaganza, listed in his memorandum of living expenses as 'amusements at home' without any figure placed against the item. Such junketings had never belonged to his notions of domestic or social life, and the only question is whether he willingly indulged his wife's tastes on this occasion.

Cochrane's own enthusiasm during this year was the harnessing of the power of steam under pressure. It was natural that he and Marc Brunel, who had both suffered from Admiralty obtuseness and each attempted to solve the problems of tunnelling, should have sought one another's acquaintance, and this soon flowered into active collaboration. Brunel's letters to Cochrane commented on the unreliability of the locomotive engines that were being manufactured at this time, and on 17 May 1833 he wrote: 'My Lord, I propose making a Report to the Admiralty on the performance of Tuesday last; but without a certainty as to the consumption of coals to produce an effect I cannot satisfy their Lordships. If you have, as I understand you have, a pumping apparatus moved by a similar machine, I can ascertain by that means, and with the greatest precision, the effect produced by a given quantity of coals. Let me know, if you please, when you may be prepared to make the experiment in question, that we may come to a conclusion on the most important point which is the consumption of coals; or otherwise the effect produced independent of loss by friction.'

Back came the desired information in a matter of days, and in

addition to the use of his invention in tunnelling and in ships, Cochrane
now explored whether it might also be of service to the railways. On 26
May Brunel informed him that his report had been submitted to the
Admiralty and added: 'With respect to Locomotive Engines for land
use, considering the rapid deterioration of those engines that are now in
use, I think that yours would be a valuable agent, the more particularly
so as it may be relieved by springs of the jarring which so soon affects
the others.' He suggested that Cochrane would probably hear further
from the Admiralty on the subject of their proposals, and wrote crossly
on 29 May: 'My Lord, I have had no answer from the Admiralty about
further experiments which I have suggested should be carried on a
larger scale . . .' It was what both men might have expected.

This correspondence opens the door on the last service which
Cochrane performed for the British Navy. It may not appear so spectacular as his feats of war in the *Speedy* and the *Impérieuse*, but it played a
fundamental part in maintaining his country's naval supremacy for
another century when it might otherwise have been lost. 'Their Lordships,' announced Melville in his office as First Lord, at the time when
the *Karteria* was showing her capabilities in Greek waters, 'feel it their
bounden duty to discourage to the utmost of their ability the employment of steam vessels, as they consider that the introduction of steam
is calculated to strike a fatal blow to the naval supremacy of the
Empire.' By 1824 the First Lord, in a reformed Parliament, could say
to Cochrane: 'It is impossible to over-estimate the paramount importance of steam in future naval operations and it is fortunate that you
have directed so much of your attention to the subject.' What Sir James
Graham might also have recalled was that it was Cochrane who had
for years been trying to direct other people's attention to the subject.
In this year of 1834 he brought out one of the earliest rotary engines
and published a pamphlet to explain its advantages over earlier types,
which was supported by the contemporary verdict that it was 'the most
perfect engine of the class that has yet been projected'.

It was a form of steam turbine, which he had already used to operate
a circular saw and to propel his boat on the Thames, where her engineer
started racing another craft on the river until her boilers exploded. As
in the case of the *Karteria*, the problem was that the boilers of those times
were not strong enough to withstand a high pressure of steam, and it
was only a matter of time before Cochrane would turn his powers of
invention to the correction of this defect. Meanwhile some locomotive
engineers and directors of the Liverpool and Manchester Railway
became interested in his experiments, and they came to London to
examine his model, in all probability when it was installed in the steam-

boat. For the railway engine which the Stephensons had constructed in 1825 was not without its faults, and in particular Cochrane claimed that his rotary engine would operate more smoothly—a claim which Brunel supported.

After their initial survey the directors of the Liverpool and Manchester Railway offered to lend Cochrane Stephenson's *Rocket*, which had by this time broken down and been withdrawn from service, and to pay £30 towards the cost of converting it to his form of locomotion. When the trials were held in October 1834 George Stephenson did not attend them, but gave his opinion that Cochrane's invention would not work. Certainly they proved too inconclusive to convince the railway directors, so Cochrane removed his apparatus from the *Rocket* and transported it back to London, where he succeeded in arousing greater enthusiasm in the directors of the London and Greenwich Railway Company. Its line passed over a high viaduct, which gave added importance to a smooth-running engine 'freeing the locomotive carriages from the alternating push and pull of common engines (so dangerous by the breaking of cranks and destructive to the wheels and machinery)'. Cochrane claimed to have found the 'means of preventing the oscillating and rocking motions (so disagreeable to passengers) and to remove the double cause of the splitting and breaking of rails, and tottering of their supports—(which oscillating, rocking and tottering would occasion rapid disjunction of the upper strata of the Viaduct, and insupportable noise in the arches below)'.

The directors of the London and Greenwich Railway wrote to Cochrane on 5 December, offering to build two of his rotary engines at their own expense, and as he approached his fifty-ninth birthday he had the satisfaction of replying to George Walter, the Company secretary: 'As the Revolving Engine is patented, and as I have no motive whatsoever to abstain from permitting a full examination of its powers and properties, the Proprietors of the Greenwich railway are at liberty to construct, or cause to be constructed, the pair of Engines, and to apply them to any locomotive or other purpose they shall judge proper—paying as an acknowledgment one farthing to me.' He did emphasise at this early stage, however, that the introduction of his engine would involve certain improvements and modifications to the carriages, the braking system, and even the track; and since George Walter undertook the management of Cochrane's patent a few months later, in which they were specified, he knew what these were. 'I consider that the engines, however useful their properties, especially on your elevated viaduct, are a minor consideration unless united to the advantages which the company would ensure by putting in practice the suggestions I have confidentially made to Colonel Landmann and to you.' Landmann was a civil engineer.

On 24 June 1835 the first locomotive driven by rotary engines was put through its trials on the track of the London and Greenwich Railway in the presence of Cochrane, Walter, Landmann and several of the company's directors. They were sufficiently satisfied to order the construction of another and to pay £100 for each one that was built. By this time Cochrane had spent the colossal sum of £4000 on his invention, but at last there was the hope that his losses would be converted into gain.

The trials did not include carriages of Cochrane's new design, perhaps because W. J. Curtis, their builder in Deptford, had written to George Walter on 3 June, expressing his disapproval. 'The Earl of Dundonald this morning laid before me plans of alterations in the carriages, which are at present in hand at the works: viz a roller before each wheel on the principal of my brake, and a method of hanging the frame from the axle of the wheel by a link, instead of suspending them from the springs, as I have already done those upon the line. I am decidedly of opinion that the adoption of either of these plans will be highly prejudicial to the carriages as, in the case of the roller, the wheel axle breaking the advantage of the frame becoming a drag is entirely lost or the wheel quitting the rail the roller affords no additional security, whereas the stoppers and joggles which I have long since proposed fixing to the frame effectually and at a trifling cost meets the case exactly . . .' After more of this breathless, unpunctuated censure of the noble interloper who had invaded his pitch, W. J. Curtis informed the secretary to the Railway Company that he could not carry out Cochrane's instructions 'as I cannot consent to incur a responsibility which would charge me with the consequences of any accident which might happen'. Walter sent these comments to Cochrane and, undeterred, they arranged to have the carriages modified elsewhere.

The new locomotive worked well at first despite Stephenson's cheerful forecast that it would be incapable of pulling even empty carriages. But gradually, like all the other engines designed during this experimental period, it developed defects which culminated in a complete breakdown towards the end of 1835. With undiminished confidence the railway directors ordered the construction of a new one, while Cochrane held discussions with Walter, the company secretary, and Landmann, the engineer, on possible improvements. Cochrane wrote to Walter on 3 March 1836, sending 'my sanction to your lowering the centre of gravity of the train carriages according to the plan I suggested confidentially to Col. Landmann and to you'; and he suggested, 'I think you should also try the Drag for stopping the locomotive trains which I likewise described to you;—for, on your elevated viaduct, the arresting of the trains suddenly may at times be highly important.' In order to protect the fruits of his invention he added: 'Of course, the permission to try my plans does not imply my sanction to use them, except under an arrangement; which I shall be glad to render amply conducive to the interests of the proprietors of the viaduct.'

When he had heard nothing for 3 months concerning the progress of his proposals, Cochrane wrote to Walter at the end of May: 'I shall be obliged if you will inform me of the result of any trials you may have made on lowering the centre of gravity, from which I expect considerable benefit must result; and also if you approve of my means of arresting the trains, by transferring the moving weight from revolving wheels to sledges.' A few days later he travelled from Hanover Lodge to examine the work which was being carried out on the carriages and found that it was not being 'executed by your engineer quite in the manner best adapted to attain all the objects contemplated in my Patent'. However, he remained good-natured as he expressed the hope that the alterations to the carriages would soon be completed correctly and would satisfy the directors at their trials.

The reply which he received to this letter brought these friendly relations to an abrupt end and precipitated a bitter dispute over Cochrane's rights in the brakes and carriages which added the expenses of a lawsuit to those which his experiments had already cost him. 'Lord Dundonald,' he wrote formally from Hanover Lodge on 9 June 1836, 'presents his respects to Mr Walter, and begs to say that he cannot receive any explanation verbally regarding the contents of the extraordinary letter to which his name is affixed as Secretary to the London and Greenwich Railway Company: and he assures Mr Walter that it will be with the greatest reluctance if he is compelled to resort to measures which will introduce his name as in any way coupled with an attempt, on the part of the Board of Proprietors, to do that which Lord Dundonald will leave the Public to describe by an appropriate appellation.'

While this quarrel gathered momentum, work continued at Seaward's factory in Limehouse on Cochrane's new rotary engines. Brunel had just resumed work on his tunnel beneath the Thames, and had written to Cochrane in April 1836: 'My Lord, I have been to Mr Seaward to view the rotary engine of your invention, which I am ready to put to a fair trial and in the most conspicuous place of our platform at the Tunnel. If your Lordship concurs in the arrangement I shall immediately make such dispositions as will demonstrate its power as a high pressure engine. Our engine works at 40 to 45th pressure; consequently the present boiler or one of them will do very well.' By this time Brunel's son Isambard was already 30 years old, and he gave his father the greatest assistance in solving the problems (including three more eruptions of the river into the tunnel) before it was completed in 1843. It was naturally in such a service as this that Cochrane's rotary engine could operate most effectively, since the size and weight of the boiler presented no problem when it stood at the entrance to a tunnel, as they did when it had to be mounted on a locomotive engine.

This, and not the dispute between Cochrane and the Railway Company, was the cause of the final breakdown in his current experiments. He wrote to Walter on 5 September: 'I have delayed answering your note of the 19th August (requesting an interview) until my attorney had completed the documents, and arranged the evidence to compel those who would unjustly wrest from me the fruits of years' consideration devoted to the subject of locomotion, the purport of which I had confidentially communicated to you. These documents being ready to be laid before the Lord Chancellor, I once more offer to the Greenwich Railway Company a licence to use my Patent Improvements in "Machinery and apparatus applicable to locomotion" on terms to be agreed on . . .' Ten days later, Cochrane was informed that the 'engine constructed under the directions of your Lordship is now ready for delivery', although it was not until November that it reached the railway for its trials. Here it was found that the boiler lay so low as to foul the track, and the engine could not pass the first set of points. In fact it required the deep trench between the tracks which had been specified in the patent.

Nothing was done to rectify this fault. The engine was towed back to Deptford works while 1837 was spent in the lawsuit which added further to the costs of Cochrane's invention. When it had ended with profit to nobody except the lawyers, his engine was broken up in October 1838, and so ended his ruinous association with railways. On a more disastrous scale than ever before it had repeated his father's record as an inventor.

Cochrane now drew a British Admiral's pay, though he had not been granted the arrears that would be due to him if it were conceded that he had been removed unjustly from the Navy List in 1814. However, it was not merely in the expectation of such amends as these that he had incurred the expense of establishing himself at Hanover Lodge. Ten years had elapsed since he had left South America, and during that time he might reasonably have expected to receive the payments due to him under precise and solemn contracts, especially in view of his stupendous services, services for which scarcely any reward would have been adequate. But of the sums owed to him in Chile he had received not a penny while his unrealised assets in Brazil were jeopardised by the premature death of the Emperor. Pedro had handed the Brazilian throne to his son in 1831 and had travelled to Europe to place his daughter on the throne of Portugal. Had Cochrane accepted Grenfell's invitation, he would have been presented with an opportunity to win the only fleet action of his career, though his engagement would probably have been terminated when Pedro succumbed to tuberculosis at the age of 36 in 1834.

In Greece the first President of the independent Republic, Capo d'Istria, had been murdered in 1831 and Prince Otto, son of the King of Bavaria, had accepted an invitation to establish a monarchy there. In 1833 King Otto made amends for the shabby circumstances of Cochrane's departure by investing him with the Greek Order of the Saviour, which he was given formal permission to wear at the British court in 1835. The honour was augmented when the former Admiral of Greece was raised to a higher rank in the Order in 1837, but in his present circumstances Cochrane may well have regretted that he had waived the £20,000 due to him under the terms of his engagement. All would have been well, however, if Cochrane's scientific experiments had proved to be a source of profit rather than of gigantic loss.

His second account of annual expenses for Hanover Lodge shows a reduction from £3960 to £3153, and the third is only slightly larger, £3455. Perhaps it is significant that his next account (the last which he kept in this way) totals £9235 for two years, including £1500 described as 'Lady Dundonald's subsidy'. Whatever had been going on during those years in which Cochrane had been so preoccupied with his railway engines and carriages, the expenses of his home had increased greatly, while his wife's allowance had almost trebled.

But by this time a source of financial worry had arisen of a far more alarming nature. Cochrane evidently had no suspicion of it when he wrote to his wife at Tunbridge Wells where she was staying in April 1835, saying that he expected complete success in the trials of his engine, and adding that Horace would be joining her for two days' leave. 'He has obtained an excellent character at Sandhurst, and I have no doubt will do well through life.'

Since Cochrane had inherited the earldom of Dundonald he and his entire family had naturally addressed his eldest son by the courtesy title of Lord Cochrane which he had himself formerly enjoyed. But inasmuch as the Admiral has been known throughout the world from that day to this by the name which he immortalised, it would be improper to deprive him of it in favour of his namesake-son, although it is that son who is referred to henceforth as Cochrane in the family correspondence. That son, and his brother Horace, had been deprived throughout their formative years of any settled home, and of the influence of their father's constant presence. For them, the attempt to establish a permanent home at Hanover Lodge came too late to be effective, and by 1836 Cochrane became aware of the serious consequences of having raised a family without adequate thought to the responsibilities that this involves.

On 7 June Cochrane wrote from Hanover Lodge to inform Horace that he had been made aware of certain sums of money which Horace had drawn since he obtained his commission, and warned him with ill-advised good-nature: 'Mind my dear Horace what you are about; no horses and no expenses must be incurred until I can enable you so to amuse yourself.' It is clear from this remark that in Cochrane's eyes the crock of gold was almost within his reach, and that he longed to pour it into the laps of his family. Unfortunately it appears that they had all been anticipating it—Cochrane himself, his wife, Horace, and his eldest son most seriously of all. 'I am afraid that your Brother has wholly ruined himself,' Cochrane told Horace. 'He is yet here, without leave of absence; not daring to return to Plymouth where, under existing circumstances, not an officer would speak to him. He has been reported to the Horse Guards as having obtained money and drawn bills under false pretences; and I should not be surprised if he is compelled to quit the army—and God knows then what will become of him: I am now trying to get him off to India, where if he is not more prudent he will leave his bones.'

Thus all the adults in the family had contributed to undermine Cochrane's attempt to establish a permanent home for them in London, though the men who had destroyed it were those whose countries he had liberated in South America, and who had dishonoured their debts to him. Cochrane still possessed the £37,000 that he had been paid by the Greek Committee, invested in French bonds, and in 1839 he settled this entire sum on his wife to ensure her future security while he lived in future on his naval pay. In this arrangement can be seen the provision for Kitty's desertion of her husband and of London, in favour of life on the continent.

'My dear Horace,' Cochrane wrote to his son from Hanover Lodge on 11 April 1839, 'I am just embarking in the Cab for the steam conveyance from London Bridge to Boulogne. I shall endeavour to prevail on Dear Mam to permit two thousand of the French stock to be sold to prevent your ruin, and I shall give any security I have got to make up the difference of her little income, already too small to keep up a decent appearance; for where she is there is our home. As to myself I am accustomed to live in a very quiet and cheap way in every respect.' Horace's debts had evidently increased monumentally since his father's warning 3 years earlier, but if his father hoped to shame him by his latest remarks he was to be disappointed once more.

These financial embarrassments had caused a further complication. His only daughter Lizzie was engaged to be married to John Fleming, heir to Stoneham Park in Hertfordshire, whose family no longer considered her to be such a desirable match. 'Old Fleming,' Cochrane continued the letter to his son Horace, 'is spreading all manner of reports and has been talking most disrespectfully of all our family to Sir Robert Wilson and others. Cochrane'—that is, his eldest son— 'must gull John or I must refuse my sanction to any marriage of Dearest Lizzie with him. We shall be disgraced by being reported to have entrapped John.'

As soon as Cochrane had returned from visiting Kitty in Boulogne, he sat down at Hanover Lodge to write to his 15-year-old son Arthur. It was not too late to ensure that his two younger boys should escape the fate of their elder brother. 'You have been well and religiously reared by your dear Mamma,' he reminded Arthur, 'which gives me great confidence in you. I am indebted to the instruction of my most worthy Grandmother for having avoided every kind of vice which surrounded me on entering the Navy. Never let a cigar or pipe get into your mouth; it is a practice that leads to drinking, and drinking leads to ruin. God bless you and make you that which dearest Mamma has endeavoured to effect, an open, true and honourable man, and being so success in life is sure.' By this time Arthur was already in the navy, which may have blunted the shock of his mother's departure abroad and of the dissolution of the only family home he had ever known. Yet he preserved the brief, precious memory of it throughout his long un-married life and 56 years later he wrote to his brother Horace: 'Yester-day I walked past Hanover Lodge, and could not refrain from plucking two or three sprigs of holly from the hedge inside the wooden paling near the front gate. I send them to you as you might like to have a living memento of the days of Hanover Lodge. I plucked them from the hedge facing the drawing room windows, between which used to stand in our time great China vases or jars; so large were they that one day I was put bodily into one, either by you or our eldest brother . . .' So the elderly bachelor in the United Services Club recalled his father's ill-fated attempt to build a family home, too late, and upon financial expectations that had failed to materialise.

Cochrane wrote gently to his young son in the Navy, telling him in May 1840 that 'Mamma is still at Boulogne', that his eldest brother intended to go to Chile 'to get my money and recover my estate there; and Lizzie is at Dresden with her lord and master'. He did not mention that Tom was going about incognito to avoid his creditors, nor that Lizzie had married John Fleming in the end against the advice of her parents, thereby gravely increasing her mother's neurotic condition. But to Horace, who was older, he spoke more frankly in October. 'Dear Mamma has come over, but is sadly broken in health from letting real evils, and imaginary evils, prey too much on her very susceptible nerves. She has taken Lizzie's cruel and I may say inhuman conduct deeply to heart, and I really think she will never recover it.' Lizzie had always been her mother's favourite, and perhaps she had been spoiled. But she had also grown past the age of puberty without a settled family background, like her two elder brothers.

Contemplating his daughter's marriage, which was to end as unhappily as it had begun, Cochrane continued his letter to Horace with some remarks that might be taken merely as advice to economise and to choose a well-endowed wife. But while he remained loyal to Kitty to his dying day, it is impossible to read his words without recalling that they were those of a man whose own marriage had collapsed. 'I hope your Brother and yourself, if such an event shall be contemplated, will *secure* enough, not for your living alone, but for the consequences of married life: for, believe me, that after the honeymoon is past there is the education of children to provide for, their advancement too in life—But *ABOVE* all, there is the necessity that the Hon. Mrs Horace shall not get out of humour, and make your life *one continued scene of bickering and reproach*, because the Hon. Mrs somebody else keeps a carriage; can give better or more numerous parties—or dress better! My dear boy, guard against this species of ever-preying misery above all else! For, like the perpetual drop of water, it will wear the heart, or harden it to stone.' Since he invariably wrote henceforth to his children praising or excusing their mother, urging them to write to her or to visit her, he presumably would not have expected Horace to recognise his description as a portrait of her, even if he was aware of it himself.

Kitty was developing symptoms by this time, as painful as they are familiar. Having abandoned her husband and her children, taking what remained of the family's capital with her, she saw each misfortune that befell any of them as her own personal affliction. She became obsessed that they did not visit her, remember all that she had done for them, write to her, realise how ill she was. 'Poor dear Mamma,' wrote Cochrane to Horace in December, 'I am grieved to say, has been very unwell lately, and I fear is in such a nervous state of excitement, through the conduct of Lizzie and Fleming and the whole combination of evils and annoyances, that until some decisive change takes place in my affairs to enable her to look on things with a more cheerful prospect she will not be better. I hope, however, that *this* time draws near, for my engine continues to have the *most complete* success and the Admiralty are considering about putting a pair in a Government steamer. Besides, I have heard of the arrival in Chile of my memorial, which Cochrane was to have taken out, praying the Government and Congress to grant me the sums justly due for my services to that state.' With incurable optimism he announced that he had renewed possession of Hanover Lodge for another year 'and hope before that time all will be well'. For home was where Kitty was and this was the bait to lure her back. Whether or not the debts of Horace had been settled by the sale of her stock, he was disabled for the time being from contracting any more, and an unsuitable marriage was all his father had to fear. For Horace spent that Christmas of 1840 serving with the rank of Lieutenant in the 92nd Regiment stationed at Malta.

But 1841 did not fulfil Cochrane's expectations. He was promoted to the rank of Vice-Admiral and granted a pension for meritorious service, which must have helped to maintain the remarkable buoyancy of his spirits, but no payment came from Chile or Brazil, his inventions continued to drain his resources without reward, while his eldest son caused him fresh humiliation. Notices were posted about the town giving a description of the young Lord Cochrane which disclose that he had not grown into a tall man like his father, although he had inherited his colouring. 'The said Lord Cochrane is aged about 28 years, round visage, complexion fair, height 5 ft 8 in, wore moustaches when last seen.'

The press gave young Cochrane sympathetic coverage, telling how he had borrowed no more than £700 from a money-lender named Kelly during the past 3 years, yet was now being pursued for a sum of £4800 in repayment.

'As the parties in this affair have caused to be circulated and stuck on and above pumps, posts, and nuisance-corners of the metropolis the annexed hand-bill, with a view to the annoyance of the family and friends of his lordship, we feel bound to go a little more at length into a matter fraught with so large a share of combined knavery and persecution.

'The man Kelly is, as our readers well know, a bill discounter, whose usual rate of premiums for the loan of money is 60 *per cent*—and a little more when he can get it! It is hardly necessary to add that charges of this kind assist materially in filling debtors' prisons, and have brought more young men to ruin than half the gambling dens in the metropolis.' Kelly was offered repayment at 10 per cent interest with a bonus to repay his trouble, while Cochrane succeeded in hustling his son away to the China station, where he served as Assistant Quartermaster-General in Hong Kong from 1842 until 1847.

But Horace had also been borrowing from the same source—Cochrane spelt his name Keily in his letters—and for this son he proposed a different solution. 'Not only were you under age when Keily led you to borrow money, but all his charges were usurious, at a time when the usury laws were in force; and it is clear that a transaction commenced in fraud could not be legalised by any subsequent Act of Parliament which had not a restrospective clause.' Horace had returned from Malta by the time his father wrote him this letter, addressed to him under an assumed name in Manchester Square, on 2 April 1841. 'I am willing, in all, to help you both to the extent of my power—in money, I can do no more—but by exertion in your behalf I shall always endeavour to promote your welfare. *You*, I am persuaded, can get rid of your debt to Keily . . .'

He was in Portsmouth, working on his engine. 'I am sorry that there is no possibility of my leaving this until the cooler is properly attached to the engine; for such things have happened during my absence before that I am quite certain that mischief of some sort will occur if I leave this, even for a day.' He gave this as his excuse for not coming to meet Lizzie and her husband on their return to England, where Lizzie would soon suffer her first miscarriage. But Cochrane ended his olive-branch of a letter to his son-in-law: 'Pray let me know how long you continue on this side of the water, and believe me, with best love to Lizzie, yours affectionately.'

As soon as he could, he tore himself away from his experiments to visit his wife, of whom he had received a disturbing report from her doctor during the previous January. 'My Lord, I was called upon to visit the Countess Dundonald on the 1st January in consequence of the most severe attack of Haemorrhage from the womb, which I am sorry to say has continued to the present time, with but slight abatement. I have no doubt it was occasioned, and I fear is kept up, by mental emotion. I feel it therefore to be my imperative duty to impress upon your Lordship the necessity of keeping her Ladyship as quiet as possible, otherwise the result might be most serious.' Defensively, sardonically, Cochrane scribbled below those words: 'This Doctor thought that I had been the cause, and wrote me this letter!' At the age of 45 Kitty might well have been suffering a change of life, aggravated by a condition that can be cured today by a simple hysterectomy operation. But it is clear from the doctor's report that she bludgeoned his ears with the family misfortunes to which she attributed her ill-health.

Cochrane tried the benefits of change, and reported to his son Arthur on 3 August, after he was back in Portsmouth: 'I have just returned from Paris where I took dear Mamma and left her in order to divert her thoughts, by a change of scene, from the dull monotony of Boulogne.' Arthur had recently passed the examinations that led to his promotion to the rank of midshipman and a tour of duty in the Mediterranean. His proud father gave him precepts—not all of which he had followed in his own career—then added prophetically: 'Attending to these (which will be all sources of lasting enjoyment to you) your success in life will be secure. You will have bye-and-bye to become the protector and assistant of those who have acted in direct contravention of every counsel I have given for their governance in life. I allude to your two elder Brothers who, I may say, are completely ruined by their thoughtless folly'. It is possible that with those words Cochrane had planted a thought in the mind of his 17-year-old son which helps to account for the most inexplicable act of Arthur's career.

Cochrane told his son that he might still address letters to Hanover Lodge, but by 1842 the dream that it would once again be the family home, presided over by Kitty, had faded for ever. Cochrane took lodgings for himself in 2 Victoria Square, Pimlico, from where he sent Arthur increasingly explicit details of the family misfortunes. He was now over 66 years old, and he had decided to prepare this lad with such a mature head on young shoulders to take over the appalling family responsibilities in the event of his own death. So he told Arthur in July: 'As to Horace, he is seemingly determined to effect total ruin, beyond the possibility of my being able to save him. I look with deep grief on the prospect of his future fate—he seems to have lost all sense, and to have his mind perfectly unsettled and regardless even of his most manifest interests.'

A week later he wrote to Arthur equally frankly about his sister. 'Lizzie poor thing was brought to bed last night of another stillborn female child. She never will have a living one, in the way she goes on, racketing at Almacks, the Caledonian meetings, operas, plays and other places.' He was in a hurry to post the same sad news to 'dear Mamma', but found time to assure Arthur of his efforts to find another ship for him, now that he had returned from his Mediterranean tour.

So regularly did Cochrane and his wife write to one another as a rule that he told Arthur in September: 'I have had a letter from Mamma

T.S.W.—2B

today, which has greatly relieved my mind; for I feared that she was unwell, not having heard from her for ten days.' He also wrote to Arthur every few days, and promised to come from Pimlico to see him on his birthday in Portsmouth, bringing some salmon and a bottle of champagne and a gun as a birthday present. But he confessed that when he went to collect the new gun, the gunsmith would not hand it to him without a cash payment, even though Cochrane's own gun was in his hands as well as his silver-mounted pistols. 'I am grieved at this affair of the gun, not only as it may vex you, but as a mark how low my credit has been brought by all the doings of your brothers amongst tradesmen, who of course talk amongst themselves of such affairs.'

So it was that although Cochrane strove to prevent the bonds that united his family from being entirely sundered, he was determined that his two youngest sons should be protected from the example of their elder brothers and sister; when Ernest became old enough he would be placed in the navy under Arthur's care. During this same month of September Cochrane blocked an attempt by Lizzie to invite Arthur to visit her in the country home which she and John Fleming had leased. 'I have had a few lines from Lizzie asking leave for you to come there. Now my dear Arthur, this cannot be. I have told her that her two eldest Brothers are both ruined, and that you must stick to your profession and save the family, by having at least one well-doing member.' Cochrane's eldest son was indeed safely in Hong Kong, and satisfactorily employed there, but there were still his unpaid debts at home for his father to meet when the rewards of his inventions or of his services in South America should enable him to do so.

So it was not simply from a desire to modernise the ships of his country's navy that Cochrane pursued his researches into engines, boilers and screw propellers designed to replace paddle-wheels; and in an era that was becoming so enlightened and progressive it is astonishing that the Admiralty should have maintained its resistance to his ideas. In the civilian sphere the government had revolutionised the mail service between Britain and America when it attracted Samuel Cunard from Halifax in Nova Scotia, who harnessed the coastal steamship firms of Glasgow and Liverpool, and in 1840 inaugurated the first voyage across the Atlantic by Cunard Steamer. Yet when the First Lord asked Cochrane to report on the state of the navy 2 years later, he was obliged to reply: 'Timidity as to change caused many years to elapse, after the commercial use of steam vessels, before the Navy department possessed even a tug-boat. Hence the mischievous economy manifested by the purchase of worthless merchant steamers; hence the subsequent parsimonious project of building small steam vessels fitted with engines immersed beyond their bearing, and deficient in every requisite for purposes of war.'

The same mentality evidently still operated in the Admiralty as in the days when it had purchased that old collier, the *Arab*, in which Cochrane had wasted a year off Orkney. By the time he submitted his report to the First Lord, the Earl of Haddington, he was already working on his new design of screw propeller, in which the blades formed a right-angle with the shaft in order to compensate for the centrifugal action of the screw. In 1843 the first naval vessel was built with Cochrane's propeller in it, and subjected to a tug-of-war with a paddle steamer that heralded the emergence of the modern warship. Such improvements, Cochrane had warned the First Lord in the previous year, had generally 'been effected by the gradual changes which time occasions, or by following the example of America, or even France, than by encouraging efforts of native genius'.

He had suffered much personal experience of this, and he now ventured to suggest where the roots of the trouble lay in the bureaucratic system. 'This has arisen from causes easily remedied; one of which is that the rejection or adoption of proffered improvements has depended on the decision of several authorities, who consequently feel little individual responsibility, and imagine themselves liable to censure only for a change of system.' Probably he did not know how recently the Lords of the Admiralty had actually declared 'their bounden duty to discourage to the utmost of their ability the employment of steam vessels'. But in 1844 they retreated so far as to build a steam vessel to Cochrane's specifications.

She was named HMS *Janus*, and the Science Museum in London possesses a model of one of the four boilers that Cochrane designed for her, each heated by three furnaces. The shortcoming of marine boilers in the days of the Greek war had been their tendency to burst under too great a head of steam; but by now Cochrane had identified and provided against a greater danger than this, the risk that boilers might collapse under atmospheric pressure if the steam pressure were lowered, rather as Brunel's tunnel had collapsed before Cochrane found the solution. On the front of each boiler he had installed an internally opening valve by which air could enter when the steam pressure was reduced. He also experimented in the introduction of hot air into the combustion chamber. Despite all the worries of his family and his finances, his mind remained as inventive as ever.

During these years that followed Kitty's removal to Boulogne and his own installation in Pimlico, while he divided his time between his experiments, voluminous correspondence with his scattered family and periodical visits to his wife, she too was writing letters to her children, and very odd some of them were. It can only be surmised that her eldest sons were displeased by her abandonment of their father, and especially that all the money which might have paid their debts had been placed in her hands. 'Remember, my own Horace,' she wrote from Paris in 1842, 'that there is no heart so true or so sincere as a mother's.' But the reminder was of no practical assistance to him as he hid from his creditors under an assumed name.

It seems possible that young Arthur came to the assistance of Horace under an arrangement with their mother that she would reimburse him, according to a somewhat puzzling letter which Arthur wrote to Horace from Portsmouth in July 1842. 'I am surprised at Mamma's extraordinary conduct in not dating her orders from the time I entered the service although I may say that I have no right to expect it, because as the money was paid, she will say it does not matter to you by whom. However I will write to her on the chances. How are you going to manage about your commission, and in case you lose it what are you going to do? Your leave is up tomorrow, is it not?' Thus the 18-year-old Arthur began his lifetime's involvement in his brother's troubles.

Soon afterwards he received a commission which enabled him to take up his father's claims personally in Chile, and it was while he was still in South America during 1844 that his mother sent another of her characteristic letters, this time to her eldest son in Hong Kong. She wrote from London on 27 December, so perhaps she had crossed the Channel to spend her husband's sixty-ninth birthday and also Christmas with him. There was little enough to celebrate for even the intervention of the Foreign Minister, the Earl of Aberdeen, had failed to extract from the Chilean government an admission that they owed Cochrane any more than £6000, and after having waited for 20 years he could not bring himself to accept such a sum in settlement. Kitty wrote to Tom in Hong Kong, telling him that she still awaited news of him. 'I am sadly grieved, my dearest child, that you should suspect my *deep and true* and warm affection for you. Oh, you little dream the great and vexing wrong these and other groundless suspicions cause me.' She then informed Tom of the marriage of one of his relatives and added 'marriage is at best a lottery and I hope he may have drawn a prize'. Coming from Kitty, the remark is as suggestive as her husband's observations on the married state.

Tom's mother told him that she longed for his return home, 'but I confess I see no likely chance of that happiness to me if it depends upon money affairs, for the Steam makes but slow progress in my mind, but I am not a sanguine person as you know. Your father however says that he is right and I confess my ignorance in all matters of that kind, having no sort of mechanical genius. I hate the inventive faculty.' Cochrane was equally bored by the kind of social life for which she craved. Once he had dazzled her as the celebrated nobleman, the glamorous naval hero, while she had captivated him as the beautiful young girl of his dreams. In those early, romantic days it had not mattered that she possessed no dowry, he no inheritance. Neither had their compatibility been tested by living together permanently under one roof until they moved into Hanover Lodge, and it is open to question whether their relationship would have survived the test even if financial worries had not placed an even more severe strain upon it. When Kitty visited London during that December of 1844 she did not join Cochrane at his address in Pimlico, but stayed at 3 Berkeley Square.

Her need to reassure Tom may have had a different cause from her protestations to Horace. By the whole family he was addressed as Lord Cochrane, heir to the earldom, but both he and Horace had been born after the extremely unusual marriage ceremony of their parents at Annan, and the very fact of their marriage had been kept a secret until the conventional ceremony that took place in Kent in 1818. Arthur was the elder son born after that wedding, and if the earlier one were held to be invalid, he would be heir to the earldom. It would be perfectly easy for his parents to pronounce this to be the case, and they had considerable grounds for deciding to do so, now that Tom and Horace had behaved so irresponsibly, while Arthur gave such early signs of dependability and talent. For the remainder of his father's life, Tom was worried over the question of his legitimacy, and he may have had misgivings over that all-important witness, his mother. For it might well be that after his father's death she would be free to choose to which of two sons she wished to hand his coronet.

By the autumn of 1845 Tom (or Cochrane, as the family called him) had returned to his mother's favour and it was Arthur in South America who was the target for lengthy reproaches. 'I have felt deeply your silence for I see letters constantly from you to your father, but not one line to me. You will understand how bitter these feelings are to me, feeling that in your youth I did all I could and tried all that was in my poor power to contribute to your future welfare.' The reason why she saw Arthur's letters to his father was that she had yielded to persuasion to return to London, although she did not go to her husband in Pimlico, but moved into 8 Chesterfield Street, Mayfair. Here she was soon pouring out her complaints on monogrammed and coroneted notepaper of a quality very much better than her husband used.

The fortunes of Horace might have given her satisfaction, but that
he had once again ignored his father's advice by marrying a wife who
possessed no more fortune than he did, with exactly the consequences
that Cochrane had predicted although they had not as yet materialised.
'I think Horace is well,' Kitty told Arthur. 'He is now employed as a
Director in one of the Rail Road concerns and he gets £600 a year
which is a great blessing for it will give him habits of application and
reflection.' Unfortunately it was to give him neither. 'I have not seen
him for months or his wife either,' Kitty complained, 'neither have I
seen or heard from Lizzie since last July she has taken offence with me
and we do not now write.' It would have seemed almost inconceivable
that she could have found grounds for self-pity in the affairs of little
Ernest also, but she succeeded. 'Ernest is going to the Navy College
next January to be a Mid. He says he likes this profession better than
any other. I hope he may never regret the liking he has for this way of
life but I never will try to dissuade either of my children for that which
they might hereafter throw blame upon me for having done so. Mine
indeed has been a most difficult card to play . . .'

There was a reason why Arthur had recently been exchanging so
many letters with his father, whether or not Kitty knew it. Since the
failure of Cochrane's agent in Chile to extract the payments due to him,
he had naturally wondered whether this was due to any shortcomings
on the agent's part. As soon as Arthur became 21 years old in September
1845, Cochrane sent him a Power of Attorney with instructions to use
it only if he judged that any inadequacy in the agent justified his intervention. It was an extremely delicate assignment, for 'I wish you produce your enclosed power only in the event of total neglect, and even
then not to blame his conduct or find fault with it to a single mortal.'
Cochrane's scrupulousness in financial matters, so often questioned
during his lifetime and since his death, is well exemplified in the instructions he sent to his son. 'If you feel *obliged* to interfere officially, let Mr
Caldeclough know that he is to have *all* the benefits of *the Agency* that
may be due, and that, on my obtaining the amount that may be finally
decreed, it shall be paid to his order.' Arthur's commission would also
involve him in conversations with Walpole, the British Consul in
Santiago, who had received instructions from Aberdeen, the Foreign
Minister in London, to make approaches to the Chilean Government
on the subject. 'Colonel Walpole has been most obliging in reference to
my affairs, and I am sure will give you any advice on the subject you
may require. Lord Aberdeen also feels warmly on the subject, and has
done me the favour to write to the Colonel.' Cochrane was placing a
high degree of confidence and trust in the son to whom he wrote: 'I beg

you to observe that I wish you to act in this matter as if you had an old head on your shoulders—and I believe though yourself young it is pretty mature.'

Cochrane told Arthur with perennial optimism that 'I am on the point of succeeding with the Janus'. But his mother included the *Janus* in her long catalogue of complaints, saying that poor Tom in Hong Kong could not come home until his debts were paid and that it was the *Janus* that was swallowing all the money which might have been used to redeem Tom from his exile. 'Your Father never will have it in his power to relieve him of these worries for from the outlay he has thought it right to make regarding his plans about Steam Janus etc. I think there is little chance of any money. I had hoped that the debts from Chile would have been paid. I had sincerely hoped this might have been accomplished but alas! nothing has yet been done there, which I think is so very cruel, knowing as I do that that money was so hardly earned.' It does not appear as though Kitty knew anything about the Power of Attorney which Cochrane had sent to Arthur, and this would explain why he had not forwarded Arthur's letters to Kitty as he usually did. He thus avoided the risk of further rows over the favour he had shown to a younger son, though he exposed them both instead to Kitty's jealousy and resentment.

For Arthur it should have been relatively easy to placate his mother and recover her favour. Unlike Tom and Horace he had never disgraced the family by defaulting on his debts; unlike Horace and Lizzie he had not incurred an imprudent marriage. However, Kitty was able to make even this a matter for censure related to herself. 'I am glad to hear that you have been brushing yourself up a little—a little *good* female society is the best thing for a young man possible—it cannot fail to soften the durity, *dûreté* of a harsh nature. It improves the expression of the ugliest face, it makes a man feel his superiority over the weaker sex and gives him confidence without hardness. Arthur, you require to be softened, you have formed a wrong estimate of women—and I fear you will require much to change your idea. I myself like to see a man *show* feeling and I am, believe me, not a *singular* instance. I thought you might have called upon me (your Mother) and have said some little word of fond regret, some little affectionate natural kiss, on leave taking upon a separation of so long!' She has steered her way back once more to her favourite theme.

Since Arthur never married, the question naturally arises whether experience of his mother had made him wary of women, or alternatively whether he was disabled by lack of the normal heterosexual instinct from understanding them. The best evidence about this is a surviving letter which an actress of the Gaiety theatre, who signed herself Augusta, once wrote to him after he had sailed abroad. She appears to have been an enchanting girl, humorous, intelligent and devoted to Arthur. But it is an aspect of Arthur's character that is most clearly revealed in her words, for they show him to have been as fully capable as any man of a mature relationship with a woman. Nor do his efforts to maintain an equilibrium with his neurotic mother (though his profession generally enabled him to do this from a safe distance) reveal less.

It is common in such cases that those who are nearest incur the brunt of disapproval, while a little luck and discretion are sufficient to protect those who are far away. Arthur had been unlucky when his reference to feminine society triggered off another lengthy outburst of recrimination, but it was not long before the domestic misfortunes of Horace and Lizzie erupted to take Kitty's mind off Arthur's emotional shortcomings.

They put an end to a period of tranquillity and hopefulness. No good news had arrived from Chile or from Brazil, but on the birthday of Queen Victoria, 24 May 1846, Cochrane won another objective that was near to his heart. He was not only invested with the Order of Knight Grand Cross of the Bath, but the honour was enhanced by Prince Albert, who sent him the insignia direct so that he could wear it at court when the Queen held her birthday drawing-room on the 27th. Since the time when Cochrane had been invested previously with the Order, the original K.B. had been expanded into the hierarchy of Grand Cross, Knight, and Commander of the Order. Knights of the Bath of earlier creation had become Knights Grand Cross under the new dispensation, so this was the precise rank which represented his reinstatement. In July he was installed in the chapel of the Order in Westminster Abbey, when it fell to Lord Ellenborough, son of the Chief Justice who had sentenced him to the pillory, to act as one of the sponsors. Almost as bizarre was the meeting on this occasion between Cochrane and the Duke of Wellington, probably for the first time in their lives. Wellington was the elder by 6 years when Britain's most outstanding soldier and sailor, whose lives had been so diametrically different, exchanged civilities amid the pageantry that had outlasted the age of chivalry. Queen Victoria also granted permission to Cochrane to wear the insignia of the Grand Cross of Brazil, bestowed on him by the Emperor Pedro before Britain had recognised his flag.

Of more practical importance was a letter which Cochrane received from Commodore Lord John Hope at the Admiralty on 14 January 1847. 'I am so thoroughly convinced of the numerous advantages of having one boat (at least) in all our large ships fitted with a high-pressure engine, that I had great satisfaction in recommending the plan you sent to the Board for adoption—and I should like to have one or more ready for the ship that carries your Flag.

'Bermuda of all our possessions is the island to be defended by Gun Boats, equal to carry one 68 pounder with an engine of 10 horse power.' As the year wore on to summer Cochrane received reports from Portsmouth that his engine excelled all others in the yard, while at Woolwich the *Janus* was being prepared for her final trials.

Such were his grounds for buoyancy of spirit, and they were augmented by the continued presence of his wife in London and the return of Tom from Hong Kong and of Arthur from South America. Then Lizzie abandoned her husband for the society of another man, accusing John Fleming of brutality, while Horace once again fled underground to escape from his creditors.

At first Cochrane remained remarkably phlegmatic, writing to Horace concerning Lizzie on 25 September: 'Poor thing, she stands much in need of a friend and counsellor, for she has no knowledge of the world, nor in truth how to conduct herself in a ladylike manner. I wish to God that she (as well as you) would reflect, there might then be some hope.' However, the exile of Cochrane's heir in Hong Kong appears to have steadied him considerably, and he now contracted a marriage that would stabilise him for the remainder of his life. His bride was a daughter of the Mackinnon Chief, offspring of a family that had forfeited all its Scottish property after the Jacobite uprising of the previous century, only to recover its fortunes in the West Indies. This union restored the Dundonald tradition of making Scottish marriages, broken by the marriage of Cochrane to someone of entirely unknown genetic stock.

Kitty's solution to the fresh troubles that had engulfed her family was to return to France, taking Lizzie with her. The recently-engaged Tom accompanied them to Paris, from where Cochrane presently received ominous tidings that Lizzie's male friend had arrived also. For his part Cochrane gave advice where he could, informed Horace that he did not possess the means to rescue him, immersed himself in his mechanical inventions, and pinned his faith increasingly in Arthur. 'You shall have all the fruits of sixty years' knowledge in naval affairs placed at your discretion.' Arthur appears to have been the only member of the family who gave a thought to the feelings of the elderly Titan at its head, and on 18 November Cochrane reassured him: 'Do not make yourself the least uneasy about me or my anxieties. I am, like the eels, accustomed to be skinned.' Brave words from a man near breaking-point.

A week later his eldest son wrote from Paris: 'I am requested by my Mother in *aid* of poor Lizzie to beg of you not to delay *an hour* after you receive this but to come to Paris.' He suggested that Arthur should come too as Lizzie would probably listen to him, 'but of that you are the best judge'. Kitty wrote a similar letter, in an attempt to drag the only two members of the family who were doing a job of work to Paris, at a moment's notice, to try to disentangle Lizzie's affairs. Cochrane told Arthur: 'That which I have long foreseen has come to pass—evil example and bad company corrupt good manners.' He remained impartial in the quarrel between Lizzie and her husband. 'I fear there are errors on both sides; *would* I believed otherwise, then the scoundrel could be horsewhipped as undoubtedly he richly deserves. I fear they will *all* find themselves in Paris without the means to return!—and, to make the matter worse, they want me there, without the possibility of my aiding them—advice being useless and heavy expense certain.' At last he revealed the strain he felt: 'I am too full of this calamity to think of Janus or boilers or anything else.'

Arthur offered to visit him but he replied: 'Pinched as we all are in our finances, I do not like to say come up.' Neither did he go to Paris, where he feared that Tom's forthcoming marriage was being jeopardised by his involvement in the family scandal. 'I am overwhelmed with the prospect of difficulties on all sides. Cochrane's debts are not yet settled. A trick is intended to make me answerable to some extent which I intend to frustrate.'

The final blow was a disastrous accident at the trials of the *Janus*. It was caused by carelessness on the part of Robinsons, the engineers, though Cochrane might possibly have prevented it, had he not been distracted by his family's misfortunes. 'Whether the intimation of the Admiralty will be adhered to I know not,' he told Arthur on 20 December, 'but they have declined to make farther trial of the Janus's engines. I have today offered to complete them and obtain a satisfactory result if they will place at my disposal £100 worth of work and materials in Woolwich Yard. Our late mishap was solely because the Robinsons did not put a proper oil holder on the plenum side of the engines.'

His thoughtfulness for Kitty remained undiminished. Spending Christmas alone with his worries, he wrote to Arthur: 'I hope you have written to your Mama. You ought not to neglect that whatever you do to me. I make allowance for thoughtlessness or want of leisure, or other causes, which Mama does not take to account.' Arthur was in fact preparing to sail on his next tour of duty.

There was a little lightening of the sky before the year 1847 ended. For one thing, Lizzie's husband proposed a not-ungenerous settlement.

'*John* is resolved not to take her back, and offers to give her £600 a year! with the stipulation that she shall reside in England and not run him in debt.' Tom's intended marriage to the Mackinnon's daughter did not founder; and one day the First Lord of the Admiralty paid a surprise visit to the *Janus* and found the former protégé of honest Jack Larmour, now over 70 years old, in a place in which Vice-Admirals were not often encountered. 'I was on board the Janus yesterday,' he told Arthur on 28 December, 'when who should come down into the engine room but Lord Auckland; I was glad he found me there, with a tallow candle in my hand, for it proved that I was in earnest.'

The hand which held that tallow candle was beginning to falter at last. 'My hand is so much swelled from some bad state of my blood,' he confessed to Arthur on the following day, 'that I can scarcely hold a pen. I attribute this to worry of the mind from circumstances with which you are generally acquainted, and over which I have no control. I have heard nothing from John Fleming, nor of him save what you are already acquainted with. Poor Lizzie, I know not what will be her fate, whether public exposure or private wretchedness.' Poor Lizzie was soon reported to be taking a succession of young men back from the theatre to her lodgings, where they frequently spent the night.

Out of the gloom of the new year came an invitation from the First Lord to command a British fleet for the first time, as Commander-in-Chief of the North American and West Indian stations. 'Will you accept the appointment? I shall feel it to be an honour and a pleasure to have named you for it; and I am satisfied that your nomination will be agreeable to her Majesty, as it will be to the country—and particularly to the Navy.' One member of the service proved the truth of Auckland's assertion by expressing his satisfaction in verse. He described himself as 'One who served in the Basque Roads', that triumph of long ago over the French at Rochefort, and his poem of eight verses was published in the *Naval and Military Gazette*.

Before he hoisted his flag aboard the seventy-two-gun warship *Wellesley* on 7 March 1848, Cochrane had found time to publish his *Observations on Naval Affairs*, his first essay in the curious mixture of autobiography, technical advice and outspoken comment on the people and events of his time that he was to expand in later volumes. To his great satisfaction, Arthur had not yet sailed and was permitted to join the *Wellesley* as his Flag Lieutenant.

CHAPTER FIFTEEN

Prometheus Bound

The *Wellesley* was a sailing ship, but Cochrane's squadron also contained steamships and for these the British Navy did not yet possess any fuel supply on the west side of the Atlantic. Looking as he did towards a future in which every vessel would be powered by steam, Cochrane used the opportunity which a peacetime tour offered him to carry out a systematic survey of the British possessions which lay in his path, in search of coal deposits. The exhilaration of finding his feet on a quarter-deck once more, the miraculous release from all the distresses that had beset him on land, these seem to have heightened the vitality and intellectual curiosity which he had retained to such an advanced age. They drove him to explore the commerce and mineral wealth, the social conditions and administrations of the islands that he visited, and he kept a journal in which he added his observations on all the people he met, from Governors to freed slaves. In Newfoundland he began the collection of mineral specimens that he presented to the institution of Practical Geology on his return.

Here is a typical entry from 1849. 'At daybreak on Monday the 30th July we weighed anchor and stood along the peninsular promontory called Cape St George. About midway a remarkable change takes place to the northward of the Table Mountain, where the vertical strata become in appearance horizontal along the whole shore of the project-ing isthmus. The colour of the strata is chiefly grey, in parallel layers of varying hardness, as appears from its projections and indentations. I could not, without delaying the ship longer than I wished, procure samples of the strata, but there was no appearance of carboniferous minerals.' He was anxious to discover coal, not only for the benefit of the British Navy, but also to assist the island's economy. 'In New-foundland there is no income whatsoever derived from the soil—no mines in activity'—while there was destitution in the fishing industry.

Cochrane was scandalised by the decline in the Newfoundland fisheries and by the cause of it. The British government had granted fishing rights in these waters to France and to the United States, and both countries had granted bounties to their fishermen which made competition with them impossible, and had driven 400 British boats from the fishing grounds. Worse still, the inhabitants of Newfoundland, a country larger than Ireland, were crippled by penal taxation, a subject on which the Bishop of the island provided him with detailed information. And yet, as Cochrane observed of St George's harbour, in its deep inlet facing the huge mouth of the St Lawrence, 'no village can be better placed for the herring fishery, as these gregarious fish, at the season of their arrival on the coast, enter this harbour as it were into the cod of a net, whence they are lifted into the boats by scoops and buckets. With such slender means possessed by the inhabitants, the average catch amounts to 22,000 barrels, but hundreds of thousands might be taken were encouragement afforded.'

Throughout his tour, he kept a sharp eye on the appearance of ordinary people, as evidence of the kind of administration under which they lived. 'It is grievous to observe the difference in the mode of carrying on the British fishery compared to that of the French. The former in rudely constructed skiffs with a couple of destitute-looking beings in party-coloured rags; the latter in fine well-equipped schooners (which may be called tenders to their larger ships), the seamen uniformly dressed in blue with Joinville hats, looking as men ought, and may be expected to look, whose interests and those of the Parent State are understood to be in unison and attended to as such.'

He was heartened by the contrast he found at Forteau Bay on the mainland coast of Labrador opposite, in the latitude of Scotland. 'The activity apparent here in the fishing department I ascribe to the British fishery on the coast of Labrador being still free from the exactions now imposed in Newfoundland, for the maintenance of the excessive retinue of a Government, by the taxation of every article of food and clothing imported, together with imposts placed on all existing property.' He described the different kind of craft in Forteau Bay, and observed: 'The small boats at the mouth of the bay have seemingly an excellent fishing ground. The people are all hard at work. No sooner is one line hauled up than the second requires attendance. The fish flakes are numerous on the beach, and so are the men turning the fish, although so many are out in the boats. I counted forty-eight men hauling up a fishing boat by main force, there being no crab, windlass or tackle employed. There are heaps of fish cured and stacked up, like diminutive hayricks, the fish being nicely arranged to throw off the rain, like thatch.'

But when he sailed south across the mouth of the St Lawrence to Nova Scotia, the picture that faced him was once again a depressing one. He had come here last in the *Thetis*, over half a century earlier. 'I cannot say that I perceived much improvement in the city of Halifax since my first visit in 1794. There are more houses, but few are in a better condition. Such limited portion of the country as I visited had not made the progress that might have been anticipated in one-tenth of that period. There seems to be no encouragement either to agriculture or commerce, and consequently there is a lack of exertion. A few establishments for rude manufacturers were undertaken some years ago, but have all been given up in consequence of the one-sided free-trade with the United States, whose produce and manufactures under-sell those of the British provinces whilst articles originated in the Colonies are subject to heavy duties in the Union. As an instance of the strictness with which duties are thus levied, the proprietor of a gypsum quarry (a substance in great demand by agriculturists in the States), having ground that material in Nova Scotia, was charged with duty upon it as a manufactured article.' And where did this money go? 'Here, as in Newfoundland and indeed in each of the Colonies, there are officials sufficient to stock a kingdom.' Cochrane was observing colonial paternalism at its worst, and he commented on another of its ills, the withholding of crown lands from the inhabitants.

'If I am asked what remedy is there, besides alleviation of fiscal exactions, for this paralysing state of affairs, I answer, let the Crown land be *given* to respectable agricultural emigrants in portions proportioned to their means of cultivation, thus leaving in their pockets the amount requisite for clearing and cultivating the soil, nine-tenths of which, under the present system, lies unproductive in the hands of penniless and incompetent occupants.'

In his strictures, Cochrane was careful to defend the various colonial governors whose hospitality he enjoyed in the course of his travels. 'Colonial distress cannot be remedied by Authorities less powerful than those who sanctioned or enacted the measures that produced it. It is not therefore to Colonial Governors abroad, or to Colonial Secretaries at home, that we are to look for the removal of evils.' Several of these governors were doing everything possible with their inadequate powers, and all of them were eager to feed Cochrane with the information he sought, as well as to meet and entertain the almost legendary hero who had arrived amongst them. As for returning hospitality, there is the example of what occurred at Sydney in the island of Cape Breton, which lies beside Nova Scotia. 'The town contains many very respectable inhabitants, whom I had the pleasure of seeing on board at a little morning's dance that was given to them.' The hour of this entertainment helps to confirm an impression that Cochrane was one of those who had preserved his energy late in life, partly by avoiding the human weakness for turning night into day.

His sailors must have marvelled at some of the tasks that they were called upon to perform. 'There is an enormous boulder about three miles from Halifax called the Rocking Boulder, often visited by the surrounding population from its vibrating, on a base of granite rock, at its point of contact.' Such erratic blocks, as geologists call them, had been moved by glaciers during the ice ages, and Cochrane's insatiable curiosity prompted him to explore from whence this one had travelled. 'I therefore took some marines and a boat's crew to clear away the mossy soil and uncover the rut (if such there was), by which it had arrived at its extraordinary position, on the apex of a mount of smooth and solid granite. A deep rut in the granite was presently uncovered on the S.E. side, which was traced from the stone into a contiguous lake, over which it had probably been forced.' If the seamen and marines were relieved to see the track disappear into the water, their satisfaction was shortlived. 'We endeavoured to trace its route on the opposite shore of the lake, but our efforts were unsuccessful, the whole margin being covered with wood, the roots of which it would have required much time and labour to clear away.' His men may well have been surprised that he did not attempt it all the same.

The devotion of the sailors to their Admiral was expressed by a certain Thomas Branton not long after he relinquished his command. 'During the whole commission I was one of the crew of the Admiral's galley, and I was never tired of hearing of the fine old fellow's exploits when, as young Lord Cochrane, he fought the French and Spaniards in Nelson's days. He was a fine old man with typical Scotch features. He was an ideal officer, and was so beloved by the men that his name on the lower deck was "Dad". He would not allow flogging, greatly to the disgust of some of the other officers, who considered that such leniency was bad for discipline. When he was in the galley he would talk to his coxwain and the crew as though we were his equals.' Cochrane had never resorted to flogging to maintain efficiency although he had opposed its abolition—probably because he had no means of learning how brutally it had been abused by bad commanders during his earlier career.

Late in the year 1849 the squadron sailed south from the north Atlantic and called at Bermuda on its way to the Caribbean. The visit evoked in Cochrane a rare sense of nostalgia. 'My early impressions in relation to the Island of Bermuda, where I spent many happy days when youthful vigour made me more sensible of pleasurable scenes, are still vivid in my recollection. The beauty of its scenery has not changed, nor are its inhabitants less steady and judicious than in former days.' He was delighted with the present appearance of the native people. 'The coloured population of this island are a fine race, incomparably superior to the generality of the coloured population in the West Indies. They are accustomed to navigate in their commercial vessels—their lives are almost spent in boats, and no better crews could be got for the defence of their own island than they would prove themselves to be.'

Instead, ridiculous systems of fortification had been partially built before work on them was suspended, 'blunders which, were I to set them forth, would seem incredible. The measures which have tardily been resolved to stop the progress of an interminable series of fortifications I hope may be followed by putting a stop to the extravagance perpetrated in the erection of this naval arsenal.' Here, Cochrane discovered that work was still in progress. 'It has proved a subject so vexatious to me that I shall not proceed in detail, but express my earnest hope that those who have the power will investigate the subject.' It must have been a tense day in the Bermudan naval yard when the Commander-in-Chief arrived for his tour of inspection, snorting that instead of this useless extravagance, all the island required for its defence were gunboats manned by the excellent native seamen.

But the civil administration delighted him. 'The civil government is conducted in a manner highly creditable to the Governor and to his Council, who seem to have but one view—the prosperity of the island, in which success attends their endeavours in so far as they possess the necessary power.' He noted the marketing of early vegetables for the United States, the orange groves, the potatoes unaffected by blight, the shelter-belts of reeds grown to protect crops from the wind.

It was a party of officers who went on a caving expedition with their elderly Admiral. 'There is one on Tucker's Island where these stalactites reach from the top of the cave far below the surface of the salt water it contains. I am not aware of any other instance where similar crystallisations have taken place under sea water. It seems to lead to the belief that this island was at some time less submerged.' Evidently they entered this one by boat, but 'there are other caves much larger, and one which goes in so far that the officers who accompanied me did not scramble to its end'. Their recreations ashore do not appear to have resembled the fooleries and drinking bouts of Cochrane's last visit to this theatre, when he had been a junior officer.

They also examined the coral reefs 'raised by the industry of the numerous species of coral insects in from six to ten fathoms of water and to the extent of 45 miles in length—exceeding in magnitude all the works of man for the protection of anchorages throughout the world. I have broken off some curious specimens of their work, but still more curious is the bottom in ten or twelve fathoms of water, where forests of large submarine productions of innumerable kinds luxuriate like plants, exhibiting in appearance through the clear and pellucid water varieties of form and colour such as are nowhere to be seen on the surface of the earth.'

After they had spent Christmas and the New Year in these delightful surroundings the Admiral set sail on 26 January 1850, or rather, he ordered the steamship *Scourge* to tow the *Wellesley* out of harbour, since the wind was light and adverse. 'At the end of forty-eight hours a breeze sprang up from the N.E., whereby the *Wellesley* was enabled to return a similar service to the *Scourge* which, like most steam vessels, is inadequately rigged and thereby deprived of more than half the power of performing useful service. This defect is however in some degree remedied when a sailing vessel is in company, for the *Scourge* advanced the *Wellesley* 220 miles, and during the next three days we towed that steam vessel 360 miles; thus we alternatively proceeded until our arrival at Carlisle Bay, Barbados, on Monday morning, the 5th February.' Until some local source of fuel could be found it was essential to conserve the coal supplies of the *Scourge*, and Cochrane continued to use this method throughout the remainder of his tour of duty.

As he was returning from a visit to the Governor his alert eye fell on a strange sight. 'On our way out we observed from fifty to sixty men, peculiarly dressed, working with an energy which I had rarely seen in any climate, and never within the tropics. On enquiring what they were (supposing them to be Coolies), I was informed that delinquents here were sentenced to a certain amount of task-work, instead of a specified duration of punishment—an admirable mode of administering justice, which ought to be adopted generally throughout the islands.' Cochrane took an especial interest in social conditions throughout the islands in which slavery had been abolished by Earl Grey's administration in 1833, and he was glad to find here 'that the negroes, who are much more numerous on this island than on any other in the West Indies, appear to be well-fed and cheery in their dispositions. They live in small wooden houses resting on clumps of wood or blocks of stone, a mode of construction which enables them, when tired of or displeased with their locality, to transport them elsewhere.' He was impressed with this 'locomotive propensity' of theirs—so akin to his own.

There was a high mortality rate from fever among the troops stationed in the island's barracks, for which the medical staff could find no explanation. Tossing sleeplessly one night aboard his ship in a temperature of 84° Fahrenheit—for tropical conditions had never agreed with his constitution—Cochrane determined to visit these barracks, and by daylight he was on his way ashore with the Captain and Doctor of the *Wellesley* as well as his son Arthur, the First Lieutenant. The cause of mortality appears obvious enough from his description of what he found, and his solution was a simple one. 'Troops, if now required on these islands, ought to be barracked on rising grounds, where they can breathe pure air which, with good water, contribute more to health than the efforts of all the medical staff in tropical climates.' That dawn inspection, arising out of the thoughts of a fretful night, reveals him as attentive to detail in his seventy-fifth year as he had been on active service half a century before.

Throughout his tour he found repeated shortcomings in the military and naval establishments, causing a wanton waste of lives and of public money, and he was punctilious in carrying out inspections and submitting reports which were probably more welcome to the island authorities than to the distant masters who held them like puppets on a string. But his deepest concern of all appears to have been one that was entirely outside his responsibilities, the welfare of the emancipated negroes, and it was their plight in Jamaica that moved him to his most passionate anger and eloquence.

'It is lamentable to see the negroes in rags, lying about the streets of Kingston; to learn that the gaols are full, whilst the Port is destitute of shipping, the wharves abandoned, and the storehouses empty; while much, if not all of this might be remedied.' The cause, Cochrane thundered, was precisely the same which had undermined the prosperity of Newfoundland, where slavery had never existed. 'Never can this wretched state of affairs be remedied, so long as taxes on the necessaries of life are heaped on an impoverished population. Never can the peasantry raise their heads with a contented aspect, whilst every animate and inanimate thing around them is taxed to the utmost.' Their ills resembled those of Newfoundland in another respect: just as the fishermen of the north found it impossible to compete with those of foreign nations who were aided by subsidies, so the British sugar estates which now employed free labour could not compete with those in countries that had not yet abolished slavery. In both cases the home government was simply strangling a dying economy by raising taxes in an attempt to make its administration pay.

As for some of the ways in which this money was spent, Cochrane recorded in Kingston on 24 March 1850: 'I went to the top of a tower (which has been erected at a cost of £1300 to accommodate a clock worth £50), not only that I might judge of the thoughtless extravagance of this building, but that I might have a view of the swamps on the promontory from which pestilential vapours exhale.' Cochrane described the place in fact as 'the dirtiest place I ever beheld' and found it 'a matter of regret that the ships of war must be detained in this vile anchorage'. The reason they were there was a court-martial of officers and engineers of the steam sloop *Vixen* for reasons that the Admiral did not make public.

As for the state of the hospital to which sick members of his squadron were sent, Cochrane not only introduced improvements there on his own authority and reported its condition to the Admiralty, but he subsequently wrote to the Mayor of Kingston in these terms. 'I communicated to the Admiralty, on my visit to Port Royal last year, the great injury arising to the seamen consigned to the hospital, not only from the numerous small enclosures which intervene between that establishment and the trade wind, but from the excessively dirty condition in which these and the whole of the streets are suffered to remain, apparently without the slightest attention being paid to the sanitary condition of the town, or to the prejudice that may be incurred by the seamen of her Majesty's ships who of necessity frequent this place.

'It is my anxious wish that a sanitary commission should be named, to which I have desired Commodore Bennett, with your sanction, to appoint such officers as may be in port at that time, to aid in an investigation, with a view to remedy these evils. Never have I seen, in the whole course of my life, a place so disgustingly filthy, or which could give so bad an opinion to foreigners of British Colonial Administration, as the town of Port Royal.' It does not sound likely that the Mayor of Kingston would have dared to withhold his sanction from the irate old Admiral, in whom the autocratic streak in his character had been so thoroughly aroused.

It was in Trinidad, the southernmost island within the sphere of his responsibilities, that Cochrane made his most exciting discovery. First he paid his courtesy visit to the Governor, Lord Harris, who invited him to stay in the residency amidst grounds that were maintained as a botanical garden, '. . . which I declined—having learnt that excellent timber for ship-building was to be procured in Trinidad, which I was anxious to ascertain the practicability of embarking in the bays on the northern shore'. He set off on the very next day in the steamship *Scourge*, accompanied by his son Arthur 'who is zealous and active in aiding in whatever can conduce to the interests of the service'. Two days later, indefatigable as ever, Cochrane went to inspect the bitumen lake, 'which I hoped might be rendered useful as fuel for our steam ships'.

He noticed that all excavation had ceased there, although earlier attempts had been made to apply the pitch to useful purposes. 'It occurred to me that were the inner bars of the furnaces of the *Scourge* withdrawn, and a quantity of ashes heaped up until the ash-pits beneath the removed bars were nearly filled, the bitumen thrown on would be absorbed as it melted, and would be gradually given out and converted into flame and heat by a current of air permitted to enter between the fire and the bitumen so absorbed by the heated ashes.'

The experiment worked perfectly when put to the test. 'During this short trip the bitumen was used in the furnaces of the *Scourge* in the proportion of 2 to 1 of coal, and produced an effect on the engines nearly equal to that which double *that* quantity of coal would give— that is, 2 parts of bitumen, under the foregoing arrangement, were equal to 1 of coal; 8 measures of coal, considered to be cwts., and 16 measures of bitumen were used per hour, and produced on an average seven revolutions of the paddle-wheels per minute and $4\frac{1}{2}$ knots per hour without sail. It must be remarked that only eight out of the twelve furnaces were used, and that the amount of fuel consumed was little more than half the quantity appropriated to such engines.' Further tests convinced him that bitumen produced one half of the power of the best coal.

By this time Cochrane had thought of all sorts of other uses for bitumen, as he explained to the Governor after he had returned to hustle him aboard his ship for a tour of inspection. Lord Harris agreed to discover whether it could be used 'as a manure for the growth of sugar on the worn-out estates of the long-cultivated West India islands' and also as a means of preventing potato disease and turnip blight. 'The seamen and marines of the *Scourge* and some blacks who were hired were employed for some hours in quarrying and embarking a farther supply of pitch, and on the same evening we returned to the Port of Spain.' He had sent his son Arthur scrambling all over the place, collecting mineral samples, and as he mused on the untapped riches of Trinidad, 'an unpleasant feeling was experienced by the reflection that many valuable treasures, from parsimony, or rather the small influence of scientific men, may be unknown and neglected, whilst so many and such heavy salaries are paid to persons whose duties are merely nominal or of little utility'.

Cochrane acquired proprietary rights in Trinidad and at the end of his tour of duty he brought home a consignment of bitumen with which to conduct experiments into its possible uses. To begin with, he obtained permission to lay an experimental asphalt surface on part of a street in Westminster. The horses found it alarmingly smooth and slippery (for horses are generally scared of the unfamiliar), and although the horses of the Metropolitan Mounted Police continue to patrol the asphalt streets of London to this day, the consequences of that first experiment was that the bulk of Cochrane's shipload was taken out to sea and dumped in it. Nevertheless he continued to believe that Trinidad might provide him with the crock of gold that had so far eluded him in Chile, Brazil and his own country. Once again his judgment was a perfectly sound one although his efforts brought no profit to himself. Just as the governments of Britain, Chile and Brazil ultimately paid their debts to his descendants, so the Trinidad concession became immensely profitable to those who took it up after these descendants had abandoned it.

Ten years after Cochrane's return, Anthony Trollope gazed over the Pitch Lake, and reflected on the uses to which he had considered putting it. 'That indefatigable old hero Lord Dundonald tried hard to make wax candles and oil for burning. The oil and candles he did make but not, I fear, the money which should be consequent on their fabrication. I have no doubt however that we shall all have wax candles from thence, for Lord Dundonald is one of those men who are born to do great deeds of which others shall reap the advantages. One of these days his name will be duly honoured for his conquests as well as for his candles.'

One of the most imaginative proposals with which he returned home in 1851 at the end of his term of command was the embankment of the Thames, using a composition of bituminous concrete. He also envisaged the use of pitch in the improvement of drains, the insulation of wire, and in the production of substances (pregnant phrase) 'useful in the arts and manufactures'. During his absence work had gone forward on the improved kind of ship's boiler that he had been promoting, and he returned to discover that by now it was being installed in British naval vessels. It was to his son Arthur that he bequeathed his maritime patents, and after his father's death Arthur secured trials for a new kind of boiler which conducted water in tubes through the heat, rather than heat through the water. This water-tube boiler was believed to be the invention of Arthur, rather than his father's.

What Cochrane did not return to discover was that any of the outstanding debts to him had been paid. He claimed £100,000 from Brazil, which paid £40,000 to his family after his death in settlement. He claimed £4000 from the British Treasury in compensation for the eighteen years he had been deprived of half-pay since he was struck off the Navy List. This debt was not settled until 1877, when Parliament voted £5000 to his grandson 'in respect of the distinguished services of his grandfather', thus leaving the nature of the obligation unspecified. By Chile he had been offered a mere £6000 of the £26,000 he claimed. He therefore found himself back amidst his family's misfortunes without the financial means to cope with them.

Letters that he had received in the West Indies had warned him of the trouble in store for him on his return, especially one in which Horace had accused him of taking Kitty's part against her son, and he had scarcely stepped ashore at Spithead on 10 June before the storm broke over his head. Less than a fortnight later he was writing to Arthur from the house of his brother William, 162 Albany Street: 'I am now at my brother's until I can get into a place of my own.' Kitty was evidently impatient to have the first word, though not sufficiently so to cross the Channel. 'Mam is in Paris tormenting me to go over immediately and leave my accounts unpassed and consequently my pocket without a shilling. Nothing can satisfy her that I am *really usefully* engaged, and that such employment is not in some way disgraceful to myself and injurious to her.' It was perhaps the most bitter of his disappointments to discover that his wife's mental condition had deteriorated in this way. It had reached the point, in fact, when he could only excuse her conduct by finding sympathetic causes of her derangement. 'I do not however, my dear Arthur, despair so long as I have you to look forward to as my support in age, should God preserve my life until I am unable to defend myself.' Arthur had been promoted Commander a few weeks earlier.

He returned to unfashionable Pimlico where he found lodgings at 2 Belgrave Road, and it was from here that he informed Arthur of the predicament of Horace on 6 July. 'Never, never were such transactions *perpetrated* as he has been *guilty* of. No wonder your poor Mama was distressed, and obliged to leave the country. I dare not tell you in plain terms by letter how matters stand . . . how completely Horace is ruined—irretrievably ruined. Never, never can he raise his head in the society of gentlemen again.' It was a pitiful welcome to have received on his homecoming. 'I have been so tortured by Horace,' Cochrane wrote to Arthur on 20 July, 'who if caught will undoubtedly be transported, and with duns for the payment of poor Mam's old bills, that I have had no peace—nor leisure to go to Paris to *see* her, at which she is very angry—but I cannot leave matters here of such importance while she, for some reason, will not come here, I believe on account of Horace.' During Cochrane's absence Horace had increased his debts, by means that his father would not commit to paper, to nearly £8000.

In August Cochrane went to Kitty in Paris and took her back to Boulogne. 'Poor Mama is no better in health than she was', he told Arthur, but at least Horace had escaped safely to the Netherlands, where his father enabled him 'to draw quarterly for £25 until something turns up—what that can be I do not know, for he is not fit to be trusted with any place where money is to come into his hands. There is not one mortal of his acquaintance that he has not cheated out of sums of money.' His sister was exploring more distant pastures. 'Poor Liz is lost, incurably gone. She is living at Florence in the society of young men, not one but in the plural number, the females, though virtue is there not much prized, having cut her. These facts, my dear Arthur, are very painful . . .'

The contribution that Arthur made was to look after his younger brother Ernest, now an officer in the navy, who expressed his gratitude by addressing him as 'my dearest Best of Arthurs' and 'my best of Brothers'. Cochrane did not miss his first opportunity since that sad year 1847 to join Kitty in celebration of her birthday. 'Mama is still at Boulogne,' he told Arthur on 1 October, 'and I am going over in a few days to spend the twelfth with her, and take her back to Paris. I regret to say that she is in no better health or spirits than formerly. She lets everything vex her. No doubt she has enough, but things that are beyond remedy ought not to be suffered to destroy every pleasure of life. I try to reason her out of this distressing habit of thought, but I really despair.' His eldest son appears to have been keeping his distance from the family troubles since his marriage, and Cochrane told Arthur that he 'is at his place in Scotland, Auchintoul house, Banff. N.B. Horace is on the continent out of the way, Lizzie at Florence. You are well out of the mess for here there is no happiness.'

By the following spring all the benefit of the foreign tour to Cochrane's health and spirits had been dissipated. From his lonely lodgings in Pimlico he wrote to Arthur on 2 April 1852: 'Poor Mama has been very very ill, and so have I, so much so that I have not been able to go over to see her. She is a little better, and so am I, but out of the door I have not been these three weeks.' However, he had found time since his return to publish his *Notes on the Mineralogy, Government and Condition of the British West India Islands and the North-American Maritime Colonies*. As soon as his health returned, he enlisted the help of his sons in developing the projects that had occurred to him during his tour of these lands. Instead of leaving Horace to live idly in Europe on his allowance of £100 a year, Cochrane despatched him to New York to take out two patents, one for the insulation of wire, the other for a plough to lay pipes in drains. It was a hazardous chance to take with the most improvident of his sons, and by October 1852 Horace had exhausted his credit with his father, and was begging Arthur for a loan with which to repay him. 'I cannot help borrowing for the present from

Peter to pay Paul,' he explained artlessly. 'On the day of my leaving England you gave me a substantial proof of the sincerity of your Brotherly affection towards me. I now take advantage of that, and *must* ask you to accept a bill for £200 for me.'

Evidently this was too much for Arthur, whose reply provoked Horace to protest: 'I deeply regret that I placed myself in such a position as to draw down from any Younger Brother so much animadversion and stern censure. . . . It is the first and the *last* time, Arthur, that I shall put it in your power or subject myself to be so dealt by.' Arthur relented, and thus exposed himself to another 40 years of similar demands, and comparable recrimination when he attempted to resist them. His part in the present enterprise was to supervise the manufacture of the plough for which Horace was taking out his patent in New York. On 19 August 1853 William Dray and Company, the implement makers of Swan Lane in London, wrote to him: 'We have the pleasure to inform you the first experiment was made with the Draining Plough yesterday most satisfactorily.' Arthur was at Woolwich, from where they asked him to come to attend a second trial, since 'we have just seen the Earl of Dundonald, who unfortunately will be unable to attend, owing to his being troubled with a severe cold'.

Arthur was also involved at this time in negotiations with the agents in New York through whom a consignment of pitch from Trinidad had been shipped to Britain, at unexpectedly heavy expense. Once again Cochrane's brilliant ideas were threatening to involve him in ruin, while Horace in New York continued his requests for more money. 'Surely,' he wrote to his father on 12 September, 'you can arrange to give me the temporary assistance I ask when it will be returned to you ten fold.' This appeal had hardly arrived when William Dray reported from Swan Lane: 'The plough as it stands, though proved to be capable of laying the pipes, will yet require a great deal doing to it, and a considerable increase in cost to render it a saleable implement.'

However, Horace was able to write to Arthur in December, thanking him for having accepted his bill for £200, and adding optimistically: 'No doubt money will be got for the Patents out here, if I could only get them granted, and the necessary specimens to prove their goodness. I am now going to New York to hear if anything has been heard from Washington. I have also written to the Patent Office to ask when they think the first Patent will be granted, which was said by them to have been under consideration 7 weeks since.' Cochrane retained such a confident belief in the merits of his new form of insulation that he wrote to Horace 'to put you on your guard not to dispose (if properly you can avoid it) of the Pitch Patent, until you shall receive the samples now making'. He had received a report from the manufacturer that 'the coating of wire is perfect and the *flexible* pipes will exceed all that ever has been produced'.

The new year of 1854 brought fresh grounds for confidence. Cochrane's solicitors in London wrote to Arthur on 18 March telling him that his father appeared well pleased by the sale of his French patents, and informing him that a shipping company had agreed to install Cochrane's boilers in three of their boats. 'He shall have an opportunity I hope of convincing the Admiralty of the injustice they have inflicted.'

But a few days later an event occurred which caused Cochrane to fling all his remaining energy into an attempt to convince the Admiralty that the time had come to use another of his inventions. On 28 March Britain and France declared war on Russia, setting in motion what became known as the Crimean War. Cochrane decided that the opportunity had arrived to employ the secret weapon which he had once promised the Prince Regent that he would never employ except in the defence of his own country. The conflict called for the presence of British fleets both in the Baltic and in the Black Sea. Cochrane begged for the command of the Black Sea fleet which was then vacant, although he was now approaching his eightieth year, and recommended that Russia could be defeated at a stroke by the reduction of the fortresses of Kronstadt in the Gulf of Finland and of Sebastopol in the Crimea with poison gas. Sir James Graham was First Lord of the Admiralty once more, and he addressed to Queen Victoria a remarkable memorial, revealing the aged Sea Wolf as the government of the day saw him.

'Sir James Graham with humble duty begs to lay before your Majesty certain important considerations which were discussed at the Cabinet yesterday with respect to the election of a Commander-in-Chief for the fleet about to be appointed for service in the Baltic.

'Lord Dundonald is seventy-nine years of age; and though his energies and faculties are unbroken, and though, with his accustomed courage, he volunteers for the service, yet, on the whole, there is reason to apprehend that he might deeply commit the Force under his command in some desperate enterprise, where the chances of success would not countervail the risk of failure and of the fatal consequences which might ensue. Age has not abated the adventurous spirit of this gallant officer, which no authority could restrain; and being uncontrollable it might lead to most unfortunate results.'

To this Cochrane replied in the autobiography that still remained to be written: 'When on the coast of Chile I captured a province with 120 men only, and that by storming its fortifications. These were thirteen in number and were garrisoned by 2000 men. I was accused of rashness for the attempt: yet no more doubted the fact of my success than I doubted the reality of the attack.' Then he had forborne to use his secret weapon, in order to retain the element of surprise for just such an emergency as the present one. He believed it could save very many more lives than it could destroy (and nobody in military history has ever won larger victories with smaller loss of life). He also hoped it might, by its effectiveness, help to dissuade men from making war at all. 'What is to become of us?' he replied to his critics, 'What? Universal peace.' But the humane and pacific Earl of Aberdeen who was now Prime Minister was not the man to experiment with a new weapon of war that had been condemned by a committee of experts as infallible but too terrible for use.

So the Cabinet not only turned down Cochrane's request to be appointed to the Baltic command, but it also decided not to use the secret weapon against the fortress of Kronstadt. Sir James Graham, the First Lord, gave him the verdict of the Admiralty Committee that had reported on it. 'On the whole after careful consideration they have come to the unanimous conclusion that it is inexpedient to try the experiment in present circumstances. They do full justice to your Lordship and they expressly state that if such an enterprise were to be undertaken it could not be confided to fitter or abler hands than your Lordship's, for your professional career has been distinguished by remarkable instances of bravery and courage in all of which you have been foremost in the way and by your personal heroism you have gained an honourable celebrity in the naval history of this country.'

By the time those words were written on 15 August 1854 both Arthur and his brother Ernest were serving with the British fleet in the Baltic, and Kitty had presumably paid a visit to England, since she was able to send a copy of them to Arthur. It was a most improper thing to do, unredeemed by the nature of her remarks about the First Lord and other members of Aberdeen's administration. 'So much for the sword of this diplomat. They have got out of Lord D all they wanted to know, what his plan was, and now they tell him what we all knew before, that he is a great minded man, but that they do not want to employ him. Keep all this to yourself, for I have no permission from headquarters to send you this.'

At the top of her letter Kitty referred to her forthcoming birthday, remarking: 'I am sorry to say I shall be 56!!' Either she was understating her age or she had been only 14 years old at the time of her elopement to Annan for her first ceremony of marriage.

In the Baltic the British Commander-in-Chief was Sir Charles Napier, who was by now old and timid although he was just over 10 years younger than Cochrane. 'Any attack on Cronstadt by ships would be impracticable,' he reported to an Admiralty as cautious as himself. The British fleet therefore sailed to reduce a Russian fort at Bomarsund in the Åland Islands, that confetti of rocks and isles at the entrance to the Gulf of Bothnia whose waterways were so treacherous to large warships. Small steam-driven gunboats of the kind Cochrane had been promoting for so long would have been exactly the craft for such an operation, just as his sulphur fumes would probably have induced the Russian garrison to abandon Kronstadt.

Nevertheless a British ship did succeed in navigating a channel between the islands to within a few hundred yards of the fort of Bomarsund, and on 1 August Arthur wrote to inform his father: 'Being worked almost to death I have scarce energy left to write but a few lines to hope you are well and say that I am alive. We attack Bomarsund in two or three days. The French troops have arrived and I am this moment taking in a cargo of shot and shell for the ships off Bomarsund.' Arthur knew how deeply his father yearned to be present and therefore, weary though he was, he filled his letter with details of the intended attack. Finally he composed the remarks that so many men sat down to write on the eve of an action which they might not survive. 'Please on no account vex yourself about my not being promoted, as I believe it would be my greatest misfortune at present as I should lose my ship and I do not know what I should do, and I really like the sea, and do not know what I should do on shore. Hoping you have inherited your good fortune, that you preserve your health, and may be enabled to carry out all those beneficial and vast projects you have ever had in view is the earnest wish of your affectionate son.' He concluded by reassuring Cochrane that he was keeping an eye on his younger brother. 'Ernest is looking well.'

No great damage was done to the fortress of Bomarsund, but the attack persuaded the commanding General that his position was desperate and he surrendered. Arthur was among those promoted Captain immediately after the victory. The timid Lords of the Admiralty were sufficiently satisfied to order Napier to retire from the Baltic without attempting to reduce any of Russia's more important strongholds there.

In September Kitty was back in Boulogne and Cochrane visited her there at the time when Prince Albert was paying a visit to Napoleon III and his Empress in a nearby château. This was the kind of society in which Kitty loved to exert her influence. 'I prevailed upon Lord D.,' she wrote to Arthur on 11 September, 'to go to the old Chateau and write his name upon the Prince Albert and the Empress Book. He has

been sent for expressly to go and see Prince Albert at 3 o'clock today
so at least his calling has done some good. I have helped him to dress,
cut his hair and trimmed his nails, brushed up his sword, cleaned the
gold of his coat, put on his *Stars*, and now he has no white gloves so a
pair of mine is substituted and with hard stretching they will do: and
now I find the Red Ribbon looks *greasy* and the daylight shows it has
not been always in right handling. I trust when I see you Sir Arthur
Auckland C.G.C.B. and no doubt I shall, that you will take more care
of your Ribbon than has one of our Noble Lords.' These remarks from
a woman who had forsaken her husband from the time when he was
sixty-five years old until he had now reached eighty were not the most
painful that Kitty saw fit to send to her son Arthur in the Baltic.

During this period he had been considerably closer to his father than
Kitty had been, yet she now told him: 'I think that the Admiralty were
afraid to put him in command, and I am sure I should be for I think his
mental and bodily powers are alas! very *greatly* on the wane. His mind
is broken or breaking fast—although he is pretty well in health and eats
and sleeps. He keeps up for a few hours and then I see he goes to bed
and is either half-dozing or stupid. In short my Arthur your Father is
now an old man and ought as Sir James Graham tells him to rest upon
his laurels. Do not when you write say that *he ought* to go to Cronstadt
for he gets so excited and so annoyed that I think it will be better to
let the subject alone, for I am sure the Admiralty will never employ him
upon active service again.'

Another passage in this long letter, as inconsiderate as a mother
could conceivably have sent to a son on foreign service in wartime,
reveals one of the roots of her quarrel with Cochrane. 'Your Father is
becoming very shaking in his mind and memory and indeed I think
through his *terrible* deafness that he will lose all power of business
powers. He says he is still without money although he had £6000 last
year and he has had a legacy from a cousin Scott Moncreiff of £3000,
making £9000 within eighteen months besides his Admiral's pay and
his service pension. These appear very large sums and no result besides
all that was sacrificed in the Wellesley. What will be the ending of these
alarming outgoings a cleverer person than myself can best tell.' She
implored Arthur to cease from assisting his father in what he had described as 'those beneficial and vast projects you have ever had in view',
making it clear how largely they had contributed to her unhappiness.

'I hope, my dearest Arthur, that you will not imbue your hands in
that hateful Pitch and dirt. For forty years and more I have been your
Father's wife and I have seen two noble fortunes spent, and not one
penny of money spent *ever returned*: £10,000 lost in Lamp concerns,

nearly as much in Copper rolling machinery, then came the fatal Janus of ruinous memory, and now these most dreadful Pitch affairs. Oh Arthur, it is fearful, to say nothing of £70,000 spent in two Elections in younger days, our little place sold at Holly Hill which he paid £13,600 was sold for £8000. The house Hanover Lodge cost £16,000 besides nearly £5000 laid out upon it, was sold to pay for the outlays for that hateful Janus. *That home* was sold over my head for (I think) £7,500. There are hard startling facts such of the little Plate I had saved from the wreck is held by Coutts in consequence of your Father having raised £1000 or £1500 upon it. I merely tell you these horrifying facts which are not half which I do know. I tell you because I love you tenderly, and as a mother ought I am reposing a deep confidence in your mind, and it is to entreat of you, not to speculate, not to be led into the same course of ruinous and endless expense. Look at the result, see what wretchedness this most fearful and most unprofitable line of life has led to. I do not believe a more miserable man breathes upon earth, dissatisfied with himself and everyone else he moans over the years which are past in perfect uselessness, money squandered without any real friends or supporters he is left to end a life which might have been the brightest that mortal man ever had a chance of possessing. . . .'

After returning to the hateful subject of pitch (not for the last time), Kitty reverted to Cochrane's secret weapon. 'I do really think in the first outset that he might have gone to Cronstadt had he set the right way to work, but he was on and off and did not appear in the least anxious, really anxious about it until it was too late, and then when it was so he appeared particularly to wish to undertake his sulphur plan which has been declined and I think *he never will* be employed again. They say in the Government that he is so very Pugnacious upon all occasions and I am sure that the Pamphlet about the West Indies *pecking* at Lord Grey has decided the question of his non-employ-ment.' Kitty is at her silliest when reading the minds of leading statesmen.

Since Cochrane never declined into senility during the 6 years of life that remained to him, some other explanation must be found for his wife's remarks on this subject. Old people do generally curtail their activity and retire early, but it may be that Cochrane also went into a doze on occasion to protect him from his wife's recriminations, or alternatively Kitty may have been trying deliberately to undermine Arthur's faith in his father's judgment in order to lure him away from the pitch enterprises.

The letter which Cochrane sent to the First Lord on 11 November combines a rebuttal of the charge that he was senile with a renewed

plea for the use of his secret weapon as the solution to Britain's set-
backs in the war. 'The unreasoning portion of the public have made an
outcry against old admirals, as if it were essential that they should be
able to clear their way with a broadsword. But, my dear Sir James,
were it necessary—which it is not—that I should place myself in an
armchair on the poop with each leg on a cushion, I will undertake to
subdue every insular fortification at Kronstadt within four hours from
the commencement of the attack.' But while Florence Nightingale
laboured to mitigate the appalling hardships of the wounded troops in
the Crimea and thousands perished in gallant actions such as the charge
of the Light Brigade without bringing any prospect of victory, the use
of Cochrane's weapon was again rejected.

Then an adverse vote in the House of Commons on the conduct of
the war led to Aberdeen's resignation, and to the succession of Palmerston as Prime Minister in February 1855. Cochrane submitted his
proposal directly to Palmerston, who had come so near to accepting it
by August that he wrote to Lord Panmure at the War Office: 'I agree
with you that if Dundonald will go out himself to superintend and
direct the execution of his scheme, we ought to accept his offer and try
his plan. If it succeeds, it will as you say save a great number of English
and French lives; if it fails *in his hands*, we shall be exempt from blame,
and if we come in for a small share of ridicule, we can bear it, and the
greater part will fall on him. You had best therefore make arrangements
with him without delay, and with as much secrecy as the nature of
things will admit of.'

This was proving to be nothing very much, and on 9 June an article
on Cochrane in the *Illustrated Times* hoped that the mystery of his all-
conquering weapon would soon be unveiled. It published a graphic
description of the old Admiral accompanied by a sketch of him. 'Fancy
to yourself a broad-built Scotchman, rather seared than conquered by
age, with hair of snowy white, and a face in which intellect still beams
through traces of struggle and sorrow, and the marks of eighty years
of active life. A slight stoop takes away from a height that is almost
commanding. Add to these a vision of good old-fashioned courtesy
colouring the whole man, his gestures and speech, and you have some
idea of the Earl of Dundonald in this present June, 1855.' The journal
told its readers that 'the public waits with a patience such as the present
war is schooling us all into, for some evidence of a curiosity on the part
of the Government about his secret "discovery". It was, indeed,
"shelved" by Lord Aberdeen, but since that time Aberdeen has been
shelved himself; and among other happy results of that event, let us
hope to have fair play to an old man of various fortune at sea and ashore,

a long-enduring hero in victory and in distress who, having done so much and suffered so much for three generations of his countrymen, deserves to die with the sound of their gratitude in his ears.'

Cochrane, who had no immediate intention of dying, suggested that his son Arthur should direct the operation employing his secret weapon; but before it could be carried out Sebastopol fell to the awes, and so the weapon remained unused, the secret intact.

But it passed into the Panmure papers and was published with them in 1908. Even Cochrane's senior grandson, General the Earl of Dundonald, was unaware of this disclosure when the Great War broke out in 1914, and it is likely that the Germans were ignorant of it also. The General took the precaution of keeping the formula in two parts, one at his home in Scotland and the other in London, but he brought the Scottish section to London on the outbreak of war in order to recommend the weapon's use. After demonstrating the smoke screen he wrote to Winston Churchill at the Office of the Duchy of Lancaster on 14 July 1915 : 'Dear Mr Churchill, You take a great interest in the Smoke Committee work which 1 tried to make a success. I send you a copy of my report and the plates of my Smoke practices.' The photographs of the smoke-screen trials were impressive and, largely through Churchill's initiative, Cochrane's smoke-screen played an important part in the naval warfare of the ensuing years. But whilst the British government rejected the use of sulphur as an asphyxiant, the Germans had their own plans and introduced gas warfare within weeks of that rejection. The two halves of Cochrane's formula had been stolen from Lord Dundonald's house at Wimbledon (for which he suspected his butler) but its secret could have been discovered in the Panmure papers, as well as by independent research.

So, rightly or wrongly, Cochrane was deprived of his last opportunity to add to the long list of unique achievements in war which had begun with the capture of the *Gamo* so many decades ago, and this had been due to mere procrastination on the part of government.

His youngest son Ernest returned from the Crimean war unharmed and with encomiums on his conduct. Arthur had sustained four wounds including 'a shot hole which went quite through my left leg'. He attempted to visit his mother at Boulogne on his way home, only to discover that she had gone to Paris. For a woman so repeatedly and seriously ill she did a remarkable amount of travelling, especially as she complained that travelling also made her ill. Arthur wrote to her in September 1855 to apologise that 'I am quite unable at present to go to Paris, and shall therefore miss the pleasure of seeing you for some time.' To her extraordinary remarks about his father he replied in November merely: 'My dear Father is still well though within the last day or two he has caught a cold but not I think of any consequence.'

Cochrane had much to hearten him as he nursed his November cold. All his sons had returned safely home, and Tom had been looking after the bitumen affairs during Arthur's absence abroad. There had been endless delays but Tom wrote to Arthur confidently in November: 'I am glad you approve the prospectus. It is all ready for starting and only wants the money market to be easier. It would never do to start it and have it fail, after all the very great trouble one has to get it so well filled up.' As the brothers were to meet in a few days Tom did not descend to detail in his letter, but he also told Arthur that 'Lord D has voted him a considerable sum of money from the Brazils as also £2000 a year'.

Tom told Arthur that once again 'Lady D has been very ill but is better now'. Evidently diabetes was suspected, for Arthur wrote to her a few days later recommending a recently published book on the treatment of the disease—which could have been of little help before the discovery of insulin.

In May 1856 Arthur was offered a posting to the Far East in command of the 14-gun screw-propelled warship *Niger*, and sailed away leaving his elder brother Tom once more in charge of his family's business affairs. 'Ernest, poor boy,' Tom told Arthur in August, 'drags on at Portsmouth and Horace vegetates in Scotland. Lady D exists in a state of mental excitement at Boulogne.' The cause of their mother's condition is revealed in the hysterical letter which she wrote to Arthur for his birthday in September.

Like his great contemporaries Wellington and Nelson, Cochrane had not been blessed with a successful marriage. Unlike them, he had not enjoyed the consolation of other attachments so far as is known, and in the case of such public figures it was virtually impossible for them to enter into a liaison without comment. Even Maria Graham's friendship with Cochrane in South America has given rise to the flat statement that she was his mistress, although there is not the slightest evidence or likelihood that this was so. It was not until Cochrane was over 80 years old that his wife first brought an accusation against him of this sort. She did so, in terms that reveal her as something less than every inch a Countess, in that venomous letter which she sent to Arthur in the Baltic, and it could have been the case that the woman whom she named was simply acting as Cochrane's housekeeper. For by this time she would even attack Cochrane's brother William and William's wife when he went to stay with them, and she developed a virulent animosity against his secretary William Jackson, while to her own children she was increasingly critical of her husband's health, mental capacity, and even of his past career.

But while it would be unwise to accept her statements without corroboration, there is the testimony of her son Tom, writing to Arthur in that letter of August 1856, that their 82-year-old father had indeed formed the affection which excited Kitty so much. According to both of them the association seems to have consisted of little more than regular evening strolls in Regent's Park, as might be expected at Cochrane's age, but Kitty's birthday letter to Arthur in September launched into a diatribe on the subject. She quoted a 'correspondent who appears to keep a very sharp look out upon the imprudent doings of a very weak old headstrong old dotard wilfully independent, who is lowering his position to the level of idiotancy'. Thereafter her entire letter is filled with reflections on Cochrane's past career that reveal a sadly disturbed state of mind.

Regrettable though it may appear that Arthur should have preserved this distressing letter, it does help to explain the furore caused by another that Kitty evidently wrote to Lizzie in Florence at this time, and which she must have forwarded to her brothers before it was destroyed. Remaining loyal as ever to his wife, Cochrane wrote to Horace in February 1857: 'The letter is obviously written with a view to set Cochrane' (that is Tom) 'you and myself by the ears. That she has not had sense enough to see the state of her mother's mental health is a deep misfortune, but one into which you also fell.' After reminding his son of the puerperal convulsions of 1829 that had been followed by the birth of a still-born son, and the decline in Kitty's health ever since, Cochrane told Horace 'had you reflected I believe you would have spared all the ill will that has been produced under another impression regarding the conduct of your mother'. The domestic tragedy of Cochrane's later years peeps through the tact and reticence of these words.

One complaint Kitty never made, so that it is evident she was never given cause. She could afford to travel wherever she wished, and a French relative of her husband's, the Duke de Gramont, helped to give her access to the social world for which she possessed a parvenu's enthusiasm. She was able to visit her family in England as often as she was unable to summon them to see her in France. Cochrane insisted upon the children's duty to her, though they may have become hardened to her own appeals to 'think sometimes of the lonely mother who gave you life and love, when there were few else to think or care for you'.

Cochrane was still doing his best with such means as he possessed. Ernest, who had by now been posted to the north American station, was given a quarterly allowance of £30 by his father. Tom had been made independent by his marriage, but Cochrane had made him heir to patented inventions which might make his fortune one day. Horace and his family were supported entirely by Cochrane, who protested in March 1857 when he was asked for more, 'to do more than I have done is quite impossible. My income (arising from pay) is anticipated. I have outlived credit, and from the circumstances in which I have been placed have no friends, and scarcely an acquaintance—assuredly not one that would lend me money even on the prospect of a Brazilian remittance.' Yet he was assisting his daughter also. 'Your sister has two pounds ten a day—and her living cannot cost more than mine.' This man who had been accused so often of greed and avarice had spent his gigantic energies in the service of four nations, flung the proceeds into projects, every one of which was sound and beneficial in its conception, distributed the residue fairly amongst his family, and left himself with scarcely anything.

If he derived solace from the feminine society that outraged Kitty, it could not have been very much, for he wrote to Arthur in April 1857 of 'the mental oppression which I have suffered ever since your departure and long before'. He could not have known what Kitty had been saying to Arthur when he tried to reassure him: 'Mam has had a severe illness but has recovered and thank God is now out of danger.' He had always been close to his brother William, now an old man like himself. 'I propose to take my Brother and Mrs Cochrane down to the neighbourhood of the Crystal Palace, where there are so many objects to divert attention, and stay there for a month or more to change this monotonous state of existence.'

The monotony was relieved that summer by news from Santiago that the Government of Chile had decided to bestow a medal on him in commemoration of his services and to give him the pay of a Vice-Admiral. His former shipmate Robert Simpson wrote to him on 15 August 1857: 'Be pleased to accept them with the efforts that, from circumstances, I have been enabled to make in order to bring about this testimony (however late) of national feeling: as a tribute of admiration and esteem for your lordship: I would add, of gratitude for many kindnesses received in former days.

'I have been requested to procure a biographical sketch of your lordship's eventful life in order to its publication in this country; also of your portrait. I need not say that I shall feel highly honoured by your lordship's attention to their humble demands from the many admirers, and a few old friends, of the famous Vice-Admiral of Chile, Lord Cochrane!

'That my very noble and gallant old Chief may live many, many years in health, and in the enjoyment of somewhat improved circumstances, is the sincere wish of his faithful friend and most obedient, humble servant.'

But Cochrane no longer hoped to live for many years, and he could not accept as a favour what amounted to short change in the settlement of a debt that had been recognised formally by Chile over a decade earlier. He wrote to the President: 'The grant of full pay, only prospectively, to one who is upwards of eighty years of age is little more than nominal, as my life in all human probability is approaching its close.' Manuel Montt had been President of Chile for over 5 years, and his firm rule had contributed effectively to the stability of a country which Cochrane had left in a state of disorder. Cochrane could not close his letter without expressing his personal respect for the President and his gratitude for the compliment that had been paid to him. 'Be assured, most Excellent Sir, that it is only my advanced age that prevents me from attempting to revisit your now peaceful and prosperous country, personally to acknowledge your Excellency's courtesy.'

According to Kitty's latest birthday letter to Arthur in September Cochrane was still enjoying his liaison. 'I think it most disgraceful conduct for a man at 82 and will be in the course of a very few months 83 years old.' Meanwhile she was still indulging her taste for ducal society, having abandoned the waters of Vichy for the villa of the Duke and Duchess de Gramont at Cannes, who were about to leave for Rome where the Duke had been appointed French Ambassador. She had moved on to Nice, and from her delightful villa there she wrote that Tom 'has bought a house in Albert Road. I believe it is beyond his means to keep it up but I have not seen it or was I in England when it was bought. Your father has given him four thousand five hundred pounds out of the Brazilian money.' It was at this house, 12 Prince Albert Road, Kensington, that Cochrane would spend the remainder of his life.

One of his first acts there was to settle the rest of Horace's debts. Cochrane wrote to him on 20 February 1858: 'I shall try to muster up courage to sell £2000 of the money yet saved next week; and pay off at once all you owe and some other scores that press heavily on my mind.' The bitumen project was at a standstill, which may have been the cause of his depression, but the request from Chile for a biographical sketch roused him to his final task, the compilation of his four volumes of autobiography. In 1858 appeared the first two volumes, describing his services in Chile, Peru and Brazil, a story made easier for him to recall by the published testimonies of Captain Hall and Major Miller,

John Miers, Maria Graham and William Stevenson. In addition, his secretary William Jackson had rescued many of his papers from Herradura during the Chilean earthquake, while a number of documents of his Brazilian service were still in his hands. But by now the events themselves were the fading memories of a very old man, so although these volumes contain precious historical material, the narrative does not match the epic quality of the theme.

It is also marred by the secondary objective of these books, which was to present the evidence of the debts of Chile and Brazil to their former Admiral. Cochrane's correspondence with his secretary Jackson illustrates the manner in which this ulterior motive forced itself upon the story. He told his secretary on 15 June 1858: 'I have received a letter from Rio remitting that which I scarcely expected, namely my half pay, accompanied with the . . . decision of the Rascally Prize tribunal that no more Prizemoney is due to me!!! It is lucky my Memorial is in hand shewing what they really do owe me. I have no doubt but that the same conclusion is to come in all other cases—for our captures were all given back to their Portuguese owners as the price of the acknowledgment of Brazilian independence.' The circumstances were comparable to those in which he had lost the Rio Clara estate that had been granted to him in southern Chile as a reward for his services.

'I am glad you think the Chilean memorial good. It is all derived from the documents of the time, many of which will be photographed in proof of ineradicable facts therein contained.' Cochrane had soon spotted the benefits of photo-copying, though by now he was too old to attempt any contribution of his own to the new techniques of photography.

Even a less argumentative man than he might have found it difficult to tell the South American story without descending to personal advocacy in such circumstances as these. On 25 November he was writing to Jackson: 'The proofs received from the Printers were so filled with alterations that they were sent back to be amended, and now further additions of great importance to the result—have been made; when received in a state to be revised by you, they will be forwarded.

'This morning I have had a very mournful letter from Grenfell, saying that in addition to the charges made against me of every shilling that passed through my hands—amounting to all and more than my share of Prize money—they have served him the same trick regarding his accounts at Para . . . The Memorials will be made irresistible; not a harsh expression will be used, but all smooth as oil yet corrosive as caustic. I shall recover my spirits if all goes as I hope and anticipate. The preface to the Memorials I propose shall expose the conduct pursued towards me by our own Government, which I am convinced led to that adopted by the S. American Rascals.' These business letters correct the statements which Kitty had been making to her children, that their father was by now in his dotage, as well as the later accusations of the Ellenborough apologists that the literary productions of his last year were ghosted for him by others.

He was, besides, providing wholly for Horace and his family, as well as giving financial assistance to all his other children. He was writing to those who were absent as dutifully as ever and pursuing his scientific and commercial projects with unabated enthusiasm. When his wife returned from her travels to Boulogne and required attention, he still crossed the Channel to see her. He wrote to Ernest at the Atlantic station in April 1858: 'Mam has been during all the winter at Nice and Sardinia in order to avoid the winter, having been afraid to encounter the cold of this country after the severe attack she had last autumn . . . Horace, poor fellow, is in the country, without occupation or resource of his own, with a penniless wife hanging upon him, notwithstanding that I have done my best to relieve him by compromising his debts.' Nostalgically Cochrane asked his son to 'tell me all about the plants at Bermuda and whatsoever you think will interest me, in those scenes in which I delighted'.

In September he was able to tell Ernest: 'I was over at Boulogne last week, and dear Mamma, though not well, is better than for some time past in health, and what is more cheering, in mind. I have there-fore hope of happiness yet to come, of which she has been deprived for many years by the most perverse circumstances.' Alas for his optimism! When Arthur was injured at the China station and invalided home, he aroused her most distressing symptoms by failing to visit her instantly. 'I am in perfect ignorance as to what I have done to offend you in the slightest degree, and it does distress me most painfully so I assure you to feel that you have entirely overlooked me and for no earthly cause that I am aware of.' Since Arthur never replied (so far as is known) to the dreadful attacks on his father which his mother had been sending him in letter after letter, it is impossible to tell whether these help to account for his failure to visit her, or whether his injury and his naval duties offer a sufficient explanation.

'I have had enough suffering,' she continued. 'I have gone through misery such as I pray to God you may never know much less feel—be assured my child I do not need one other drop in the cup of affliction.' And so on for several pages more, before setting off, not to see her wounded son in England but to resume her European wanderings.

Meanwhile the publication of Cochrane's books about his career in South America had inspired him to attempt an account of his earlier life; and once he had decided to expose the treatment he had received from the British government it was a short step to embark on his autobiography from the beginning. Such was the last, mammoth task which he set himself. He commissioned G. B. Earp, the author of a recent history of the Crimean war, to assemble his papers for the enterprise, and Earp approached Jackson for additional material. Of both men Cochrane never ceased to speak with appreciation, calling Jackson 'my steady friend and former secretary' and Earp 'my friend and literary coadjutor', a man without whose help he could never have undertaken his task.

Nevertheless he found time to discuss the marketing of oil during April and May 1859 with his convalescent son, and in July he crossed to Boulogne to visit Kitty, from where he wrote to Arthur: 'Mam does not come over with me as I have advised her by no means to go to London during this hot weather.' But she elected to cross the Channel with her husband to Deal, whither Cochrane asked Arthur to travel on 5 August in order to 'accompany your Mamma to Boulogne when she goes'. From Deal Cochrane himself rejoined his brother William at Crystal Palace, where he had found refreshment during the previous year. Here he acknowledged a touching invitation from Horace 'to accommodate me in case of need—and not only me but Mr Earp, to whom I am so greatly indebted. He has been indefatigable and the result I have no doubt will set our family on their feet.' His unselfish devotion to his entire family had survived every strain placed upon it. On 18 October he wrote to Arthur: 'I have concentrated all the remaining powers of my mind to devise the result (under *present* circumstances) of your kind endeavours to bring the Boiler into use.'

On the following day it was the turn of Ernest to hear from his father. 'Cochrane,' (that is, Tom) 'and Arthur have taken up a project of making grease for Locomotives which, by saving one half, besides wear and tear, will enable a good profit to be made. I am quite busy about my Book and hope to get it out by the beginning of next month or soon after. Mamma is still at Boulogne, but proposes to go southward during the winter. Poor soul, she is by no means well, and is very despondent, being so much alone.' Arthur had tried to comfort her by promising to visit her on her birthday if he could. 'If duties and other urgent matters permit me I shall certainly do myself the pleasure to come over to you by the 12th and paying my devoirs. I hope to be enabled to come but am unable to say positively.' The reason was that he had recently been given a post on a Government committee, and there is no evidence whether this prevented him from visiting his mother on her birthday or not.

The first volume of Cochrane's autobiography came out shortly before his eighty-fifth birthday, and carried his story as far as his return from the final achievement of his British naval service, the operation in Basque Roads. The reader was left on the threshold of those convulsive events, the Gambier court-martial and the trial before Lord Chief Justice Ellenborough. 'I fear the second volume will require a great deal of trouble,' Cochrane wrote on 15 December 1859, 'by reason of the notes I have lost of past events. It will however be far the most interesting, as matters treated of will be of *Public* importance, not of a private nature. I anticipate that the world at large will scarcely give credit to the facts I have to state in regard to the proceedings at Gambier's Court Martial.'

But this resurrection of old animosities was not doing him any good, and although he still possessed the clarity of mind to realise this, it did not prevent him from disfiguring his narrative and giving, at the end of the day, a distorted picture of his own character. 'I am very low in spirits,' he continued that letter to Jackson from his son's house in Prince Albert Road as his last Christmas approached, 'why, I cannot conceive for everything is going well with me, at least so it appears. I conceive therefore it must arise from the numerous facts—raised as if from their graves, that have lately been pressed on my attention.'

The fabrication of charts to support the false statements of Admiral Gambier at his court-martial concerning the dangers of shoals was a matter which Cochrane was particularly concerned to prove beyond question in his book. He wrote on 2 February 1860: 'The villainy is not exceeded by the Star Chamber, Jeffreys, Titus Oates or all the doings in the reign of the Stuarts.' But his anger was assuaged by the fact 'that the Brazilian Minister has opened a correspondence, to which I have given an answer that I hope will shame them out of the course they have been pursuing—as I hope will also be the case with our own Government. I feel myself getting better, mentally, now that things seem to be progressing favourably.' He continued thus until 8 March, when he expected the proofs of his second volume to arrive at any moment and told Jackson, 'do you exercise your judgment *freely* in this important matter' of correcting them.

But in fact he was already suffering from the complaint that would kill him, stones in the kidneys, and he remarked: 'Thank God I am getting better, but dare not move out whilst this easterly wind continues, the part which has been affected being very susceptible of cold—and cold productive of inflammation.' He remained buoyant in spirit: 'I think I may say with confidence that all my matters are going on well, and will succeed.'

Six days later he was still bothered over the manner in which the charts produced in evidence at Gambier's court-martial were illustrated and expounded in the book, though he conceded that ill-health was perhaps clouding his judgment. 'The state of my health probably renders me less susceptible of being pleased with any description or explanation of the charts, but Mr Earp has several times declared himself satisfied. I will however have my own way in this vital matter, and the book shall never be published unless I am.' He was heartened by the reception of the first volume of his life-story, for it was 'making a great stir. I have been asked, for the first time in 80 years, to dine with the Secretary of the Admiralty ! ! ! Lord Clarence Paget.' Paget would rise to the rank of Admiral and publish his own autobiography one day, but he had missed his opportunity to entertain the Grand Old Man of his Service. 'I have declined,' Cochrane told Jackson, 'on account of my health.'

By 19 March 'my hand shakes so much I can hardly write legibly—but I dare say you will make it out. I am a little better than I have been, and the Doctor says I will get over it.' To the pain he must have been suffering he made no reference, while he clung to the business of life, the costs of publication, the prospect of meeting his expenses out of the resources of Trinidad; until the tired, resentful mind wandered off to earlier years.

'You shall be enabled to pay your publisher, though I shall borrow it.

'The oil speculation—which I may say is *certain* of success—has left me just where I was a twelve-month ago—except that my plate is not in pawn. I look forward however to brighter prospects at no distant date . . .

'Never, never has such an exposure been made of any Pious government, in early or in present time.

'That a *Distributor* of Tracts should prompt forgery and perjury will astonish the Saints!'

A day later: 'I am far from being well, and fear that this is the beginning of the end.' On 4 April, having undergone his first operation, he felt more optimistic. 'I have been very, very ill, but an operation under the wonderful effect of chloral—which takes off all sense of pain both at the time and—in my case—after, has relieved me, so that I have hope of getting better.' He emerged from his coma still obsessed about

Gambier: 'The cursed explanation of the forgeries and falsehoods perpetrated both in regard to the charts and in the evidence has almost given me a death blow.' Then he was heartened by news of the return of Ernest from his tour of duty, to whom he wrote on 9 April: 'Do you come straight here; I have things to tell you.' He mentioned that he had been very ill for 2 months before reassuring him: 'I hope it is not quite over with me and that I shall live to see you Post Captain.'

But 3 days later Arthur told his mother: 'I think my Father's state of health precarious to the last degree. He underwent another operation yesterday under Bruce Jones, Lee and others and a large quantity of stone was brought away. He may or may not have power to rally . . . Ernest you of course know has arrived.' Nobody invited Kitty to come, nor did she ever cross the Channel to see her husband again.

On 17 April he was still sufficiently miserable to write: 'I have been confined to bed ever since the last cruel operation, quite unable to attend a magistrate or take my declaration about the pay or to attest my receipt for Chilean pay. This is the first day I have been able to raise my head.'

Yet he rallied gradually during the spring and summer until Earp told Jackson, 'he is now in a fair way of recovery'. Earp was concerned that they should not try to hustle the second volume of Cochrane's autobiography through the press. 'Hurry is a fatal mistake in book-making, if a book is intended to live after its author.' But by now Cochrane's two assistants found that they must fall back on documents in the completion of the work. 'I am very much obliged for the parcels you have sent me,' Earp told Jackson on 3 May. 'They are of great use, as bringing up matters which Lord Dundonald's memory no longer retains, and of which his sons have only imperfect remembrance.' He was still pleased with Cochrane's progress. 'I am happy to say he is better, but is still confined to his bedroom. He has gone through that which would have killed many men only half his age, and his having lived through it shows the finest constitution possible.'

By the end of May he was well enough to correct the work that Earp and Jackson had been attempting during his illness. 'He took a favourable turn last Saturday, and was dressed yesterday, though not downstairs. He was so much better as to be able to go over a proof sheet with me and make some very judicious remarks thereon. I have now hopes of his recovery, provided another operation is not necessary, but if it be, no one can tell the result, which will either be death from inflammation or prolonged life, perhaps for many years.'

In June William Miller in Lima wrote him a long letter which must have reconciled him to cutting his losses in South America, when neither Admiral Grenfell in Brazil nor General Miller in Peru had succeeded in obtaining better treatment by remaining in the service of those countries. 'The ingratitude of the Chileans towards your Lordship will be a sad blot in their history,' Miller wrote. 'I applied, a year ago, for the payment of my arrears; for my share of prize-money for the taking of Valdivia, and some compensation for disabling wounds, which have embittered and will shorten my life.' He had received no better satisfaction than Cochrane had done.

Miller reviewed his services to the British and Peruvian governments during the past 16 years and remarked: '*No* sort of duty is required of me and I receive my pay, to which I am entitled so long as I remain in Peru. But this, in virtue of existing Regulations, I shall probably lose when I leave the country to return to the Sandwich Islands, as I purpose doing in a few months, since I prefer a comparatively small salary, which I consider certain there, to a larger but precarious salary here—in this distracted country. I would fain pay another visit to England but I am too poor, the climate, I fear, would be too cold for me, and I should not like to again be obliged to become a rambling guest.' Outliving Cochrane by only a few months, Miller died before he could take up his British government post in the Sandwich Islands.

Cochrane's recovery lasted until the end of the summer, by which time it had occurred to Kitty to emulate her husband's generosity in distributing the money that came into his hands amongst his family. Arthur wrote to her on 15 September: 'Of your own kindness and free will you mentioned to me that so anxious were you for me to go to sea that you would settle on me £2500 if I would go. Would you kindly let me know if on my telling you I am prepared to go you will take legal steps to make your promise binding. 'It appears an odd time to have attempted to deprive her sick husband of the presence of his favourite son, but in any case Kitty changed her mind. 'Ladies have been at all periods allowed the privilege of changing their minds,' Arthur responded, 'courtesy says under all circumstances. Your letter has concluded the subject of financial matters.' If Arthur had been in actual need of money, his father would not have been able to supply it, for Ernest approached on the subject in October and Cochrane replied: 'I can not supply you with money, there not being *above* ground wherewith to put me below it.'

In these last days he experienced the Scotsman's yearning to return to his own country, as he wrote on 25 October to his friend Lyon Playfair, Professor of Chemistry at Edinburgh University. But 5 days later he had to undergo an emergency operation, from which he died on the 31st.

'One of the great characters of a past generation has just departed,' announced *The Times*. 'After attaining to an age beyond man's ordinary lot; after outliving envy, obloquy and malice; after suffering much, doing more, and triumphing at last, Lord Dundonald has closed in peace and honour the days of his eventful life.

'History can produce few examples of such a man or of such achievements. There have been greater heroes, because there have been heroes with greater opportunities; but no soldier or sailor of modern times ever displayed a more extraordinary capacity than the man who now lies dead. He not only never knew fear, but he never knew perplexity, and was invariably found master of the circumstances in which he was placed.'

Nevertheless he was not awarded a state funeral, although his family were offered the option of burial in St Paul's cathedral or Westminster Abbey. They chose the resting-place whose neighbourhood had been lit, so many years before, by his lamps and by his oratory. The funeral cortège consisted of a hearse drawn by six horses. Behind it followed eight mourning coaches-and-four, and then a long line of carriages containing people from near and far. There was the 82-year-old former Lord Chancellor Brougham, who had travelled all the way from Cannes to attend, and Admiral Pascoe Grenfell from Brazil, and Admiral Sir George Seymour of the British Navy, who shared with Cochrane the glory of their escapade in Aix Roads. The procession moved from Queen's Gate to Piccadilly, down St James's Street, along Pall Mall to Parliament Street, and so arrived at the Broad Sanctuary at 1 o'clock on 14 November 1860. On the previous day Queen Victoria and Prince Albert had ordered that his banner of a Knight of the Bath should be replaced in the chapel of Henry VII, and the regalia was recovered from a junkshop just in time to be installed amongst the insignia of the Order before his corpse was brought in through the same door from which his banner had been kicked over half a century before. Large crowds stood round the abbey entrances and spectators in mourning encircled the grave that had been dug in its central nave. The pall was borne there by the Brazilian Minister, Admirals Seymour and Grenfell and five other naval officers. Sir Francis Burdett's sole heiress, the future Baroness Burdett Coutts, was present among the host of people, famous and obscure, who had come to pay their last respects. But Lord Brougham exclaimed as he scanned their faces:

'What? No Cabinet Minister here, no officer of state to grace this great man's funeral?'

In the following month a committee was appointed to raise funds for erecting a statue in his memory. The faithful Earp became its secretary, and it was supported by the Dukes of Wellington and Bedford, Lords Brougham and Ebrington, Professor Playfair, and five admirals, one of whom was the son of Admiral Sir Alexander Cochrane and a namesake of the cousin they were trying to honour. But Cochrane had rarely received in life the recognition which was his due, and it eluded him at his death also. No memorial was raised in Scotland to her greatest sailor, no memorial in England to the seaman whose name was being coupled already with that of Nelson.

'Great Britain (says the *Daily News*, whose words we endorse) has lost the last of her ancient Sea-Kings. The paragon of the British Navy in its heroic age, the brilliant rival in desperate service and dauntless exploit of Nelson himself, the cynosure of Nelson's bravest captains ...' Somebody tried to enshrine the same sentiments in verse:

> A Sea King, whose fit place had been by Blake
> Or our own Nelson, had he but been free
> To follow glory's quest upon the sea,
> Leading the conquered navies in his wake.

His son, now the eleventh Earl of Dundonald, recalled in his tribute the quality that had struck so many others—Mary Mitford, Charles Greville, Maria Graham. 'Kindness, indeed, was as much a character-istic of him as valour. While the world was full of the fame of his war-like achievements, all who came within the circle of his acquaintance marvelled to find a man so simple, so tender, so generous, so courteous.' Alas, it is not the most immediate impression of his character left by the more cantankerous passages of his autobiography, and how many would recognise these as the work of a sick old man in a hurry?

Certainly not the Ellenborough muck-rakers, attempting to salvage the reputation of the Lord Chief Justice by demolishing that of Cochrane. The numerous inaccuracies in the autobiography, although immaterial to the issue, provided them with the means of undermining the general credibility of Cochrane's story. His association with Earp and Jackson also enabled them to question whether it really was the Admiral's own story, and they reached conclusions about this which are totally con-tradicted by the correspondence between the three collaborators. But the dirtiest sewer in which these sleuths tunnelled was naturally the one which involved the personal characters of the men under attack.

Cochrane's anxiety to recover the money owed to him by various governments when he was over 80 years old was aggravated, as he approached nearer to his death, by the fear that he would not be able to provide adequately for his dependants. The press remarked that his 'will is of a peculiar character, and very many of the bequests depend entirely upon the realisation of sums of money which the late Earl claimed from various Governments, our own included, should the exertions of the executors, conjointly with the late Earl's private secretary, procure a liquidation of them'. But Cochrane had preserved the reward of his Greek services for his wife, and to this he was able to add £6000 that he had received belatedly from Brazil. He bequeathed to her all the furniture and plate that he had provided for her residence at Boulogne, and the use of all the family plate lodged at present at Coutts' bank for the remainder of her life. This was a wise precaution, inasmuch as Kitty passed all her jewellery to her daughter Lizzie in Florence, who died shortly afterwards leaving it to an adopted child.

The eleventh Earl's portion was by contrast meagre, except in its potential. He inherited the inalienable symbol of his earldom, the ruined castle of Dundonald in Renfrewshire with its baronial lands, and all his father's interests in the island of Trinidad—as speculative a gift as a share in the outstanding debts to his late father. Arthur received the maritime patents and Horace and Ernest 'the profits (if any) which may arise from a share in the manufacture of certain compounds for the use of railways, but in no case are they to interfere in the management of the business'. William Jackson was left £100; a female servant £50 and an annuity. Earp was rewarded with a royalty on the sale of the books he had helped to put together, which soon proved to have been among Cochrane's most profitable enterprises. It was thus clear, declared the apologists of Ellenborough, that here were men who had fabricated an autobiography which represented a rogue as a hero for their personal profit.

It is true that Cochrane's literary assistants were left to patch together the uncompleted second volume of his autobiography. 'Can you remember anything about the Countess being in Brazil?' Earp asked Jackson on 12 February 1861. 'Not that I want to say much about her; but if not correct as to fact she may and would contradict me. She is not overpleased that the honour of the Earl has been vindicated and nothing said about herself. Knowing what the Earl has suffered for the past thirty years, I am not greatly inclined to puff her . . .' By this time the faithful Jackson was an ailing man of 78 and he was also extremely hard-up, for he had served his master without making financial demands on one whose embarrassments he knew as well as any. He had taken the trouble to preserve a large number of Cochrane's letters over the entire period since 1814 when he had been employed for the first time by him, and in his difficulties he wrote to the eleventh Earl, asking whether he would be prepared to acquire them. 'I think they would be cheap at a hundred pounds.'

On 25 April Dundonald replied, sending £25 and explaining that he was 'sorry that the heavy payments I have been called on to make since the death of my poor father does not enable me to do more for so old and valued a friend of his. Better days may come, and if I obtain a pension from the Government for my father's services I will do more for you.' Kitty's attitude to Jackson was very different. 'I have always despised the man,' she announced after her husband's death, 'and look upon him as the greatest enemy my husband had in life, and the ruin of his purse and character. Alas! Lord Cochrane had much more confidence in him than he deserved.' The Ellenborough apologists who seized upon this judgment were unaware of the even more extravagant remarks she had made to her own children about her own husband, apart from her erratic criticism of others. In his books she was able to read, by contrast, his devoted tributes to her, reminding her of his life-long loyalty to her.

But a step that her son Arthur took enabled her to make amends. He decided to appeal to the House of Lords that he was the true heir to the Dundonald earldom on the ground that his parents had not con-tracted a valid marriage at Annan, so that neither of his elder brothers was legitimate. Kitty wrote to warn him that such a claim would 'cost mines of money and no good result can possibly be achieved. Letters placed in the hands of the Lords will prove what here I have asserted to you.' She proved to be right; but Arthur's persistence enabled Kitty to step before the footlights once more in the role of Dowager Countess of Dundonald, and this time her sense of occasion, her concern for her honour and (one hopes) her memories of a deep devotion transformed her once more into the Sea Wolf's wife.

'I cannot bear to be sitting here to vindicate the honour of such a man,' she expostulated to those who had come to Boulogne to question her. 'It is too much to speak and tell my feelings, it would be impossible. He was a glorious man. He was incapable of deception such as is imputed to him by the world, I know.' Gradually his image expanded in her mind. 'Such a God of a man! A man who could have ruled the world upon the sea. That I, his wife, should sit here to vindicate the honour of such a man as that. Oh God have mercy upon me and upon us. It is too much, I cannot stand it.'

Thus she reached her peroration. 'That honoured name! That name for ages, for ages and for ages that has run the world with his deeds. The hero of a hundred fights. I have followed the fortunes of that great man. I have stood upon the battle deck. I have seen the men fall. I have raised them. I have fired a gun to save the life of a man for the honour of my husband and would do it again. He was a glory to the nation in which he was born, and there is not a member of the family of Dundonald that need not be proud of belonging to such a noble man as he was.'

POSTSCRIPT

The Secret War Plan
of Lord Dundonald

Charles Stephenson

Admiral Sir John 'Jacky' Fisher's 1899 observation that 'Moderation in
war is imbecility . . .'[1] places him squarely amongst the proponents of
what we now call 'Total War'. Not for him the gentlemanly ideals of
'fair play' that motivated his rival Lord Charles Beresford to propose
utilising only half his force against the Russian Baltic Fleet in 1904 on
the grounds of chivalry.* Cochrane however had such a modernistic
outlook on his profession almost a century before such ideas began to
gain common currency. The prime exemplar of this was his conception,
adoption, and unremitting urging of methods of chemical warfare some
104 years before they actually made their debut on the battlefield, and
the fact that they were, in almost their original form, still considered at
that later date.

Cochrane first became aware of the potential of sulphur fumes
during a visit he made to the island of Sicily in July of the year 1811. One
of the principle industries of Sicily at that time was the manufacture
of sulphur. As quarried or mined free sulphur is contaminated with
clay, limestone, gypsum etc., its extraction depended on melting it and
running it off from the earthy residue—a process known as liquation.
The method he saw employed involved placing a mass of the ore in
a kiln and igniting a portion of it, the resultant heat melting the rest
which was run off into damp wooden moulds. The ensuing fumes—
when burned, sulphur produces sulphur dioxide, an extremely toxic
gas—caused '. . . the abandonment of the country around the sulphur
mines in the melting season (which is restricted by law to two months
of the year) . . .'[2] He observed that the fumes '. . . though first
elevated by heat, soon fell to the ground, destroying all vegetation,

---

*This was following the 'Dogger Bank Incident' of 22 October 1904, when the Rus-
sian Baltic Fleet under Admiral Rozhestvensky, en route to its fateful rendezvous at
Tsushima, opened fire on the Hull fishing fleet in the mistaken belief that there were
Japanese torpedo boats amongst them. The incident brought Russia and Britain to the
brink of war.

and endangering animal life to a great distance . . .'[3] Here, to his warrior's eye, was a method of attacking an enemy no matter where and how he might shield himself from conventional forms of attack; a method that would, a century or so later, become known as chemical warfare: '. . . chemicals do not strike a physical target—they pervade the atmosphere over an area.'[4]

As he himself was to later put it, 'An application of these facts was immediately made to Military and Naval purposes, and after mature consideration, a Memorial was presented on the subject to His Royal Highness the Prince Regent on 12 April 1812 . . .'[5] Cochrane was being somewhat modest; this 'Memorial' (penned by his uncle, Mr Cochrane Johnstone,[6] and actually dated the 2nd of March 1812) was far more than a mere appreciation of the utility of sulphur dioxide as a weapon. It was actually a blueprint for the destruction of the entire French Navy and advocated an entirely new strategy for using British naval superiority as an alternative to that which it was then employing.

> . . . The French Squadrons . . . are not yet formidable . . . however . . .
> they . . . require a force to blockade them . . . on so many, and on such
> distant stations . . . [that] this apparently endless, and harassing, and at
> certain seasons impracticable, mode of warfare, [is] destructive of the
> spirit of the British Navy.[7]

This reaction to a potential 'fleet in being' was forced onto the British by the difficulties of overcoming the maritime fortifications behind which the enemy protected their dispersed strength. The fundamentals of the problem were tactical; how to overcome stone-built land-based works with wooden ships. As Lord Nelson himself had styled it, how to 'lay wood before walls.[8] Merely blockading the French navy is a defensive mode of warfare; what he proposes is taking the offensive to the enemy, and rather than being content to "bottle up" the various flotillas, to seek them out and destroy them.' He goes on to 'proceed to the chief object . . . the means of destroying the whole navy and flotilla of France'.

Basically put, Cochrane envisaged the saturation bombardment of the French vessels in their protected harbours by what he termed 'temporary mortars' and the reduction of their maritime fortifications, where necessary, by 'sulphur vessels'. A temporary mortar was a ship whose hold had been specially adapted—the bottoms and sides strengthened with extra timbers and lined with clay in order to project explosive force upwards—to hold a large quantity of powder, over the top of which was laid 'carcasses, shells and grenades'. The idea behind the weapon was 'of the simplest kind; and founded on the known principle of the expansion of ignited powder; is in the line of least resistance; and that bodies will receive an impulse therefrom, in proportion to the quantity of powder used, and the opposition given to its efforts in other directions'.

Cochrane proposes to modify three old hulks per target to be attacked; these would in effect be huge, as he states it, mortars, which, when fired, would hurl in an instant in the region of 6000 carcasses and shells over the protective moles and ramparts and destroy any ships within. He states the result of a trial carried out in Sicily during February 1811, when a wine pipe* 'converted into one of these mortars, threw 28 eight-inch shells over a wider space than the principle fortifications of Corfu [230 yards] although there were only three pounds of powder to each shell'. Temporary mortars were not for the purposes of distant bombardment and in order for them to 'hurl destructive missiles into naval depots; and lift them over moles, and basins, amidst the vessels they contain', they would have to get in close, which would make them vulnerable to shore based defences. To neutralise these defensive works and fortifications, Cochrane had devised another weapon—'sulphur ships, placed during night on the windward side of such fortifications'. He attached a generic plan, though the explanation above hardly needed much expansion, for the mode of attack. He also included a drawing of such a craft, with the notation: 'It is unnecessary to suggest that the vapour will pervade the innermost recesses of bomb-proofs, fill batteries or cones, and that it will roll along under the lee of walls and parapets to a great distance.' The sulphur vessels in reality formed only a small portion of the overall plan, though nevertheless by far the most novel and therefore controversial.

The Prince Regent, later to become George IV, placed the memorial before a commission '. . . consisting of the . . . Duke of York, as President, Lord Keith, Lord Exmouth, and the two Congreves, one of whom, Sir William, was the celebrated inventor of the rocket which bears his name'.[9] Admiral Lord Keith contributed the following observation, dated 9 March, on the plan for sulphur ships:

> Of the combustible weapons I am not so able to judge as others more conversant in such affairs; but there is, no doubt, valuable matter in the plan for consideration, and, if put into skillful management tempered with prudence, may be attended with good effect.

Cochrane pursued the matter, and was writing to Keith on 23 March:

---

* A wine pipe is a large cask, equal to four barrels, holding 105 imperial gallons.

. . . His Royal Highness the Duke of York has expressed himself satisfied with the military part of the plan submitted to the Regent; and His Royal Highness also informed me that Mr Congreve, after some days consideration, gave a favourable opinion as to the practibility of using Explosion and Sulphur vessels as pointed out.[10]

There were further papers by Cochrane on 2 and 11 May, the former concerning the tactical use of 'Explosion Vessels' and the latter, entitled 'Additional Observations', enumerating the advantages to be accrued by the Royal Navy pursuing amphibious operations. In fact, despite the commission reporting favourably on the efficacy of the secret weapons—'These officers . . . gave it as their opinion that . . . such a mode of attack would be irresistible. And the effect of the power and means proposed, infallible . . .'[11]—nothing was done. Cochrane was summoned to Carlton House and commanded to secrecy on his part, and 'not long' after that interview Lord Melville informed him that it was intended to put into action a portion of the war-plan, requesting his [Cochrane's] attendance at the Admiralty 'for the purpose of conferring on the subject'. To this he demurred on the grounds that '. . . development of a portion might give the enemy such an insight of the whole as would enable him to turn it against ourselves on a large scale . . .'[12] However he was prevailed upon by Lord Keith, and accordingly formulated a plan to destroy enemy ships in the outer roads of Toulon. Part of his reasoning here was the assurance that '. . . a success once achieved, the popular voice would place it in my power to enforce the execution of the more destructive portion of the invention within the enemy's inner harbours'.[13] On 12 May 1812 Cochrane wrote to Lord Melville stating what force he considered necessary for executing the plan for the destruction of the Toulon fleet: one seventy-four [a line-of-battle ship armed with that many cannon]; two 38-gun frigates; two 18-gun brigs; two cutters or schooners; '. . . requisite as an escort and to protect the boats'.[14]

It is clear from the above, since the fleet was situated in the *outer* roads of Toulon, that the portion of the plan the Admiralty was interested in utilising concerned the explosion vessels or temporary mortars. In his original memorial he had enunciated his belief that with three such vessels '. . . the French fleet may be burnt at their anchors or driven onto the rocks in the outer roads, where they anchor during the summer months . . .' Even the reduced plan was not put into effect, which Cochrane was to blame on '. . . ill feeling against me at the Admiralty . . . [as it] would have placed me in command of a squadron, with my flag flying in a line-of-battle ship . . . and the project after long fruitless expectation was dropped'.[15] Despite being again offered the prospect of attacking Toulon on a small scale—an offer dismissed by Cochrane as '. . . preposterous . . . [and] not altogether free from the suspicion that failure would be more acceptable than success . . .'[16]—his plan was not to be resurrected during the course of the rest of the conflict, whilst the Royal Navy continued its ultimately successful blockading strategy 'which no sailing navy before had ever attempted'.[17]

It must be reiterated that the usage of sulphur dioxide formed, as stated, only a small portion of the overall plan Cochrane had developed, though by far the most original. His 'Temporary Mortars' bear a striking resemblance to the vessels he had actually utilised during his action at Aix Roads and were merely a development of an existing, conventional weapon. The proposal to utilise sulphur vessels was novel—perhaps too novel—and certainly a sharp departure from ordinary methods. He included a drawing of a 'Sulphur Ship' in an appendix to the 'Memorial', but did not include any detailed tactical plan as to their usage; one hardly being necessary, for if the weapon were adopted the means by which it would be employed were obvious.

The demise of Napoleonic France and the ensuing peace did not, following his return to Britain and rehabilitation,* deter Cochrane from attempting to gain official adoption of his methods; in this he was relentless. He badgered, which is not too strong a word, successive First Lords of the Admiralty, the newly crowned William IV, and various other political figures, all to no avail; '. . . the fact that England was at peace . . . [being] . . . a sufficient reason for not discussing the value of a new instrument of war'.[18] As his son and biographer put it: 'Lord Dundonald,† however . . . thought otherwise.'[19] His frustration and annoyance at the huge cost of the, useless in his view, maritime defences then being constructed at various British ports, led him, on 29 November 1845, to compose a 'vigorous' (and very long) letter to *The Times*. His opening paragraph contained a stinging attack on those too hidebound, in his view, to embrace his ideas:

> Had gunpowder and its adaptation to artillery been discovered and perfected by an individual, and had its wonderful power been privately tested, indisputably proved, and reported to a Government, or to a

---

*'He might have used his secret in Chili, Brazil, and Greece; but his promise to the Prince Regent, and patriotic feelings . . . restrained him.' Cochrane, Thomas Barnes, 11th Earl of Dundonald, and Bourne, H. R. Fox, *The Life of Thomas, Lord Cochrane, 10th Earl of Dundonald*, published 1869, p. 247.
† Thomas Cochrane became the 10th Earl of Dundonald on 1 July 1831.

council of military men, at the period when the battering-ram and cross-bow were chief implements in war, it is probable that the civilians would have treated the author as a wild visionary, and that the professional council . . . would have spurned the supposed insult to their superior understanding . . .

He went on to argue that the advent of steam-powered warships need not necessitate the construction of the great, and expensive, fixed maritime defences then under consideration, as a counter. He considered of course that his secret plan, of saturation bombardment of vessels in harbours and the gassing of the personnel in the fixed defences, had rendered such structures obsolete:

> . . . I am desirous of showing that the use of steam-ships of war, though at present available by rival nations . . . need not necessarily endanger our national existence, which appears to be apprehended by those who allege the necessity of devoting millions of money to the defence of our coasts. I contend that there is nothing in the expected new system of naval warfare, through the employment of steam-vessels, that can justify such expensive and derogatory precautions, because there are equally new, and yet secret, means of conquest, which no devices hitherto used in maritime warfare could resist or evade.
>
> . . . with this all powerful auxiliary invasion may be rendered impossible . . . by the speedy and effectual destruction of all assemblages of steam-ships, and, if necessary, of all the navies of the whole world . . . [a]way with the projected plans of 'protective forts and ports' . . . ports on the margin of the Channel cannot be better protected than those which exist, respecting which I pledge any professional credit I may possess, that whatever hostile forces might therein be assembled could be destroyed within the first twenty-four hours favourable for effective operations, in defiance of forts and batteries, mounted with the most powerful ordnance now in use . . .
>
> . . . Protective harbours . . . may be likened to nets wherein fishes, seeking to escape, find themselves inextricably entangled . . . [n]o effective protection could be afforded in such ports against a superior naval force equipped for purposes of destruction . . . [t]he hasty adoption of such measures, and the voting of the vast sums required to carry them into execution, are evils seriously to be deprecated. It is therefore greatly to be desired that those in power should pause before proceeding further in such a course. It behoves them to consider . . . the overwhelming influence of the secret plan which I placed in their hands, similar to that which I presented in 1812 to . . . the Prince Regent . . .

The conclusion of this missive contained a scarcely veiled threat that he would, unless his plan was given serious consideration by the government, and unless that government reversed its policy on maritime defence, reveal all.

> Thirty-three years is a long time to retain an important secret, especially as I could have used it with effect in defence of my character when cruelly assailed . . . and could have practically employed it on various occasions to my private advantage. I have now, however, determined to solicit its well merited consideration, in the hope, privately, if possible, to prove the comparative inexpedience of an expenditure . . . for the construction of forts and harbours, instead of applying ample funds at once to remodel and renovate the navy . . .
>
> . . . However injudicious it might be thought to divulge my plan . . . if its disclosure is indispensable to enable a just and general estimate to be formed of the merits of the mongrel terraqueous scheme of defence now in contemplation, as compared with the mighty power and protective ubiquity of the floating bulwarks of Britain, I am satisfied that the balance would be greatly in favour of publicity.

This somewhat crude attempt at coercion may well have worked, at least after a fashion, or it may have been due, as his son suggested, to the appointment of 'his friend' Lord Auckland as First Lord of the Admiralty, for within 'a few months' his plan was put before a 'competent committee of officers' for their consideration. [20] As was pointed out in the letter to *The Times,* the methods under consideration were similar to those propounded in the 'Memorial' of 1812. They had however been distilled (Britain being no longer at war with France of course, though the French were still seen as the most likely potential enemy) and consisted now of two components—the use of sulphur dioxide as an offensive weapon, and the utilisation of smokescreens. The committee, consisting of Sir Thomas Hastings, Surveyor-General of the Ordnance, Sir John Fox Burgoyne, and Lt. Col. J. S. Colquhoun, reported their findings on 16 January 1847.

They were of the opinion that the idea of using smoke for '. . . concealing or masking offensive warlike operations . . . under many particular circumstances . . . may be made available . . . and we therefore suggest that a record of this part of Lord Dundonald's plans should be deposited with the Admiralty, to be made use of when, in the judgement of their lordships, the opportunity for employing it may occur'. [21] They were however unimpressed with the idea of chemical warfare:

After mature consideration, we have resolved that it is not desirable that any experiment should be made. We assume it to be possible that the plan . . . contains power for producing the sweeping destruction the inventor ascribes to it; but it is clear this power could not be retained exclusively by this country, because its first employment would develop both its principle and its application. We considered, in the next place, how far the adoption of the proposed secret plans would accord with the feelings and principles of civilised warfare. We are of unanimous opinion that . . . [the] . . . plans would not be so. We therefore recommend that, as hitherto, . . . [the] . . . plans should remain concealed.[22]

Dundonald's response was, given the acerbic tone of his *Times* letter and his impatient nature, somewhat muted. Writing to Auckland on 27 January he said:

Permit me to express . . . my deep sense of obligation to your lordship in causing my plans of war to be thoroughly investigated by the most competent authorities . . . [w]ith regard to their disposal, I submit that it would be advisable to retain them inviolate until a period shall arrive when the use of them may be deemed beneficial to the country.

He took issue, though again in a restrained manner, with the committee's conclusion that the use of sulphur dioxide would not accord with the 'principles and feelings of civilised warfare', arguing that the adoption of

. . . a new method resorted to by the French, of firing horizontal shells and carcases [sic], is stated by a commission of scientific and practical men appointed by the French Government to ascertain their effects, to be so formidable that 'it would render impossible the success of any enterprise attempted against their vessels in harbour', and that, 'for the defence of roadsteads, or for the attack of line-of-battle ships, becalmed or embayed, its effect would be infallible'—namely, by blowing up or burning* our ships, to the probable destruction of the lives of all their crews. I submit that, against such batteries as these, the adoption of my plans . . . would be perfectly justifiable.[23]

---

* Two vital changes in the technology of naval warfare were the invention of the explosive shell and the rifled gun. Though adopted by military forces some years before, it was not until the 1830s that explosive shell was taken aboard ships. The detonation of such a missile in a wooden structure caused a primary fire at the site of the explosion, and secondary conflagrations where the red-hot splinters landed, and fire was one of the things that the sailors of wooden ships feared the most. It was rare for such vessels to be sunk in engagements where solid shot was the only ordnance, but fire on a wooden ship meant almost certain destruction. The development of the

In fact it was to be against similar batteries that the next usage of the plans were to be mooted; however they were not to be French but Russian, during the Crimean War. Naval and military forces were despatched to aid the Turks, landing at Varna on the Western shore of the Black Sea, at which the the Russians withdrew leaving the Allies searching for somewhere to bring their power to bear. Eventually it was decided to attack Sevastopol on the Crimean peninsula.

The Baltic was another location where it was felt operations may have been conducted profitably and to that end a fleet under Vice-Admiral Sir Charles Napier had been despatched. Cochrane had been considered for the command of this fleet, but, in a backhanded tribute to his abilities, Sir James Graham, the First Lord of the Admiralty, had vetoed the appointment:

> Lord Dundonald is seventy nine years of age; and though his energies and faculties are unbroken, and though, with his accustomed courage, he volunteers for the service, yet, on the whole, there is reason to apprehend that he might deeply commit the force under his command in some desperate enterprise, where the chance of success would not countervail the risk of failure and of the fatal consequences, which might ensue. Age has not abated the adventurous spirit of this gallant officer, which no authority could restrain; and being uncontrollable it might lead to most unfortunate results. The Cabinet, on the most careful review of the entire question, decided that the appointment of Lord Dundonald was not expedient.[24]

Russian naval strength in the region consisted of some 27 ships of the line and a host of smaller vessels, a fleet superior to the force commanded by Napier who could initially muster only six ships of the line, an equal number of steam frigates and several other vessels. Moreover, the British fleet was undermanned with crews largely untrained. The Admiralty ordered Napier to prevent the Russian fleet from leaving the Gulf of Finland and to report on the possibilities of offensive action against the enemy bases. The Russian defences in the region were based on four strong points: Kronstadt, Sveaborg, Revel and Bomarsund.

---

rifled gun meant that such missiles could be delivered with greater accuracy over longer ranges than had been possible with smooth bore cannon. A practical example concerned the action off Sinope in 1853, when the Russian Black Sea fleet surprised a part of the Turkish fleet and completely destroyed it by using explosive shell, against which the Turks could only reply with the traditional solid shot. Not only did the Russian shell incinerate the fleet, but the town itself was set ablaze and a good part reduced to ashes.

The supreme prize was the Russian Baltic fleet which had withdrawn to the naval fortress of Kronstadt. Situated on the island of Kotlin, guarding the approaches to St Petersburg, the Russian capital, it was a position of immense strength. Napier studied the island and attendant fortifications for several days before despatching a signal to the Admiralty, to the effect that the position was impregnable with the forces at his disposal; accordingly the Allied fleet left the waters around Kronstadt on 4 July 1854 without a shot being fired.

Disappointing as this news may have been to an expectant British public, it was undoubtedly the correct decision for Napier to make. The defences of Kronstadt were well equipped with shell and incendiary missiles and against them the Allied vessels would have been at a severe disadvantage; for although the French navy had adopted shell in 1837, with the Royal Navy following suit in in 1839, neither had evolved any protective measures for their wooden ships. Had the [wooden] Russian fleet given battle the outcome may have been uncertain, against the stone forts guarding Kronstadt the Allied fleet would have been committing suicide. The conventional way to deal with such matters was to land a military force and assault or lay siege to the works, which of course is what happened at Sevastopol, though a purely naval attack was attempted on 17 October 1854 which achieved nothing beyond the loss of 6 ships and some 500 men.

It was therefore with a great degree of interest that Sir James Graham studied a letter, dated 22 July 1854, sent to him by Dundonald:

> . . . I am desirous through you to offer for the consideration of Her Majesty's cabinet ministers a simple yet effective plan of operations, showing that the maritime defences of Kronstadt (however strong against ordinary means) may be captured and their red hot and incendiary missiles prepared for the destruction of our ships turned on those they protect . . .
>
> Permit me therefore, in the event of my plans being approved, unreservedly to offer my services (under the passive protection of the fleet) to put them in execution, without command or authority, except over the very limited means of attack . . .[25]

As can be imagined, Sir James was mightily interested in such a plan, and he replied to Dundonald on 26 July:

> You offer for the consideration of H.M. Government a plan of operations, by which the maritime defences of Kronstadt in your opinion may be captured; and in the most handsome manner you disclose your

readiness to assist and superintend the execution of your plan should it be adopted.

When the great interests at stake are considered, and when the fatal effects of a possible failure are duly regarded, it is apparent that the merits of your plan and the chances of success must be fully investigated and weighed by competent authority . . .

. . . The question is a naval one, into which professional considerations must enter largely. Naval officers of experience and high character are the judges, to whom in the first instance the question ought to be submitted . . .

Sir James then proposed that Dundonald lay his plan before a committee of 4 senior officers, 3 naval and 1 military. Under the chairmanship of Admiral-of-the-Fleet Sir Byam Martin, the comptroller of the navy, he nominated; Admiral Sir William Parker,* C-in-C Plymouth, Rear-Admiral Berkeley, a Lord of the Admiralty, and General Sir John Fox Burgoyne, the Inspector-General of fortifications. His letter continued:

I am sure that you will not regard this mode of treating your proposal as inconsistent with the respect which I sincerely entertain for your high professional character, resting on past services of no ordinary merit, which I have never failed to recognise, but my duty on this occasion prescribes caution and deliberate care, and you will do justice to the motives by which this answer to your request is guided.

Sir James wrote to Sir Byam on 29 July informing him that Lord Dundonald accepted the proposed reference and on 2 August, with Sir Byam taking notes, they:

. . . assembled at the Admiralty . . . and entered into a discussion with Lord Dundonald respecting his plans, but it was, in the first instance, indicated to his Lordship that we thought he might be desirous to have the assurance of perfect secrecy regarding his plans, and that we would at once set him at ease on that point, by an unqualified declaration that nothing relating to his plan would be mentioned by any member of the committee, except in their report to Sir James Graham, we therefore urge his lordship to enter unreservedly into an explanation of his plans, and his mode of carrying them out.

The notes go on to explain that after much conversation, sadly unrecorded, the committee put several questions to Dundonald, and

---

*Sir William Parker provides a direct link between Horatio Nelson and 'Jacky' Fisher. He had served as a captain under the former, and sponsored the latter at the outset of his career.

he delivered several memoranda. The questions and answers were recorded, apparently verbatim, and they go on at some length.

In order to carry out his plan, Lord Dundonald explained he would require 24 old iron colliers or iron lighters; 16 of these would be fitted out as smoke vessels and 8 as sulphur craft. They would require to be crewed by 210 officers and men. The smoke craft would be filled with bituminous coal and other smoke producing substances; the sulphur vessels with coke, charcoal, and sulphur—some 200 tons of 'common, crude sulphur'. The boats from the fleet, 'at least one from each ship', would be required to support the attack but the fleet itself would not be required to join in.

The committee were concerned about the composition of the fumes generated by the sulphur vessels: 'Do you wish to withhold from us a knowledge of the component parts of this noxious matter?' They were reassured: 'No, sulphur, charcoal and coke will completely decompose all the atmospheric air that comes in contact during combustion.'

They also sought clarification on some of the wording contained in the original letter to Sir James Graham, relating to his statement that the defences may be captured. They enquired whether military forces would have to be landed to effect this capture. Dundonald replied: 'If you want to capture it there must be men provided, but if the destruction of the fleet be the only object it may be affected without landing.' What he proposed was the obscuring or disabling of two or three of the outlying works to facilitate the passage of the ships boats. The crews of these would occupy the defences along the sea wall, the garrison of which would have previously been disabled by sulphur fumes, and using the weapons of these works, destroy the Russian fleet: '. . . their red hot shot and incendiary projectiles . . . turned on those they protect.'

The committee expressed concern that this implied a large landing force would be required, they were also worried about the effectiveness of the methods advocated: 'What practical proof have you ever had, on a large scale that the smoke will have a sufficient spread to conceal your operations? . . .'

Lord Dundonald replied that he had only experienced such phenomena on a small scale whilst he was near sulphur works in Sicily. He then delivered a paper for the committee's consideration:

> Red hot shot and missiles being now generally used in maritime fortifications, it is manifest that attacking ships are infinitely more endangered than formerly when cold shot were the only missiles— especially during their approach, when elaborate aim can safely be taken from casemates and embrasures before the guns of the ships can bear.

To avert this peril it is proposed that iron vessels containing large masses of combustible materials [bituminous coal or other matter] shall be kindled at a proper distance to windward of the fortifications or batteries to be attacked so that dense vapours—more obscure than the darkest night—shall conceal the ships from the batteries, until they arrive at a position to [illegible].

If the assailing force, as there is great reason to believe, is still endangered by incendiary missiles, sulphur vessels may be conducted to appropriate positions, the fumes from which will expel artillery men from the strongest casemates, and drive them from their guns, wherever situated, within a mile of the burning sulphur carried down the breeze. The works at Kronstadt are particularly exposed to this mode of attack—being partly isolated and partly situated on a long sea wall running in the usual course of the prevailing wind, whereby one or two smoke and sulphur vessels would clear the whole range.

The committee once again raised doubts about the effectiveness of the smoke:

As your opinion of the spread of the smoke is founded only on what you have witnessed when passing near sulphur works, it seems evidently a matter of conjecture as to the degree to which you may be capable of spreading over a large space 'a dense vapour more obscure than night' so as to conceal your operation from the enemy. The smoke will naturally take a lateral direction when sent forth from each smoke vessel . . . but it is difficult to envisage its density continuing for any length of time, over a space so great as to shut out the garrison and the fleet from discovery of your position and proceedings—even if other smokers contribute an additional supply is it not probable that the smoke would pass off in a narrow current, or at best provide only a transient eclipse of the light, you have already stated that the operation must not be undertaken in a calm.

Lord Dundonald could only reply that he did not expect the smoke to behave in the way the committee expected. They again returned to the subject of the need for men to land and take possession of the defensive works: 'What additional force of men do you consider necessary to attack and take possession of Fort Alexander and other isolated forts in the event of their garrison being temporarily paralysed by the fumes of the sulphur craft.' Dundonald replied: 'If the fleet is the object there is no occasion to take possession of the isolated forts, paralysing the garrison of fort Alexander and obscuring the others would suffice. It is obvious however that if animation is suspended a boats crew would suffice, if not, an army would not accomplish the storming of such structures.'

The committee also asked for a complete list of all the requirements for mounting an attack as proposed, and requested that it be delivered within 2 days. Dundonald replied that he would comply, but pointed out that the questions he had answered left little more to say. Nevertheless, the next day his memorandum entitled 'Preliminary Requisites' was delivered:

> In order to enable a full explanation to be drawn up, showing the practicability of successfully attacking Kronstadt, a large outline chart of the island and anchorage is essential—say on a scale three times greater than those sold in the shops.
>
> Enquiry ought to be made as to the number of old iron vessels and large Thames lighters that can be procured. Also as to the practicability of procuring two or three hundred tons of sulphur [common crude sulphur].
>
> Coals, coke, gas tar and such like articles can be had in abundance at a moments warning, and these consist of the chief requisites.
>
> The whole except the old vessels being of trifling value.

He had already informed the committee that he estimated the total cost of the operation to be £200,000. This concluded the interview with Dundonald and the committee set out to deliberate. They drew up a list of 7 questions which they transmitted to him, and also communicated details of the scheme, presumably with his concurrence, to the most eminent scientist of the day, Professor Michael Faraday, together with the same set of questions. It may be inferred from the tone of the verbal questioning that they viewed the plan in a somewhat less than favourable light; this tone was reflected in the written questions:

> 1. Can it be shown by any *proof* the different requirements for vessels, the quantity of matter to be ignited, the distance at which it will be of avail, and the amount of wind to render it effective; must these be nicely adjusted or do each of them admit of considerable latitude?
> 2. What is the amount of effect in intensity anticipated on the individuals, and if not totally destructive, to what period of time would it paralyse them?
> 3. What proof is there that supposing the vapours to be intolerable along the surface over which the wind carries them, that under cover of the parapets or by closing the windows or shutters, which probably exist at the embrasures of the casemates, the same vapour would penetrate and extend with sufficient intensity?

4. If the smoke is to conceal the ships from the view of the batteries how are the ships and smoke vessels themselves to approach, by *probably an intricate passage*, through the same smoke?

5. Where the batteries are dispersed as at Kronstadt, there must be separate smoke vessel sufficient for each, and as the bearing of their guns are in complicated lines and distances mutually flanking each other, would it not be a matter of difficulty to obtain a simultaneous effect on each, which would be very necessary?

6. The extent laterally that would be covered *with effect* by the vapours from each vessel—would need proof?

7. How are the smoke and vapour vessels to be brought into position with sufficient rapidity. [Once on] the position are they to lay to, or to anchor, or to move on; if the first two how are our own boats to pass through the smoke; and if the last how are these vapour vessels to direct their course?

Lord Dundonald's reply was dated 5 August:

1. No practical proof exists of the different requirements for vessels, though inferences may be drawn as to the quantity of matter to be ignited, by the effects on a small scale. The more combustible matter ignited the greater will be the effect. No nice adjustment is necessary, the wind should not be too strong so as to alleviate the smoke or dilute the emanation of sulphurous fumes.

2. We breathe about a dozen of times in a minute so that even by holding the breath it is probable that one minute would suspend animal life.

3. No embrasures are so closely fitted as to exclude *atmospheric air*, which in point of stability is in no degree different from *decomposed air*.

4. The smoke vessels are guided by vessels placed in a line with the fort to be attacked, and cross bearings may in like manner denote when the attacking force has arrived at a proper distance to anchor.

5. One or more forts may be attacked at a time, provided that the view of the others is intercepted by dense fumes—which, in that case, may prevent intervention without actually embracing the objects.

6. The vapour that issues from the funnel of a steam vessel when fresh fuel is thrown on, being produced by a few shovels of bituminous coal, may afford some idea what would be the amount occasioned by the ignition of hundreds of tons—soaked, if necessary, with tar.

7. The smoke vessels will burn for many hours, perhaps for days, in iron vessels. They need not however be counted on in this latter period. In certain cases such as an attack on fort Alexander they might be anchored, but if on a dead wall or rampart such as commanding the docks at Kronstadt they may be left to drift alongside that which they cannot but encounter . . .

On 7 August he submitted 2 more papers for consideration, one entitled 'Brief outline of a proposed means of attacking Kronstadt in reference to the accompanying chart':

> The British fleet may be anchored at four or five miles distant from the enemies' isolated fortifications. The small steam vessels and regularly fitted smoke vessels may be brought up anywhere contiguous.
>
> Coasters, or captured coasting vessels, may be fitted as explosion vessels, and placed at a greater distance from the fleet. Some of these may be prepared as sulphur vessels by filling them with compressed straw, reeds, shavings or chips of wood, or other combustible materials soaked with tar. Which equipment will have the advantage of enabling them to float though pierced by shot. Indeed it seems probable that this mode of fitting—aided by a ground tier of empty casks—might be substituted for iron vessels containing bituminous coal.
>
> Guide vessels must be placed [at three or four miles distant from the enemy] so that a line drawn through these vessels shall bisect the fort to be attacked. The wind being Westerly and steady, and all in readiness for the attack, small craft crammed with the tarred materials may be sent down along shore and anchored off certain points in order that when kindled the smoke shall obscure the operations, about to take place, from the enemy.
>
> Several modes of attack may be adopted, but it seems indispensible that the lofty fort called 'Alexander' should be taken or silenced, lest the mast heads of the attacking force should be seen from its summit.
>
> To capture this fort it is essential that the other isolated forts shall be obscured—or simultaneously assailed, but to avoid detail, let the former be exemplified, and let the the assailing force proceed along the line direct towards Fort Alexander—each tug vessel having two smokers in tow by quarter hawsers of such length that the towing vessel shall not be involved in the smoke during the two mile run after the smokers are kindled.
>
> Astern of the smoke vessels the sulphur craft—towed in like manner—must keep the guide vessels 'on with each other' so as not only to follow in the direct course themselves but to be able to indicate to the smoke tug when 'my cross bearing is on' in order so the smokers being 'brought up' by an anchor attached to their tow lines in the tug. The sulphurous craft are to be anchored to leeward of these.
>
> It is obvious that a second and third dose of sulphur may be administered if required, which in the case of the lofty castle called 'Alexander' may be necessary—a circumstance which doubtless may be ascertained if the top of the castle is visible from the fleet above the smoke.

The hundred gun tower being taken or silenced, Fort Constantine, Fort Peter and Fort Risbank may simply be obscured, so that the grand attack might at once take place against the Western and Southern ramparts, and against Fort Kronstadt, which forcibly protect the anchorage of the hostile fleet.

The effect to be produced by numerous small smoke vessels [to deter the enemy boats] and by sulphur craft sent adrift before the wind against that broad space indicating the channel between Kronstadt and Fort Menshekof is so obvious that detail seem unnecessary.

His other paper was entitled simply 'Preliminary Observations'.

Before enlarging on the explanation of arrangements necessary to mask, silence or capture the detached forts, and assail the long line of ramparts that protect the fleet at Kronstadt, it may be well to refer to a more simple case [now in progress of execution at Bomarsund] where the British ships of war—with good reason—have been restrained from acting until the arrival of an army to co-operate on land.

The chief battery, is said to have seventy guns in casemates, supported by two towers on the heights—the former being close to the water's edge, where there is sufficient depth to permit the near approach of ships of any size.

Now, it is submitted that neither prudent hesitation on the part of the naval force, nor the presence of an army would have been necessary, had it occurred, that half a dozen of captured coasting vessels—crammed with reeds, compressed hay, straw, shavings, or chips of wood soaked with tar, on being kindled and run on the weather side of the battery— would have produced obscurity more intense than night—and had as many more sulphur vessels [or had the tar in the smoke vessels been imbued with sulphur] would have enabled the British ships to approach with without risk, and to have pounded the walls without opposition.

Whether afloat or onshore these means must supercede all tedious modes of attack. Narrow channels may be passed or 'ground may be opened' without traverses on the very glacis of fortifications, where mounds may be raised and batteries situated commanding the interior defences, whence the enemy inevitably would be driven.

Professor Faraday's reply was received on the same day as Dundonald's two papers:

Very few of the questions are so put that I, in reference to their chemical or physical character, can give any consistent or distinct answer to them. The proposition is correct in theory, i.e. dense smoke will hide objects, and burning sulphur will yield fumes that are intolerable, and able to render men involved in them incapable of action, or even to kill them. But whether this proposition is *practicable* on the scale proposed and required, is a point so little illustrated by any experience, or by facts that can be made to bear upon it, that for my own part I am unable to form a judgement . . . I should hesitate in concluding that ten or twenty vessels could give a body of smoke, the columns of which at a mile to leeward, would coincide and form an impervious band to vision a mile broad; but I have no means of judging . . .

I may remark, that as 400 tons of sulphur have been spoken of, perhaps the following consideration may help to give some general ideas, in the present state of the proposition, as to the probable effect of its fumes. If a ship charged with sulphur were burning in a current of air, a continuous stream of sulphuric acid fumes, mingled with air, would pass off from it. This stream, being heavier than air, would descend and move along over the surface of the water; and, I suppose, would sink perpendicularly and expand laterally, so as to form a low broad stream. The noxious height would probably soon be less than 15, or perhaps even 10 feet [but I cannot pretend to more than a guess] and its width by degrees more and more. The water . . . would tend continually to take part of the noxious vapour out of it. Now 400 tons of sulphur would require 400 tons of oxygen; and that it would find in about 1740 tons of air. Supposing that this product were mixed with ten times its bulk of unaltered air, it would make nigh upon 20,000 tons of a very bad mixture; and one, which if a man were to be immersed in it for a short time, would cause death . . .

In respect of the seven questions, there is hardly a point in them to which I am able to give an answer of any value.

1. I suspect much larger quantities of matter will be required than is supposed—I do not imagine that if burnt in heaps coals would burn fast enough to give the smoke required.
2. The data is wanting.
3. I suspect the upper part of high buildings would frequently be free from the sulphurous vapours; and that jets or eddies of fresh air from above would occur behind.
4. (Left unanswered).
5. (Left unanswered).
6. The lateral extent at the distance of a mile very doubtful—would need proof.
7. (Left unanswered).

The proposition is . . . correct in theory, but in its result must depend entirely on practical points. These are of so untried a character . . . that

I have the utmost difficulty in speaking at all on the matter . . . All I
need add is, that if the project were known or anticipated, it would not
be difficult for the attacked party to provide respirators, which would
enable the men, in a very great degree or even altogether, to resist a
temporary invasion of an atmosphere such as that described.

Sir John Fox Burgoyne had also put pen to paper and delivered his view
of the plan to Sir Byam Martin and the committee. He outlined his
doubts as to whether the smoke produced to mask the movements of
the attackers would be effective:

. . . it is extremely doubtful that it would be obtained to the ammount
[sic] of preventing occasional glimpses . . . of what was proceeding behind
it, the forts being generally lofty . . . and the smoke alone would not
prevent the service of the guns . . . [and] their fire would as soon as the
process began be directed at the front of the smokers and whatever might
be behind them . . . probably with damaging effects . . . At the same
time it would be extremely difficult to regulate the movements of the
assailants . . . behind this great cloud of smoke, nor is it comprehended
how any great advantage is to be obtained . . . against works that are
enclosed all round, or against any considerable strength of garrison.

He was equally dismissive of the sulphur ships:

As regards the application of the sulphurous vapour, independent of the
barbarous and uncivilised character that would be given to it, there are
very great doubts of its efficacy which are itemised by Mr Faraday who
has been consulted as one of the highest authorities on such subjects.

There is no proof, nor should I think . . . that any trials should be
recommended.

He also related his belief that the complement of the works to be
'sulphured' would escape from the worst effects of the fumes due to
the expected properties of the cloud of vapour, '. . . its weight being
greater than atmospheric air would tend to keep it low'. Concerning
the physical characteristics of the defences: 'Now as the lowest tier of
batteries are probably not less than fifteen feet above the water and the
rest twenty four and upwards, this quality would be conclusive against
the efficacy of the undertaking.'

With these various negative pieces of advice, and taking into account
the sceptical tone of the verbal questioning, it comes as little surprise
to note that the committee advised Sir James Graham against adopting
the plan. In their written submission to him they reiterated Michael
Faraday's observations and alluded to Sir John Fox Burgoyne's paper in

handsome terms: '. . . we can with much satisfaction refer to a paper delivered to the committee . . . in which everything is said that can be said on the subject.' Sir John added his own rider to the letter sent to Sir James: 'I am quite of the opinion that the project is very little likely to be succesful on any great scale, and if not so the attempt would be attended with considerable odium.'

It fell to Sir James Graham to write to Dundonald explaining that his plan was not to be adopted at that time, but making an attempt to mollify him by paraphrasing the committee's conclusion that:

> . . . if such an enterprise were to be undertaken we are certain it could not be in better hands than Lord Dundonald's whose professional career has been distinguished by remarkable instances of skill and courage in all of which he has been the foremost to lead the way and by his personal heroism has gained an unfading celebrity in the naval history of the country.

Dundonald dismissed the committee's findings and continued to press the Government for his scheme to be given a chance; alluding in letters to the press that he had powerful methods which would equalise the disparity between wooden ships and stone forts: 'There is but one means to place these parties on an equal footing, and that I confidentially laid before the Government.' He again wrote to Sir James Graham in November stating that '. . . I will undertake to subdue every insular fortification at Kronstadt within four hours from the commencement of the attack'. He offered to apply his methods to the capture of Sevastopol, and repeated this offer in a letter to the Prime Minister, Lord Aberdeen. Sir James was obliged to reply stating that as his proposals had been rejected by the committee then: 'Neither Lord Aberdeen nor I can venture to place our individual opinions in opposition to a recorded judgement of the highest authority.'

In one of his earlier replies to Dundonald's canvassing he had expressed the hope that Sevastopol would fall without recourse to unconventional methods. The failure of this to happen was to cause a change of ministry, replacement for Sir James and a new opportunity for Dundonald to press his schemes.

Kronstadt and the Russian Baltic fleet were to remain unmolested, by conventional or other methods, and the Allies concentrated on the 'southern theatre', landing their armies on the Crimean peninsula and moving on Sevastopol. Unfortunately, after winning the battles of The Alma, Inkerman and Balaclava, Lord Raglan's expeditionary force failed to move quickly enough and gave the defenders time to fortify. Sevastopol was somewhat analogous to Singapore in the next century;

in that it had minimal permanent defences against a land approach but was heavily fortified against attack from the sea.

The south and east sides of the city were the only realistic approaches open to the attackers, the north being bounded by the harbour and dominated by a modern fortification, Fort Severnaya or 'Star Fort', whilst the permanent southern defenses consisted only of the Malakoff tower, a 2 storey masonry affair. Thanks to the breathing space allowed them, however, the Russians constructed an earthworks system to augment their defence, which grew to a size and complexity previously unknown. That this was done was primarily due to Colonel Franz Todleben, an engineer of some genius, and Admiral Kornilov, the chief-of-staff of the garrison, who mobilised all available resources to aid Todleben. They had 3 weeks of uninterrupted peace to complete their preparations whilst the Allies brought up siege guns; this time they used well. Todleben's opposite number on the British side, the chief engineering officer, was Sir John Fox Burgoyne.

Orthodox military opinion held that only permanent defensive works were of use and that earthworks were of limited utility. Orthodox opinion was wrong and the siege was to last for 349 days, not merely due to the static component but also to Todleben's dynamic direction of the defence. The Allied cause was also hampered by the fact that for a large portion of the operations they were inferior in artillery. The Russians had augmented their military guns with naval ones, removed from the ships of the Black Sea fleet which lay sunk; not due to enemy action but done on the orders of Todleben who had scuttled them in the harbour mouth to deny access to Allied vessels.

The failure to destroy the Russian Baltic Fleet and the bogging down of the Crimean campaign before Sevastopol caused the crisis in the British government which led to the Aberdeen ministry falling in February 1855, and a new ministry under Lord Palmerston taking its place. The new secretary for war, in whose office was combined the 2 posts formerly responsible for army affairs, was Lord Panmure.

The scandal caused by reports of the conditions under which the British army served during the winter of 1854–5, combined with the apparent failure of the Allies to progress their siege successfully, made Panmure and Palmerston receptive to any idea which promised an end to the venture. It was in this light that Lord Dundonald next proposed his 'plan'.

Dundonald, though a professional sailor, had envisaged the use of smoke and noxious fumes to aid military operations previously, as per his paper 'Preliminary Observations' of 7 August 1854, delivered to the

Martin Committee. Exactly a year later he delivered his opinion on the matter to Lord Panmure:

Materials required for the expulsion of the Russians from Sevastopol:

Experimental trials have shown that about five parts of coke effectively vapourise one part of sulphur. Mixtures for land service, where weight is of importance, may, however, probably be suggested by Professor Faraday, as to operations on shore I have paid little attention.

Four or five hundred tons of sulphur and two thousand tons of coke would be sufficient.

Besides these materials, it would be necessary to have, say, as much bituminous coal, and a couple of thousand barrels of gas or other tar, for the purpose of masking fortifications to be attacked, or others that flank the assailing positions.

A quantity of dry firewood, chips, shavings, straw, hay or other such combustible materials, would also be requisite quickly to kindle the fires, which ought to be kept in readiness for the first favourable and steady breeze.

The objects to be accomplished being specially stated, the responsibility of their accomplishment ought to rest on those who direct their execution.

Suppose that the Malakoff and Redan are the objects to be assailed, it might be judicious merely to *obscure* the Redan [by the smoke of coal and tar kindled in 'The Quarries'] so that it could not annoy the Mamelon, where the sulphur fire would be placed to expel the garrison from the Malakoff, which ought to have all the cannon that can be turned towards its ramparts employed in overthrowing its *undefended* ramparts.

There is no doubt but that the fumes will envelop all the defences from the Malakoff to the barracks, and even to the line-of-battle ship, *The Twelve Apostles*, at anchor in the harbour.

The two outer batteries, on each side of the port, ought to be smoked, sulphured, and blown down by explosion vessels and their destruction completed by a few ships of war anchored under *cover* of the smoke.[26]

Lord Dundonald had offered to supervise the execution of the plan himself, and Palmerston and Panmure were prepared to let him try.*

---

*Dundonald had been asked if he would instruct two engineer officers in applying his plan. His answer was 'No, I have offered to risk my own life and reputation on their efficacy, but will not impart my mode of applying them to others, who may not, either from preconceived notions or professional jealousy of naval inventions, comprehend them.' Cochrane, *Autobiography*, vol. II, p. 236.

There were no committees to assess its worth on this occasion; the political embarrassment caused by the army's failure to take Sevastopol saw to that. The politicians were also aware of the need to shift the blame should the Dundonald plan miscarry, as is made plain by Lord Palmerston's communication with his Secretary for War of 7 August:

> I agree with you that if Dundonald will go out himself to superintend and direct the execution of his scheme, we ought to accept his offer and try his plan. If it succeeds, it will, as you say, save a great number of English and French lives; if it fails in his hands, we shall be exempt from blame, and if we come in for a small share of the ridicule we can bear it, and the greater part will fall on him. You had best, therefore, make arrangements with him without delay, and with as much secrecy as the nature of things will admit of.[27]

That the scheme was never put into operation, and that Sevastopol fell following conventional, and in terms of casualties, expensive, operations are matters of historical fact. This was, no doubt, a great disappointment to Dundonald, who would have relished ending his long and illustrious naval and military career, at the age of 79, with a full scale use of his long secret plan. Dundonald died in London on 30 October 1860 and was buried in Westminster Abbey, his plans however did not die with him, for he left them to his friend Lyon Playfair. Playfair was professor of chemistry at Edinburgh University from 1856 to 1869, and shortly before his own death in 1898 he handed them back to the family; to Dundonald's grandson, the 12th Earl.[28]

The 12th Earl was a distinguished soldier, eventually reaching the rank of Lt. General, and during the Boer War (1899–1902) he commanded the Mounted Brigade in Natal under General Sir Redvers Buller. Recounting his thoughts following the failure of the second advance on Ladysmith and the disaster of Spion Kop in January 1900, he seriously considered revealing the plan to his superior:

> In my mind's eye I saw the great banks of smoke, producing an atmosphere . . . 'dark as the darkest night'; then I thought of this same atmosphere impregnated with sulphur. I saw the lines of Boer riflemen in their trenches, waiting for our men, with Mausers useless, for those that held them could not see . . . But I restrained myself and kept the secret.[29]

The reason for this restraint was the pledge he had given Playfair to divulge them only in a national emergency, and he was not to calculate that just such an emergency had arrived until some 14 years later following the outbreak of the Great War.

Winston Churchill, at the time 'responsible to Crown and Parliament for all the business of the Admiralty',[30] was probably the first senior Great War political figure to seriously entertain proposals for utilising methods of asphyxiating an enemy. He records the matter in his monumental account of the war, *The World Crisis*, quite openly, quoting at length a letter he had sent to H. H. Asquith on 5 January 1915 and telling him that, with regards to the manufacture of smoke barrels, there are '. . . other matters closely connected with this to which I have already drawn your attention, but which are of so secret a character that I do not put them down on paper'.[31]

Churchill must have considered the matters secret in the extreme if he could not write of them to the Prime Minister, but he divulges all, explaining how Lieutenant-General Lord Dundonald '. . . the grandson of the famous Admiral Cochrane . . .'[32] had visited Lord Kitchener and appraised him of various plans 'left by his ancestor' for making smoke screens and for '. . . driving an enemy from his position by means of noxious though not necessarily deadly fumes'.[33] The enemy in question at this time was of course the army of Imperial Germany and the position from which they were to be driven was the Western Front in Northern France. The seeming stalemate in that area had, as is well known, resulted from the failure of Germany's Schlieffen Plan, the plan for defeating— within six weeks —France. This dislocation and the subsequent inability of offensive measures to defeat entrenched opposition—trench warfare—baffled those who sought answers to it in the tactical sphere.

The reason for the approach to Churchill was simple. Having informed the army of his grandfather's plans, via the Secretary of State for War Lord Kitchener, during September 1914, and despite having given thought to their application for land usage, he had been rebuffed. Kitchener had immediately pronounced '. . . that the idea was of no use for land operations, and as it was the invention of an Admiral he advised me to see the Admiralty about it'.[34] The 12th Earl accordingly called on the Second Sea Lord, Admiral Sir Frederick Hamilton and '. . . explained fully the value of the plans for Naval operations . . . and also for land warfare'.[35] Hamilton wrote to Dundonald on 29 September.

> I have talked the matter over with Prince Louis [of Battenberg, the First Sea Lord] and he thinks you had better see Churchill. . . . he agrees with me that at present we can see no probability of naval use, especially seeing that a failure would be giving the whole thing away without any corresponding gain; as for land, when a sufficiently grave crisis arrives, there can be no doubt of its use.

He agrees with me that the best thing to ask Churchill for would be a small joint Naval and Military Commission to consider the whole matter and in the meantime to divulge as little as possible.

You had better write a note to Churchill asking him for an interview on a private matter.[36]

Churchill, as always, receptive to new ideas and sensing that a key to the trench dead-lock may have been discovered had an interview with Dundonald during the course of which he asked to see the plans of 'the illustrious Cochrane', which after a few days' consideration Lord Dundonald felt justified in revealing due to the current 'national emergency'. Churchill was given the papers in the middle of October, which he (mistakenly) recounts as having '. . . once before, in the Crimean War . . . been placed at the disposal of the British Government'.[37] Churchill describes, and indeed reproduces a facsimile of, the words inscribed on the 'inner covering of the packet': 'To the Imperial mind one sentence will suffice: All fortifications, especially marine fortifications, can under cover of dense smoke be irresistibly subdued by fumes of sulphur kindled in masses to windward of their ramparts.'[38]

Churchill, considering himself the possessor of an 'Imperial Mind' no doubt, wrote that 'the reader, captivated by the compliment, will no doubt rise to the occasion and grasp at once the full significance of the idea'.[39] A 'prolonged' discussion with Prince Louis of Battenberg ensued, and an opinion of the practicalities of the scheme sought from Sir Arthur Wilson.[40] Wilson was a past First Sea Lord and one of the few living men who had actually fought in the Crimean War, and later, in 1884, at the Second Battle of El Teb in The Sudan, gained a Victoria Cross—in the days when there were both naval and military versions. He has been described as '. . . once an outstanding fleet commander and in his later years a consultant on almost every naval enterprise of the First World War'.[41] Churchill describes him as having a 'practical and inventive turn of mind' which 'seemed specially adapted to the task' of assessing the scheme.[42] This assessment is however somewhat at odds with his earlier (in the same book) characterisation of Wilson as '. . . a man of the highest quality and stature, but, as I thought, dwelling too much in the past of naval science, not sufficiently receptive of new ideas when conditions were changing so rapidly, and of course

---

*This was following Wilson's somewhat dismal performance at a meeting of The Committee of Imperial Defence held on 23 August 1911, to consider 'Action to be taken in the event of Intervention in a European War'. This event revealed the fundamentally divergent war strategies of the army and the navy, or rather the lack of any such in the case of the latter.

tenacious and unyielding in the last degree'.[43] This opinion, though written post-war, is consistent with his pre-war appraisal: '. . . I cannot feel much confidence in Wilson's sagacity . . .'* Wilson then seems a strange choice to adjudicate in the matter, and perhaps the result was predictable.

Churchill was soon writing to Dundonald, on 18 October, appraising him of Sir Arthur's findings: 'Sir Arthur Wilson thought the scheme obsolete on account of modern conditions, and it was useless to pursue it with him. I do not share these views and am considering how and when progress may be made.'[44] Sir Arthur Wilson had evidently made his mind up, and being 'tenacious and unyielding in the last degree', Churchill could not persuade him to reconsider. Dundonald was, unsurprisingly, none too happy, replying on 24 October: 'The term obsolete does not describe a novel departure. You I know place an accurate value on the criticism . . . I feel sure that you will help my wish to conduct land operations under the plan if agreed that the navy is out of it.'[45]

Churchill himself, not accepting that the 'navy was out of it', and obviously taken with the plan, sought to pursue it with his customary vigour, giving 'decisive instructions' to make experiments and later enjoining Dundonald to lay his scheme before Colonel Hankey, the Secretary for the Committee of Imperial Defence, who was as Churchill stated '. . . pursuing considerable investigations in a similar though not identical direction'.[46] Hankey was in pursuit of 'special material' with which to overcome the tactical impasse, and he records how 'Under the seal of the strictest secrecy [removed by subsequent publicity*] I became the repository of the secret passed down through several generations of the Dundonald family for using sulphur to asphyxiate an enemy'.[47]

Another repository of the 'secret' was Sir Douglas Haig, the future Field Marshal and c-in-c of the British Army on the Western Front, who was visited by Lord Dundonald on 11 March 1915. Haig recorded that Dundonald was '. . . studying the conditions of the war in the hopes of being able to apply to modern conditions an invention of his great grandfather [sic] for driving a garrison out of a fort by using sulphur fumes. I asked him how he arranged to have a favourable wind.'[48] Dundonald had actually consulted the Meteorological Office[49] on the question, and had discovered '. . . the wind statistics from the

---

*The secrecy, obviously unknown to Hankey or the Dundonald clan, had been comprehensively breached in 1908, when the papers of Lord Panmure, Minister for War during the latter portion of the Crimean War, had been published. These included a brief, though detailed, account of the genesis of the plan, and an appreciation of its specific use.

coast of Holland to Berlin show that the wind from [westerly directions] is far more prevalent than from the opposite or eastern section of the compass, especially is this so during November, December, January and February . . .'[50] The prevailing winds over north-west Europe do indeed blow from the west or south-west,[51] and later in the war the British army especially was to utilise this to launch massive cloud gas attacks.

It is a matter of record that no attempts were made to attack the German trenches with sulphur fumes and that researches into such matters were terminated by the British, though efforts to perfect and enhance smoke-screens were to continue. It must have been clear to Dundonald that the 'smoke' aspects of his plan were receiving greater consideration than the 'sulphur', and this was confirmed on 21 March, when Churchill ordered the Admiralty Smoke Screen Committee be formed under the chairmanship of the unflagging Earl. It was made clear to him in which direction his, and the committee's, efforts should be directed in a letter sent from Churchill's private secretary, James Masterton-Smith, on 31 March:

> Mr Churchill asked me to write and confirm a decision already communicated to you by Colonel Hankey, that while the smoke experiments are to be continued it is not intended for the present to proceed with the more important proposal [i.e. experiments in noxious fumes]. Mr Churchill agrees that it would not be expedient to introduce into the war elements which might justify the enemy in having recourse to inhuman reprisals.† At the same time Mr Churchill wishes me to convey to you his sense of deep obligation for the ungrudging manner in which you have placed at his disposal your exceptional knowledge.[52]

Churchill wrote: 'There can be no question but that Lord Dundonald had grasped at this time the whole idea of gas and smoke warfare, and that he had derived it directly from the papers of his grandfather.'[53] Dundonald had proposed that 'An attack on miles of entrenchment would be made on sectional fronts by sulphur and smoke, the intervening blocks where sulphur would not be employed being smoked only, in order to blind the hostile artillery'.[54] These proposed tactics bore a strong resemblance to those utilised later in the war, following the outbreak of chemical warfare. Lord Dundonald had indeed conceived the 'whole idea' of gas and smoke warfare some time before it came into being as such, and there is no doubt that his grandfather, 'the illustrious Cochrane', had provided the basis for this idea.

---

†On 22 April, the Germans attacked the Ypres salient with chlorine gas.

The basis, the 10th Earl of Dundonald's Secret War Plan, had been scrutinised, during his lifetime, on three occasions; by the Duke of York's Committee in 1812; the Hastings Committee in 1847; and the Martin Committee in 1854.* They had recommended against its adoption, not solely on the grounds of its uncivilised nature, as it might be termed, but, certainly on the latter occasion, also on the grounds that it was unlikely to be effective. Palmerston and Panmure, somewhat cynically perhaps, had been willing to allow it to be tried, though circumstances prevented this, and Churchill, long after Dundonald's death, had been keen to at least investigate it further, whilst Sir Arthur Wilson had pronounced it 'obsolete'. The question that therefore remains for the armchair warrior to peruse is then: would the plan have worked?

The core of the plan was the use of sulphur dioxide, a very toxic gas, as a chemical weapon. We have data concerning the use of noxious gases from the Great War, and whilst sulphur dioxide was never itself used, it can be compared with similar agents that were. Using the classifications system introduced during the war, sulphur dioxide would fall into that group of chemical agents known as toxic lung-injurants. The lung-injurant gases included chlorine, chloropicrin, and phosgene, whose '. . . principal physiological action was injury of the pulmonary system of the body. The main result of this injury was to cause fluid to pass from the blood into the minute air sacs of the lungs and thus obstruct the supply of oxygen to the blood. Death from one of these substances may be compared to death by drowning, the water in which the victim drowns being drawn into his lungs from his own blood vessels.'[55] Sulphur dioxide, though, also has toxic properties, and Great War toxic lung-injurants were a much rarer group of agents, comprising three liquids used for shell fillings, and not introduced until 1917–18. This class of agent, in addition to its lung injurant effect, also '. . . exerts an additional systemic poisoning effect . . .'[56]

Postwar research into the effectiveness of chemical warfare, indicated that lung injurants '. . . secured the bulk of the gas fatalities in the war'.[57] This needs to be somewhat qualified, because a high proportion of those fatalities would have been caused during the opening phases of gas warfare (in 1915) and thus before any protective measures had been introduced, and the effect of gas on those unprepared has always been significant, whilst its effect on troops equipped to deal with it is much

---

*The inclusion of Sir John Fox Burgoyne on the Martin Committee, it may be argued, could have given that body an intrinsic bias against the plan—that is unless Sir John's views had altered since his previous perusal of the matter. This does not appear to have been the case.

less. A judgement concerning how effective sulphur dioxide might have been may be formed by comparing it with the first German gas attack on 22 April 1915. The Germans, using some 160 tons of chlorine gas, caused 15,000 allied casualties, including 5000 deaths. Chlorine is lethal in concentrations of 1000 parts per million of air—exactly the same level as sulphur dioxide.

Cochrane then had discovered an effective chemical warfare agent, and had worked out a generic tactical scheme for its use—a scheme moreover that relied on contemporary technology and readily available material; it was thus realistic.* So, as to answering the question, the answer must be a hesitant 'yes'. Hesitant because the scheme remains hypothetical, but yes because a practical warrior of Cochrane's experience must be credited with knowing his business, and with the inestimable benefit of hindsight we can judge what the effect of a surprise chemical warfare attack was likely to be. As the 12th Earl says in one of his memoranda quoted by Churchill '. . . these plans were invented by Admiral Lord Dundonald in 1811 . . .'[58] It follows therefore that some 104 years before chemical warfare actually made its debut onto the battlefield, it had been conceived *in detail* by a Scots seaman— Thomas Cochrane, later the 10th Earl of Dundonald.

---

*At least for maritime operations. The logistical difficulties associated with military operations would probably have precluded anything more than a small scale operation—quite simply, what a ship could carry with ease would involve a major logistical effort on land. By way of example; in comparing the gunnery power of Nelson's fleet at Trafalgar (27 ships) with the artillery of Napoleon's Army of the North at Waterloo (366 guns) John Keegan states it thus: '. . . six times as many guns, of much heavier calibre, could be transported daily by Nelson's fleet as by Napoleon's army, at one fifth of the logistic cost and at five times the speed.' *The Price of Admiralty*, Hutchinson, 1988, p. 67.

REFERENCES

1 Bacon, Reginald *The Life of Lord Fisher of Kilverstone,* Hodder & Stoughton, 1929, vol. 1, p. 121.

2 The Melville Papers (2nd Series) British Library, Add. MS 41083 vol. V (ff. 220.)

3 Douglas, G. and Ramsay, G. D. *The Panmure Papers,* 1908, p. 341.

4 Prentiss, A.M. *Chemicals in War: A Treatise in Chemical Warfare,* McGraw-Hill Book Company Inc, 1937, p. 3.

5 Douglas and Ramsay op. cit., p. 341.

6 Cochrane, Thomas, 10th Earl of Dundonald *The Autobiography of a Seaman,* 1860, vol. II, p. 228.

7 The Melville Papers, op. cit., (all quotations in this portion of the work, unless otherwise stated, are from this source).

8 Clarke, Sir George Sydenham *Fortification: Its Past Achievements, Recent Developments, and Future Progress,* 1890, p. 231.

9 Cochrane op. cit., p. 227

10 Lloyd, Christopher(ed.) *The Keith Papers,* Navy Records Society, 1955, p. 316.

11 Cochrane op. cit., pp. 227–8

12 ibid., p. 228.

13 ibid., p. 229.

14 ibid., p. 229.

15 ibid., p. 231.

16 ibid., p. 232.

17 Price, Anthony *The Eyes of the Fleet: A Popular History of Frigates and Frigate Captains, 1793–1815,* Hutchinson, 1990, p. 45.

18 Cochrane, Thomas Barnes, 11th Earl of Dundonald, and Bourne, H. R. Fox *The Life of Thomas, Lord Cochrane, 10th Earl of Dundonald,* 1869, pp. 250–1.

19 ibid., p. 251.

20 ibid., p. 257.

21 ibid., pp. 257–8.

22 ibid., p. 258.

23 ibid., pp. 259–60.

24 Benson, A. C. and Viscount Esher (eds.) *Letters of Queen Victoria,* vol. III, p. 9.

25 The Martin Papers. British Library, Add MS 41370 (ff 302–367). (All quotations in this portion of the work, unless otherwise stated, are from this source).

26 Douglas and Ramsay op. cit., pp. 341–2.

27 ibid., p. 340.

28 Dundonald, Lt-Gen., 12th Earl of, *My Army Life,* Arnold, 1926, p. 330.

29 ibid., p. 135.

30 Churchill, Winston S. *The World Crisis: 1911–1918,* two-volume edition, Odhams Press Ltd, 1938, p. vii.

31   ibid., p. 511.

32   ibid., p. 516.

33   ibid., p. 516.

34   Dundonald (12th Earl) op. cit., p. 331.

35   ibid., p. 331.

36   ibid., p. 331–2

37   Churchill op. cit., p. 517.

38   ibid., p. 518.

39   ibid., p. 517.

40   ibid., p. 517.

41   Palmer, Alan *The Banner of Battle. The Story of the Crimean War*, Weidenfield and Nicolson, 1987, p. 251.

42   Churchill op. cit., p. 517.

43   ibid., p. 60.

44   ibid., p. 517.

45   ibid., p. 517.

46   ibid., p. 519.

47   Hankey *The Supreme Command 1914–1918*, two volumes, George Allen and Unwin Ltd, 1961, vol. I, p. 230.

48   Quoted in Terraine, John *White Heat: The New Warfare 1914–18*, Guild, 1982, p. 161, n7.

49   Dundonald (12th Earl) op. cit., p. 330.

50   Churchill op. cit., p. 519.

51   Cowper, Henry *World War One and its Consequences —The Nature of the War*, The Open University, 1990, p. 19.

52   Churchill op. cit., p. 520.

53   ibid., p. 519.

54   ibid., p. 519.

55   Prentiss op. cit., p. 147.

56   ibid., p. 147.

57   ibid., p. 169.

58   ibid., p. 519.

APPENDIX ONE

(To Cochrane's Memorial of 1812)

Temporary Mortars

It would be unnecessary to say more on the effect of Temporary Mortars, or Explosion Ships, did not the understanding naturally revolt at Plans which violate preconceived opinions, and search for difficulties to embarrass, rather than facilities that are to surmount them; and thus whilst the mind admits, as if by instinct, the prodigious violence exerted by ignited powder on surrounding objects, it may involuntarily withhold assent from the application of the principle to the projection of Carcasses and Shells. Therefore let,

ABC	be the segment of a ships hold,
DEF	Old Cannon and pigs of iron bedded in clay,
GHIK	transverse logs of old Ships Timber
LMN	another tier crossing these, and bolted,
OPQR	upright beams of Ditto
STUW	old mooring chains cables and hawsers surrounding and binding the upright logs,
XY	Stones, clay, and other tenacious and ponderous matter

The Mortar thus chambered and bound together, is ready to be charged for service, then let,

pp	represent the powder
w	junk wadding
cvg	carcasses, shells grenades

It is demonstrable that the expansive effort of the powder (being a ratio to the quantity) will be exerted equally on the bed and on the shells, and that these aggregate masses will recede from the impulse in an inverse ratio of the matter they contain and of the opposition made by water to instantaneous motion, to that of air.

Hence the Carcasses Shells and Grenades will be impelled by a force nearly equal to the whole power of the powder inflamed and the flight of such will be in the line of least resistance, or between the angle of 45 degrees and the zenith

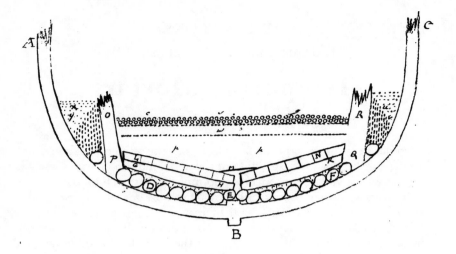

APPENDIX TWO

(To Cochrane's Memorial of 1812)

Sulphur Ships

The plan proposed for neutralising Marine Batteries, Bastions, and Works, by means of vessels containing large quantities of sulphur and charcoal, is not liable to some of the objections alluded to in Appendix One; for instance they cannot be blown up, and therefore if conducted at a proper time to a fit situation, their effect is inevitable

Let BCD be the Works of Flushing, or the Cones of Cherbourg,
E, a stink vessel,
W, the direction of the wind,
S,U,L, Sulphur and Charcoal, on a Bed of Clay on the Main Deck

It is unnecessary to suggest that the vapour will pervade the innermost recesses of Bomb-Proofs, fill Batteries or Cones, and that it will roll along under the lee of Walls and Parapets to a great distance. The effect when compared to the Stink Ball now in use will probably be in the ratio of the ignited masses

Note. The intention of placing the Charcoal and Sulphur on the Upper Deck, and on a bed of Clay, is to admit air beneath and to prevent the vessel from consuming soon. The melted sulphur, if any falls, will drop into the sand and water admitted into the hold

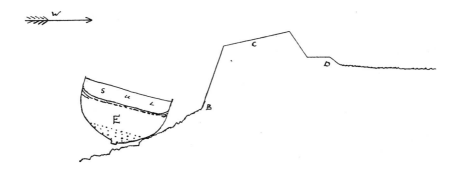

Bibliography

The following list includes previous lives of the Admiral, other books that have been consulted, and those from which quotations have been taken. The use of periodical material is indicated in the text. Since the unpublished material quoted in this book is not calendared, it has simply been described in each instance as fully as was possible without interrupting the flow of the narrative.

Allen, Joseph, *Life of the Earl of Dundonald*, 1861.

Armitage, John, *History of Brazil*, 2 vols., 1836.

Atlay, James B., *The Trial of Lord Cochrane before Lord Ellenborough*, 1897.

Bamford, Samuel, *Autobiography*, ed. W. H. Chaloner, 2 vols., 1967.

Berenger, Charles Random de, *The Noble Stock-Jobber*, 1816.

Brenton, Edward, *Life and Correspondence of John, Earl of St Vincent*, 2 vols., 1838.

Bunster, Enrique, *Lord Cochrane*, Santiago, 1966.

Caldeclough, A., *Travels in South America*, 2 vols., 1825.

Campbell, John, Lord, *Lives of the Chief Justices*, 3 vols., 1849–57.

Cecil, Henry, *A Matter of Speculation: The Case of Lord Cochrane*, 1965.

Chatterton, Georgiana, Lady, *Memorials Personal and Historical of Admiral Lord Gambier*, 2 vols., 1861.

Clissold, Stephen, *Bernardo O'Higgins and the Independence of Chile*, 1968.

Clowes and Markham, *The Royal Navy: A History*, 7 vols., 1897–1903.

Cochrane, Basil, *An Improvement in the Mode of Administering the Vapour Bath*, 1809.

Cochrane, Douglas F., *The Case of Lord Cochrane: Henry Cecil Examined*, 1965.

Cochrane, Thomas, Lord, *The Trial of Lord Cochrane for a Conspiracy*, 1814.

Cochrane, Thomas, Lord, *An Address from Lord Cochrane to his Constituents the Electors of Westminster*, 1815.

Cochrane, Thomas, Lord, *Lord Cochrano á los Habitantes de Chile*, Quintero, 1823.

Cochrane, Thomas, Earl of Dundonald, *Observations on Naval Affairs,* 1847.

Cochrane, Thomas, Earl of Dundonald, *Notes on the Mineralogy, Government and Condition of the British West Indian Islands,* 1851.

Cochrane, Thomas, Earl of Dundonald, *Brief Extracts . . . on the Use . . . of the Bitumen and Petroleum of Trinidad,* 1857.

Cochrane, Thomas, Earl of Dundonald, *Narrative of Services in the Liberation of Chili, Peru and Brazil,* 2 vols., 1858.

Cochrane, Thomas, Earl of Dundonald, *The Autobiography of a Seaman,* 2 vols., 1860.

Cochrane, Thomas, 11th Earl of Dundonald, *The Life of Thomas Cochrane, 10th Earl of Dundonald,* 1869.

Cochrane, Thomas, Earl of Dundonald, *The Autobiography of a Seaman,* ed. 12th Earl of Dundonald, 1890.

Cruz, Ernesto de la, *Epistolario de D. Bernardo O'Higgins,* 2 vols., Santiago, 1916.

Cruz, Ernesto de la, *La Entrevista de Guayaquil: El Libertador y San Martín,* Santiago, 1917.

Douglas and Ramsay ed., *The Panmure Papers,* 2 vols., 1908.

Dundonald Peerage Claim, *House of Lords Papers,* 1861–3.

Ellenborough, Lord, *The Guilt of Lord Cochrane in 1814,* 1914.

Encina, F. A., *Historia de Chile,* Santiago, 1954.

Finlay, George, *History of the Greek Revolution,* 2 vols., 1861.

Floriano: Brazilian Warship, *Brazilian Tribute to Lord Cochrane 28 June 1901,* 1901.

Fortescue, J. W., *Dundonald,* 1895.

Gambier, Lord, *Minutes of a Court Martial . . .,* 1809.

Gambier's Memoirs, see Chatterton.

Gordon, Thomas, *History of the Greek Revolution,* 2 vols., 1832.

Graham, Maria (Lady Callcott), *Journal of a Residence in Chili,* 1824.

Graham, Maria, *Journal of a Voyage to Brazil,* 1824.

Gurney, W. B., *Minutes of . . . the Trial of Lord Gambier,* 2nd edn., 1809.

Gurney, W. B., *Notes on the Minutes of . . . the Trial of Lord Gambier,* 1810.

Hall, Basil, *Extracts from a Journal written on the Coasts of Chile, Peru and Mexico in the Years 1820, 1821 and 1822,* 2 vols., Edinburgh, 1824.

Haswell, F. R. N., 'Cochrane's First Lieutenant': *Northern Notes and Queries.*

Humphreys, R. A., *Liberation in South America,* 1952.

Jellez, I., *Historia Militar de Chile,* Santiago, 1946.

Knight, Francis, *Rebel Admiral,* 1968.

Knollys, William, *The Intrepid Exploits of Lord Cochrane,* 1877.

Larraín, José, *San Martín y sur Enigmas*, 2 vols., Santiago, 1949.

Lloyd, Charles Christopher, *Lord Cochrane*, 1947.

Louriotes, A., *Correspondence respecting the Steam Vessels which were intended to form the Expedition to Greece*, 1827.

Mallalieu, J. P. W., *Extraordinary Seaman*, 1957.

Marryat, Florence ed., *Life and Letters of Captain Marryat*, 2 vols.,1872.

Martel, Alamiro de Avila, *Cochrane y la Independencia del Pacifico*,Santiago, 1976.

Miers, John, *Travels in Chile and La Plata*, 2 vols., 1826.

Miller, John, *Memoirs of General Miller*, 2 vols., 1828.

Mitre, Bartólomé, *Historia de San Martín y de la Emancipación Sudamericana*, 6 vols., Buenos Aires, 1937.

O'Higgins, Bernardo, *Archivo de Don Bernardo O'Higgins*, Santiago, 1946.

Otero, J. P., *Historia del Libertador Don José de San Martín*, 4 vols., Buenos Aires, 1932.

Pezuela, Joaquín de la, *Memoria de Gobierno*, Seville, 1947.

Ross, Sir John, *Treatise on Navigation by Steam*, N.D. (*Rising Star*)

Rothpletz, Emile, *Correspondence entre le Docteur Louis-André Gosse et l'Amiral Lord Thomas Cochrane (1827–1828)*, Paris, 1919.

Scott, Sir Walter, *Life of Napoleon*, 9 vols., 1827.

Silva, P. C. da, *Historia de Brazil desde 1807 até ao presente*, 6 vols., 1819–34.

Smith, F. E., Earl of Birkenhead, *Hutchinson's Magazine*, vol. XV, 1926.

Stevenson, William Bennet, *A Historical and Descriptive Narrative . . .* , 3 vols., 1825.

Strachey and Fulford, *The Greville Memoirs*, 8 vols., 1938.

Tute, Warren S., *Cochrane*, 1965.

Twitchett, E. G., *Life of a Seaman*, 1931.

Zenteno, J. L., *Documentos justificativos sobre la Espedición Libertadora del Perú*, Santiago, 1861.

Index

Roxas, Chilean soldier, 209.
Russell, H.M.S., 143.
Russia, 77, 162, 361, 363.

St George, 349.
St Helens, 55.
St Lawrence river, 349.
St Vincent, Earl of, *see* Jervis.
Sandhurst, 331.
Sandwich Islands, 378.
San Lorenzo, 197-9.
San Martín, José de (1778-1850),
    189-92, 194, 203, 212-14, 216-20,
    224-6, 228-9, 231-41, 243, 246-8,
    250-1, 254, 257-8, 260, 271, 285,
    290, 294.
San Martín, Chilean warship, 218.
Santiago, 190, 194, 198-200, 204, 208,
    210, 247, 250, 256, 286, 370.
Sardinia, 29.
Saumarez, Admiral James, 1st Lord
    de (1757-1836), 38-9.
Sauveur, Greek warship, 297, 299, 306,
    315.
Scarlett, James, 1st Lord Abinger
    (1769-1844), 161, 164-5.
Scheldt, 120, 124-6, 128, 135, 209.
Scott, John, 1st Earl of Eldon (1751-
    1838), 142, 170.
Scott, Sir Walter, Bart. (1771-1832),
    45, 82-3, 92, 102, 191, 288.
Scott, Sir William, 1st Lord Stowell
    (1745-1836), 131, 142.
Scourge, H.M.S., 353, 355-6.
Seawards factory, 329.
Sebastopol, 361, 367.
Sesostris, merchant vessel, 265.
Sewell, Dr, 138-40.
Seymour, Admiral Sir George (1787-
    1870), 61, 103-4, 112, 122-3, 379.
Seymour-Conway, Francis, Earl of
    Yarmouth, 6th Marquess of Hertford
    (1777-1842), 154, 161, 163.
Sheerness, 9, 16, 20-1, 30, 55, 132, 136.
Shelley, Percy Bysshe (1792-1822),
    182-3.
Shepherd, Captain, 289.
Sheppey, 9.
Sheridan, Richard Brinsley (1751-
    1816), 66-9, 169.

Sheriff, Captain of *Sesostris*, 265.
Shetland, 48.
Sicily, 25, 116, 138.
Simpson, John, 149.
Simpson, Robert, 370.
Slade, Adolphus, 299.
Smith, Frederick, 1st Earl of
    Birkenhead (1872-1930), 165-6.
Smith, Sir Sydney (1771-1845), 92.
Smithfield, 294-5.
Southampton, 324.
Southwark, 320.
Spa Fields, 180, 183.
Spain, King of, *see* Ferdinand VII.
Spartan, H.M.S., 83-4.
Speedy, H.M.S., 28-37, 39-43, 50-4,
    62, 71, 73, 137, 171, 193, 197, 293,
    326.
Spetsae, 306.
Spiridion Monastery, 302.
Spithead, 19-21, 25, 45, 55, 95, 110,
    143, 284-5, 295, 358.
Spry, Captain, 193, 195, 209-10, 212,
    220, 227, 235, 237, 257, 259.
Stephenson, George (1781-1848),
    327-8.
Stevens, Deputy Marshal, 139.
Stevenson, William Bennet, 194, 209,
    216, 221, 234, 236-8, 246, 286, 318,
    372.
Stewart, Charles, 3rd Marquess of
    Londonderry (1778-1854), 313, 322.
Stewart, Professor Dugald (1753-
    1828), 45.
Stewart, Admiral Sir Houston (1791-
    1875), 72.
Stewart, Robert, 2nd Viscount
    Castlereagh, 2nd Marquess of
    Londonderry (1769-1822), 168, 171,
    216-17, 313.
Stikes, Chart Master, 123.
Stopford, Admiral Sir Robert (1768-
    1847), 94, 110-11, 113.
Strachan, Admiral Sir Richard (1760-
    1828), 124.
Stuart, General James (1741-1815), 14.
Stuart, Jean, Dowager Countess of
    Dundonald (1723-1808), 14.
Sucre, General Antonio José (1793-
    1830), 243-5, 290.